New Concise
SPELLING
DICTIONARY

New Concise
SPELLING
DICTIONARY

Prepared by

Donald O. Bolander, M.A., Litt. D.

LEXICON PUBLICATIONS, INC.

Copyright © 1986 by
Lexicon Publications, Inc.
95 Madison Avenue
New York, NY 10016

ISBN 0-7172-4502-0

SPELLING DICTIONARY

A

aard·vark
ab·a·cus
abaft
ab·a·lo·ne
aban·don
  aban·doned
  aban·don·ment
abase
  abased
  abas·ing
  abase·ment
abate
  abat·ed
  abat·ing
  abate·ment
ab·at·toir
ab·axial
ab·bey
ab·bot
  ab·bess
a·bre·vi·ate
  ab·bre·vi·at·ed
  ab·bre·vi·at·ing
  ab·bre·vi·a·tion
ab·di·cate
  ab·di·cat·ed
  ab·di·cat·ing
  ab·di·ca·tion
ab·do·men
  ab·dom·i·nal
ab·duct
  ab·duc·tion
  ab·duc·tor
ab·er·rant
  ab·er·ra·tion
  ab·er·rance
  ab·er·ran·cy
abet
  abet·ted

abet·ting
abet·ment
abey·ance
ab·hor
  ab·horred
  ab·hor·ring
  ab·hor·rence
  ab·hor·rent
abide
  abode
  abi·ded
  abid·ing
abil·i·ty
  abil·i·ties
ab·ject
  ab·ject·ly
  ab·ject·ness
ab·jure
  ab·jured
  ab·jur·ing
  ab·ju·ra·tion
ab·late
  ab·lat·ed
  ab·lat·ing
  ab·la·tion
  ab·la·tive
able
  ably
able-bod·ied
ab·lu·tion
ab·ne·gate
  ab·ne·gat·ed
  ab·ne·gat·ing
ab·normal
  ab·normal·i·ty
  ab·normal·i·ties
abol·ish
  abol·ish·a·ble
  abol·ish·ment
ab·o·li·tion
  ab·o·li·tion·ism
  ab·o·li·tion·ist
A-bomb

abom·i·nate
  abom·i·nat·ed
  abom·i·nat·ing
  abom·i·na·tion
abom·i·na·ble
  abom·i·na·bly
ab·o·rig·i·ne
  ab·o·rig·i·nal
abort
  abortion
  abor·tion·ist
  abor·tive
above·board
ab·ra·ca·dab·ra
abrade
  abrad·ed
  abrad·ing
  abra·sion
  abra·sive
abreast
abridge
  abridged
  abridg·ing
abroad
ab·rogate
  ab·ro·gat·ed
  ab·ro·gat·ing
  ab·ro·ga·tion
ab·rupt
ab·scess
  ab·scessed
ab·scis·sa
ab·scis·sion
ab·scond
ab·sence
ab·sent
  ab·sen·tee
  ab·sent-mind·ed
ab·sinthe
ab·so·lute
  ab·so·lute·ly
ab·so·lu·tion
ab·solve

1

ab·solved
ab·solv·ing
ab·sol·vent
ab·sorb
ab·sorb·ent
ab·sorp·tion
ab·sorp·tive
ab·sorb·a·ble
ab·sorb·en·cy
ab·stain
ab·sten·tion
ab·sti·nence
ab·sti·nent
ab·ste·mi·ous
ab·stract
ab·strac·tion
ab·stract·ed
ab·struce
ab·surd
ab·surd·i·ty
ab·surd·ness
abund·dant
abun·dance
abuse
abused
abus·ing
abus·er
abu·sive
abu·sive·ly
abu·sive·ness
abut
abut·ted
abut·ting
abut·ment
abys·mal
abyss
ac·a·dem·ic
ac·a·dem·i·cal
acad·e·mi·cian
acad·e·my
acad·e·mies
ac·cede
ac·ced·ed
ac·ced·ing
ac·ce·le·ran·do
ac·cel·er·ate
ac·cel·er·at·ed
ac·cel·er·at·ing

ac·cel·er·ant
ac·cel·er·a·tion
ac·cel·er·a·tor
ac·cent
ac·cen·tu·ate
ac·cen·tu·at·ed
ac·cen·tu·at·ing
ac·cen·tu·a·tion
ac·cept
ac·cept·ed
ac·cept·ance
ac·cept·a·ble
ac·cept·a·bil·i·ty
ac·cess
ac·ces·si·ble
ac·ces·si·bil·i·ty
ac·ces·sion
ac·ces·so·ry
ac·ci·dence
ac·ci·dent
ac·ci·den·tal
ac·claim
ac·cla·ma·tion
ac·cli·mate
ac·cli·mat·ed
ac·cli·mat·ing
ac·cli·ma·tion
ac·cli·ma·tize
ac·cli·ma·tized
ac·cli·ma·tiz·ing
ac·cli·ma·ti·za·tion
ac·cliv·i·ty
ac·cliv·i·ties
ac·co·lade
ac·com·mo·date
ac·com·mo·dat·ed
ac·com·mo·dat·ing
ac·com·mo·da·tive
ac·com·mo·da·tion
ac·com·pa·ny
ac·com·pa·nied
ac·com·pa·ny·ing
ac·com·pa·ni·ment
ac·com·pa·nist
ac·com·plice
ac·com·plish
ac·com·plished
ac·com·plish·ing

ac·com·plish·ment
ac·cord
ac·cord·ing
ac·cord·ance
ac·cor·di·on
ac·cost
ac·couche·ment
ac·count
ac·count·a·ble
ac·count·a·bil·i·ty
ac·count·ant
ac·count·ing
ac·cred·it
ac·cred·i·ta·tion
ac·cre·tion
ac·cre·tive
ac·cru·al
ac·crue
ac·crued
ac·cru·ing
ac·cu·mu·late
ac·cu·mu·lat·ed
ac·cu·mu·lat·ing
ac·cu·mu·la·tion
ac·cu·mu·la·tive
ac·cu·rate
ac·cu·ra·cy
ac·cu·rate·ly
ac·cu·rate·ness
ac·curs·ed
ac·curst
ac·cu·sa·tive
ac·cuse
ac·cused
ac·cus·ing
ac·cu·sa·tion
ac·cu·sa·to·ry
ac·cus·tom
ac·cus·tomed
acer·bi·ty
ac·e·tate
ace·tic
acet·i·fy
ac·e·tone
acet·y·lene
ache
ached
ach·ing

achieve
  achieved
  achiev·ing
  achiev·a·ble
  achieve·ment
ach·ro·mat·ic
ac·id
  acid·ic
  acid·i·fy
  acid·i·ty
ac·i·do·sis
acid·u·late
  acid·u·la·tion
acid·u·lous
ac·knowl·edge
  ac·knowl·edged
  ac·knowl·edg·ing
  ac·knowl·edge·a·ble
  ac·knowl·edg·ment
ac·me
ac·ne
ac·o·lyte
ac·o·nite
acous·tic
  acous·tics
  acous·ti·cal
ac·quaint
ac·quaint·ance
ac·qui·esce
  ac·qui·esced
  ac·qui·esc·ing
  ac·qui·es·cence
  ac·qui·es·cent
ac·quire
  ac·quired
  ac·quir·ing
  ac·quire·ment
  ac·qui·si·tion
ac·quit
  ac·quit·ted
  ac·quit·ting
  ac·quit·tal
  ac·quit·tance
acre
  acre·age
ac·rid
  acrid·i·ty
ac·ri·mo·ny

ac·ri·mo·ni·ous
ac·ro·bat
  ac·ro·bat·ic
ac·ro·nym
ac·ro·pho·bia
across
acryl·ic
act·ing
ac·tion
  ac·tion·a·ble
  ac·tion·a·bly
ac·ti·vate
  ac·ti·vat·ed
  ac·ti·vat·ing
  ac·ti·va·tion
  ac·ti·va·tor
ac·tive
  ac·tive·ly
  ac·tive·ness
ac·tiv·ism
ac·tiv·ist
ac·tiv·i·ty
  ac·tiv·i·ties
ac·tor
ac·tress
ac·tu·al
  ac·tu·al·ly
  ac·tu·al·i·ty
ac·tu·al·ize
  ac·tu·al·i·za·tion
ac·tu·ary
  ac·tu·ar·ies
  ac·tu·ar·i·al
ac·tu·ate
  ac·tu·at·ed
  ac·tu·at·ing
  ac·tu·a·tion
  ac·tu·a·tor
acu·i·ty
acu·men
ac·u·punc·ture
acute
  acute·ly
  acute·ness
ad·age
ada·gio
ad·a·mant
ad·a·man·tine

adapt
  adapt·a·ble
  adapt·a·bil·i·ty
  ad·ap·ta·tion
  adap·tive
ad·dend
ad·den·dum
  ad·den·da
ad·dict
  ad·dict·ed
  ad·dic·tive
  ad·dic·tion
ad·di·tion
  ad·di·tion·al
ad·di·tive
ad·dle
ad·dress
ad·dress·ee
ad·duce
ad·e·noid
  ad·e·noi·dal
adept
  adept·ly
ad·e·quate
  ad·e·qua·cy
  ad·e·quate·ly
ad·here
  ad·hered
  ad·her·ing
  ad·her·ence
ad·her·ent
ad·he·sion
ad·he·sive
  ad·he·sive·ness
ad·hib·it
adi·a·bat·ic
a·dieu
ad in·fi·ni·tum
adi·os
ad·i·pose
  ad·i·pose·ness
ad·ja·cent
  ad·ja·cent·ly
  ad·ja·cen·cy
  ad·ja·cen·cies
ad·jec·tive
ad·join
  ad·join·ing

ad·journ
  ad·journ·ment
ad·judge
  ad·judged
  ad·judg·ing
ad·ju·di·cate
  ad·ju·di·cat·ed
  ad·ju·di·cat·ing
  ad·ju·di·ca·tion
ad·junct
  ad·junc·tive
ad·jure
  ad·jured
  ad·jur·ing
  ad·ju·ra·tion
ad·just
  ad·just·a·ble
  ad·just·er
  ad·just·ment
ad·ju·tant
ad·lib
  ad·libbed
  ad·lib·bing
ad·min·is·ter
ad·min·is·trate
ad·min·is·tra·tion
  ad·min·is·tra·tive
  ad·min·is·tra·tor
ad·mi·ral
ad·mi·ral·ty
ad·mire
  ad·mired
  ad·mir·ing
  ad·mi·ra·ble
  ad·mi·ra·bly
  ad·mi·ra·tion
  ad·mir·er
  ad·mir·ing·ly
ad·mis·si·ble
  ad·mis·si·bil·i·ty
ad·mis·sion
ad·mit
  ad·mit·ted
  ad·mit·ting
ad·mit·tance
ad·mix·ture
ad·mon·ish
  ad·mo·ni·tion

ad·mon·i·to·ry
ado·be
ad·o·les·cence
ad·o·les·cent
adopt
  adopt·a·ble
  adopt·er
  adop·tion
  adop·tive
adore
  adored
  ador·ing
  ador·a·ble
  ad·o·ra·tion
adorn
  adorn·ment
ad·re·nal
adren·a·line
adrift
adroit
  adroit·ly
  adroit·ness
ad·sorb
  ad·sor·bent
  ad·sorp·tion
ad·u·late
  ad·u·lat·ing
  ad·u·la·tion
  ad·u·la·to·ry
adult
  adult·hood
adul·ter·ate
  adul·ter·at·ed
  adul·ter·at·ing
  adul·ter·ant
  adul·ter·a·tion
adul·tery
  adul·ter·er
  adul·ter·ess
  adul·ter·ous
ad va·lo·rem
ad·vance
  ad·vanc·ing
  ad·vance·ment
ad·van·tage
  ad·van·tag·ing
  ad·van·ta·geous
ad·vent

ad·ven·ti·tious
ad·ven·ture
  ad·ven·tur·ing
  ad·ven·tur·er
  ad·ven·ture·some
  ad·ven·tur·ous
ad·verb
  ad·ver·bi·al·ly
ad·ver·sary
  ad·ver·sar·ies
ad·verse
  ad·verse·ly
  ad·verse·ness
ad·ver·si·ty
  ad·ver·si·ties
ad·vert
  ad·vert·ence
  ad·vert·ent
ad·ver·tise
  ad·ver·tised
  ad·ver·tis·ing
  ad·ver·tis·er
  ad·ver·tise·ment
ad·vice
ad·vise
  ad·vis·ing
  ad·vis·a·bil·i·ty
  ad·vis·a·ble
  ad·vis·a·bly
  ad·vis·er
  ad·vis·ed·ly
  ad·vise·ment
  ad·vi·so·ry
ad·vo·cate
  ad·vo·cat·ed
  ad·vo·cat·ing
  ad·vo·ca·cy
  ad·vo·ca·tion
ae·on
ae·o·ni·an
aer·ate
  aer·at·ed
  aer·at·ing
  aer·a·tion
  aer·a·tor
aer·i·al
  aer·i·al·ist
aero·dy·nam·ics

4

aero·log·i·cal
  aerol·o·gist
aero·naut·ics
  aero·nau·ti·cal
aero·sol
aero·space
aes·thete
aes·thet·ic
  aes·thet·i·cal·ly
af·fa·ble
  af·fa·bil·i·ty
  af·fa·bly
af·fair
af·fect
  af·fect·ing
af·fect·ive
af·fec·ta·tion
af·fect·ed
  af·fect·ed·ly
  af·fect·ed·ness
af·fec·tion
  af·fec·tion·ate
af·fi·ance
af·fi·da·vit
af·fil·i·ate
  af·fil·i·at·ed
  af·fil·i·a·tion
af·fin·i·ty
af·firm
  af·fir·ma·tion
  af·firm·a·tive
af·flict
  af·flic·tion
af·flu·ence
  af·flu·ent
af·ford
af·fray
af·fright
af·front
af·ghan
afore·men·tioned
afore·said
afore·thought
afraid
Af·ri·can
Af·ri·kan·der
af·ter·birth
af·ter·burn·er

af·ter·ef·fect
af·ter·glow
af·ter·math
af·ter·most
af·ter·noon
af·ter·thought
af·ter·ward
again
against
agape
ag·ate
aga·ve
age
  aged
  ag·ing
  age·ing
age·less
agen·cy
  agen·cies
agen·da
agent
ag·glom·er·ate
  ag·glom·er·at·ing
  ag·glom·er·a·tion
ag·glu·ti·nate
  ag·glu·ti·nat·ing
  ag·glu·ti·na·tion
  ag·glu·ti·na·tive
ag·gran·dize
  ag·gran·dized
  ag·gran·diz·ing
  ag·gran·dize·ment
ag·gra·vate
  ag·gra·vat·ed
  ag·gra·vat·ing
  ag·gra·va·tion
ag·gre·gate
  ag·gre·gat·ed
  ag·gre·gat·ing
  ag·gre·ga·tion
  ag·gre·ga·tive
ag·gress
  ag·gress·ive
  ag·gress·or
  ag·gres·sion
ag·grieve
  ag·grieved
  ag·griev·ing

aghast
ag·ile
  ag·ile·ly
  agil·i·ty
ag·i·tate
  ag·i·tat·ed
  ag·i·tat·ing
  ag·i·ta·tion
  ag·i·ta·tor
agleam
ag·nos·tic
  ag·nos·ti·cism
ag·o·nize
  ag·o·niz·ing
ag·o·ny
  ag·o·nies
ag·o·ra·pho·bia
agrar·i·an
agree
  agreed
  agree·ing
  agree·ment
  agree·a·ble
  agree·a·bil·i·ty
  agree·a·bly
ag·ri·cul·ture
  ag·ri·cul·tur·al
  ag·ri·cul·tur·ist
agron·o·my
  ag·ro·nom·ic
  ag·ro·nom·i·cal
  agron·o·mist
aground
ague
aide-de-camp
ai·grette
ail·ing
  ail·ment
ai·ler·on
aim·less
air·less
air·borne
air·brush
air-con·di·tion
  air-con·di·tioned
  air con·di·tion·ing
  air con·di·tion·er
air·craft

air·drop
  air·dropped
  air·drop·ping
Aire·dale
air·field
air·foil
air·plane
air·port
air pres·sure
air·sick·ness
air·space
air·tight
air·wave
air·worthy
airy
  air·i·er
  air·i·est
  air·i·ness
  air·i·ly
aisle
ajar
akin
al·a·bas·ter
a la carte
alac·ri·ty
alarm
  alarm·ing
al·ba·core
al·ba·tross
al·be·it
al·bi·no
  al·bi·nos
  al·bi·nism
al·bum
al·bu·men
al·bu·min
  al·bu·mi·nous
al·che·my
  al·che·mist
al·co·hol
  al·co·hol·ic
  al·co·hol·ism
al·cove
al·der·man
alert
  alert·ness
al·fal·fa
al·fres·co

al·ga
  al·gae
al·ge·bra
  al·ge·bra·ic
  al·ge·bra·ic·al
al·go·rithm
ali·as
  ali·as·es
al·i·bi
al·ien
  al·ien·a·ble
al·ien·ate
  al·ien·at·ed
  al·ien·at·ing
al·ien·ist
  al·ien·ism
alight
  alight·ed
  alit
  alight·ing
align
align·ment
aline·ment
alike
al·i·ment
  al·i·men·tal
  al·i·men·ta·ry
al·i·mo·ny
al·ka·li
  al·ka·lies
  al·ka·line
  al·ka·lin·i·ty
  al·ka·lize
  al·ka·lized
  al·ka·liz·ing
  al·ka·li·za·tion
  al·ka·loid
  al·ka·loi·dal
all-Ameri·can
all-around
al·lay
  al·layed
  al·lay·ing
al·lege
  al·leged
  al·leg·ing
  al·le·ga·tion
  al·lege·a·ble

al·le·giance
al·le·go·ry
  al·le·go·ries
  al·le·gor·ic
  al·le·gor·i·cal
al·le·gret·to
al·le·gro
al·ler·gen
al·ler·gy
  al·ler·gies
  al·ler·gic
  al·ler·gist
al·le·vi·ate
  al·le·vi·at·ed
  al·le·vi·at·ing
  al·le·vi·a·tion
  al·le·vi·a·tive
  al·le·vi·a·to·ry
al·ley
  al·leys
al·li·ance
al·lied
al·li·ga·tor
al·lit·er·ate
  al·lit·er·at·ed
  al·lit·er·at·ing
  al·lit·er·a·tive
  al·lit·er·a·tion
al·lo·cate
  al·lo·cat·ed
  al·lo·cat·ing
  al·lo·ca·tion
al·lop·a·thy
  al·lo·path·ic
al·lot
  al·lot·ted
  al·lot·ting
  al·lot·ment
  al·lot·ta·ble
al·low
  al·low·ing
  al·low·a·ble
  al·low·ed·ly
  al·low·ance
al·loy
all·spice
al·lude
  al·lud·ed

6

al·lud·ing
al·lure
  al·lured
  al·lur·ing
  al·lure·ment
al·lu·sion
  al·lu·sive
  al·lu·sive·ly
al·lu·vi·al
al·lu·vi·um
al·ly
  al·lies
al·lied
  al·ly·ing
  al·li·ance
al·ma ma·ter
al·ma·nac
al·mighty
almond
almost
al·oe
aloft
alo·ha
alone
  alone·ness
along
along·side
aloof
  aloof·ness
al·pha
al·pha·bet
  al·pha·bet·ic
  al·pha·bet·i·cal
  al·pha·bet·ize
al·pha·nu·mer·ic
al·ready
al·so
al·tar
al·ter
  al·ter·a·bil·i·ty
  al·ter·a·ble
  al·ter·ant
  al·ter·a·tion
  al·ter·a·tive
al·ter·cate
  al·ter·ca·tion
al·ter e·go

al·ter·nate
  al·ter·nat·ed
  al·ter·nat·ing
  al·ter·nate·ly
  al·ter·na·tion
al·ter·na·tor
al·ter·na·tive
al·though
al·tim·e·ter
al·ti·tude
al·to
al·to·geth·er
al·tru·ism
  al·tru·ist
  al·tru·is·tic
al·um
a·lu·min·na
alu·mi·num
alum·na
  alum·nae
alum·nus
  alum·ni
al·ve·o·lar
al·ways
amal·gam
  amal·gam·ate
  amal·gam·a·tion
am·a·ryl·lis
amass
  amass·ment
am·a·teur
  am·a·teur·ism
  am·a·teur·ish
am·a·to·ry
amaze
  amazed
  amaz·ing
  amaze·ment
Am·a·zon
am·bas·sa·dor
  am·bas·sa·dress
  am·bas·sa·do·ri·al
am·ber
am·ber·gris
am·bi·dex·trous
  am·bi·dex·ter·i·ty
am·bi·ance
  am·bi·ence
am·bi·ent

am·big·u·ous
  am·big·u·ous·ly
  am·bi·gu·i·ty
am·bi·tion
am·bi·tious
  am·bi·tious·ly
  am·bi·tious·ness
am·biv·a·lence
  am·biv·a·lent
am·ble
  am·bled
  am·bling
am·bro·sia
  am·bro·sial
am·bu·lance
am·bu·la·to·ry
am·bu·lant
am·bu·late
  am·bu·lat·ed
  am·bu·lat·ing
am·bus·cade
am·bush
  am·bush·ment
ame·ba
amel·io·rate
  amel·io·rat·ed
  amel·io·rat·ing
  amel·io·ra·ble
  amel·io·ra·tion
  amel·io·ra·tive
  amel·io·ra·tor
ame·na·ble
  ame·na·bil·i·ty
  ame·na·ble·ness
  ame·na·bly
amend
  amend·a·ble
  amend·ment
amen·i·ty
amerce
  amerce·ment
Amer·i·ca
  Amer·i·can
  Amer·i·cana
  Amer·i·can·ism
  Amer·i·can·i·za·tion
am·e·thyst
ami·a·ble

ami·a·bil·i·ty
ami·a·bly
am·i·ca·ble
  am·i·ca·bil·i·ty
  am·i·ca·bly
amid
  amidst
ami·go
am·i·ty
am·me·ter
am·mo·nia
am·mo·ni·um
am·mu·ni·tion
am·ne·sia
  am·ne·sic
am·nes·ty
am·ni·on
amoe·ba
  amoe·bae
  amoe·bas
  amoe·bic
  amoe·boid
amok
among
  amongst
amor·al
am·o·rous
  am·o·rous·ly
  am·o·rous·ness
amor·phous
am·or·tize
  am·or·tized
  am·or·tiz·ing
  am·or·ti·za·tion
amount
amour
am·pere
  am·per·age
am·per·sand
am·phet·a·mine
am·phib·i·an
  am·phib·i·ous
am·phi·the·a·ter
am·ple
  am·ple·ness
  am·ply
am·pli·fy
  am·pli·fied

am·pli·fy·ing
am·pli·fi·ca·tion
am·pli·fi·er
am·pli·tude
am·poule
  am·pule
am·pu·tate
  am·pu·tat·ed
  am·pu·tat·ing
  am·pu·ta·tion
am·pu·tee
amuck
am·u·let
amuse
  amused
  amus·ing
  amuse·ment
anach·ro·nism
  anach·ro·nis·tic
  anach·ro·nous
an·a·con·da
an·aes·the·sia
  an·aes·thet·ic
  an·aes·the·tize
an·a·gram
  an·a·gram·mat·ic
  an·a·gram·mat·i·cal
anal
  anus
an·al·ge·sia
  an·al·ge·sic
an·a·logue
  an·a·log
  an·a·log·i·cal
  anal·o·gize
anal·o·gy
  anal·o·gies
  anal·o·gous
anal·y·sis
  anal·y·ses
an·a·lyst
  an·a·lyt·ic
an·a·lyze
  an·a·lyzed
  an·a·lyz·ing
  an·a·ly·za·tion
an·a·pest
an·ar·chist

an·ar·chism
an·ar·chis·tic
an·ar·chy
an·ar·chic
an·ar·chi·cal
anath·e·ma
  anath·e·ma·tize
anat·o·mize
  anat·o·mized
  anat·o·mizing
  anat·o·mi·za·tion
anat·o·my
  anat·o·mies
  an·a·tom·i·cal
  anat·o·mist
an·ces·tor
  an·ces·tral
  an·ces·tress
  an·ces·try
an·chor
  an·chor·age
  an·cho·rite
  an·chor·man
an·cho·vy
an·cient
  an·cient·ness
an·cil·lary
an·dan·te
an·dan·ti·no
and·i·ron
an·dro·gen
  an·drog·y·nous
  an·drog·y·ny
an·ec·dote
  an·ec·do·tal
  an·ec·dot·ti·cal
ane·mia
  ane·mic
an·e·mom·e·ter
anem·o·ne
an·er·oid
an·es·the·sia
  an·es·thet·ic
  an·es·the·tist
  an·es·the·si·ol·o·gist
  an·es·the·tize
  an·es·the·tiz·ing
an·eu·rysm

an·eu·rism
an·gel
  an·gel·ic
  an·gel·i·cal·ly
an·ger
  an·gerily
an·gi·na pec·to·ris
an·gle
  an·gling
  angler
An·gli·can
  An·gli·can·ism
  An·gli·cism
  An·gli·cize
  An·gli·ci·za·tion
An·glo-Amer·i·can
An·glo-Sax·on
an·go·ra
an·gos·tu·ra
an·gry
  an·gri·ly
  an·gri·ness
ang·strom unit
an·guish
  an·guished
an·gu·lar
  an·gu·lar·i·ty
  an·gu·la·tion
an·hy·dride
  an·hy·drous
an·i·mad·vert
  an·i·mad·ver·sion
an·i·mal
  an·i·mal·ism
  an·i·mal·i·ty
  an·i·mal·ize
an·i·mate
  an·i·mat·ed
  an·i·mat·ing
  an·i·ma·tion
an·i·mism
  an·i·mis·tic
an·i·mos·i·ty
an·i·mus
an·ise
an·i·sette
an·kle
an·klet

an·ky·lose
an·ky·lo·sis
an·nals
  an·nal·ist
  an·nal·is·tic
An·nap·o·lis
an·neal
an·ne·lid
an·nex
  an·nex·a·tion
an·ni·hi·late
  an·ni·hi·lat·ed
  an·ni·hi·lat·ing
  an·ni·hi·la·tion
  an·ni·hi·la·tor
an·ni·ver·sa·ry
  an·ni·ver·sa·ries
an·no Do·mi·ni
an·no·tate
  an·no·tat·ed
  an·no·tat·ing
  an·no·ta·tion
  an·no·ta·tor
an·nounce
  an·nounced
  an·nounc·ing
  an·nounce·ment
  an·nounc·er
an·noy
  an·noy·ance
an·nu·al
an·nu·i·ty
an·nu·i·tant
an·nul
  an·nulled
  an·nul·ling
  an·nul·ment
an·nu·lar
an·nun·ci·ate
  an·nun·ci·at·ing
  an·nun·ci·a·tion
  an·nun·ci·a·tor
an·ode
an·od·ize
an·o·dyne
anoint
  anoint·ment
anom·a·ly

anom·a·lism
anom·a·lous
anon·ymous
  an·o·nym·i·ty
  anon·y·mous·ly
an·oth·er
an·swer
  an·swer·a·ble
ant·ac·id
an·tag·o·nist
  an·tag·o·nism
  an·tag·o·nis·tic
  an·tag·o·nize
  an·tag·o·niz·ing
ant·arc·tic
Ant·arc·ti·ca
an·te
ant·eat·er
an·te-bel·lum
an·te·cede
  an·te·ced·ed
  an·te·ced·ing
  an·te·ced·ence
  an·te·ced·ent
an·te·cham·ber
an·te·date
an·te·di·lu·vi·an
an·te·lope
an·te me·ri·di·em
an·ten·na
  an·ten·nae
  an·ten·nas
an·te·pe·nult
an·te·ri·or
an·te·room
an·them
an·thol·o·gy
  an·thol·o·gies
  an·thol·o·gist
an·thra·cite
an·thrax
an·thro·po·cen·tric
an·thro·poid
  an·thro·pol·o·gy
  an·thro·po·log·ic
  an·thro·po·log·i·cal
  an·thro·pol·o·gist
an·thro·pom·e·try

an·thro·po·mor·phic
an·ti·air·craft
an·ti·bac·te·ri·al
an·ti·bal·lis·tic
an·ti·bi·ot·ic
an·ti·body
  an·ti·bod·ies
an·tic
An·ti·christ
an·tic·i·pate
  an·tic·i·pat·ed
  an·tic·i·pat·ing
  an·tic·i·pa·tion
  an·tic·i·pa·tive
  an·tic·i·pa·to·ry
an·ti·cler·i·cal
an·ti·cli·max
  an·ti·cli·mac·tic
an·ti·dote
  an·ti·dot·al
an·ti·freeze
an·ti·gen
an·ti·his·ta·mine
an·ti·log·a·rithm
an·ti·ma·cas·sar
an·ti·mis·sile
an·ti·mo·ny
an·ti·pas·to
an·tip·a·thy
  an·ti·pa·thet·ic
an·ti·pode
an·ti·quar·i·an
an·ti·quary
  an·ti·quar·ies
an·ti·quate
  an·ti·quat·ed
  an·ti·quat·ing
an·tique
  an·tiqued
  an·tiqu·ing
  an·tique·ness
an·tiq·ui·ty
an·ti-Sem·i·tism
an·ti·sep·sis
an·ti·sep·tic
  an·ti·sep·tical·ly
an·ti·se·rum
an·ti·slav·ery

an·ti·so·cial
an·tith·e·sis
  an·tith·e·ses
  an·ti·thet·i·cal
an·ti·tox·in
  an·ti·tox·ic
an·ti·trust
ant·ler
  ant·lered
an·to·nym
anus
an·vil
anx·i·e·ty
  anx·i·e·ties
anx·ious
  anx·ious·ness
any·body
  any·bod·ies
any·how
any·more
any·one
any·place
any·thing
any·way
any·where
any·wise
aor·ta
  aor·tal
  aor·tic
apace
apart
apart·heid
apart·ment
ap·a·thy
  ap·a·thet·ic
  ap·a·thet·i·cal·ly
aper·ri·tif
ap·er·ture
apex
  apex·es
  api·ces
ap·i·cal
apha·sia
aphid
aph·o·rism
aph·o·rist
  aph·o·ris·tic
aph·ro·dis·i·ac

api·ar·i·an
api·a·rist
api·ary
  api·ar·ies
api·cul·ture
  api·cul·tur·al
  api·cul·tur·ist
apiece
ap·ish
aplomb
apoc·a·lypse
  apoc·a·lyp·tic
apoc·o·pe
apoc·ry·pha
ap·o·dic·tic
ap·o·gee
apol·o·get·ics
apol·o·gist
apol·o·gize
  apol·o·gized
  apol·o·giz·ing
apol·o·gy
  apol·o·gies
apol·o·get·ic
apol·o·get·i·cal
ap·o·plec·tic
ap·o·plex·y
apos·ta·sy
  apos·tate
  apos·ta·tize
a pos·te·ri·o·ri
apos·tle
  apos·to·late
  ap·os·tol·ic
  ap·os·tol·i·cal
apos·trophe
apoth·e·cary
  apoth·e·car·ies
ap·o·thegm
apoth·e·o·sis
  apoth·e·o·size
Ap·pa·la·chi·an
ap·pall
  ap·palled
  ap·pal·ling
ap·pa·rat·us
  ap·pa·rat·us
  ap·pa·rat·us·es

ap·par·el
ap·par·ent
ap·pa·ri·tion
ap·peal
  ap·peal·a·ble
  ap·peal·ing·ly
ap·pear
ap·pear·ance
ap·pease
  ap·peased
  ap·peasing
  ap·pease·ment
  ap·peas·er
ap·pel·late
  ap·pel·lant
  ap·pel·la·tion
  ap·pel·la·tive
ap·pend
  ad·pen·dage
  ap·pend·ant
ap·pen·di·ci·tis
  ap·pen·dec·to·my
ap·pen·dix
  ap·pen·dix·es
  ap·pen·di·ces
ap·per·cep·tion
ap·per·tain
ap·pe·tite
  ap·pe·tiz·er
  ap·pe·tiz·ing
ap·plaud
  ap·plause
ap·ple
ap·pli·ance
ap·pli·ca·ble
  ap·pli·ca·bil·i·ty
ap·pli·cant
ap·pli·ca·tion
ap·pli·ca·to·ry
ap·pli·ca·tor
ap·pli·que
ap·ply
  ap·plied
  ap·ply·ing
ap·point
  ap·point·ee
  ap·poin·tive
  ap·point·ment

ap·por·tion
  ap·por·tion·ment
ap·pose
  ap·posed
  ap·pos·ing
ap·po·site
ap·po·si·tion
ap·pos·i·tive
ap·praise
  ap·praised
  ap·prais·ing
  ap·prais·er
  ap·prais·al
ap·pre·ci·a·ble
  ap·pre·ci·a·bly
ap·pre·ci·ate
  ap·pre·ci·at·ing
  ap·pre·ci·a·tion
  ap·pre·ci·a·tive
ap·pre·hend
  ap·pre·hen·si·ble
  ap·pre·hen·sion
  ap·pre·hen·sive
ap·pren·tice
ap·prise
  ap·prised
  ap·pris·ing
ap·proach
  ap·proach·a·ble
ap·pro·ba·tion
  ap·pro·ba·to·ry
ap·pro·pri·ate
  ap·pro·pri·at·ed
  ap·pro·pri·at·ing
  ap·pro·pri·ate·ness
  ap·pro·pri·a·tion
ap·prov·al
ap·prove
  ap·proved
  ap·prov·ing
ap·prox·i·mate
  ap·prox·i·mate·ly
  ap·prox·i·ma·tion
ap·pur·te·nance
  ap·pur·te·nant
ap·ri·cot
a pri·o·ri
apron

ap·ro·pos
apt
  apt·ly
  apt·ness
  ap·ti·tude
aq·ua
  aqua·cul·ture
  aq·ua·lung
  aq·ua·ma·rine
  aq·ua·naut
  aq·ua·plane
aquar·i·um
aquat·ic
aq·ue·duct
aque·ous
aq·ui·line
ar·a·besque
Ara·bi·an
Ara·bic
ar·a·ble
arach·nid
ar·ba·lest
ar·bi·ter
ar·bi·trary
  ar·bi·trar·i·ly
  ar·bit·ra·ment
ar·bi·trate
  ar·bi·trat·ed
  ar·bi·trat·ing
  ar·bi·tra·tor
  ar·bi·tra·tion
ar·bor
  ar·bo·re·al
  ar·bo·re·tum
arc
  arced
  arc·ing
ar·cade
ar·chae·ol·o·gy
  ar·che·ol·o·gy
  ar·chae·o·log·i·cal
  ar·che·o·log·i·cal
  ar·chae·ol·o·gist
  ar·che·ol·o·gist
ar·cha·ic
  ar·cha·ism
arch·an·gel
arch·bish·op

arch·dea·con
arch·di·o·cese
  arch·di·oc·e·san
arch·du·cal
arch·duke
  arch·duch·ess
arch·er
arch·ery
arch·e·type
arch·fiend
ar·chi·e·pis·co·pal
ar·chi·pel·a·go
ar·chi·tect
ar·chi·tec·ton·ic
ar·chi·tec·ture
  ar·chi·tec·tur·al
ar·chive
  ar·chi·val
  ar·chi·vist
arc·tic
ar·cu·ate
ar·dent
ar·dor
ar·du·ous
ar·ea
are·na
ar·go·sy
ar·got
ar·gue
  ar·gued
  ar·gu·ing
  ar·gu·a·ble
ar·gu·ment
  ar·gu·men·ta·tion
  ar·gu·men·ta·tive
  ar·gu·men·tive
ar·gyle
ar·ia
ar·id
  ar·id·i·ty
ar·ise
  ar·ose
  ar·is·en
  ar·is·ing
ar·is·to·crat
  ar·is·to·crat·ic
  ar·is·toc·ra·cy
  ar·is·toc·ra·cies

arith·me·tic
  ar·ith·met·i·cal
  arith·me·ti·cian
arm
  armed
  arm·ing
ar·ma·da
ar·ma·dil·lo
Ar·ma·ged·don
ar·ma·ment
ar·ma·ture
ar·mi·stice
ar·moire
ar·mor
  ar·mored
ar·mory
  ar·mo·ries
ar·my
  ar·mies
aro·ma
  ar·o·mat·ic
  ar·o·mat·i·cal
around
arouse
  aroused
  arous·ing
  arous·al
ar·peg·gio
ar·raign
  ar·raign·ment
ar·range
  ar·ranged
  ar·rang·ing
  ar·range·ment
ar·rant
ar·ray
  ar·ray·al
ar·rear
  ar·rear·age
ar·rest
  ar·rest·er
ar·rive
  ar·rived
  ar·riv·ing
  ar·ri·val
ar·ro·gant
  ar·ro·gance
  ar·ro·gant·ly

ar·ro·gate
  ar·ro·gat·ed
  ar·ro·ga·tion
ar·row
  ar·row·head
ar·royo
ar·se·nal
ar·se·nic
ar·son
  ar·son·ist
ar·te·ri·al
ar·te·ri·o·scle·ro·sis
ar·tery
  ar·ter·ies
ar·te·sian
art·ful
  art·ful·ly
ar·thri·tis
  ar·thrit·ic
ar·thro·pod
ar·ti·choke
ar·ti·cle
ar·tic·u·lar
ar·tic·u·late
  ar·tic·u·lat·ed
  ar·tic·u·lat·ing
  ar·tic·u·late·ly
  ar·tic·u·late·ness
  ar·tic·u·la·tor
  ar·tic·u·la·tion
ar·ti·fact
  ar·te·fact
ar·ti·fice
ar·ti·fi·cial
  ar·ti·fi·ci·al·i·ty
  ar·ti·fi·cial·ly
ar·til·lery
ar·ti·san
art·ist
  ar·tiste
ar·tis·tic
  ar·tis·ti·cal·ly
art·ist·ry
art·less
arty
  ar·ti·ness
as·bes·tos
  as·bes·tus

as·cend
  as·cend·ance
  as·cend·ence
  as·cend·an·cy
  as·cend·en·cy
as·cend·ant
  as·cend·ent
as·cent
  as·cen·sion
as·certain
  as·cer·tain·a·ble
  as·cer·tain·ment
as·cet·ic
  as·cet·i·cism
as·cot
as·cribe
  as·cribed
  as·crib·ing
  as·crib·a·ble
  as·crip·tion
asep·sis
asep·tic
asex·u·al
  asex·u·al·i·ty
ashamed
  asham·ed·ly
ash
  ash·en
  ash·es
  ashy
Asi·at·ic
as·i·nine
  as·i·nin·i·ty
askance
askew
asleep
aso·cial
as·par·a·gus
as·pect
as·pen
as·per·i·ty
as·perse
  as·persed
  as·pers·ing
  as·per·sion
as·phalt
as·phyx·ia
  as·phyx·i·ate

as·phyx·i·at·ed
as·phyx·i·at·ing
as·phyx·i·a·tion
as·pic
as·pir·ant
as·pir·rate
  as·pi·rat·ed
  as·pi·rat·ing
  as·pi·ra·tion
  as·pi·ra·tor
as·pire
  as·pir·ing
  as·pi·rin
as·sail
  as·sail·a·ble
  as·sail·ant
as·sas·sin
  as·sas·si·nate
  as·sas·si·nat·ed
  as·sas·si·nat·ing
  as·sas·si·na·tion
  as·sas·si·na·tor
as·sault
as·say
  as·say·er
as·sem·blage
as·sem·ble
  as·sem·bled
  as·sem·bling
  as·sem·bler
as·sem·bly
  as·sem·blies
  as·sem·bly·man
as·sent
  as·sen·ta·tion
as·sert
  as·ser·tion
as·ser·tive
  as·ser·tive·ness
as·sess
  as·sess·a·ble
  as·sess·ment
  as·sess·or
as·set
as·sev·er·ate
  as·sev·er·at·ed
  as·sev·er·at·ing
  as·sev·er·a·tion

as·si·du·i·ty
  as·sid·u·ous
as·sign
  as·sign·a·ble
  as·sign·a·bly
  as·sign·ment
  as·sig·na·tion
as·sim·i·late
  as·sim·i·lat·ed
  as·sim·i·lat·ing
  as·sim·i·la·ble
  as·sim·i·la·tion
as·sist
  as·sist·ance
as·sis·tant
as·size
as·so·ci·ate
  as·so·ci·at·ed
  as·so·ci·at·ing
  as·so·ci·a·tion
  as·so·ci·a·tive
as·so·nance
  as·so·nant
as·sort
  as·sort·ed
  as·sort·ment
as·suage
  as·suaged
  as·suag·ing
  as·suage·ment
as·sua·sive
as·sume
  as·sumed
  as·sum·ing
  as·sump·tion
as·sure
  as·sured
  as·sur·ing
  as·sur·ance
  as·sur·ed·ly
  as·sured·ness
as·ter·isk
as·ter·oid
asth·ma
  asth·mat·ic
astig·ma·tism
  as·tig·mat·ic
as·ton·ish

as·ton·ish·ing
as·ton·ish·ment
as·tound
astrad·dle
as·tra·khan
as·tral
astray
astride
as·trin·gent
as·trin·gen·cy
as·tro·dome
as·tro·labe
as·trol·o·gy
as·trol·o·ger
as·trol·log·ic
as·tro·log·i·cal
as·tro·naut
as·tro·nau·tics
as·tro·nau·ti·cal
as·tro·nom·ic
as·tro·nom·i·cal·ly
as·tron·o·my
as·tron·o·mer
as·tro·phys·ics
as·tro·phys·i·cist
as·tute
as·tute·ly
as·tu·cious
asun·der
asy·lum
asym·me·try
asym·met·ric
asym·met·ri·cal
at·a·vism
at·a·vis·tic
at·el·ier
athe·ism
athe·ist
athe·is·tic
athe·is·ti·cal
ath·er·o·scle·ro·sis
ath·lete
ath·let·ic
ath·let·ics
ath·let·i·cal·ly
athwart
at·las
at·las·es

at·mos·phere
at·mos·pher·ic
at·mos·pher·i·cal
at·oll
at·om
atom·ic
atom·i·cal
at·om·ism
at·om·ize
at·om·ized
at·om·iz·ing
at·om·iz·er
atonal
ato·nal·i·ty
atone
atoned
aton·ing
atone·ment
atri·um
atro·cious
atroc·i·ty
atroc·i·ties
at·ro·phy
at·ro·phies
at·ro·phied
at·ro·phy·ing
atroph·ic
at·tach
at·tach·ment
at·ta·che
at·tack
at·tain
at·tain·a·ble
at·tain·ment
at·tain·der
at·taint
at·tar
at·tempt
at·tend
at·tend·ance
at·tend·ant
at·ten·tion
at·ten·tive
at·ten·u·ate
at·ten·u·at·ed
at·ten·u·at·ing
at·ten·u·a·tion
at·test

at·test·ta·tion
at·tic
at·tire
at·tired
at·tir·ing
at·tire·ment
at·ti·tude
at·ti·tu·di·nize
at·tor·ney
at·tor·neys
at·tract
at·trac·tive
at·trac·tion
at·tri·bute
at·trib·ut·ed
at·trib·ut·ing
at·trib·ut·a·ble
at·tri·bu·tion
at·trib·u·tive
at·tri·tion
at·trite
at·tune
at·tuned
at·tun·ing
atyp·i·cal
au·burn
auc·tion
auc·tion·eer
au·da·cious
au·dac·i·ty
au·di·ble
au·di·bil·i·ty
au·di·bly
au·di·ence
au·dio
au·dio·phile
au·di·o·vis·u·al
au·dit
au·di·tion
au·dit·or
au·di·to·ri·um
au·di·to·ry
aught
aug·ment
aug·men·ta·tion
au grat·in
au·gust
au·gust·ly

auld·lang syne
au·ral
  au·ral·ly
au·re·ate
au·re·ole
au·re·o·my·cin
au re·voir
au·ri·cle
  au·ric·u·lar
au·ro·ra
au·ro·ra aus·tra·lis
au·ro·ra bor·e·al·is
aus·pice
  aus·pic·es
aus·pi·cious
aus·tere
  aus·ter·i·ty
au·then·tic
au·then·ti·cate
  au·then·ti·cat·ed
  au·then·ti·cat·ing
  au·then·ti·ca·tion
  au·then·tic·i·ty
au·thor
  au·thor·ess
  au·thor·ship
au·thor·i·tar·i·an
au·thor·i·ta·tive
au·thor·i·ty
  au·thor·i·ties
au·thor·ize
  au·thor·ized
  au·thor·iz·ing
  au·thor·i·za·tion
au·to·bi·og·ra·phy
  au·to·bi·og·ra·phies
  au·to·bi·og·ra·pher
  au·to·bi·o·graph·ic
  au·to·bi·o·graph·i·cal
au·toc·ra·cy
  au·toc·ra·cies
au·to·crat
  au·to·crat·ic
  au·to·crat·i·cal·ly
au·to·graph
au·to·mate
  au·to·mat·ed
  au·to·mat·ing

au·to·mat·ic
  au·to·mat·i·cal
au·to·ma·tion
au·tom·a·tism
  au·tom·a·ton
au·to·mo·bile
au·to·mo·tive
au·ton·o·mous
  au·ton·om·ic
au·ton·o·my
  au·ton·o·mies
au·top·sy
au·tumn
  au·tum·nal
aux·il·i·a·ry
  aux·il·ia·ries
avail
  avail·a·ble
  avail·a·bil·i·ty
av·a·lanche
  av·a·lanch·ing
avant·garde
av·a·rice
  av·a·ri·cious
Ave Ma·ria
avenge
  avenged
  aveng·ing
  aveng·er
av·e·nue
aver
  averred
  aver·ring
  aver·ment
av·er·age
  av·er·aged
  av·er·ag·ing
averse
  averse·ly
  aver·sion
avert
  avert·a·ble
avi·ary
  avi·aries
avi·a·tion
  avi·a·tor
  avi·a·trix
av·id

avid·i·ty
  av·id·ly
av·o·ca·do
av·o·ca·tion
avoid
  avoid·a·ble
  avoid·ance
av·oir·du·pois
avow
  avow·al
  avowed
avun·cu·lar
await
awake
  awoke
awaked
awak·ing
awak·en
award
aware
  aware·ness
away
awe
  awed
  aw·ing
aweigh
awe·some
awe·strick·en
  awe·struck
aw·ful
  aw·ful·ly
  aw·ful·ness
awhile
awhirl
awk·ward
  awk·ward·ness
awn·ing
awry
ax
  ax·es
ax·i·om
  ax·i·o·mat·ic
  ax·i·o·mat·i·cal
ax·is
  ax·es
  ax·i·al
ax·le
azal·ea

az·i·muth
az·ure

B

bab·bitt
bab·ble
 bab·bled
 bab·bling
ba·boon
ba·bush·ka
ba·by
 ba·bies
 ba·bied
 ba·by·ing
ba·by·sit
 ba·by·sit·ting
 ba·by·sit·ter
bac·ca·lau·re·ate
bac·ca·rat
bac·cha·nal
 bac·cha·na·li·an
bach·e·lor
ba·cil·lus
 ba·cil·li
back·ache
back·bite
back·board
back·bone
back·drop
back·field
back·fire
back·gam·mon
back·ground
back·hand
back·hand·ed
back·ing
back·lash
back·log
back·side
back·slide
 back·slid·den
 back·slid·er
back·spin
back·stage
back·stairs
back·stop
back·talk

back·ward
 back·ward·ness
back·wash
ba·con
bac·te·ria
 bac·te·ri·um
 bac·te·ri·al
bac·te·ri·cide
 bac·te·ri·ci·dal
bac·te·ri·ol·o·gy
 bac·te·ri·ol·o·gist
 bac·te·ri·o·log·i·cal
bad
 worse
 worst
badge
badg·er
bad·i·nage
bad·land
bad·ly
bad·min·ton
baf·fle
 baf·fled
 baf·fling
bag
 bagged
 bag·ging
bag·a·telle
ba·gel
bag·gage
bag·gy
 bag·gi·er
 bag·ging
ba·gnio
bag·pipe
ba·guette
bail·a·ble
bail·iff
bail·i·wick
bails·man
baize
bake
 baked
 bak·ing
bak·er
bak·er·y
 bak·er·ies
bak·sheesh

bal·a·lai·ka
bal·ance
 bal·anced
 bal·anc·ing
 bal·anc·er
bal·co·ny
 bal·co·nies
bald
 bald·ness
bal·der·dash
bald·head
bale
 baled
 bal·ing
bale·ful
balk
balky
 balk·i·est
bal·lad
bal·last
bal·le·ri·na
bal·let
bal·lis·tic
 bal·lis·tics
 bal·lis·ti·cian
bal·loon
bal·lot
 bal·lot·ed
 bal·lot·ing
ball·room
bal·ly·hoo
balmy
 balm·i·er
ba·lo·ney
bal·sa
bal·sam
bal·us·ter
 bal·us·trade
bam·bi·no
bam·boo
bam·boo·zle
 bam·boo·zled
 bam·boo·zling
ban
 banned
 ban·ning
ba·nal
 ba·nal·i·ty

ba·nana
band·age
  band·aged
  band·ag·ing
ban·dana
  ban·dan·na
ban·deau
ban·de·role
ban·dit
  ban·dit·ry
ban·do·leer
  ban·do·lier
band·stand
band·wag·on
ban·dy
  ban·died
  ban·dy·ing
bane·ful
ban·gle
ban·ish
  ban·ish·ment
ban·is·ter
  ban·nis·ter
ban·jo
bank·book
bank·er
  bank·ing
bank·rupt
  bank·rupt·cy
  bank·rupt·cies
ban·ner
banquet
ban·quette
ban·shee
ban·tam
ban·ter
  ban·ter·ing·ly
ban·yan
ban·zai
bap·tism
  bap·tis·mal
Bap·tist
Bap·tis·tery
bap·tize
  bap·tized
  bap·tiz·ing
bar
  barred

barring
bar·bar·ic
  bar·bari·an
  bar·ba·rism
  bar·ba·rous
bar·bar·i·ty
  bar·bari·ties
bar·be·cue
  bar·be·cued
  bar·be·cu·ing
bar·ber
bar·bi·can
bar·bi·tal
bar·bi·tu·rate
bar·ca·role
bare
  bare·ness
bare·back
bare·faced
bare·foot
bare·ly
bar·gain
barge
  barged
  barg·ing
bari·tone
bari·um
barley
bar mitz·vah
bar·na·cle
bar·o·graph
ba·rom·et·er
  baro·met·ric
bar·on
  bar·on·ess
  ba·ro·ni·al
bar·on·et
ba·roque
bar·rack
bar·ra·cu·da
bar·rage
bar·rel
  barreled
  barrel·ing
bar·ren
  bar·ren·ness
bar·rette
bar·ri·cade

bar·ri·cad·ed
bar·ri·cad·ing
bar·ri·er
bar·row
bar·ten·der
bar·ter
  bar·ter·er
ba·sal
  bas·al·ly
ba·salt
base
  based
  bas·ing
base·ball
base·less
base·ment
bash·ful
  bash·ful·ly
ba·sic
  ba·si·cal·ly
ba·sil
ba·sil·i·ca
bas·i·lisk
ba·sin
ba·sis
  ba·ses
bas·ket·ball
bas·ket·ry
bas-re·lief
bas·si·net
bas·so
  bas·sos
bas·soon
bas·tard
  bas·tard·ize
  bas·tard·ly
baste
  bast·ed
  bast·ing
bat
  bat·ted
  bat·ting
  bat·ter
bate
  bat·ed
  bat·ing
bathe
  bathed

17

bath·ing
bath·y·sphere
ba·tiste
bat·on
bat·tal·ion
bat·ten
bat·ter
bat·tery
bat·tle
  bat·tled
  bat·tling
bat·tle·field
bat·tle·ment
bau·ble
baux·ite
bawdy
bay·o·net
bay·ou
ba·zaar
ba·zoo·ka
beach·comb·er
beach·head
bea·con
bead·ed
bead·like
beak·er
beamed
bear
  bore
  borne
bear·ing
bear·a·ble
  bear·a·bly
beard·ed
  beard·less
bear·ish
beast
  beast·li·ness
  beast·ly
beat
  beat·en
  beat·ing
be·a·tif·ic
be·at·i·fy
  be·at·i·fied
  be·at·i·fy·ing
  be·at·i·fi·ca·tion
be·at·i·tude

beat·nik
beau
  beaus
  beaux
beau geste
beau·te·ous
beau·ti·cian
beau·ti·fy
  beau·ti·fied
  beau·ti·fi·ca·tion
beauty
  beau·ti·ful
beaux-arts
bea·ver
be·calm
be·cause
beck·on
be·cloud
be·come
  be·came
  be·com·ing
bed
  bed·ded
  bed·ding
be·daz·zle
  be·daz·zled
  be·daz·zling
  be·daz·zle·ment
be·dev·il
  be·dev·iled
  be·dev·il·ing
  be·dev·il·ment
be·dim
  be·dimmed
  be·dim·ming
bed·lam
bed·drag·gle
  be·drag·gling
bed·rid·den
bed·room
beech-nut
beef
  beeves
beef·eat·er
beef·steak
beefy
  beef·i·er
bee·hive

bee·line
Bee·tho·ven
bee·tle
be·fall
  be·fell
  be·fall·en
  be·fall·ing
be·fit
  be·fit·ted
  be·fit·ting
be·fog
  be·fogged
  be·fog·ging
be·fore
be·friend
be·fud·dle
  be·fud·dled
  be·fud·dling
beg
  begged
  beg·ging
be·get
  be·got
  be·got·ten
beg·gar
  beg·gar·ly
be·gin
  be·gan
  be·gun
  be·gin·ning
be·gin·ner
be·gone
be·go·nia
be·got·ten
be·grime
be·grudge
  be·grudged
  be·grudg·ing
be·guile
  be·guiled
  be·guil·ing
be·half
be·have
  be·haved
  be·hav·ing
be·hav·ior
  be·hav·ior·ism
  be·hav·ior·ist

be·head
be·he·moth
be·hest
be·hind
be·hold
  be·held
  be·hold·ing
be·hold·en
be·hoove
beige
be·ing
be·la·bor
be·lat·ed
  be·lat·ed·ly
be·lay
  be·layed
  be·lay·ing
belch
be·lea·guer
bel·fry
  bel·fries
be·lie
  be·lied
  be·ly·ing
be·lief
be·lieve
  be·lieved
  be·liev·ing
  be·liev·a·ble
  be·liev·er
be·lit·tle
  be·lit·tled
  be·lit·tling
bel·la·don·na
belles let·tres
bel·li·cose
  bel·li·cos·i·ty
bel·lig·er·ence
  bel·lig·er·en·cy
bel·lig·er·ent
  bel·lig·er·ent·ly
bel·low
bel·ly
  bel·lies
  bel·lied
  bel·ly·ing
bel·ly·ache
  bel·ly·ach·ing

be·long
  be·long·ings
be·loved
be·low
belt·ed
be·mire
  be·mired
  be·mir·ing
be·moan
be·muse
  be·mused
  be·mus·ing
bend
  bent
  bend·ing
be·neath
ben·e·dict
ben·e·dic·tion
  ben·e·dic·to·ry
ben·e·fac·tion
ben·e·fac·tor
  ben·e·fac·tress
ben·e·fice
  ben·e·ficed
  ben·e·fic·ing
be·nef·i·cent
  be·nef·i·cence
ben·e·fi·cial
ben·e·fi·ci·ar·y
  ben·e·fi·ci·ar·ies
ben·e·fit
  ben·e·fit·ed
  ben·e·fit·ing
be·nev·o·lence
  be·nev·o·lent
be·night·ed
be·nign
  be·nign·ly
be·nig·nant
  be·nig·nan·cy
be·numb
ben·zene
ben·zine
be·queath
be·quest
be·rate
  be·rat·ed
  be·rat·ing

be·reave
  be·reaved
  be·reft
  be·reav·ing
be·ret
ber·ga·mot
ber·i·beri
ber·ke·li·um
ber·ret·ta
  bir·ret·ta
berry
  berries
ber·serk
berth
ber·yl
be·ryl·li·um
be·seech
  be·sought
  be·seeched
  be·seech·ing
be·set
  be·set·ting
be·side
be·siege
  be·sieged
  be·sieg·ing
  be·sieg·er
be·smear
be·smirch
be·sot·ted
be·speak
  be·spoke
  be·spok·en
  be·speak·ing
bes·tial
  bes·tial·ly
  bes·ti·al·i·ty
be·stir
  be·stirred
  be·stir·ring
be·stow
  be·stow·al
be·stride
  be·strode
  be·strid·den
  be·strid·ing
bet
  bet·ted

bet·ting
bet·tor
be·take
  be·took
  be·tak·en
  be·tak·ing
be·ta·tron
be·tel
beth·el
be·tide
  be·tid·ed
  be·tid·ing
be·to·ken
be·tray
  be·tray·al
  be·tray·er
be·troth
  be·troth·al
  be·trothed
bet·ter
  bet·ter·ment
bet·tor
be·tween
be·twixt
bev·el
  bev·eled
  bev·el·ing
bev·er·age
bevy
  bev·ies
be·wail
be·ware
be·wil·der
  be·wil·der·ing·ly
  be·wil·der·ment
be·witch
  be·witch·ing
  be·witch·ment
be·yond
bi·an·nu·al
bi·as
  bi·ased
  bi·as·ing
bi·ax·i·al
bi·be·lot
Bi·ble
Bib·li·cal
bib·li·og·ra·phy

bib·li·og·ra·phies
bib·li·og·ra·pher
bib·li·o·graph·ic
bib·li·o·ma·nia
  bib·li·o·ma·ni·ac
bib·li·o·phile
bib·u·lous
bi·cam·er·al
bi·car·bo·nate
bi·cen·ten·ni·al
  bi·cen·te·nary
bi·ceps
bi·chlo·ride
bick·er
bi·cus·pid
bi·cy·cle
  bi·cy·cled
  bi·cy·cling
  bi·cy·cler
  bi·cy·clist
bid
  bade
  bid·den
  bid·ding
  bid·da·ble
  bid·der
bide
  bode
  bid·ed
  bid·ing
bi·en·ni·al
  bi·en·ni·al·ly
  bi·en·ni·um
bier
bi·fo·cals
bi·fur·cate
  bi·fur·ca·tion
big
  big·ger
  big·gest
big·a·my
  big·a·mist
  big·a·mous
big-heart·ed
big·ot
  big·ot·ed
  big·ot·ry
bi·jou

bi·ki·ni
bi·la·bi·al
bi·lat·er·al
bilge
bi·lin·gual
bil·ious
billed
  bill·ing
bil·let
bil·let-doux
bil·liards
bil·lion
  bil·lionth
bil·lion·aire
bil·low
  bil·low·y
bi·met·al·lism
bi·month·ly
bi·na·ry
bind
  bound
  bind·ing
  bind·er
bind·ery
binge
bin·go
bin·na·cle
bin·oc·u·lar
bi·nom·i·al
bi·o·chem·is·try
  bi·o·chem·i·cal
  bi·o·chem·ist
bio·de·grad·able
bi·o·e·col·o·gy
bi·o·en·gi·neer·ing
bi·o·gen·e·sis
bi·og·ra·phy
  bi·og·ra·pher
  bi·o·graph·ic
  bi·o·graph·i·cal
bi·ol·o·gy
  bi·o·log·i·cal
  bi·ol·o·gist
bi·om·e·try
  bi·o·met·rics
bi·on·ics
bi·o·nom·ics
bi·o·phys·ics

bi·op·sy
  bi·op·sies
bi·par·ti·san
bi·par·tite
bi·ped
bi·plane
bi·po·lar
bi·ra·cial
birch
bird·brained
bird·ie
bird's-eye
bi·ret·ta
  be·ret·ta
birth·day
birth·mark
birth·place
birth·stone
bis·cuit
bi·sect
  bi·sec·tion
  bi·sec·tor
bi·sex·u·al
bish·op
  bish·op·ric
bis·muth
bi·son
bisque
bis·tro
bitch
  bit·chy
bite
  bit
  bit·ten
  bit·ing
bit·ter
  bit·ter·ly
  bit·ter·ness
bit·tern
bi·tu·men
  bi·tu·mi·nous
bi·va·lent
  bi·va·lence
bi·valve
  bi·val·vu·lar
biv·ou·ac
  biv·ou·acked

biv·ou·ack·ing
bi·week·ly
bi·zarre
  bi·zarre·ness
blab
  blabbed
  blab·bing
black·ball
black·ber·ry
black·bird
black·board
black·en
black·eyed
black·guard
black·head
black·jack
black·ly
black·mail
black·out
black·top
blad·der
blade
  blad·ed
blame
  blamed
  blam·ing
  blam·a·ble
  blame·less
  blame·wor·thy
blanch
blanc·mange
bland
  bland·ly
  bland·ness
blan·dish
  blan·dish·ment
blank
  blank·ly
blan·ket
blare
  blared
  blar·ing
blar·ney
bla·se
blas·pheme
  blas·phemed
  blas·phem·ing
  blas·phem·er

blas·phem·ous
blas·phemy
  blas·phem·ies
blast·ed
bla·tant
  bla·tan·cy
  bla·tant·ly
blaze
  blazed
  blaz·ing
bleach·er
bleak
  bleak·ly
bleary
  blear·i·ness
bleed
  bled
  bleed·ing
blem·ish
blend·er
bless·ed
  blest
  bles·sing
blind
  blind·ing
  blind·ness
blind·er
blink·er
bliss·ful
blis·ter
blithe·ly
blitz·krieg
bliz·zard
block·ade
  block·ad·ed
  block·ad·ing
block·bus·ter
blond·ness
blood·curd·ling
blood·hound
blood·less
blood·shed
blood·shot
blood·stained
blood·suck·er
blood·thirsty
bloody
  blood·i·est

blood·ied
blood·y·ing
bloom
bloom·ing
bloop·er
blos·som
blot
blot·ted
blot·ting
blotch
blotchy
blot·ter
blow
blew
blown
blow·ing
blow·er
blow·torch
blub·ber
bludg·eon
blue
blu·est
blu·ing
blue·ness
blue·bell
blue·ber·ry
blue·bird
blue·blood·ed
blue·col·lar
blue·print
blun·der
blun·der·ing
blun·der·buss
blunt·ly
blunt·ness
blur
blurred
blur·ring
blur·ry
blush
blushed
blush·ing
blus·ter
blus·ter·ing·ly
blus·ter·ous
blus·tery
boar
board·er

board·walk
boast
boast·fulness
boast·ing·ly
boat·house
boat·swain
bob
bobbed
bob·bing
bob·bin
bob·ble
bob·bled
bob·bling
bob·o·link
bob·sled
bob·white
bode
bod·ed
bod·ing
bod·ice
bod·kin
bod·y
bod·ies
bod·i·ly
bod·y·guard
bog
bog·gy
bo·gey
bog·gle
bog·gled
bog·gling
bo·gus
bogy
bo·he·mi·an
boil·er
bois·ter·ous
bois·ter·ous·ness
bold
bold·ly
bold·face
bo·le·ro
boll·worm
bo·lo
bo·lo·gna
bo·lo·ney
Bol·she·vik
Bol·she·vism
bol·ster

bol·ster·er
bolt
bolt·ed
bom·bard
bom·bard·ment
bom·bar·dier
bom·bast
bom·bas·tic
bom·bas·ti·cal·ly
bomb·er
bomb·proof
bomb·shell
bomb·sight
bo·na fide
bo·nan·za
bon·bon
bond·age
bond·ed
bond·man
bone
boned
bon·ing
bone·head
bon·fire
bon·go
bon·ho·mie
bon·net
bon·ny
bo·nus
bo·nus·es
bon voy·age
bony
bon·i·er
boo·by
boo·bies
boo·by trap
boo·dle
book·bind·er
book·case
book·end
book·ie
book·ish
book·keep·ing
book·keep·er
book·let
book·mark
book·mo·bile
book·plate

book·sell·er
book·shelf
book·worm
boom·er·ang
boon·dog·gle
boor
  boor·ish
boost
  boost·er
booth
boot·leg
  boot·legged
  boot·leg·ging
  boot·leg·ger
boot·ty
booze
  booz·er
  boozy
bo·rax
Bor·deaux
bor·der
  bor·dered
bor·der·land
bor·der·line
bore
  bored
  bor·ing
  bor·er
  bore·dom
bor·ough
bor·row
  bor·row·er
borsch
  borscht
bos·om
bossy
  boss·i·est
  boss·i·ness
bo·sun
bot·a·ny
  bo·tan·i·cal
  bot·a·nist
  bot·a·nize
botch
  botchy
  botch·i·est
both·er
  both·er·some

bot·tle
  bot·tled
  bot·tling
  bot·tle·ful
bot·tle·neck
bot·tom
  bot·tom·less
bot·u·lism
bou·doir
bouf·fant
bough
bought
bouil·lon
boul·der
boul·e·vard
bounce
  bounced
  bounc·ing
bound
bound·a·ry
  bound·a·ries
bound·less
boun·te·ous
boun·ti·ful
boun·ty
  boun·ties
bou·quet
bour·bon
bour·geois
bour·geoi·sie
bou·tique
bou·ton·niere
bo·vine
bow·el
bow·er
bow·ery
bow·ie
bow·ing
bow·knot
bowl
bow·leg
  bow·leg·ged
bowl·er
bow·line
bowl·ing
bow·string
box·car
box·er

box·ful
box·ing
boy
  boy·hood
  boy·ish
boy·cott
boy·friend
boy·sen·ber·ry
brace
  braced
  brac·ing
brace·let
brac·er
  bra·ces
brack·et
brack·ish
brad
  brad·ded
  brad·ding
brag
  bragged
  brag·ging
brag·ga·do·cio
brag·gart
Brah·ma
Brah·min
  Brah·man
braid
  braid·ing
braille
brain·child
brain·less
brain·pow·er
brain·storm
brain·wash·ing
brainy
  brain·i·er
  brain·i·est
braise
  braised
  brais·ing
brake
  brak·ing
bram·ble
  bram·bly
branch
  branch·ed
brand

brand·er
bran·dish
bran·dy
  bran·dies
  bran·died
bra·sier
bras·siere
brassy
  brass·i·er
brat
  brat·tish
  brat·ty
bra·va·do
brave
  braved
  brav·ing
  brave·ness
  brav·ery
  brav·er·ies
bra·vo
bra·vu·ra
brawl
  brawl·er
brawn
  brawny
  brawn·i·er
  brawn·i·ness
braze
bra·zen
bra·zier
breach
bread
  bread·ed
bread·win·ner
break
  broke
  bro·ken
  break·ing
  break·a·ble
break·age
break·down
break·er
break·fast
break·neck
break·out
break·through
break·wa·ter
breast·bone

breath
breathe
  breathed
  breath·ing
  breath·less
breath·tak·ing
breathy
breech·es
breech·load·er
breed
  bred
  breed·ing
breeze
  breezy
  breez·i·ness
breth·ren
bre·vet
  bre·vet·ted
  bre·vet·ting
bre·vi·a·ry
  bre·vi·a·ries
brev·i·ty
brew·ery
  brew·er·ies
bri·ar
bribe
  bribed
  brib·ing
  brib·a·ble
brib·ery
  brib·er·ies
bric·a·brac
brick·lay·er
brick·yard
bride
  brid·al
  bride·groom
  brides·maid
bridge
  bridge·work
bri·dle
  bri·dled
  bri·dling
brief
  brief·ly
  brief·ing
bri·er
bri·gade

brig·a·dier
brig·and
brig·an·tine
bright
  bright·ness
  bright·en
bril·liance
  bril·lian·cy
  bril·liant
brim·ful
brim·ming
brim·stone
brine
  briny
bring
  brought
  bring·ing
brink
bri·quette
  briquet
brisk
  brisk·ly
  brisk·ness
bris·ket
bris·tle
  bris·tled
Brit·ain
  Bri·tan·nia
  Brit·ish
  Brit·on
Brit·ta·ny
britch·es
brit·tle
broach
  broached
  broach·ing
broad·cast
  broad·cast·ed
  broad·cast·ing
broad·cloth
broad·mind·ed
broad·side
bro·cade
  bro·cad·ed
  bro·cad·ing
broc·co·li
bro·chure
broque

broil·er
bro·ken
bro·ken-heart·ed
bro·ker
bro·ker·age
bro·mide
bron·chi
bron·chi·al
bron·chi·tis
bron·co
bron·to·sau·rus
bronze
  bronzed
  bronz·ing
brooch
brood
  brood·ing
broth·el
broth·er
  broth·er·hood
broth·er-in-law
broth·er·ly
  broth·er·li·ness
brow·beat
  brow·beat·en
brown
brown·ie
browse
  browsed
  brows·ing
bru·in
bruise
  bruised
  bruis·ing
bruis·er
bru·net
brush-off
brusque
brusk
bru·tal
  bru·tal·i·ty
bru·tal·ize
  bru·tal·ized
  bru·tal·iz·ing
  bru·tal·i·za·tion
brut·ish
bub·ble
  bub·bled

bub·bling
bu·bon·ic
buc·ca·neer
buck·a·roo
buck·board
buck·et·ful
buck·le
buck·ram
buck·skin
buck·tooth
buck·wheat
bu·col·ic
bud
  bud·ded
  bud·ding
Bud·dha
  Bud·dhism
  Bud·dhist
bud·dy
budge
budg·et
buf·fa·lo
  buf·fa·loed
buff·er
buf·fet
buf·foon
  buf·foon·ery
bug
  bugged
  bug·ging
bug·a·boo
bug·gy
bu·gle
  bu·gling
  bu·gler
build
  built
  build·ing
bulb
  bul·bous
bulge
  bulged
  bulg·ing
  bulgy
bulk·head
bulky
  bulk·i·er
  bulk·i·ness

bull·doze
  bull·dozed
  bull·doz·ing
  bull·doz·er
bul·let
bul·le·tin
bul·let-proof
bull·fight
bull·frog
bull·head·ed
bul·lion
bull·ock
bull's-eye
bul·ly
  bul·lies
  bul·lied
  bul·ly·ing
bul·rush
bul·wark
bum
  bummed
  bum·ming
bum·ble·bee
bump·er
bump·kin
bump·tious
bumpy
  bump·i·est
  bump·i·ness
bunch
  bunchy
bun·co
bun·dle
  bun·dled
  bun·dling
bun·ga·low
bun·gle
  bun·gled
  bun·gling
bun·ion
bunk·er
bun·ny
  bun·nies
Bun·sen burner
bun·ting
bu·oy
buoy·ant
  buoy·an·cy

bur·den
  bur·den·some
bu·reau
  bu·reaus
  bu·reaux
bu·reauc·ra·cy
  bu·reauc·ra·cies
  bu·reau·crat
  bu·reau·crat·ic
bur·geon
bur·gess
bur·gher
bur·glar
  bur·glar·ize
  bur·glar·ized
  bur·glar·iz·ing
bur·gla·ry
  bur·gla·ries
bur·gle
  bur·gled
  bur·gling
Bur·gun·dy
bur·i·al
bur·lap
bur·lesque
  bur·lesqued
  bur·les·quing
bur·ly
  bur·li·ness
burn
  burned
  burnt
  burn·ing
burn·er
bur·nish
bur·noose
burr
  burred
  bur·ring
bur·ro
bur·row
bur·sa
bur·sar
bur·sa·ry
bur·si·tis
burst
  burst·ing
bury

bur·ied
bur·y·ing
bus
  bus·es
bush·el
Bu·shi·do
bush·ing
bush·man
bush·mas·ter
bush·whack
bushy
bus·i·ly
busi·ness
busi·ness·like
busi·ness·man
bus·tle
  bus·tled
  bus·tling
busy
  bus·ied
  bus·y·ing
  bus·i·ly
  bus·i·er
bu·tane
butch·er
butch·ery
but·ler
butt
butte
but·ter·fin·gered
but·ter·fly
  but·ter·flies
but·ter·scotch
but·tery
but·tock
but·ton·hole
  but·ton·hol·ing
but·tress
bux·om
buy
  bought
  buy·ing
buy·er
buz·zard
buzz·er
by·law
by·line

by·pass
by·play
by·prod·uct
by·stand·er
byte
by·way
by·word
Byz·an·tine

C

ca·bal
  ca·ball·ed
  ca·ball·ing
ca·bal·le·ro
ca·ba·na
cab·a·ret
cab·bage
cab·in
cab·i·net
ca·ble
  ca·bled
  ca·bling
ca·ble·gram
ca·boose
cab·ri·o·let
ca·cao
cache
  cached
  cach·ing
ca·chet
cack·le
  cack·led
  cack·ling
ca·coph·o·ny
  ca·coph·o·nous
cac·tus
  cac·ti
cad
  cad·dish
ca·dav·er
  ca·dav·er·ous
cad·die
  cad·died
  cad·dy·ing
cad·dy
ca·dence
ca·den·za

ca·det
cadge
  cadged
  cadg·ing
cad·mi·um
ca·dre
ca·du·ce·us
Cae·sar
cae·sar·e·an
  ces·ar·ean
ca·fe au lait
caf·e·te·ria
caf·feine
caf·tan
cage
  caged
  cag·ing
cagey
  ca·gi·ly
cai·man
cais·son
ca·jole
  ca·joled
  ca·jol·ing
Ca·jun
cake
  caked
  cak·ing
cal·a·bash
cal·a·boose
cal·a·mine
ca·lam·i·ty
  ca·lam·i·ties
  ca·lam·i·tous
cal·ci·fy
  cal·ci·fied
  cal·ci·fy·ing
  cal·ci·fi·ca·tion
cal·ci·mine
cal·ci·um
cal·cu·la·ble
  cal·cu·la·bil·i·ty
cal·cu·late
  cal·cu·lat·ed
  cal·cu·lat·ing
  cal·cu·la·tion
cal·cu·la·tor
cal·cu·lus

cal·dron
cal·en·dar
calf
  calves
cal·i·ber
cal·i·brate
  cal·i·brat·ed
  cal·i·brat·ing
  cal·i·bra·tion
cal·i·co
  cal·i·coes
cal·i·per
ca·liph
cal·is·then·ics
cal·lig·ra·phy
  cal·lig·ra·pher
call·ing
cal·li·o·pe
cal·lous
  cal·loused
cal·low
cal·lus
calm·ly
ca·lor·ic
cal·o·rie
  cal·o·ries
ca·lum·ny
  cal·um·nies
cal·lum·ni·ate
  ca·lum·ni·at·ed
  ca·lum·ni·at·ing
  ca·lum·ni·a·tion
Cal·va·ry
calve
  calved
  calv·ing
ca·lyp·so
ca·ma·ra·de·rie
cam·ber
cam·bric
cam·el
ca·mel·lia
Cam·em·bert
cam·eo
cam·era
cam·i·sole
cam·ou·flage
  cam·ou·flaged

cam·ou·flag·ing
cam·paign
camp·er
cam·phor
cam·pus
  cam·pus·es
cam·shaft
can
  canned
  can·ning
Can·a·da
  Ca·na·di·an
ca·nal
can·a·pe
ca·nary
ca·nas·ta
can·can
can·cel
  can·celed
  can·cel·ing
  can·cel·la·tion
can·cer
can·de·la·brum
  can·de·la·bra
can·des·cent
  can·des·cence
can·did
can·di·da·cy
  can·di·da·cies
can·di·date
can·died
can·dle
  can·dled
  can·dling
can·dor
can·dy
  can·dies
  can·died
cane
  caned
  can·ing
ca·nine
can·is·ter
can·ker
canned
can·nery
  can·ner·ies
can·ni·bal

can·ni·bal·ism
can·ni·bal·ize
  can·ni·bal·iz·ing
can·non
can·ny
  can·ni·ly
  can·ni·ness
ca·noe
  ca·noed
  ca·noe·ing
  ca·noe·ist
can·on
can·on·ize
  can·on·iz·ing
  can·on·i·za·tion
can·o·py
  can·o·pies
  can·o·pied
  can·o·py·ing
can·ta·loupe
  can·ta·lope
can·tan·ker·ous
can·ta·ta
can·teen
can·ter
can·ti·lev·er
can·to
can·tor
can·vas
can·vass
can·yon
cap
  capped
  cap·ping
ca·pa·bil·i·ty
  ca·pa·bil·i·ties
ca·pa·ble
  ca·pa·bly
ca·pa·cious
ca·pac·i·tate
  ca·pac·i·tat·ed
  ca·pac·i·tat·ing
ca·pac·i·ty
  ca·pac·i·ties
ca·per
cap·il·lar·i·ty
cap·il·lary
  cap·il·lar·ies

cap·i·tal
cap·i·tal·ism
  cap·i·tal·is·tic
  cap·i·tal·ist
cap·i·tal·ize
  cap·i·tal·i·za·tion
cap·i·tal·ly
cap·i·ta·tion
ca·pit·u·late
  ca·pit·u·lat·ed
  ca·pit·u·lat·ing
  ca·pit·u·la·tion
ca·pon
ca·pric·cio
ca·price
  ca·pri·cious
cap·ri·ole
  cap·ri·oled
  cap·ri·ol·ing
cap·size
  cap·siz·ing
cap·stan
cap·sule
  cap·su·lar
cap·tain
  cap·tain·cy
cap·tion
cap·tious
cap·ti·vate
  cap·ti·vat·ed
  cap·ti·vat·ing
  cap·ti·va·tion
cap·tive
  cap·tiv·i·ty
cap·tor
cap·ture
  cap·tured
  cap·tur·ing
cara·cole
car·a·cul
ca·rafe
car·a·mel
car·at
car·a·van
car·a·way
car·bide
car·bine
car·bo·hy·drate

car·bol·ic
car·bon
  car·bo·na·ceous
  car·bo·na·tion
  car·bon di·ox·ide
  car·bon·ize
  car·bon·ized
  car·bon·iz·ing
  car·bon·i·za·tion
  car·bon mon·ox·ide
car·bo·run·dum
car·boy
car·buncle
car·bu·re·tor
car·cass
car·cin·o·gen
  car·cin·o·gen·ic
car·ci·no·ma
car·da·mom
card·board
car·di·ac
car·di·gan
car·di·nal
car·di·o·graph
  car·di·og·ra·phy
car·dio·vas·cu·lar
card·sharp
care
  cared
  caring
ca·reen
ca·reer
care·free
care·ful
  care·ful·ly
care·less
  care·less·ness
ca·ress
  ca·ress·ing·ly
caret
care·tak·er
car·go
Car·ib·be·an
car·i·bou
car·i·ca·ture
  car·i·ca·tured
  car·i·ca·tur·ing
  car·i·ca·tur·ist

car·il·lon
car·mine
car·nage
car·nal
  car·nal·i·ty
  car·nal·ly
car·na·tion
car·nel·ian
car·ni·val
car·ni·vore
  car·niv·o·rous
car·ol
  car·oled
  car·ol·ing
car·om
ca·rouse
  ca·roused
  ca·rous·ing
  ca·rous·al
  car·ou·sel
car·pen·ter
  car·pen·try
car·pet
car·pet·bag·ger
car·pet·ing
car·rel
car·riage
car·ri·er
car·ri·on
car·rot
  car·roty
car·ry
  car·ried
  car·ry·ing
cart·age
carte blanche
car·tel
  car·te·lize
car·ti·lage
  car·ti·lag·i·nous
car·tog·ra·phy
  car·tog·ra·pher
  car·to·graph·ic
car·ton
car·toon
car·tridge
carve
  carved

carv·ing
car·y·at·id
ca·sa·ba
cas·cade
  cas·cad·ed
  cas·cad·ing
case
  cased
  cas·ing
case·ment
ca·se·ous
cash·ew
cash·ier
cash·mere
ca·si·no
cas·ket
cas·sa·ba
cas·se·role
cas·sette
cas·sock
cast
  cast·ing
cas·ta·net
cast·a·way
caste
cast·er
cast·ing
cas·ti·gate
  cas·ti·gat·ed
  cas·ti·gat·ing
  cas·ti·ga·tion
cast i·ron
cas·tle
cas·tor
cas·trate
  cas·trat·ed
  cas·trat·ing
  cas·tra·tion
cas·u·al
  cas·u·al·ness
cas·u·al·ty
  cas·u·al·ties
cas·u·ist
  cas·u·is·tic
  cas·u·ist·ry
cat·a·clysm
  cat·a·clys·mal
  cat·a·clys·mic

cat·a·comb
cat·a·falque
cat·a·lep·sy
  cat·a·lep·tic
cat·a·log
  cat·a·logue
  cat·a·loged
  cat·a·log·ing
ca·tal·y·sis
  cat·a·lyt·ic
cat·a·lyst
cat·a·lyze
  cat·a·lyz·ing
cat·a·ma·ran
cat·a·pult
cat·a·ract
ca·tarrh
ca·tas·tro·phe
  cat·as·troph·ic
Ca·taw·ba
catch
  caught
  catch·ing
  catch·er
catchy
  catch·i·er
cat·e·chism
cat·e·chize
  cat·e·chized
  cat·e·chiz·ing
  cat·e·chi·za·tion
  cat·e·chist
cat·e·gor·i·cal
cat·e·go·ry
  cat·e·go·ries
  cat·e·gor·ize
  cat·e·gor·iz·ing
ca·ter
  ca·ter·er
  cat·er·pil·lar
cat·er·waul
cat·fish
ca·thar·sis
  ca·thar·tic
ca·the·dral
cath·e·ter
cath·ode
cath·o·lic

cath·o·lic·i·ty
ca·thol·i·cize
Cath·o·lic
Ca·thol·i·cism
cat·nap
cat·nap·ping
cat·nip
cat·tle
cat·tle·man
cat·ty
cat·ti·ness
Cau·ca·sian
cau·cus
cau·cus·es
cau·cus·ing
caul·dron
cau·li·flow·er
caulk
caus·al
cau·sal·i·ty
cause
caused
caus·ing
cau·sa·tion
cause·less
cause·way
caus·tic
cau·ter·ize
cau·ter·ized
cau·ter·iz·ing
cau·ter·i·za·tion
cau·tery
cau·tion
cau·tion·ary
cau·tious
cav·al·cade
cav·a·lier
cav·al·ry
cave
caved
cav·ing
ca·ve·at
cav·ern
cav·ern·ous
cav·i·ar
cav·il
cav·iled
cav·il·ing

cav·i·ty
cav·i·ties
ca·vort
cay·enne
cay·man
cay·use
cease
ceased
ceas·ing
cease·less
cease·fire
ce·dar
cede
ced·ed
ced·ing
ceil·ing
cel·e·brate
cel·e·brat·ing
cel·e·bra·tion
cel·e·brant
cel·e·bra·tor
ce·leb·ri·ty
ce·leb·ri·ties
ce·ler·i·ty
cel·ery
ce·les·tial
cel·i·ba·cy
cel·i·bate
cel·lar
cel·lo
cel·list
cel·lo·phane
cel·lu·lar
cel·lu·lose
ce·ment
cem·e·tery
cem·e·ter·ies
cen·o·taph
cen·ser
cen·sor
cen·so·ri·al
cen·sor·ship
cen·so·ri·ous
cen·sure
cen·sured
cen·sur·ing
cen·sur·er
cen·sur·a·ble

cen·sus
cen·sus·ing
cen·taur
cen·te·nar·i·an
cen·te·na·ry
cen·te·na·ries
cen·ten·ni·al
cen·tes·i·mal
cen·ter·board
cen·ter·piece
cen·ti·grade
cen·ti·gram
cen·ti·li·ter
cen·ti·me·ter
central
cen·tral·ize
cen·tral·ized
cen·tral·iz·ing
cen·trif·uge
cen·trif·u·gal
cen·trip·e·tal
cen·tro·bar·ic
cen·tu·ri·on
cen·tu·ry
cen·tu·ries
ce·ram·ic
ce·ram·ics
ce·re·al
cer·e·bral
cer·e·bel·lum
cer·e·bric
cer·e·brum
cer·e·mo·ny
cer·e·mo·nies
cer·e·mo·ni·al
cer·e·mo·ni·ous
ce·rise
cer·tain
cer·tain·ly
cer·tain·ty
cer·tain·ties
cer·tif·i·cate
cer·ti·fi·ca·tion
cer·ti·fy
cer·ti·fied
cer·ti·fy·ing
cer·ti·fi·a·ble
cer·ti·fi·er

cer·ti·tude
ce·ru·le·an
cer·vix
  cer·vi·cal
ce·sar·ean
  cae·sar·ean
ces·sa·tion
ce·ta·cean
Cha·blis
chafe
  chafed
  chaf·ing
chaff
cha·grin
  cha·grined
  cha·grin·ing
chain
chair·man
  chair·per·son
  chair·wom·an
chaise longue
chal·et
chal·ice
chalk
  chalky
chal·lenge
  chal·lenged
  chal·leng·ing
cham·ber
cham·bray
cha·me·le·on
cham·ois
cham·pagne
cham·pi·on
  cham·pi·on·ship
chance
  chanced
  chanc·ing
  chancy
chan·cel·lor
chan·de·lier
change
  changed
  chang·ing
  change·a·ble
  change·ful
  change·less
chan·nel

chan·nel·ing
chan·teuse
chan·tey
chan·ti·cleer
cha·os
  cha·ot·ic
chap
  chapped
  chap·ping
chap·ar·ral
cha·peau
chap·el
chap·e·ron
chap·lain
chap·ter
char
  charred
  char·ring
char·ac·ter
  char·ac·ter·is·tic
char·ac·ter·ize
  char·ac·ter·ized
  char·ac·ter·iz·ing
  char·ac·ter·i·za·tion
cha·rade
char·coal
charge
  charged
  charging
charge d'af·faires
charg·er
char·i·ot
  char·i·ot·eer
cha·ris·ma
char·i·ta·ble
  char·i·ta·bly
char·i·ty
  char·i·ties
char·la·tan
charm
  charm·er
  charm·ing
char·ter
char·treuse
chary
  char·i·er
  char·i·est
chase

chased
chas·ing
chasm
chas·sis
chaste
  chaste·ness
  chas·ti·ty
chas·ten
  chas·tise
  chas·tis·ing
  chas·tise·ment
chat
  chat·ted
  chat·ting
cha·teau
chat·tel
chat·ter
chat·ty
  chat·ti·ly
  chat·ti·ness
chauf·feur
chau·vin·ist
  chau·vin·ism
  chau·vin·is·tic
cheap
  cheap·ness
  cheap·en
cheap·skate
cheat
  cheat·er
check·book
check·er·board
check·list
check·mate
check·point
check·room
ched·dar
cheek·bone
cheeky
  cheek·i·ness
cheer·ful
  cheer·ful·ness
  cheer·less
cheery
  cheer·i·er
  cheer·i·ness
cheese
  cheesy

chee·tah
chef
chem·i·cal
  chem·i·cal·ly
che·mise
chem·ist
  chem·is·try
chem·o·ther·a·py
che·nille
cher·ish
cher·ry
  cher·ries
cher·ub
  cher·ubs
  che·ru·bic
chess·man
chest·nut
chesty
  chest·i·er
chev·ron
chew
  chew·er
  chewy
Chi·an·ti
chi·a·ro·scu·ro
chi·can·ery
chi·chi
chick·a·dee
chic·ken
chic·le
chic·o·ry
chide
  chid·ed
  chid·ing
chief
  chief·ly
chief·tain
chif·fon
chif·fo·nier
chig·ger
chi·gnon
Chi·hua·hua
chil·blain
chil·dren
child·bear·ing
child·birth
child·hood
child·ish

child·like
chili
chill
  chill·ing
chilly
  chill·i·er
  chill·i·ness
chime
  chim·ing
chim·ney
chim·pan·zee
chin
  chinned
  chin·ning
chi·na
Chi·na
  Chi·nese
chin·chil·la
chintz
chintzy
chip
  chipped
  chip·ping
chip·munk
Chip·pen·dale
chip·per
chi·rog·ra·phy
  chi·rog·ra·pher
chi·rop·o·dist
chi·ro·prac·tic
  chi·ro·prac·tor
chis·el
  chis·eled
  chis·el·ing
  chis·el·er
chit·chat
chit·ter·ling
chiv·al·ry
  chiv·al·ric
  chiv·al·rous
chlo·rine
chlo·ro·form
chlo·ro·phyll
chock·full
choc·o·late
choice
  choice·ness
choir·boy

choke
  choked
  chok·ing
chok·er
chol·er
chol·era
cho·les·te·rol
choose
  chose
  cho·sen
  choos·ing
choosy
  choos·i·est
chop
  chopped
  chop·ping
chop·per
chop·py
chop·pi·ness
chop su·ey
cho·ral
  cho·ral·ly
cho·rale
chord
chore
cho·reo·graph
  cho·re·og·ra·phy
  cho·re·og·ra·pher
  cho·re·o·graph·ic
chor·tle
  chor·tled
  chor·tling
cho·rus
  cho·rus·es
chor·is·ter
  cho·rus·ing
chos·en
chow·der
chow mein
Christ
chris·ten
  chris·ten·ing
Chris·ten·dom
Chris·tian
  Chris·ti·an·i·ty
  Chris·tian·ize
  Chris·tian·ized
Christ·like

Christ·mas
chro·mat·ic
  chro·mat·i·cal·ly
  chro·mat·ics
chrome
  chro·mi·um
chro·mo·lith·o·graph
chron·ic
  chron·i·cal·ly
chron·i·cle
  chron·i·cled
  chron·i·cling
chron·o·log·i·cal
chro·nol·o·gy
  chro·nol·o·gies
chro·nom·e·ter
chrys·a·lis
chry·san·the·mum
chub·by
  chub·bi·ness
chuck·full
chuck·le
  chuck·ling
chuck·ker
chum·my
chunk
  chunky
  chunk·i·est
church
  church·li·ness
church·go·er
church·man
church·war·den
church·yard
churl·ish
  churl·ish·ness
churn·ing
chut·ney
chutz·pah
ci·ca·da
cic·e·ro·ne
ci·der
ci·gar
cig·a·rette
cil·ia
  cil·i·ar·y
cinc·ture
cin·der

cin·e·ma
cin·e·mat·o·graph
  cin·e·ma·tog·ra·pher
cin·e·rari·um
cin·na·bar
cin·na·mon
ci·pher
cir·ca
cir·cle
  cir·cled
  cir·cling
cir·clet
cir·cuit
cir·cu·i·tous
cir·cu·lar
cir·cu·lar·ize
  cir·cu·lar·iz·ing
  cir·cu·lar·i·za·tion
cir·cu·la·tion
cir·cu·late
  cir·cu·lat·ed
  cir·cu·lat·ing
cir·cu·la·tive
cir·cu·la·to·ry
cir·cum·am·bi·ent
cir·cum·cise
  cir·cum·cised
  cir·cum·cis·ing
  cir·cum·ci·sion
cir·cum·fer·ence
cir·cum·flex
cir·cum·flu·ent
cir·cum·fuse
cir·cum·lo·cu·tion
  cir·cum·lo·cu·to·ry
cir·cum·nav·i·gate
  cir·cum·nav·i·ga·tion
cir·cum·scribe
cir·cum·scrip·tion
cir·cum·spect
cir·cum·stance
cir·cum·stan·tial
  cir·cum·stan·ti·ate
  cir·cum·stan·ti·a·tion
cir·cum·vent
cir·cum·ven·tion
cir·cus
  cir·cus·es

cir·rho·sis
cir·rus
cis·soid
cis·tern
cit·a·del
cite
  cit·ed
  cit·ing
  cit·ta·tion
cit·i·zen
  cit·i·zen·ship
cit·i·zen·ry
  cit·i·zen·ries
cit·re·ous
cit·ron
cit·ron·el·la
cit·rus
city
  cit·ies
civ·ic
  civ·ics
civ·il
civ·il·ly
ci·vil·ian
ci·vil·i·ty
  ci·vil·i·ties
civ·i·li·za·tion
civ·i·lize
  civ·i·lized
  civ·i·liz·ing
civ·et
claim
  claim·a·ble
  claim·ant
clair·voy·ance
  clair·voy·ant
clam
  clammed
  clam·ming
clam·my
  clam·mi·ness
clam·or
  clam·or·ous
clamp·er
clan
  clan·nish
clan·des·tine
clang·or

clang·or·ous
clans·man
clap
  clapped
  clap·ping
clap·board
clap·per
claque
claret
clar·i·fy
  clar·i·fied
  clar·i·fy·ing
  clar·i·fi·ca·tion
clar·i·net
  clar·i·net·ist
clar·i·on
clar·i·ty
clas·sic
clas·si·cal
clas·si·cism
  clas·si·cist
clas·si·fy
  clas·si·fied
  clas·si·fy·ing
  clas·si·fi·ca·tion
classy
  class·i·er
clat·ter
clause
  claus·al
claus·tro·pho·bia
clav·i·chord
clav·i·cle
clay·ey
clean·cut
clean·er
clean·ly
  clean·li·ness
cleanse
  cleansed
  cleans·ing
  cleans·er
clear
  clear·ly
  clear·ness
clear·ance
clearcut
clear·ing

clear·sight·ed
cleav·age
cleave
  cleaved
  cleav·ing
cleav·er
clef
cleft
clem·en·cy
  clem·ent
clergy
  cler·gies
cler·gy·man
cler·ic
  cler·i·cal
cleri·cal·ism
clev·er
  clev·er·ness
clev·is
clew
cli·ché
cli·ent
cli·en·tele
cli·mac·ter·ic
cli·mate
  cli·mat·ic
  cli·mat·i·cal
cli·max
  cli·mac·tic
climb
  climb·er
clinch·er
cling
  clung
  cling·ing
clin·ic
  clin·i·cal
clink·er
clin·quant
clip
  clipped
  clip·ping
clip·per
clique
  cliqu·ish
clit·o·ris
clo·a·ca
clob·ber

clock·wise
clod
  clod·dish
clog
  clogged
  clog·ging
cloi·son·ne
clois·ter
  clois·tral
close
  closed
  clos·ing
  clos·est
  close·ly
  close·ness
clos·et
  clos·et·ed
  clos·et·ing
close·up
clo·sure
clot
  clot·ted
  clot·ting
clothe
  clothed
  cloth·ing
cloth·ier
cloth·ing
clo·ture
cloud·burst
cloudy
  cloud·i·ness
clo·ven
clo·ver
clown
  clown·ish
cloy
  cloy·ing·ly
club
  clubbed
  club·bing
club·foot
club·house
clue
clump
clum·sy
  clum·si·ly
  clum·si·ness

cluster
clutter
coach·man
co·ag·u·late
  co·ag·u·lat·ed
  co·ag·u·lat·ing
  co·ag·u·la·tion
co·a·lesce
  co·a·lesced
  co·a·les·cing
  co·a·les·cence
  co·a·les·cent
co·a·li·tion
coarse
  coars·en
  coarse·ness
coast·er
coast·guard
coast·line
coat·ing
co·au·thor
coax
  coax·ing·ly
co·balt
cob·ble
  cob·bler
cob·ble·stone
co·bra
cob·web
co·ca
co·caine
coc·cyx
cock·ade
cock·a·too
cock·er·al
cock·le
cock·le·bur
cock·le·shell
cock·ney
cock·roach
cock·tail
cocky
  cock·i·ly
  cock·i·ness
co·coa
co·co·nut
co·coon
cod·dle

cod·dled
cod·dling
code
  cod·ed
  cod·ing
co·deine
codg·er
cod·i·cil
cod·i·fy
  cod·i·fied
  cod·i·fy·ing
  cod·i·fi·ca·tion
co·ed
co·ed·u·ca·tion
co·ef·fi·cient
co·e·qual
co·erce
  co·erced
  co·erc·ing
  co·er·cion
  co·er·cive
co·ex·ist
  co·ex·ist·ence
co·ex·tend
cof·fee
cof·fer
cof·fin
co·gent
  co·gen·cy
  co·gent·ly
cog·i·tate
  cog·i·tat·ed
  cog·i·tat·ing
  cog·i·ta·tive
co·gnac
cog·nate
  cog·nat·tion
cog·ni·tion
cog·ni·tive
cog·ni·zance
cog·ni·zant
co·hab·it
  co·hab·i·ta·tion
co·here
  co·hered
  co·her·ing
co·her·ent
  co·her·ence

co·her·ency
co·her·ent·ly
co·he·sion
co·he·sive
co·he·sive·ness
co·hort
coif
coif·feur
coif·fure
coin·age
co·in·cide
  co·in·cid·ed
  co·in·cid·ing
  co·in·ci·dence
  co·in·ci·dent
  co·in·ci·den·tal
co·i·tion
co·i·tus
col·an·der
cold
  cold·ly
  cold·ness
cold·blood·ed
cole·slaw
col·ic
  col·icky
col·i·se·um
co·li·tis
col·lab·o·rate
  col·lab·o·rat·ed
  col·lab·o·rat·ing
  col·lab·o·ra·tion
  col·lab·o·ra·tor
col·lage
col·lapse
  col·lapsed
  col·laps·ing
  col·lap·si·ble
col·lar
col·late
  col·lat·ed
  col·lat·ing
  col·la·tion
col·lat·er·al
col·league
col·lect
  col·lect·ed
  col·lect·i·ble

col·lect·or
col·lec·tion
col·lec·tive
col·lec·tiv·i·ty
col·lec·tiv·ism
col·lec·tiv·ize
col·lec·tiv·i·za·tion
col·lege
col·le·gian
col·le·giate
col·lide
col·lid·ed
col·lid·ing
col·li·sion
col·lie
col·li·mate
col·lin·e·ar
col·lo·cate
col·loid
col·lo·qui·al
col·lo·qui·al·ly
col·lo·qui·al·ism
col·lo·quy
col·lu·sion
col·lu·sive
col·logne
co·lon
colo·nel
co·lo·ni·al
co·lo·ni·al·ism
co·lo·ni·al·ist
col·on·nade
col·o·ny
col·o·nist
col·o·nies
col·o·nize
col·o·niz·ing
col·o·ni·za·tion
col·or
col·or·ful
col·or·ing
col·or·a·tion
col·or·blind
col·or·less
co·los·sal
Col·os·se·um
co·los·sus
Co·lum·bia

col·um·bine
col·umn
co·lum·nar
col·um·nist
co·ma
co·ma·tose
com·bat
com·bat·ed
com·bat·ing
com·bat·ant
com·bat·ive
comb·er
com·bi·na·tion
com·bi·na·tive
com·bine
com·bined
com·bin·ing
com·bus·ti·ble
com·bus·tion
com·bus·tive
come
came
come
coming
co·me·di·an
co·me·di·enne
com·e·dy
com·e·dies
come·ly
come·li·ness
com·et
come·up·pance
com·fort
com·fort·a·ble
com·fort·er
com·ic
com·i·cal
com·ma
com·mand
com·man·dant
com·man·deer
com·mand·er
com·mand·ment
com·man·do
com·mem·o·rate
com·mem·o·rat·ed
com·mem·o·rat·ing
com·mem·o·ra·tion

com·mem·o·ra·tive
com·mence
com·menc·ing
com·mence·ment
com·mend
com·mend·a·ble
com·men·da·tion
com·men·su·rate
com·men·su·ra·tion
com·ment
com·men·tary
com·men·tar·ies
com·men·ta·tor
com·merce
com·mer·cial
com·mer·cial·ism
com·mer·cial·ize
com·mer·cial·i·za·tion
com·mis·er·ate
com·mis·er·at·ed
com·mis·er·at·ing
com·mis·er·a·tion
com·mis·sar
com·mis·sary
com·mis·sar·ies
com·mis·sion
com·mis·sioned
com·mis·sion·er
com·mit
com·mit·ted
com·mit·ting
com·mit·ment
com·mit·tee
com·mode
com·mo·di·ous
com·mod·i·ty
com·mod·i·ties
com·mo·dore
com·mon
com·mon·al·ty
com·mon·place
com·mons
com·mon·weal
com·mon·wealth
com·mo·tion
com·mu·nal
com·mune
com·muned

36

com·mun·ing
com·mu·ni·cant
com·mu·ni·cate
  com·mu·ni·cat·ed
  com·mu·ni·cat·ing
  com·mu·ni·ca·ble
  com·mu·ni·ca·tive
  com·mu·ni·ca·tion
com·mun·ion
com·mu·ni·qué
com·mun·ism
  com·mun·ist
  com·mu·nis·tic
com·mu·ni·ty
  com·mu·ni·ties
com·mu·nize
  com·mu·niz·ing
com·mu·ta·tion
com·mute
  com·mut·ed
  com·mut·ing
  com·mut·a·ble
  com·mut·er
com·pact
  com·pac·tor
com·pan·ion
  com·pan·ion·a·ble
  com·pan·ion·ship
com·pa·ny
  com·pa·nies
com·pa·ra·ble
  com·pa·ra·bil·ity
com·par·a·tive
com·pare
  com·pared
  com·par·ing
  com·par·i·son
com·part·ment
  com·part·ment·ed
  com·part·men·tal·ize
com·pass
com·pas·sion
  com·pas·sion·ate
com·pat·i·ble
  com·pat·i·bly
  com·pat·i·bil·i·ty
com·pa·tri·ot
com·peer

com·pel
  com·pelled
  com·pel·ling
com·pen·di·um
com·pen·sate
  com·pen·sat·ing
com·pen·sa·tive
com·pen·sa·to·ry
  com·pen·sa·tion
com·pete
  com·pet·ed
  com·pet·ing
  com·pet·i·tor
  com·pe·ti·tion
  com·pet·i·tive
com·pe·tent
  com·pe·tence
  com·pe·ten·cy
com·pile
  com·piled
  com·pil·ing
  com·pi·la·tion
com·pla·cent
  com·pla·cence
  com·pla·cen·cy
com·plain
com·plain·ant
com·plaint
com·plai·sance
  com·plai·sant
com·plect·ed
com·ple·ment
  com·ple·men·ta·ry
com·plete
  com·plet·ed
  com·plet·ing
  com·ple·tion
com·plex
  com·plex·i·ty
com·plex·ion
com·pli·ance
  com·pli·an·cy
  com·pli·ant
com·pli·cate
  com·pli·cat·ed
  com·pli·cat·ing
  com·pli·ca·tion
com·plic·i·ty

  com·plic·i·ties
com·pli·ment
com·pli·men·ta·ry
  com·pli·men·ta·ri·ly
com·ply
  com·plied
  com·ply·ing
com·po·nent
com·port
com·port·ment
com·pose
  com·posed
  com·pos·ing
com·pos·er
com·pos·ite
com·po·si·tion
com·post
com·po·sure
com·pote
com·pound
com·pre·hend
  com·pre·hen·si·ble
  com·pre·hen·si·bil·i·ty
  com·pre·hen·sion
  com·pre·hen·sive
com·press
  com·press·ing
  com·pres·si·ble
  com·pres·sion
  com·pres·sor
com·prise
  com·prised
  com·pris·ing
com·pro·mise
  com·pro·mised
  com·pro·mis·ing
comp·trol·ler
com·pul·sion
  com·pul·sive
  com·pul·so·ry
com·punc·tion
com·pute
  com·put·ed
  com·put·ing
  com·pu·ta·tion
com·put·er
com·put·er·ize
  com·put·er·iz·ing

com·put·er·i·za·tion
com·rade
con
  conned
  con·ning
con·cave
  con·cav·i·ty
con·ceal
  con·ceal·ment
con·cede
  con·ced·ed
  con·ced·ing
con·ceit
  con·ceit·ed
con·ceive
  con·ceived
  con·ceiv·ing
  con·ceiv·a·ble
  con·ceiv·a·bly
con·cen·trate
  con·cen·tra·ted
  con·cen·trat·ing
  con·cen·tra·tion
con·cen·tric
  con·cen·tri·cal
con·cept
  con·cep·tu·al
con·cep·tion
con·cep·tu·al·ize
  con·cep·tu·al·i·za·tion
con·cern
  con·cerned
  con·cern·ment
con·cert
con·cert·ed
con·cer·ti·na
con·cer·to
con·ces·sion
  con·ces·sion·aire
conch
con·cierge
con·cil·i·ate
  con·cil·i·at·ed
  con·cil·i·at·ing
  con·cil·i·a·tion
  con·cil·i·a·to·ry
con·cise
  con·cise·ness

con·cise·ly
con·clave
con·clude
  con·clud·ed
  con·clud·ing
  con·clu·sion
  con·clu·sive
con·coct
  con·coc·tion
con·com·i·tant
con·cord
  con·cord·ance
  con·cord·ant
con·course
con·crete
  con·cret·ed
  con·cret·ing
  con·cre·tion
con·cu·bine
con·cu·pis·cent
con·cur
  con·curred
  con·cur·ring
  con·cur·rence
  con·cur·rent
con·cus·sion
  con·cus·sive
con·demn
  con·dem·na·ble
  con·dem·na·tion
con·dense
  con·densed
  con·dens·ing
  con·den·sa·tion
  con·dens·er
con·de·scend
  con·de·scend·ing
  con·de·scen·sion
con·di·ment
con·di·tion
  con·di·tion·al
  con·di·tion·er
  con·di·tioned
con·dole
  con·doled
  con·dol·ing
  con·do·lence
con·do·min·i·um

con·done
  con·doned
  con·don·ing
  con·do·na·tion
con·dor
con·duce
  con·duced
  con·duc·ing
  con·du·cive
con·duct
  con·duct·ance
  con·duc·tion
  con·duc·tor
con·duit
con·fer·ence
con·fess
  con·fess·ed
  con·fes·sion
  con·fes·sion·al
  con·fes·sor
con·fet·ti
con·fi·dant
  con·fi·dante
con·fide
  con·fid·ed
  con·fid·ing
con·fi·dence
  con·fi·dent
  con·fi·den·tial
con·fig·u·ra·tion
con·fine
  con·fined
  con·fin·ing
  con·fine·ment
con·firm
  con·firmed
  con·fir·ma·tion
  con·fir·ma·tive
  con·fir·ma·to·ry
con·fis·cate
  con·fis·cat·ed
  con·fis·cat·ing
  con·fis·ca·tion
  con·fis·ca·tor
  con·fis·ca·to·ry
con·fla·gra·tion
con·flict
  con·flict·ing

con·flic·tion
con·flu·ence
  con·flu·ent
con·flux
con·form
  con·form·ist
  con·form·a·ble
  con·form·ance
  con·for·ma·tion
  con·form·i·ty
con·found
  con·found·ed
con·front
  con·fron·ta·tion
Con·fu·cius
con·fuse
  con·fused
  con·fus·ing
  con·fu·sion
con·fute
  con·fut·ed
  con·fut·ing
  con·fu·ta·tion
con·ga
con·geal
  con·geal·ment
con·gen·ial
  con·ge·ni·al·i·ty
  con·gen·ial·ly
con·gen·i·tal
con·gest
  con·ges·tion
  con·ges·tive
con·glom·er·ate
  con·glom·er·at·ed
  con·glom·er·at·ing
  con·glom·er·a·tion
con·grat·u·late
  con·grat·u·lat·ed
  con·grat·u·lat·ing
  con·grat·u·la·to·ry
  con·grat·u·la·tion
con·gre·gate
  con·gre·gat·ed
  con·gre·gat·ing
  con·gre·ga·tion
  con·gre·ga·tion·al
con·gress

con·gres·sion·al
con·gress·man
con·gress·wom·an
con·gru·ent
  con·gru·ent·ly
  con·gru·ence
  con·gru·en·cy
con·gru·ous
  con·gru·ous·ly
  con·gru·ous·ness
  con·gru·i·ty
cone
  con·ic
  con·i·cal
co·ni·fer
con·jec·ture
  con·jec·tured
  con·jec·tur·ing
  con·jec·tur·al
con·join
con·joint
con·ju·gal
  con·ju·gal·ly
con·ju·gate
  con·ju·gat·ed
  con·ju·gat·ing
  con·ju·ga·tion
  con·ju·ga·tive
con·junc·tion
  con·junc·tive
con·jure
  con·jured
  con·jur·ing
  con·ju·ra·tion
con·nect
  con·nec·tor
  con·nec·tion
  con·nec·tive
con·nip·tion
con·nive
  con·niv·ing
  con·niv·ance
con·nois·seur
con·note
  con·not·ed
  con·not·ing
  con·no·ta·tion

con·no·ta·tive
con·nu·bi·al
con·quer
  con·quer·a·ble
  con·quer·or
con·quest
con·quis·ta·dor
con·san·guin·e·ous
con·san·guin·i·ty
con·science
  con·sci·en·tious
  con·scion·able
con·scious
  con·scious·ly
  con·scious·ness
con·script
  con·scrip·tion
con·se·crate
  con·se·crat·ed
  con·se·crat·ing
  con·se·cra·tor
  con·se·cra·tion
con·sec·u·tive
con·sen·sus
con·sent
con·se·quence
con·se·quent
  con·se·quent·ly
  con·se·quen·tial
con·ser·va·tion
  con·ser·va·tion·ist
con·serv·a·tive
  con·serv·a·tism
  con·serv·a·tive·ly
con·serv·a·to·ry
  con·serv·a·to·ries
con·serve
  con·served
  con·serv·ing
con·sid·er
  con·sid·er·ing
  con·sid·er·able
  con·sid·er·a·bly
  con·sid·er·ate
  con·sid·er·a·tion
con·sign
  con·sign·er
  con·sign·or

con·sign·ment
con·sist
con·sist·en·cy
  con·sist·en·cies
  con·sist·ence
con·sist·ent
con·sis·to·ry
con·so·la·tion
  con·sol·a·to·ry
con·sole
  con·soled
  con·sol·ing
  con·sol·a·ble
con·sol·i·date
  con·sol·i·dat·ed
  con·sol·i·dat·ing
  con·sol·i·da·tion
con·som·mé
con·so·nant
con·sort
con·sor·ti·um
con·spic·u·ous
  con·spic·u·ous·ness
con·spire
  con·spired
  con·spir·ing
con·spir·a·cy
  con·spir·a·cies
  con·spir·a·tor
  con·spir·a·to·ri·al
  con·spir·er
con·sta·ble
con·stab·u·lary
con·stant
  con·stan·cy
con·stel·la·tion
con·ster·na·tion
con·sti·pa·tion
  con·sti·pate
con·stit·u·en·cy
  con·stit·u·en·cies
con·stit·u·ent
con·sti·tute
con·sti·tu·tion
  con·sti·tu·tion·al
  con·sti·tu·tion·al·i·ty
  con·sti·tu·tion·al·ly
con·strain

con·strained
con·straint
con·strict
  con·stric·tive
  con·stric·tion
  con·stric·tor
con·struct
  con·struc·tor
  con·struc·tion
con·struc·tive
con·strue
  con·strued
  con·stru·ing
  con·stru·a·ble
con·sul
  con·su·lar
  con·su·lship
  con·su·late
con·sult
  con·sul·ta·tion
  con·sult·ant
con·sume
  con·sumed
  con·sum·ing
  con·sum·a·ble
con·sum·er
  con·sum·er·ism
con·sum·mate
  con·sum·mat·ed
  con·sum·mat·ing
  con·sum·ma·tion
con·sump·tion
con·sump·tive
con·tact
con·ta·gion
  con·ta·gious
  con·ta·gious·ness
con·tain
  con·tain·er
  con·tain·ment
con·tam·i·nate
  con·tam·i·nat·ed
  con·tam·i·nat·ing
  con·tam·i·nant
  con·tam·i·na·tion
con·tem·plate
  con·tem·plat·ed
  con·tem·plat·ing

con·tem·pla·tion
con·tem·pla·tive
con·tem·po·ra·ne·ous
con·tem·po·rary
  con·tem·po·rar·ies
con·tempt
  con·tempt·i·ble
  con·tempt·i·bly
  con·temp·tu·ous
con·tend
  con·tend·er
con·tent
  con·tent·ment
  con·tent·ed
  con·tent·ed·ness
con·ten·tion
  con·ten·tious
con·ter·mi·nous
con·test
  con·test·a·ble
  con·test·ant
con·text
  con·tex·tu·al
  con·tex·ture
con·tig·u·ous
  con·ti·gu·i·ty
  con·ti·gu·i·ties
  con·tig·u·ous·ly
con·ti·nent
  con·ti·nence
  con·ti·nency
con·ti·nent
  con·ti·nen·tal
con·tin·gent
  con·tin·gen·cy
  con·tin·gen·cies
con·tin·u·al
  con·tin·u·al·ly
con·tin·ue
  con·tin·ued
  con·tin·u·ing
  con·tin·u·a·tion
  con·tin·u·ance
  con·ti·nu·i·ty
  con·tin·u·ous
  con·tin·u·um
con·tort
  con·tor·tion

con·tor·tion·ist
con·tour
con·tra·band
con·tra·cep·tive
  con·tra·cep·tion
con·tract
  con·tract·ed
  con·trac·tu·al
con·trac·tion
  con·trac·tive
  con·trac·tile
con·trac·tor
con·tra·dict
  con·tra·dic·tion
  con·tra·dic·to·ry
con·tra·dis·tinc·tion
con·tral·to
con·trap·tion
con·tra·pun·tal
con·tra·ri·wise
con·tra·ry
  con·tra·ri·ly
  con·tra·ri·ness
con·trast
  con·trast·ing·ly
con·tra·vene
  con·tra·ven·ing
con·trib·ute
  con·trib·ut·ed
  con·trib·ut·ing
  con·trib·ut·a·ble
  con·trib·u·tor
  con·trib·u·tory
  con·tri·bu·tion
con·trite
  con·trite·ness
  con·tri·tion
con·trive
  con·trived
  con·triv·ing
  con·triv·ance
con·trol
  con·trolled
  con·trol·ling
  con·trol·la·ble
con·trol·ler
con·tro·ver·sy
  con·tro·ver·sies

con·tro·ver·sial
con·tro·vert
con·tu·ma·cy
con·tu·me·ly
con·tuse
  con·tused
  con·tus·ing
  con·tu·sion
co·nun·drum
con·va·lesce
  con·va·lesced
  con·va·les·cence
  con·va·les·cent
con·vec·tion
con·vene
  con·vened
  con·ven·ing
con·ven·ience
con·ven·ient
con·vent
con·ven·tion
con·ven·tion·al
  con·ven·tion·al·ism
  con·ven·tion·al·ize
con·verge
  con·verg·ing
  con·ver·gence
  con·ver·gent
con·ver·sant
con·verse
  con·versed
  con·vers·ing
  con·verse·ly
  con·ver·sion
con·vert
  con·vert·er
con·vert·i·ble
con·vex
  con·vex·i·ty
con·vey
  con·vey·a·ble
  con·vey·ance
  con·vey·er
  con·vey·or
con·vict
  con·vic·tion
con·vince
  con·vinced

con·vinc·ing
con·vinc·i·ble
con·viv·i·al
  con·viv·i·al·ity
con·voke
  con·voked
  con·vok·ing
  con·vo·ca·tion
con·vo·lute
  con·vo·lut·ed
  con·vo·lut·ing
  con·vo·lute·ly
  con·vo·lu·tion
con·voy
con·vulse
  con·vulsed
  con·vuls·ing
  con·vul·sion
  con·vul·sive
cook·e·ry
cook·ie
cool
  cool·ish
  cool·ly
  cool·ness
cool·ant
coo·lie
coop·er·age
co·op·er·ate
  co·op·er·at·ed
  co·op·er·at·ing
  co·op·er·a·tion
  co·op·er·a·tive
co·or·di·nate
  co·or·di·nat·ed
  co·or·di·nat·ing
  co·or·di·na·tor
  co·or·di·na·tion
co·part·ner
cope
  coped
  cop·ing
cop·i·er
co·pi·lot
co·pi·ous
  co·pi·ous·ly
cop·per
  cop·pery

41

cop·pice
copse
cop·ra
cop·u·la
cop·u·late
  cop·u·lat·ed
  cop·u·lat·ing
  cop·u·la·tion
  cop·u·la·tive
copy
  cop·ies
  cop·ied
  copy·ing
copy·right
co·quet
  co·quet·ry
co·quette
cor·al
cord·age
cor·dial
  cor·dial·i·ty
  cor·dial·ly
cord·ite
cor·don
cor·do·van
cor·du·roy
core
  cored
  cor·ing
cor·nea
cor·ner
cor·net
cor·nice
cor·nu·co·pia
corny
  corn·i·er
  corn·i·est
co·rol·la
cor·ol·lary
co·ro·na
cor·o·nary
cor·o·na·tion
cor·o·ner
cor·o·net
cor·po·ral
cor·po·rate
  cor·po·rate·ly
  cor·po·ra·tive

cor·po·ra·tion
cor·po·re·al
corps
  corps·man
corpse
cor·pu·lent
  cor·pu·lence
cor·pus
cor·pus·cle
  cor·pus·cu·lar
cor·ral
  cor·ralled
  cor·ral·ling
cor·rect
  cor·rect·a·ble
  cor·rect·ness
cor·rec·tion
  cor·rec·tion·al
  cor·rec·tive
cor·re·late
  cor·re·lat·ed
  cor·re·lat·ing
  cor·re·la·tion
  cor·rel·a·tive
cor·re·spond
  cor·re·spond·ing
  cor·re·spond·ence
  cor·re·spond·ent
cor·ri·dor
cor·ri·gi·ble
  cor·ri·gi·bil·i·ty
cor·rob·o·rate
  cor·rob·o·rat·ed
  cor·rob·o·rat·ing
  cor·rob·o·rat·tion
  cor·rob·o·ra·to·ry
cor·rode
  cor·rod·ed
  cor·rod·ing
cor·ro·sion
cor·ro·sive
cor·ru·gate
  cor·ru·gat·ed
  cor·ru·gat·ing
  cor·ru·ga·tion
cor·rupt
  cor·rup·ti·ble
  cor·rup·ti·bil·i·ty

cor·rupt·ly
cor·rupt·ness
cor·rup·tion
cor·sage
cor·sair
cor·set
cor·tege
cor·tex
cor·ti·cal
cor·ti·sone
co·run·dum
cor·us·cate
cor·vette
co·sig·na·to·ry
cos·met·ic
cos·me·tol·o·gist
cos·mic
  cos·mi·cal·ly
cos·mog·o·ny
  cos·mog·o·nist
cos·mog·ra·phy
  cos·mog·ra·pher
cos·mol·o·gy
  cos·mol·o·gist
cos·mo·naut
cos·mo·pol·i·tan
  cos·mop·o·lite
cos·mos
cos·mo·tron
cost·ly
cost·li·er
cos·tume
  cos·tumed
  cos·tum·ing
cos·tum·er
co·sy
co·si·er
co·tan·gent
co·te·rie
co·til·lion
cot·tage
cot·ter
cot·ton
  cot·tony
couch
couch·ant
cough
coun·cil

coun·cil·or
coun·cil·man
coun·sel
  coun·seled
  coun·sel·ing
coun·se·lor
count
  count·a·ble
count·down
coun·te·nance
  coun·te·nanced
  coun·te·nanc·ing
coun·ter
coun·ter·act
  coun·ter·ac·tive
coun·ter·at·tack
coun·ter·charge
coun·ter·claim
  coun·ter·claim·ant
coun·ter·clock·wise
coun·ter·cul·ture
coun·ter·es·pi·o·nage
coun·ter·feit
  coun·ter·feit·er
coun·ter·in·tel·li·gence
coun·ter·mand
coun·ter·meas·ure
coun·ter·of·fen·sive
coun·ter·pane
coun·ter·part
coun·ter·point
coun·ter·poise
coun·ter·rev·o·lu·tion
coun·ter·sign
  coun·ter·sig·na·ture
coun·ter·sink
coun·ter·spy
coun·ter·weight
coun·tess
count·less
coun·tri·fied
coun·try
  coun·tries
coun·ty
  coun·ties
coup de grace
coup d'e·tat
coupé

cou·ple
  coup·ling
coup·ler
coup·let
cou·pon
cour·age
  cou·ra·geous
cour·i·er
course
  coursed
  cours·ing
cours·er
cour·te·ous
cour·te·son
cour·te·sy
  cour·te·sies
court·house
cour·ti·er
court·ly
  court·li·ness
court mar·tial
  courts·mar·tial
court·room
court·ship
cous·in
cou·tu·rier
cov·e·nant
cov·er
  cov·ered
  cov·er·ing
  cov·er·ess
  cov·er·age
  cov·er·all
  cov·er·let
cov·ert
  cov·ert·ly
  cov·er·up
cov·et
  cov·et·ous
cov·ey
cow·ard
  cow·ard·li·ness
  cow·ard·ice
cow·er
  cow·er·ing
cowl
co·worker
cow·ry

cow·rie
cox·swain
coy
  coy·ness
coy·o·te
coz·en
  coz·en·er
co·zy
  co·zi·ly
  co·zi·ness
crab
  crabbed
  crab·bing
  crab·by
crack·down
crack·er
crack·ing
crack·le
  crack·led
  crack·ling
crack·up
cra·dle
  cra·dled
  cra·dling
crafts·man
crafty
  craft·i·ly
crag
  crag·ged
  crag·gy
  crag·gi·ness
cram
  crammed
  cram·ming
cran·ber·ry
crane
  craned
  cran·ing
cra·ni·um
cranky
  crank·i·ly
  crank·i·ness
cran·ny
  cran·nies
  cran·nied
crap·shooter
crass
  crass·ly

crate
  crat·ed
  crat·ing
cra·ter
  cra·tered
cra·vat
crave
  craved
  crav·ing
  cra·ven
craw·fish
crawl
cray·fish
cray·on
craze
  crazed
  craz·ing
cra·zy
  cra·zi·er
  cra·zi·ness
creak
  creak·i·ly
  creaky
cream
  cream·i·ness
  creamy
crease
  creased
  creas·ing
  creasy
cre·ate
  cre·at·ed
  cre·at·ing
cre·a·tion
cre·a·tive
  cre·a·tiv·i·ty
cre·a·tor
crea·ture
crèche
cre·dence
cre·den·tial
cre·den·za
cred·i·ble
  cred·i·bil·i·ty
  cred·i·bly
cred·it
  cred·it·a·ble
  cred·it·a·bil·i·ty

cred·it·a·bly
cred·i·tor
cre·do
cred·u·lous
cre·du·li·ty
creek
creel
creep
  crept
  creep·ing
creepy
  creep·i·ness
creep·er
cre·mate
  cre·mat·ed
  cre·mat·ing
  cre·ma·tion
cre·ma·to·ry
  cre·ma·to·ri·um
cren·el·ate
  cren·el·la·tion
Cre·ole
cre·o·sote
crepe de Chine
crepe su·zette
cre·pus·cu·lar
cres·cen·do
cres·cent
crest
  crest·ed
  crest·less
crest·fall·en
cre·ta·ceous
cre·tonne
cre·vasse
crev·ice
crew·ed
crib
  cribbed
  crib·bing
crib·bage
crick·et
crim·i·nal
  crim·i·nal·i·ty
  crim·i·nal·ly
crim·i·nol·o·gy
  crim·i·nol·o·gist
crim·son

cringe
  cringed
  cring·ing
crin·kle
  crin·kled
  crin·kling
crin·o·line
crip·ple
  crip·pled
  crip·pling
cri·sis
  cri·ses
crisp
  crisp·ness
  crispy
  crisp·i·er
criss·cross
cri·te·ri·on
  cri·te·ria
crit·ic
crit·i·cal
  crit·i·cal·ly
crit·i·cism
crit·i·cize
  crit·i·cized
  crit·i·cizing
  crit·i·ciz·a·ble
cri·tique
croaky
cro·chet
  cro·cheted
  cro·chet·ing
crock·ery
croc·o·dile
cro·cus
crois·sant
cro·ny
  cro·nies
crook·ed
croon·er
crop
  cropped
  crop·ping
cro·quet
cro·quette
cross·bar
cross·breed
cross·coun·try

cross·ex·am·ine
cross·ex·am·i·na·tion
cross·fer·ti·li·za·tion
cross·ing
cross·pol·li·na·tion
cross·pol·li·nate
cross·ref·er·ence
crotch·ety
crotch·et·i·ness
crouch
croup
crou·pi·er
crou·ton
cru·cial
cru·ci·al·i·ty
cru·ci·ble
cru·ci·fix
cru·ci·fix·ion
cru·ci·form
cru·ci·fy
cru·ci·fied
cru·ci·fy·ing
crude
crud·est
crude·ness
cru·di·ty
cru·el
cru·el·ly
cru·el·ness
cru·el·ty
cru·et
cruise
cruised
cruis·ing
cruis·er
crul·ler
crum·ble
crum·bling
crum·my
crum·mi·est
crum·pet
crum·ple
crum·pled
crum·pling
crunchy
crunch·i·er
cru·sade
cru·sad·er

crush·er
crush·ing
crus·ta·cean
crusty
crust·i·ly
crutch
crux
cry
cried
cry·ing
cry·o·gen·ics
crypt
cryp·to·gram
cryp·to·graph
crys·tal
crys·tal·line
crys·tal·lize
crys·tal·li·za·tion
cube
cubed
cub·ing
cu·bic
cu·bi·cal
cu·bi·cle
cub·ism
cuck·old
cuck·oo
cu·cum·ber
cud·dle
cud·dled
cud·dling
cud·dle·some
cudg·el
cudg·eled
cudg·el·ing
cue
cued
cu·ing
cui·sine
cul-de-sac
cu·li·nary
cul·mi·nate
cul·mi·nat·ed
cul·mi·nat·ing
cul·mi·na·tion
cu·lottes
cul·pa·ble
cul·pa·bil·i·ty

cul·pa·bly
cul·prit
cult
cul·tist
cul·ti·vate
cul·ti·vat·ed
cul·ti·vat·ing
cul·ti·va·tion
cul·ti·va·tor
cul·tur·al
cul·ture
cul·tured
cul·tur·ing
cul·vert
cum·ber
cum·ber·some
cum·brance
cum lau·de
cum·mer·bund
cu·mu·late
cu·mu·la·tion
cu·mu·la·tive
cu·mu·lo·nim·bus
cu·mu·lus
cu·mu·lous
cu·ne·i·form
cun·ning
cun·ning·ly
cun·ning·ness
cup
cupped
cup·ping
cup·board
cup·ful
cu·pid·i·ty
cu·po·la
cur·a·ble
cur·a·bil·i·ty
cu·rate
cur·a·tive
cu·ra·tor
curb·ing
curb·stone
cur·dle
cur·dled
cur·dling
cure
cured

cur·ing
cur·few
cu·rio
cu·ri·o·sa
cu·ri·os·i·ty
  cu·ri·os·i·ties
cu·ri·ous
  cu·ri·ous·ness
curl·i·cue
curl·ing
curly
  curl·i·ness
cur·rant
cur·ren·cy
  cur·ren·cies
cur·rent
cur·ric·u·lum
  cur·ric·u·la
  cur·ric·u·lar
cur·rish
cur·ry
  cur·ried
curse
  curs·ing
  curs·ed·ness
cur·sive
cur·so·ry
  cur·so·ri·ly
curt
curt·ly
  curt·ness
cur·tail
  cur·tail·ment
cur·tain
curt·sy
  curt·sied
  curt·sy·ing
cur·va·ceous
cur·va·ture
curve
  curved
  curv·ing
cur·vi·lin·e·ar
cush·ion
cushy
  cush·i·est
cus·pid
cus·pi·dor

cuss·ed
  cuss·ed·ness
cus·tard
cus·to·di·an
cus·to·dy
  cus·to·di·al
cus·tom
cus·tom·ary
  cus·tom·ar·i·ly
cus·tom·er
cus·tom·ize
  cus·tom·ized
  cus·tom·iz·ing
cut
  cut·ting
cur·ta·ne·ous
cute
  cut·est
  cute·ness
cu·ti·cle
cut·lass
cut·lery
cut·let
cut·throat
cut·tle·fish
cy·a·nide
cy·ber·net·ics
cyc·la·men
cy·cle
  cy·cled
  cy·cling
  cy·clist
cy·clic
  cy·cli·cal
cy·clone
cy·clo·pe·di·a
cy·clo·rama
  cy·clo·ram·ic
cy·clo·tron
cyg·net
cyl·in·der
  cy·lin·dric
  cy·lin·dri·cal
cym·bal
cyn·ic
  cyn·i·cism
  cyn·i·cal
cy·no·sure

cy·pher
cy·press
cyst
czar

D

dab
  dabbed
  dab·bing
dab·ble
  dab·bled
  dab·bling
  dab·bler
dachs·hund
dac·tyl
  dac·tyl·ic
daf·fo·dil
daf·fy
dag·ger
da·guerre·o·type
dahl·ia
dai·ly
  dai·lies
dain·ty
  dain·ti·est
  dain·ti·ly
  dain·ti·ness
dai·qui·ri
dairy
  dair·ies
da·is
dai·sy
  dai·sies
dal·ly
  dal·lied
  dal·ly·ing
  da·li·ance
Dal·ma·tian
dam
  dammed
  dam·ming
dam·age
  dam·aged
  dam·ag·ing
dam·ask
damn
  dam·na·ble

46

dam·na·bly
dam·na·tion
damned
damp·en
damp·er
damp·ness
dam·sel
dam·son
dance
  danced
  danc·ing
dan·de·li·on
dan·der
dan·dle
  dan·dled
  dan·dling
dan·druff
dan·dy
  dan·dies
  dan·dy·ism
dan·ger
dan·ger·ous
dan·gle
  dan·gled
  dan·gling
dank
  dank·ness
dan·seuse
dap·per
dap·ple
  dap·pled
  dap·pling
dare
  dared
  dar·ing
dare·dev·il
dark
  dark·ish
  dark·ly
  dark·ness
dark·en
dark·room
dar·ling
  dar·ling·ness
Dar·win·ism
dash·board
dash·ing
das·tard

das·tard·li·ness
das·tard·ly
da·ta
date
  dat·ed
  dat·ing
  dat·a·ble
date·less
date·line
da·tive
da·tum
da·ta
daub
daugh·ter
daugh·ter-in-law
daunt·less
dau·phin
dav·en·port
dav·it
daw·dle
  daw·dled
  daw·dling
  daw·dler
dawn
  dawn·ing
day·break
day·dream
day·light
day·time
daze
  dazed
  daz·ing
  daz·ed·ly
daz·zle
  daz·zled
  daz·zling
dea·con
dea·con·ess
de·ac·ti·vate
  de·ac·ti·va·tion
dead·beat
dead·en
dead·end
dead·line
dead·lock
dead·ly
  dead·li·ness
deaf

deaf·ness
deaf·en
  deaf·en·ing·ly
deaf·mute
deal
  dealt
  deal·ing
dean·ship
dear
  dear·ness
dearth
death
  death·less
  death·ly
death·blow
death's·head
death·watch
de·ba·cle
de·bar
  de·barred
  de·bar·ring
  de·bar·ment
de·bark
  de·bar·ka·tion
de·base
  de·based
  de·bas·ing
  de·base·ment
de·bate
  de·bat·ing
  de·bat·a·ble
  de·bat·er
de·bauch
  de·bauch·er
  de·bauch·ment
  de·bauch·ery
deb·au·chee
de·ben·ture
de·bil·i·tate
  de·bil·i·tat·ed
  de·bil·i·tat·ing
  de·bil·i·ta·tion
de·bil·i·ty
  de·bil·i·ties
deb·it
deb·o·nair
de·brief
de·bris

debt·or
de·bunk
de·but
deb·u·tante
de·cade
dec·a·dent
   dec·a·dence
   dec·a·dent·ly
dec·a·gon
dec·a·gram
dec·a·he·dron
de·cal
Dec·a·logue
de·camp
   de·camp·ment
de·cant
de·cant·er
de·cap·i·tate
   de·cap·i·tat·ed
   de·cap·i·tat·ing
   de·cap·i·ta·tion
dec·a·pod
de·cath·lon
de·cay
de·cease
   de·ceased
   de·ce·dent
de·ceit
   de·ceit·ful
   de·ceit·ful·ness
de·ceive
   de·ceived
   de·ceiv·ing
   de·ceiv·er
de·cel·er·ate
   de·cel·er·at·ed
   de·cel·er·at·ing
   de·cel·er·a·tion
de·cen·cy
   de·cen·cies
de·cen·ni·al
de·cent
   de·cent·ly
de·cen·tral·ize
   de·cen·tral·ized
   de·cen·tral·iz·ing
   de·cen·tral·i·za·tion
de·cep·tion

de·cep·tive
dec·i·bel
de·cide
   de·cid·ed
   de·cid·ing
   de·cid·ed·ly
de·cid·u·ous
dec·i·mal
dec·i·mate
   dec·i·mat·ed
   dec·i·mat·ing
   dec·i·ma·tion
de·ci·pher
   de·ci·pher·a·ble
de·ci·sion
de·ci·sive
de·claim
   dec·la·ma·tion
   de·clam·a·tory
de·clare
   de·clared
   de·claring
   de·clar·a·tive
   de·clar·a·to·ry
   dec·la·ra·tion
de·clas·si·fy
   de·clas·si·fied
   de·clas·si·fy·ing
de·clen·sion
dec·li·na·tion
de·cline
   de·clined
   de·clin·ing
   de·clin·a·ble
de·cliv·i·ty
   de·cliv·i·ties
de·code
   de·cod·ed
   de·cod·ing
   de·cod·er
de·colle·tage
de·com·mis·sion
de·com·pose
   de·com·posed
   de·com·pos·ing
   de·com·po·si·tion
de·com·press
   de·com·pres·sion

de·con·tam·i·nate
   de·con·tam·i·nat·ed
   de·con·tam·i·nat·ing
   de·con·tam·i·na·tion
de·con·trol
   de·con·trolled
   de·con·trol·ling
de·cor
dec·o·rate
   dec·o·rat·ed
   dec·o·rat·ing
   dec·o·ra·tion
   dec·o·ra·tive
   dec·o·ra·tor
de·co·rous
de·co·rum
de·coy
de·crease
   de·creased
   de·creas·ing
de·cree
   de·creed
   de·cree·ing
de·cre·ment
de·crep·it
   de·crep·i·tude
   de·crep·it·ly
de·cre·scen·do
de·cry
   de·cried
   de·cry·ing
de·cri·al
ded·i·cate
   ded·i·cat·ed
   ded·i·cat·ing
   ded·i·ca·to·ry
   ded·i·ca·tion
de·duce
   de·duc·i·ble
de·duct
   de·duct·i·ble
   de·duc·tion
   de·duc·tive
deep
   deep·ness
   deep·en
deep·root·ed
deep·seat·ed

de·es·ca·late
  de·es·ca·lat·ed
  de·es·ca·lat·ing
  de·es·ca·la·tion
de·face
  de·faced
  de·fac·ing
  de·face·ment
de fac·to
de·fal·cate
  de·fal·ca·tion
de·fame
  de·famed
  de·fam·ing
  def·a·ma·tion
  de·fam·a·to·ry
de·fault
de·feat
de·feat·ism
  de·feat·ist
def·e·cate
  def·e·cat·ed
  def·e·cat·ing
  def·e·ca·tion
de·fect
  de·fec·tion
  de·fec·tor
de·fec·tive
de·fend
  de·fend·er
  de·fend·ant
de·fense
  de·fense·less
  de·fen·si·ble
  de·fen·si·bil·i·ty
  de·fen·sive
de·fer
  de·ferred
  de·fer·ring
  de·fer·ment
def·er·ence
  def·er·en·tial
de·fi·ance
  de·fi·ant
de·fi·cient
  de·fi·cien·cy
  de·fi·cien·cies
def·i·cit

de·file
  de·filed
  de·fil·ing
  de·file·ment
de·fine
  de·fined
  de·fin·ing
  de·fin·a·ble
def·i·nite
  def·i·nite·ly
  def·i·ni·tion
  de·fin·i·tive
de·flate
  de·flat·ed
  de·flat·ing
  de·fla·tion
  de·fla·tion·ary
de·flect
  de·flec·tion
  de·flec·tive
  de·flec·tor
de·flow·er
de·fo·li·ate
  de·fo·li·at·ed
  de·fo·li·at·ing
  de·fo·li·a·tion
de·for·est
  de·for·est·a·tion
de·form
  de·for·ma·tion
  de·formed
de·form·i·ty
  de·form·i·ties
de·fraud
de·fray
  de·fray·al
  de·fray·ment
de·frost
deft
  deft·ness
de·funct
de·fy
  de·fied
  de·fy·ing
de·gen·er·ate
  de·gen·er·at·ed
  de·gen·er·at·ing
  de·gen·er·ate·ly

de·gen·er·a·cy
  de·gen·er·a·tion
de·grade
  de·grad·ed
  de·grad·ing
  de·grad·able
  deg·ra·da·tion
de·gree
de·his·cence
  de·his·cent
de·hu·mid·i·fy
de·hy·drate
  de·hy·drat·ed
  de·hy·drat·ing
  de·hy·dra·tion
de·i·fy
  de·i·fied
  de·i·fy·ing
  de·i·fi·ca·tion
deign
de·ist
  de·ism
  de·is·tic
  de·is·ti·cal
de·i·ty
  de·i·ties
de·ject·ed
  de·jec·ted·ly
  de·jec·tion
de ju·re
de·lay
de·lec·ta·ble
  de·lec·ta·bly
  de·lec·ta·tion
del·e·gate
  del·e·gat·ed
  del·e·gat·ing
  del·e·ga·tion
de·lete
  de·let·ed
  de·let·ing
  de·le·tion
del·e·te·ri·ous
delft·ware
de·lib·er·ate
  de·lib·er·at·ed
  de·lib·er·at·ing
  de·lib·er·ate·ly

de·lib·er·a·tion
del·i·ca·cy
del·i·ca·cies
del·i·cate
del·i·cate·ly
del·i·ca·tes·sen
de·li·cious
de·li·cious·ness
de·light
de·light·ed
de·light·ed·ly
de·light·ful
de·light·ful·ly
de·lim·it
de·lim·i·ta·tion
de·lin·e·ate
de·lin·e·at·ed
de·lin·e·at·ing
de·lin·e·a·tion
de·lin·e·a·tor
de·lin·quent
de·lin·quen·cy
de·lin·quen·cies
del·i·quesce
de·lir·i·um
de·lir·i·ous
de·liv·er
de·liv·er·er
de·liv·er·ance
de·liv·er·y
de·liv·er·ies
de·louse
de·loused
de·lous·ing
del·phin·i·um
del·ta
del·toid
de·lude
de·lud·ed
de·lud·ing
del·uge
del·uged
del·ug·ing
de·lu·sion
de·lu·sive
de·lu·so·ry
de·lu·sive·ly
de·luxe

delve
delv·ing
de·mag·ne·tize
dem·a·gogue
dem·a·gog·uery
dem·a·gog·ic
dem·a·gog·i·cal
de·mand
de·mar·cate
de·mar·ca·tion
de·mean
de·mean·or
de·ment·ed
de·men·tia
de·merit
de·mesne
dem·i·god
dem·i·john
de·mil·i·ta·rize
de·mil·i·tar·i·za·tion
de·mise
de·mised
de·mis·ing
dem·i·tasse
de·mo·bi·lize
de·mo·bi·lized
de·mo·bi·liz·ing
de·mo·bi·li·za·tion
de·moc·ra·cy
de·moc·ra·cies
dem·o·crat
dem·o·crat·ic
dem·o·crat·i·cal·ly
de·moc·ra·tize
de·moc·ra·tized
de·moc·ra·tiz·ing
de·moc·ra·ti·za·tion
de·mog·ra·phy
de·mog·ra·pher
dem·o·graph·ic
de·mol·ish
de·plor·a·bly
de·plore
de·plored
de·plor·ing
de·ploy
de·ploy·ment
de·pol·ar·ize

de·pop·u·late
de·pop·u·lat·ed
de·pop·u·lat·ing
de·pop·u·la·tion
de·port
de·por·ta·tion
de·port·ment
de·pose
de·posed
de·pos·ing
de·pos·a·ble
de·pos·it
de·pos·i·tor
dep·o·si·tion
de·pos·i·to·ry
de·pot
de·prave
de·praved
de·prav·ing
de·prav·i·ty
de·pra·va·tion
dep·re·cate
dep·re·cat·ed
dep·re·cat·ing
dep·re·ca·tion
dep·re·ca·to·ry
de·pre·ci·ate
de·pre·ci·at·ed
de·pre·ci·at·ing
de·pre·ci·a·tion
de·pre·ci·a·to·ry
dep·re·di·ate
dep·re·dat·ed
dep·re·dat·ing
dep·re·da·tion
de·press
de·pres·sant
de·pressed
de·pres·sion
de·prive
de·prived
de·priv·ing
dep·ri·va·tion
depth
dep·u·rate
dep·u·ta·tion
de·pute
de·put·ed

de·put·ing
dep·u·tize
  dep·u·tized
  dep·u·tiz·ing
dep·u·ty
  dep·u·ties
de·raign
  de·raign·ment
de·rail
  de·rail·ment
de·range
  de·ranged
  de·rang·ing
  de·range·ment
der·by
der·e·lict
  der·e·lic·tion
de·ride
  de·rid·ing
de·ri·gueur
de·ri·sion
de·ri·sive
  de·ri·so·ry
der·i·va·tion
de·riv·a·tive
de·rive
  de·riv·ing
  de·riv·a·ble
der·ma·ti·tis
der·ma·tol·o·gy
  der·ma·to·log·i·cal
  der·ma·tol·o·gist
der·mis
der·o·gate
  der·o·gat·ed
  der·o·gat·ing
  der·o·ga·tion
de·rog·a·to·ry
  de·rog·a·to·ri·ly
der·rick
der·rin·ger
der·vish
de·sal·i·nate
des·cant
de·scend
  de·scend·ed
  de·scend·ing
  de·scend·ant

de·scend·ent
de·scent
de·scribe
  de·scribed
  de·scrib·ing
  de·scrib·a·ble
de·scrip·tion
  de·scrip·tive
de·scry
  de·scried
  de·scry·ing
des·e·crate
  des·e·crat·ed
  des·e·crat·ing
  des·e·cra·tion
de·seg·re·gate
  de·seg·re·gat·ed
  de·seg·re·gat·ing
  de·seg·re·ga·tion
de·sen·si·tize
des·ert
de·sert
  de·sert·ed
  de·sert·er
  de·ser·tion
de·serve
  de·served
  de·serv·ing
  de·serv·ed·ly
des·ha·bille
des·ic·cate
  des·ic·cat·ed
  des·ic·cat·ing
  des·ic·ca·tion
de·sid·er·a·tum
de·sign
  de·signed
  de·sign·ing
  de·sign·ed·ly
  de·sign·er
des·ig·nate
  des·ig·nat·ed
  des·ig·nat·ing
  des·ig·na·tion
de·sire
  de·sired
  de·sir·ing
  de·sir·a·ble

de·sir·a·bil·i·ty
de·sir·ous
de·sist
des·o·late
  des·o·lat·ed
  des·o·lat·ing
  des·o·la·tion
de·spair
  de·spair·ing
des·per·a·do
des·per·ate
  des·per·ate·ly
  des·per·a·tion
des·pi·ca·ble
  des·pi·ca·bly
de·spise
  de·spised
  de·spis·ing
de·spite
de·spoil
  de·spoil·ment
  de·spo·li·a·tion
de·spond
  de·spond·en·cy
  de·spond·ence
  de·spond·ent
des·pot
  des·pot·ic
  des·pot·i·cal·ly
  des·pot·ism
des·sert
des·ti·na·tion
des·tine
  des·tined
  des·tin·ing
des·ti·ny
  des·ti·nies
des·ti·tute
  des·ti·tu·tion
de·stroy
de·stroy·er
de·struc·tion
  de·struct·i·ble
  de·struct·i·bil·i·ty
de·struc·tive
  de·struc·tive·ness
des·ue·tude
des·ul·to·ry

des·ul·to·ri·ly
de·tach
  de·tached
  de·tach·a·ble
  de·tach·ment
de·tail
de·tain
  de·tain·ment
  de·tain·er
  de·ten·tion
de·tect
  de·tect·a·ble
  de·tec·tion
  de·tec·tor
de·tec·tive
dé·tente
de·ten·tion
de·ter
  de·terred
  de·ter·ring
de·ter·gent
de·te·ri·o·rate
  de·te·ri·o·rat·ed
  de·te·ri·o·rat·ing
  de·te·ri·o·ra·tion
de·ter·mine
  de·ter·mined
  de·ter·min·ing
  de·ter·mi·na·ble
  de·ter·mi·nant
  de·ter·mi·nate
  de·ter·mi·na·tion
  de·ter·mined·ly
de·ter·min·ism
de·ter·rent
  de·ter·rence
de·test
  de·test·a·ble
  de·tes·ta·tion
de·throne
  de·throne·ment
det·o·nate
  det·o·nat·ed
  det·o·nat·ing
  det·o·na·tion
  det·o·na·tor
de·tour
de·tract

de·trac·tion
de·trac·tor
det·ri·ment
det·ri·men·tal
de·tri·tus
deuce
de·value
  de·val·u·ate
  de·val·u·at·ed
  de·val·u·at·ing
  de·val·u·a·tion
dev·as·tate
  dev·as·tat·ed
  dev·as·tat·ing
  dev·as·ta·tion
de·vel·op
  de·vel·op·ment
  de·vel·op·er
de·vi·ate
  de·vi·at·ed
  de·vi·at·ing
  de·vi·ant
  de·vi·a·tion
de·vice
dev·il
  dev·il·ment
  dev·il·try
  dev·il·tries
  dev·il·ry
  dev·il·ish
de·vi·ous
  de·vi·ous·ness
de·vise
  de·vised
  de·vis·ing
  de·vis·a·ble
  de·vis·al
  de·vi·see
  de·vi·sor
de·void
de·volve
  de·volved
  de·volv·ing
  dev·o·lu·tion
de·vote
  de·vot·ed
  de·vot·ing
  de·vote·ment

de·vo·tee
de·vo·tion
  de·vo·tion·al
de·vour
  de·vour·ing
de·vout
  de·vout·ly
  de·vout·ness
dewy
  dew·i·ness
  dew·y·eyed
dex·ter·ous
  dex·ter·i·ty
  dex·ter·ous·ly
dex·trose
di·a·be·tes
  di·a·bet·ic
di·a·bol·ic
  di·a·bol·i·cal
di·a·crit·ic
  di·a·crit·i·cal
di·a·dem
di·ag·nose
  di·ag·nosed
  di·ag·nos·ing
  di·ag·no·sis
  di·ag·nos·tic
  di·ag·nos·ti·cian
di·ag·o·nal
di·a·gram
  di·a·gramed
  di·a·gram·ing
  di·a·gram·mat·ic
  di·a·gram·mat·i·cal
di·al
  di·aled
  di·al·ing
di·a·lect
  di·a·lec·tal
di·a·lec·tic
  di·a·lec·ti·cal
  di·a·lec·ti·cian
di·a·logue
di·am·e·ter
  di·a·met·ric
dia·mond
di·a·pa·son
dia·per

52

di·aph·a·nous
di·a·phragm
di·ar·rhea
di·a·ry
　di·a·ries
di·as·to·le
　di·as·tol·ic
di·as·tro·phism
di·a·ther·my
di·a·ton·ic
di·a·tribe
dice
　diced
　dic·ing
di·chot·o·my
　di·chot·o·mies
　di·chot·o·mous
　di·cho·tom·ic
dick·ey
dic·tate
　dic·tat·ed
　dic·tat·ing
　dic·ta·tion
dic·ta·tor
　dic·ta·tor·ship
　dic·ta·to·ri·al
　dic·ta·to·ri·al·ly
dic·tion
dic·tion·ary
　dic·tion·ar·ies
dic·tum
di·dac·tic
　di·dac·ti·cal
　di·dac·ti·cism
die
　died
　dy·ing
die·sel
di·et
　di·e·tary
　di·e·tet·ic
　di·e·tet·ics
　di·e·ti·cian
dif·fer
　dif·fer·ence
　dif·fer·ent
　dif·fer·en·tial
　dif·fer·en·ti·ate

dif·fer·en·ti·a·tion
dif·fi·cult
　dif·fi·cul·ty
　dif·fi·cul·ties
dif·fi·dent
　dif·fi·dence
dif·fuse
　dif·fused
　dif·fus·ing
　dif·fuse·ly
　dif·fuse·ness
　dif·fu·sion
dig
　dug
　dig·ging
di·gest
　di·gest·i·ble
　di·gest·i·bil·i·ty
　di·ges·tion
　di·ges·tive
dig·ger
　dig·gings
dig·it
　dig·it·al
　dig·i·tal·is
dig·ni·fy
　dig·ni·fied
　dig·ni·fy·ing
dig·ni·tary
　dig·ni·tar·ies
dig·ni·ty
　dig·ni·ties
di·gress
　di·gres·sion
　di·gres·sive
di·he·dral
di·lap·i·date
　di·lap·i·dat·ed
　di·lap·i·dat·ing
　di·lap·i·da·tion
dil·a·ta·tion
di·late
　di·lat·ed
　di·lat·ing
　di·la·tion
dil·a·to·ry
　dil·a·to·ri·ly
di·lem·ma

dil·et·tan·te
dil·i·gence
　dil·i·gent
dil·ly·dal·ly
　dil·ly·dal·lied
di·lute
　di·lut·ed
　di·lut·ing
　di·lu·tion
di·lu·vi·al
dim
　dim·mer
　dimmed
　dim·ming
　dim·ly
　dim·ness
di·men·sion
　di·men·sion·al
di·min·ish
　di·min·ish·ing
di·min·u·en·do
dim·i·nu·tion
　di·min·u·tive
dim·ple
dim·wit·ted
din
　dinned
　din·ning
dine
　dined
　din·ing
　din·er
di·nette
din·ghy
　din·ghies
din·gy
　din·gi·ness
din·ner
di·no·saur
di·o·cese
　di·oc·e·san
di·o·rama
di·ox·ide
dip
　dipped
　dip·ping
diph·the·ria
diph·thong

di·plo·ma
di·plo·ma·cy
  di·plo·ma·cies
dip·lo·mat
  dip·lo·mat·ic
  dip·lo·mat·i·cal·ly
dip·so·ma·nia
  dip·so·ma·ni·ac
dire
  dire·ness
di·rect
  di·rect·ness
di·rec·tion
di·rec·tive
di·rect·ly
di·rec·tor
  di·rec·to·ri·al
di·rec·to·rate
di·rec·to·ry
  di·rec·to·ries
dirge
di·ri·gi·ble
dirndl
dirty
  dirt·i·ness
dis·a·ble
  dis·a·bled
  dis·a·bling
  dis·a·bil·i·ty
  dis·a·ble·ment
dis·a·buse
  dis·a·bused
  dis·a·bus·ing
dis·ad·van·tage
  dis·ad·van·taged
  dis·ad·van·tag·ing
  dis·ad·van·ta·geous
dis·af·fect
  dis·af·fec·tion
  dis·af·fect·ed
dis·a·gree
  dis·a·greed
  dis·a·gree·ing
  dis·a·gree·a·ble
  dis·a·gree·ment
dis·al·low
  dis·al·low·ance
dis·ap·pear

dis·ap·pear·ance
dis·ap·point
  dis·ap·point·ment
dis·ap·prove
  dis·ap·proved
  dis·ap·prov·ing
  dis·ap·prov·al
  dis·ap·pro·ba·tion
dis·arm
  dis·ar·ma·ment
dis·ar·range
  dis·ar·ranged
  di·ar·rang·ing
  dis·ar·range·ment
dis·ar·ray
dis·as·sem·ble
dis·as·so·ci·ate
dis·as·ter
  dis·as·trous
dis·a·vow
  dis·a·vow·al
dis·band
  dis·band·ment
dis·bar
  dis·barred
  dis·bar·ring
  dis·bar·ment
dis·be·lieve
  dis·be·lieved
  dis·be·liev·ing
  dis·be·lief
  dis·be·liev·er
dis·burse
  dis·bursed
  dis·burs·ing
  dis·burse·ment
  dis·burs·er
disc
  disk
dis·card
dis·cern
  dis·cern·ing
  dis·cern·i·ble
  dis·cern·i·bly
  dis·cern·ment
dis·charge
  dis·charged
  dis·charg·ing

dis·charg·er
dis·ci·ple
dis·ci·pline
  dis·ci·plined
  dis·ci·plin·ing
  dis·ci·pli·nary
  dis·ci·pli·nari·an
dis·claim
  dis·claim·er
dis·close
  dis·closed
  dis·closing
  dis·closure
dis·coid
dis·col·or
  dis·col·or·a·tion
dis·com·fit
  dis·com·fi·ture
dis·com·fort
dis·com·mode
  dis·com·mod·ed
  dis·com·mod·ing
dis·com·pose
  dis·com·posed
  dis·com·pos·ing
  dis·com·po·sure
dis·con·cert
  dis·con·cert·ing
  dis·con·cert·ed
dis·con·nect
  dis·con·nec·tion
  dis·con·nect·ed
dis·con·so·late
  dis·con·so·late·ly
dis·con·tent
  dis·con·tent·ment
  dis·con·tent·ed
dis·con·tin·ue
  dis·con·tin·ued
  dis·con·tin·u·ing
  dis·con·tin·u·ance
  dis·con·tin·u·a·tion
  dis·con·tin·u·ous
dis·cord
  dis·cord·ance
  dis·cord·an·cy
  dis·cord·ant·ly
dis·co·théque

dis·count
dis·cour·age
  dis·cour·ag·ing
  dis·cour·age·ment
dis·course
  dis·coursed
  dis·cours·ing
dis·cour·te·ous
  dis·cour·te·ous·ly
  dis·cour·te·sy
  dis·cour·te·sies
dis·cov·er
  dis·cov·er·a·ble
  dis·cov·er·er
  dis·cov·er·y
  dis·cov·er·ies
dis·cred·it
  dis·cred·it·a·ble
dis·creet
  dis·creet·ly
dis·crep·ant
  dis·crep·an·cy
  dis·crep·an·cies
dis·crete
  dis·cre·tion
  dis·cre·tion·ary
dis·crim·i·nate
  dis·crim·i·nat·ed
  dis·crim·i·nat·ing
  dis·crim·i·nate·ly
  dis·crim·i·na·tion
  dis·crim·i·na·to·ry
dis·cur·sive
  dis·cur·sive·ness
dis·cus
dis·cuss
  dis·cus·sion
dis·dain
  dis·dain·ful
dis·ease
  dis·eased
  dis·eas·ing
dis·em·bark
  dis·em·bar·ka·tion
  dis·em·bark·ment
dis·em·body
  dis·em·bod·ied
  dis·em·bod·y·ing

dis·em·bod·i·ment
dis·em·bow·el
  dis·em·bow·eled
  dis·em·bow·el·ing
  dis·em·bow·el·ment
dis·en·chant
  dis·en·chant·ment
dis·en·cum·ber
dis·en·fran·chise
  dis·en·fran·chised
  dis·en·fran·chis·ing
dis·en·gage
  dis·en·gaged
  dis·en·gag·ing
  dis·en·gage·ment
dis·en·tan·gle
  dis·en·tan·gled
  dis·en·tan·gling
  dis·en·tan·gle·ment
dis·es·tab·lish
  dis·es·tab·lish·ment
dis·fa·vor
dis·fig·ure
  dis·fig·ured
  dis·fig·ur·ing
  dis·fig·ure·ment
dis·fran·chise
  dis·fran·chised
  dis·fran·chis·ing
  dis·fran·chise·ment
dis·gorge
  dis·gorged
  dis·gorg·ing
dis·grace
  dis·graced
  dis·grac·ing
  dis·grace·ful
dis·grun·tle
  dis·grun·tled
  dis·grun·tling
dis·guise
  dis·guised
  dis·guis·ing
dis·gust
  dis·gust·ed
  dis·gust·ing
dis·ha·bille
dis·har·mo·ny

dis·har·mo·nies
dis·heart·en
  dis·heart·en·ing
di·shev·eled
dis·hon·est
  dis·hon·est·ly
  dis·hon·es·ty
  dis·hon·es·ties
dis·hon·or
  dis·hon·or·a·ble
  dis·hon·or·a·bly
dis·il·lu·sion
  dis·il·lu·sion·ment
dis·in·cline
  dis·in·clined
  dis·in·clin·ing
  dis·in·cli·na·tion
dis·in·fect
  dis·in·fect·ant
  dis·in·fec·tion
dis·in·gen·u·ous
dis·in·her·it
  dis·in·her·i·tance
dis·in·te·grate
  dis·in·te·grat·ed
  dis·in·te·grat·ing
  dis·in·te·gra·tion
dis·in·ter
  dis·in·terred
  dis·in·ter·ring
  dis·in·ter·ment
dis·in·ter·est
  dis·in·ter·es·ted
dis·join
dis·joint
  dis·joint·ed
dis·junc·tion
disk
disc
dis·like
  dis·liked
  dis·lik·ing
  dis·lik·a·ble
dis·lo·cate
  dis·lo·cat·ing
  dis·lo·ca·tion
dis·lodge
  dis·lodged

dis·lodg·ing
dis·lodg·ment
dis·loy·al
  dis·loy·al·ly
  dis·loy·al·ty
dis·mal
  dis·mal·ly
dis·man·tle
  dis·man·tled
  dis·man·tling
dis·may
dis·mem·ber
  dis·mem·ber·ment
dis·miss
  dis·mis·sal
dis·mount
dis·o·bey
  dis·o·be·di·ence
  dis·o·be·di·ent
dis·or·der
  dis·or·dered
  dis·or·der·ly
  dis·or·der·li·ness
dis·or·gan·ize
  dis·or·gan·ized
  dis·or·gan·i·za·tion
dis·o·ri·ent
  dis·o·ri·en·ta·tion
dis·own
dis·par·age
  dis·par·aged
  dis·par·ag·ing
  dis·par·age·ment
dis·pa·rate
  dis·pa·rate·ly
dis·par·i·ty
  dis·par·i·ties
dis·pas·sion
  dis·pas·sion·ate
dis·patch
  dis·patch·er
dis·pel
  dis·pelled
  dis·pel·ling
dis·pen·sa·ble
  dis·pen·sa·bil·i·ty
dis·pen·sa·ry
  dis·pen·sa·ries

dis·pense
  dis·pensed
  dis·pens·ing
  dis·pen·sa·tion
dis·perse
  dis·persed
  dis·pers·ing
  dis·per·sion
dis·place
  dis·placed
  dis·plac·ing
  dis·place·ment
dis·play
dis·please
  dis·pleas·ing
  dis·pleas·ure
dis·port
dis·pose
  dis·pos·ing
  dis·pos·a·ble
  dis·po·si·tion
dis·pos·sess
  dis·pos·ses·sion
dis·pro·por·tion
  dis·pro·por·tion·ate
dis·prove
  dis·prov·ing
dis·pute
  dis·put·ed
  dis·put·ing
  dis·put·a·ble
  dis·pu·tant
  dis·pu·ta·tious
dis·qual·i·fy
  dis·qual·i·fied
  dis·qual·i·fy·ing
  dis·qual·i·fi·ca·tion
dis·qui·et
  dis·qui·etude
dis·qui·si·tion
dis·re·gard
dis·re·pair
dis·re·pute
  dis·rep·u·ta·ble
dis·re·spect
  dis·re·spect·ful
dis·robe
  dis·robed

dis·rob·ing
dis·rupt
  dis·rup·tion
  dis·rup·tive
  dis·rupt·er
dis·sat·is·fy
  dis·sat·is·fac·tion
  dis·sat·is·fac·to·ry
  dis·sat·is·fied
  dis·sat·is·fy·ing
dis·sect
  dis·sect·ed
  dis·sec·tion
dis·sem·ble
dis·sem·blance
  dis·sem·bled
  dis·sem·bling
dis·sem·i·nate
  dis·sem·i·nat·ed
  dis·sem·i·nat·ing
  dis·sem·i·na·tion
dis·sent
  dis·sent·ing
  dis·sen·sion
  dis·sen·tious
  dis·sent·er
  dis·sen·tient
dis·ser·tate
  dis·ser·ta·ted
  dis·ser·ta·ting
  dis·ser·ta·tion
dis·serve
  dis·served
  dis·serv·ing
  dis·serv·ice
dis·si·dence
  dis·si·dent
dis·sim·i·lar
  dis·sim·i·lar·i·ty
dis·sim·i·late
  dis·sim·i·lat·ed
  dis·sim·i·lat·ing
  dis·sim·i·la·tion
dis·si·mil·i·tude
dis·sim·u·late
  dis·sim·u·lat·ed
  dis·sim·u·lat·ing
  dis·sim·u·la·tion

dis·si·pate
  dis·si·pat·ed
  dis·si·pat·ing
  dis·si·pa·tion
dis·so·ci·ate
  dis·so·ci·at·ed
  dis·so·ci·at·ing
  dis·so·ci·a·tion
dis·sol·u·ble
dis·so·lute
dis·so·lu·tion
dis·solve
  dis·solv·ing
  dis·solv·a·ble
dis·so·nance
  dis·so·nant
dis·suade
  dis·suad·ed
  dis·suad·ing
  dis·sua·sion
dis·taff
dis·tance
dis·tant
dis·taste
  dis·taste·ful
dis·tem·per
dis·tend
  dis·ten·sion
  dis·ten·tion
dis·till
  dis·tilled
  dis·till·ing
  dis·til·la·tion
dis·til·late
dis·till·er
dis·till·ery
  dis·till·er·ies
dis·tinct
  dis·tinc·tion
  dis·tinc·tive
dis·tin·guish
  dis·tin·guished
dis·tort
  dis·tort·ed
  dis·tor·tion
dis·tract
  dis·tract·ing
  dis·trac·tion

dis·trait
  dis·traught
dis·tress
  dis·tress·ing
  dis·tress·ful
  dis·tress·ed
dis·trib·ute
  dis·trib·ut·ed
  dis·trib·ut·ing
  dis·tri·bu·tion
  dis·trib·u·tor
dis·trict
dis·trict at·tor·ney
dis·trust
  dis·trust·ful
dis·turb
  dis·turb·ance
  dis·turbed
dis·u·nite
  dis·u·nit·ed
  dis·u·nit·ing
  dis·u·ni·ty
  dis·un·ion
dis·use
  dis·used
  dis·us·ing
ditch
dith·er
dit·to
  dit·to·ing
dit·ty
di·u·ret·ic
di·ur·nal
di·va
di·va·gate
  di·va·ga·tion
di·van
dive
  dived
  dove
  div·ing
di·verge
  di·verged
  di·verg·ing
  di·ver·gence
  di·ver·gent
di·verse
  di·ver·si·fi·ca·tion

.di·ver·si·fy
  di·ver·si·fied
  di·ver·si·ty
  di·ver·si·ties
di·ver·sion
  di·ver·sion·ary
di·vert
di·vide
  di·vid·ed
  di·vid·ing
  di·vis·i·ble
  di·vi·sion
  di·vi·sive
  di·vi·sor
div·i·dend
di·vine
  di·vin·i·ty
  di·vin·i·ties
di·vorce
  di·vorc·ing
  di·vorcee
di·vulge
  di·vulged
  di·vulg·ing
  di·vul·gence
diz·zy
  diz·zi·est
  diz·zied
  diz·zy·ing
  diz·zi·ly
  diz·zi·ness
do
  did
  done
  do·ing
  does
Do·ber·man pin·scher
doc·ile
doc·tor
  doc·tor·al
  doc·tor·ate
doc·trine
  doc·tri·nal
  doc·tri·naire
doc·u·ment
  doc·u·men·ta·tion
  doc·u·men·tary
dod·der

dodge
  dodg·ing
doesn't
dog
  dogged
  dog·ging
dog·eared
dog·ged
  dog·ged·ly
dog·ger·el
dog·ma
  dog·mas
dog·mat·ic
  dog·mat·i·cal
  dog·ma·tism
  dog·ma·tist
doi·ly
  doi·lies
dol·drums
dole
  doled
  dol·ing
dole·ful
dol·lar
dol·or·ous
dol·phin
dolt
  dolt·ish
do·main
dome
  domed
  dom·ing
do·mes·tic
  do·mes·ti·cal·ly
do·mes·ti·cate
  do·mes·ti·cat·ed
  do·mes·ti·cat·ing
  do·mes·ti·ca·tion
do·mes·tic·i·ty
  do·mes·tic·i·ties
dom·i·cile
  dom·i·ciled
  dom·i·cil·ing
dom·i·nant
  dom·i·nance
  dom·i·nancy
dom·i·nate
  dom·i·nat·ing

dom·i·na·tion
dom·i·neer
  dom·i·neer·ing
do·min·ion
dom·i·no
  dom·i·noes
don
  donned
  don·ning
do·nate
  do·nat·ed
  do·nat·ing
  do·na·tor
  do·na·tion
  do·nor
don·key
doo·dle
dooms·day
dope
  doped
  dop·ing
dop·ey
  dop·i·ness
dor·mant
  dor·man·cy
dor·mer
  dor·mered
dor·mi·to·ry
  dor·mi·to·ries
dor·sal
dose
  dosed
  dos·ing
  dos·age
dos·si·er
dot
  dot·ted
  dot·ting
dot·age
dote
  dot·ed
  dot·ing
dou·ble
  dou·bled
  dou·bling
  doub·ly
dou·ble·breast·ed
dou·ble·cross

dou·ble·deck·er
dou·ble·faced
dou·ble·head·ed
dou·ble·joint·ed
dou·ble·time
doubt
  doubt·ful
  doubt·ful·ly
  doubt·less
douche
  douched
  douch·ing
dough
dough·ty
  dough·ti·ness
dour
  dour·ness
douse
  doused
  dous·ing
dove·cote
dove·tail
dow·a·ger
dow·dy
  dowd·i·ly
  dow·di·ness
dow·el
  dow·eled
  dow·el·ing
dow·er
down
  down·i·ness
  downy
down·grade
  down·grad·ed
  down·grad·ing
down·heart·ed
down·stream
down·town
down·trod·den
dow·ry
  dow·ries
dox·ol·o·gy
doze
  dozed
  dozing
doz·en
  doz·enth

drab
  drab·ness
dra·co·ni·an
draft
  draft·ee
drafts·man
drafty
  draft·i·er
drag
  dragged
  drag·ging
drag·net
drain
drain·age
drake
dra·ma
  dra·ma·tic
  dra·mat·ics
  dram·a·tist
  dram·a·tize
  dram·a·ti·za·tion
drape
  draped
  draping
dra·pery
  dra·per·ies
dras·tic
  drast·i·cal·ly
draught
draw
  drew
  drawn
  draw·ing
draw·bridge
draw·er
drawl
dread
  dread·ful
dream
  dreamed
  dreamt
  dream·ing
dream·er
dream·i·ly
dreamy
  dream·i·est
dreary
  drear·i·er

drear·i·ly
drear·i·ness
dredge
  dredged
  dredg·ing
  dredg·er
dreg
  dreg·gy
drench
dress
  dressed
  dres·sing
dress·er
dressy
  dress·i·est
drib·ble
  drib·bled
  drib·bling
dri·er
drift
  drift·age
  drift·er
drill·ing
dri·ly
drink
  drank
  drunk
  drink·ing
  drink·a·ble
  drink·er
drip
  dripped
  drip·ping
  drip·py
drive
  drove
  driv·en
  driv·ing
driv·el
  driv·eled
  driv·el·ing
driz·zle
  driz·zled
  driz·zling
  driz·zly
droll
  drol·ly
  droll·ery

drom·e·dary
  drom·e·dar·ies
drone
  droned
  dron·ing
drool
droop
  droop·ing·ly
  droop·y
drop
  dropped
  drop·ping
drop·let
drop·per
drop·sy
dross
drought
  droughty
  drought·i·est
drove
drowned
drowse
  drows·ing
  drow·sy
  drow·si·ness
drub
  drubbed
  drub·bing
drudge
  drudg·ing
  drudg·ery
drug
  drugged
  drug·ging
drug·gist
dru·id
drum
  drummed
  drum·ming
  drum·mer
drunk·ard
drunk·en
  drunk·en·ly
  drunk·en·ness
dry
  dry·ing
  dri·er
  dried

dry·ad
du·al
　du·al·i·ty
du·al·ism
　du·al·is·tic
dub
　dubbed
　dub·bing
du·bi·ous
　du·bi·e·ty
　du·bi·ous·ly
du·cal
du·cat
duch·ess
duchy
duck·ling
ducky
duct·less
duc·tile
dudg·eon
du·el
　du·eled
　du·el·ing
　du·el·ist
du·en·na
du·et
duf·fel
duff·er
dug·out
duke·dom
dul·cet
dul·ci·mer
dull
　dull·ard
　dull·ness
du·ly
dumb
　dumb·ness
dum·dum
dum·found
dum·my
　dum·mies
dump·ling
dumpy
　dump·i·er
　dump·i·ness
dun

dunned
dun·ning
dunce
dun·der·head
dune
dung·hill
dun·ga·ree
dun·geon
dun·nage
du·o·dec·i·mal
du·o·de·nal
　du·o·de·num
dupe
　duped
　dup·ing
du·plex
du·pli·cate
　du·pli·cat·ed
　du·pli·cat·ing
　du·pli·ca·tion
　du·pli·ca·tor
du·plic·i·ty
　du·plic·i·ties
du·ra·ble
　du·ra·bil·i·ty
dur·ance
du·ra·tion
du·ress
dur·ing
dusk
　dusk·i·ness
　dusky
dust·er
dust·less
dusty
　dust·i·er
　dust·i·ness
du·ti·a·ble
du·ti·ful
　du·ti·ful·ly
du·ty
　du·ties
dwarf
　dwarf·ish
dwell
　dwelt
　dwelled
　dwell·ing

dwindle
　dwin·dled
　dwin·dling
dye
　dyed
　dye·ing
dy·ing
dy·nam·ic
　dy·nam·i·cal·ly
　dy·na·mism
　dy·nam·ics
dy·na·mite
　dy·na·mit·er
dy·na·mo
　dy·na·mo·tor
dy·nas·ty
　dy·nas·ties
dy·na·tron
dys·en·tery
dys·func·tion
dys·pep·sia
　dys·pep·tic
dys·tro·phy
　dys·tro·phic·

E

ea·ger
　ea·ger·ness
ea·gle
ea·gle·eyed
ea·glet
ear·ache
ear·drum
earl·dom
ear·ly
　ear·li·est
　ear·li·ness
ear·lobe
ear·mark
earn
earn·ings
ear·nest
　ear·nest·ness
ear·ring
ear·shot
ear·split·ting
earth·bound

60

earth·en
earth·en·ware
earth·ly
earth·quake
earth·shaking
earth·work
earth·worm
earthy
  earth·i·ness
ease
  eased
  eas·ing
ea·sel
ease·ment
eas·i·ly
  eas·i·ness
east·er·ly
east·ern
East·ern·er
east·ward
easy
  eas·i·er
  eas·i·est
eas·y·go·ing
eat
  ate
  eat·en
  eat·ing
eau de co·logne
eaves·drop
  eaves·dropped
  eaves·drop·ping
  eaves·drop·per
ebb
  ebb·ing
eb·ony
ebul·lience
  ebul·lient
  eb·ul·li·tion
ec·cen·tric
  ec·cen·tric·i·ty
ec·cle·si·as·tic
  ec·cle·si·as·ti·cal
ech·e·lon
echo
  ech·oes
  ech·oed
  ech·o·ing

eclair
ec·lec·tic
  ec·lec·ti·cal·ly
  ec·lec·ti·cism
eclipse
  eclipsed
  eclips·ing
eclip·tic
ecol·o·gy
  ec·o·log·ic
  ec·o·log·i·cal
  ecol·o·gist
eco·nom·ic
  eco·nomi·cal
  eco·nom·ics
  econ·o·mist
  econ·o·mize
  econ·o·miz·ing
econ·o·my
  econ·o·mies
ec·ru
ec·sta·sy
  ec·sta·sies
ec·stat·ic
  ec·stat·i·cal
ec·u·men·ic
  ec·u·men·i·cal
  ec·u·men·ism
ec·ze·ma
  ec·zem·a·tous
e·da·cious
ed·dy
  ed·dies
  ed·died
  ed·dy·ing
edel·weiss
ede·ma
edge
  edged
  edg·ing
edgy
  edg·i·ness
ed·i·ble
  ed·i·bil·i·ty
edict
ed·i·fice
ed·i·fy
  ed·i·fied

ed·i·fy·ing
  ed·i·fi·ca·tion
ed·it
edi·tion
ed·i·tor
ed·i·to·ri·al
  ed·i·to·ri·al·ly
  ed·i·to·ri·al·ize
  ed·i·to·ri·al·iz·ing
ed·u·cate
  ed·u·cat·ed
  ed·u·cat·ing
  ed·u·ca·ble
  ed·u·ca·tive
ed·u·ca·tion
  ed·u·ca·tion·al
  ed·u·ca·tor
educe
  educed
  educ·ing
  educ·i·ble
  educ·tion
eel
  eely
ee·rie
  ee·ri·ly
  ee·ri·ness
ef·face
  ef·faced
  ef·fac·ing
  ef·face·ment
ef·fect
ef·fec·tive
  ef·fec·tive·ness
  ef·fec·tive·ly
ef·fec·tu·al
ef·fec·tu·ate
  ef·fec·tu·at·ed
  ef·fec·tu·at·ing
ef·fem·i·nate
  ef·fem·i·na·cy
  ef·fem·i·nate·ly
ef·fer·vesce
  ef·fer·vesc·ing
  ef·fer·ves·cence
  ef·fer·ves·cent
ef·fete
ef·fi·ca·cy

ef·fi·ca·cies
ef·fi·ca·cious
ef·fi·cient
  ef·fi·cient·ly
ef·fi·gy
  ef·fi·gies
ef·flo·resce
  ef·flo·resced
  ef·flo·resc·ing
  ef·flo·res·cence
  ef·flo·res·cent
ef·flu·ent
  ef·flu·ence
ef·flu·vi·um
  ef·flu·vi·al
ef·fort
  ef·fort·less
ef·fron·tery
  ef·fron·ter·ies
ef·ful·gent
  ef·ful·gence
ef·fuse
  ef·fused
  ef·fus·ing
  ef·fu·sion
  ef·fu·sive
egal·i·tar·i·an
  egal·i·tar·i·an·ism
ego·cen·tric
ego·ism
  ego·ist
  ego·is·tic
ego·tism
  ego·tist
  ego·tis·tic
  ego·tis·ti·cal
egre·gious
egress
e·gre·sion
egret
eight
  eighth
eight·een
  eight·eenth
eight·fold
eighty
  eight·ies
  eight·i·eth

ei·ther
ejac·u·late
  ejac·u·l
  ejac·u·la
·g
  ejac·u·la·tion
  ejac·u·la·to·ry
eject
  ejec·tion
  eject·ment
  ejec·tor
eke
  eked
  ek·ing
elab·o·rate
  elab·o·rat·ed
  elab·o·rat·ing
  elab·o·rate·ness
  elab·o·ra·tion
elapse
  elapsed
  elaps·ing
elas·tic
  elas·ti·cal
  elas·tic·i·ty
elate
  elat·ed
  elat·ing
  ela·tion
el·bow
eld·er
  el·er·ly
  eld·er·li·ness
  eld·est
elect
  elec·tion
  elec·tion·eer
  elec·tive
  elec·tor
  elec·tor·al
  elec·tor·ate
elec·tric
  elec·tri·cal
  elec·tri·cian
  elec·tric·i·ty
  elec·tri·fy
  elec·tri·fied
  elec·tri·fy·ing
  elec·tri·fi·ca·tion

elec·tro·car·di·o·gram
elec·tro·cute
  elec·tro·cut·ed
  elec·tro·cut·ing
  elec·tro·cu·tion
elec·trode
elec·tro·dy·nam·ics
elec·tro·en·ceph·a·lo·gram
elec·trol·y·sis
  elec·tro·lyze
  elec·tro·lyzed
  elec·tro·lyz·ing
elec·tro·lyte
  elec·tro·lyt·ic
elec·tro·mag·net
  elec·tro·mag·net·ism
  elec·tro·mag·net·ic
elec·tron
  elec·tron·ic
  elec·tron·ics
  elec·tron·i·cal·ly
elec·tro·plate
  elec·tro·plat·ed
  elec·tro·plat·ing
elec·tro·ther·a·py
el·ee·mos·y·nary
el·e·gant
  el·e·gance
  el·e·gan·cy
  el·e·gant·ly
el·e·gy
  el·e·gies
  el·e·gize
  el·e·giz·ing
el·e·ment
  el·e·men·tal
  el·e·men·ta·ry
  el·e·men·ta·ri·ly
ele·e·phant
el·e·phan·ti·a·sis
el·e·phan·tine
el·e·vate
  el·e·vat·ed
  el·e·vat·ing
el·e·va·tion
el·e·va·tor
elev·en
  elev·enth

elf
  elves
  elf·in
elic·it
el·i·gi·ble
  el·i·gi·bil·i·ty
elim·i·nate
  elim·i·nat·ed
  elim·i·nat·ing
  elim·i·na·tion
elite
  elit·ism
  elit·ist
elix·ir
Eliz·a·beth·an
el·lipse
el·lip·sis
el·lip·ti·cal
  el·lip·tic
el·o·cu·tion
  el·o·cu·tion·ary
  el·o·cu·tion·ist
elon·gate
  elon·gat·ed
  elon·gat·ing
  elon·ga·tion
elope
  eloped
  elop·ing
  elope·ment
el·o·quence
el·o·quent
elu·ci·date
  elu·ci·dat·ed
  elu·ci·dat·ing
  elu·ci·da·tion
elude
  elud·ed
  elud·ing
  elu·sion
elu·sive
  elu·so·ry
  elu·sive·ness
ema·ci·ate
  ema·ci·at·ed
  ema·ci·at·ed
  ema·ci·a·tion
em·a·nate

em·a·nat·ed
em·a·nat·ing
em·a·na·tion
eman·ci·pate
  eman·ci·pat·ed
  eman·ci·pat·ing
  eman·ci·pa·tor
emas·cu·late
  emas·cu·lat·ed
  emas·cu·lat·ing
  emas·cu·la·tion
em·balm
  em·balm·ment
em·bank·ment
em·bar·go
  em·bar·goes
  em·bar·go·ing
em·bark
  em·bar·ka·tion
  em·bark·ment
em·bar·rass
  em·bar·rassed
  em·bar·rass·ing
  em·bar·rass·ment
em·bas·sy
  em·bas·sies
em·bat·tle
  em·bat·tled
  em·bat·tling
  em·bat·tle·ment
em·bed
  em·bed·ded
  em·bed·ding
em·bel·lish
  em·bel·lish·ment
em·ber
em·bez·zle
  em·bez·zled
  em·bez·zling
  em·bez·zle·ment
  em·bez·zler
em·bit·ter
  em·bit·ter·ment
em·bla·zon
  em·blaz·on·ment
em·blem
  em·blem·at·ic
  em·blem·at·i·cal

em·bod·y
  em·bod·ied
  em·bod·y·ing
  em·bod·i·ment
em·bold·en
em·bo·lism
em·bo·lus
em·boss
  em·boss·ment
em·bou·chure
em·brace
  em·brac·ing
em·bra·sure
em·bro·cate
em·broi·der
  em·broi·dery
em·broil
  em·broil·ment
em·bryo
  em·bry·os
  em·bry·on·ic
em·bry·ol·o·gy
em·cee
  em·ceed
  em·cee·ing
emend
  emen·da·ble
  emen·da·tion
em·er·ald
emerge
  emerged
  emerg·ing
  emergence
  emergent
emer·gen·cy
  emer·gen·cies
emer·i·tus
em·ery
emet·ic
em·i·grant
em·i·grate
  em·i·grat·ing
  em·i·gra·tion
émi·gré
em·i·nence
  em·i·nent
em·i·nent do·main
em·is·sary

63

em·is·sar·ies
emis·sion
emis·sive
emit
  emit·ted
  emit·ting
emol·lient
emol·u·ment
emote
  emot·ed
  emot·ing
  emo·tive
emo·tion
  emo·tion·al·ly
  emo·tion·al·ism
em·pan·el
em·pa·thize
  em·pa·thized
  em·pa·thiz·ing
em·pa·thy
  em·pa·thet·ic
  em·path·ic
em·per·or
em·pha·sis
  em·pha·ses
em·pha·size
  em·pha·sized
  em·pha·siz·ing
em·phat·ic
  em·phat·i·cal·ly
em·phy·se·ma
em·pire
em·pir·i·cal
em·pir·i·cism
em·place·ment
em·ploy
  em·ploy·a·ble
em·ploy·ee
em·ploy·er
em·ploy·ment
em·po·ri·um
em·pow·er
em·press
emp·ty
  emp·tied
  emp·ty·ing
  emp·ti·ness
em·u·late

em·u·lat·ing
em·u·la·tion
emul·si·fy
  emul·si·fied
  emul·si·fy·ing
  emul·si·fi·ca·tion
  emul·si·fi·er
emul·sion
emul·sive
en·a·ble
  en·a·bled
  en·a·bling
en·act
  en·act·ment
enam·el
  enam·eled
  enam·el·ing
  enam·el·ware
en·am·or
  en·am·ored
en·camp
  en·camp·ment
en·cap·su·late
  en·cap·su·lat·ed
  en·cap·su·lat·ing
  en·cap·sule
en·case
  en·cased
  en·cas·ing
en·ceinte
en·ceph·a·li·tis
en·chant
  en·chant·ing
  en·chant·ment
  en·chant·ress
en·chi·la·da
en·cir·cle
  en·cir·cled
  en·cir·cling
  en·cir·cle·ment
en·clave
en·close
  en·closed
  en·clos·ing
  en·clo·sure
en·code
  en·cod·ed
  en·cod·ing

en·com·pass
en·core
en·coun·ter
en·cour·age
  en·cour·aged
  en·cour·ag·ing
  en·cour·age·ment
en·croach
  en·croach·ment
en·crust
  en·crus·ta·tion
en·cum·ber
  en·cum·brance
en·cy·clo·pe·dia
en·cy·clo·pe·dic
en·dan·ger
  en·dan·ger·ment
en·dear
  en·dear·ment
en·deav·or
en·dem·ic
  en·dem·i·cal
en·dive
end·ing
end·less
en·do·crine
en·do·cri·nol·o·gy
en·dog·a·mous
en·dorse
  en·dors·ing
  en·dors·ee
  en·dors·er
  en·dorse·ment
en·do·scope
endow
  en·dow·ment
en·due
  en·dued
  en·du·ing
en·dure
  en·dur·ing
  en·dur·a·ble
  en·dur·ance
  en·dur·ing·ness
en·e·ma
en·e·my
  en·e·mies
en·er·get·ic

en·er·get·i·cal·ly
en·er·gize
  en·er·gized
  en·er·giz·ing
  en·er·giz·er
en·er·gy
  en·er·gies
en·er·vate
  en·er·vat·ed
  en·er·vat·ing
  en·er·va·tion
en·fee·ble
  en·fee·bled
  en·fee·bling
  en·fee·ble·ment
en·fold
en·force
  en·forced
  en·forc·ing
  en·force·ment
en·fran·chise
  en·fran·chised
  en·fran·chis·ing
  en·fran·chise·ment
en·gage
  en·gaged
  en·gag·ing
  en·gage·ment
en·gen·der
en·gine
en·gi·neer
En·gland
En·glish
en·gorge
  en·gorged
  en·gorg·ing
  en·gorge·ment
en·grave
  en·graved
  en·grav·ing
  en·grav·er
en·gross
  en·grossed
  en·gross·ing
  en·gross·ment
en·gulf
en·gulf·ment
en·hance

en·hanced
en·hanc·ing
en·hance·ment
enig·ma
  en·ig·mat·ic
  en·ig·mat·i·cal
en·join
  en·join·ment
en·joy
  en·joy·a·ble
  en·joy·ment
en·large
  en·larged
  en·larg·ing
  en·larg·er
  en·large·ment
en·light·en
  en·light·en·ment
en·list
  en·list·ed
  en·list·ment
en·liv·en
en·masse
en·mesh
en·mi·ty
  en·mi·ties
en·no·ble
  en·no·bled
  en·no·bling
  en·no·ble·ment
en·nui
enor·mi·ty
  enor·mi·ties
enor·mous
enough
en·plane
  en·planed
  en·plan·ing
en·quire
  en·quiry
en·rage
  en·raged
  en·rag·ing
en·rap·ture
  en·rap·tured
  en·rap·tur·ing
  en·rapt
en·rich

en·rich·ment
en·roll
  en·roll·ment
en route
en·sconce
  en·sconced
  en·sconc·ing
en·semble
en·shrine
  en·shrined
  en·shrin·ing
en·shroud
en·sign
en·si·lage
  en·si·laged
  en·si·lag·ing
en·slave
  en·slaved
  en·slav·ing
  en·slave·ment
en·snare
  en·snared
  en·snar·ing
  en·snare·ment
en·sue
  en·sued
  en·su·ing
en·sure
  en·sured
  en·sur·ing
en·tail
  en·tail·ment
en·tan·gle
  en·tan·gled
  en·tan·gling
  en·tan·gle·ment
en·tente
en·ter
  en·ter·ing
en·ter·prise
  en·ter·pris·ing
en·ter·tain
  en·ter·tain·ing
  en·ter·tain·er
  en·ter·tain·ment
en·thrall
  en·thralled
  en·thrall·ing

en·thrall·ment
en·throne
en·throned
en·thron·ing
en·throne·ment
en·thuse
en·thused
en·thus·ing
en·thu·si·asm
en·thu·si·ast
en·thu·si·as·tic
en·thu·si·as·ti·cal·ly
en·tice
en·ticed
en·tic·ing
en·tice·ment
en·tire
en·tire·ly
en·tire·ness
en·tire·ty
en·ti·tle
en·ti·tled
en·ti·tling
en·ti·tle·ment
en·ti·ty
en·ti·ties
en·tomb
en·tomb·ment
en·to·mol·o·gy
en·tou·rage
en·trails
en·train
en·trance
en·trant
en·trap
en·trapped
en·trap·ping
en·trap·ment
en·treat
en·treat·ment
en·treaty
en·tree
en·trench
en·trench·ment
en·tre·pre·neur
en·trust
en·trust·ment
en·try

en·tries
en·twine
en·twined
en·twin·ing
enu·mer·ate
enu·mer·at·ed
enu·mer·at·ing
enu·mer·a·tion
enu·mer·a·tor
enun·ci·ate
enun·ci·at·ed
enun·ci·at·ing
enun·ci·a·tion
en·vel·op
en·vel·op·ing
en·ve·lope
en·vi·a·ble
en·vi·ous
en·vi·ous·ness
en·vi·ron
en·vi·ron·ment
en·vis·age
en·vis·ag·ing
en·vi·sion
en·voy
en·vy
en·vies
en·vied
en·vy·ing
en·vi·able
en·vi·ous
en·zyme
en·zy·mat·ic
en·vi·ron·ment
en·vi·ron·men·tal
ep·au·let
epergne
ephed·rine
ephem·er·al
ep·ic
ep·i·cal
ep·i·cen·ter
ep·i·cure
epi·cu·re·an
ep·i·dem·ic
ep·i·der·mis
ep·i·der·mal
ep·i·der·mic

ep·i·glot·tis
ep·i·gram
ep·i·gram·mat·ic
ep·i·graph
ep·i·lep·sy
ep·i·lep·tic
ep·i·logue
epis·co·pal
epis·co·pa·cy
epis·co·pate
Epis·co·pa·lian
ep·i·sode
ep·i·sod·ic
ep·i·sod·i·cal
epis·te·mol·o·gy
epis·tle
ep·i·taph
ep·i·thet
epit·o·me
epit·o·mize
ep·och
ep·och·al
ep·oxy
equa·ble
equa·bil·i·ty
equa·ble·ness
equa·bly
equal
equaled
equal·ling
equal·ly
equal·ness
equal·i·tar·i·an
equal·i·ty
equal·i·ties
equal·ize
equal·ized
equal·iz·ing
equal·i·za·tion
equa·nim·i·ty
equate
equat·ed
equat·ing
equa·tion
equa·tion·al
equa·tor
equa·to·ri·al
eques·tri·an

eques·tri·enne
equi·dis·tant
  equi·dis·tance
equil·lat·er·al
equi·li·brate
  equi·li·brat·ed
  equi·li·brat·ing
  equi·li·bra·tion
  equi·lib·ri·um
equine
equi·nox
  equi·noc·tial
equip
  equipped
  equip·ping
equ·ui·page
equip·ment
equi·poise
equ·ui·ty
  eq·ui·ties
  eq·ui·ta·ble
  eq·ui·ta·bly
equiv·a·lent
  equiv·a·lence
equiv·o·cal
equiv·o·cate
  equiv·o·cat·ed
  equiv·o·cat·ing
  equiv·o·ca·tion
erad·i·cate
  erad·i·cat·ed
  erad·i·cat·ing
  erad·i·ca·ble
  erad·i·ca·tion
  erad·i·ca·tor
erase
  erased
  eras·ing
  eras·a·ble
  eras·ure
erect
  erect·a·ble
  erec·tive
  erect·ly
  erect·ness
  erec·tor
erec·tile
erec·tion

er·mine
erode
  erod·ed
  erod·ing
  ero·sion
  ero·sive
erot·ic
  erot·i·cal·ly
  erot·i·cism
err
  err·ing·ly
err·rand
err·rant
  err·rat·ic
  err·rat·i·cal·ly
err·ra·tum
  err·ra·ta
err·ro·ne·ous
err·ror
  err·ror·less
er·satz
erst·while
er·u·dite
  er·u·dite·ness
  er·u·di·tion
erupt
  erup·tion
  erup·tive
es·ca·lade
es·ca·late
  es·ca·lat·ed
  es·ca·lat·ing
  es·ca·la·tion
  es·ca·la·tor
es·cal·lop
es·ca·pade
es·cape
  es·caped
  es·cap·ing
es·ca·pee
  es·cap·ist
  es·cap·ism
es·ca·role
es·carp·ment
es·chew
  es·chew·al
es·cort
es·crow

es·cutch·eon
Es·ki·mo
esoph·a·gus
es·o·ter·ic
  es·o·ter·i·cal
es·pal·ier
es·pe·cial
  es·pe·cial·ly
Es·pe·ran·to
es·pi·o·nage
es·pla·nade
es·pouse
  es·poused
  es·pous·ing
  es·pous·al
es·prit de corps
es·py
  es·pied
  es·py·ing
es·quire
es·say
  es·say·ist
es·sence
es·sen·tial
  es·sen·tial·ly
es·tab·lish
  es·tab·lish·ment
es·tate
es·teem
es·thet·ic
es·ti·ma·ble
  es·ti·ma·bly
es·ti·mate
  es·ti·mat·ed
  es·ti·mat·ing
  es·ti·ma·tor
  es·ti·ma·tion
es·trange
  es·tranged
  es·trang·ing
  es·trange·ment
es·tro·gen
es·tu·ary
  es·tu·ar·ies
et cet·era
etch
  etch·ing
eter·nal

67

eter·nal·ly
eter·ni·ty
eter·nize
eter·ni·za·tion
eth·a·nol
ether
ethe·re·al
ethe·re·al·ly
ethe·re·al·ize
ethe·re·al·i·za·tion
eth·ic
eth·i·cal
eth·ics
eth·nic
eth·ni·cal
eth·nog·ra·phy
eth·nol·o·gy
eth·yl
eti·ol·o·gy
eti·o·log·i·cal
et·i·quette
etude
et·y·mol·o·gy
et·y·mo·log·i·cal
eu·ca·lyp·tus
Eu·cha·rist
Eu·cha·ris·tic
Eu·cha·ris·ti·cal
eu·chre
eu·gen·ic
eu·gen·i·cal·ly
eu·lo·gize
eu·lo·gized
eu·lo·giz·ing
eu·lo·gy
eu·lo·gies
eu·lo·gis·tic
eu·nuch
eu·phe·mism
eu·phe·mist
eu·phe·mis·tic
eu·phe·mis·ti·cal
eu·phe·mize
eu·phe·mized
eu·phe·miz·ing
eu·pho·ny
eu·phon·ic
eu·phon·i·cal

eu·pho·ni·ous
eu·pho·ria
eu·phor·ic
Eu·rope
Eu·ro·pe·an
eu·tha·na·sia
evac·u·ate
evac·u·at·ed
evac·u·at·ing
evac·u·a·tion
evac·u·ee
evade
evad·ed
evad·ing
eval·u·ate
eval·u·at·ed
eval·u·at·ing
eval·u·a·tion
eval·u·a·tor
ev·a·nesce
ev·a·nesced
ev·a·nesc·ing
ev·a·nes·cent
evan·gel·i·cal
evan·gel·ic
evan·gel·i·cal·ism
evan·gel·i·cal·ly
evan·ge·lism
evan·ge·lis·tic
evan·ge·lis·ti·cal·ly
evan·ge·list
evan·ge·lize
evan·ge·lized
evan·ge·liz·ing
evan·ge·li·za·tion
evap·o·rate
evap·o·rat·ed
evap·o·rat·ing
evap·o·ra·tion
evap·o·ra·tor
eva·sion
eva·sive
eva·sive·ness
even
even·ly
eve·ning
event·ful
event·ful·ly

even·tu·al
even·tu·al·ly
even·tu·al·i·ty
even·tu·ate
even·tu·at·ed
even·tu·at·ing
ev·er·green
ev·er·last·ing
evert
ever·sion
ev·ery·body
ev·ery·day
ev·ery·one
ev·ery·thing
ev·ery·where
evict
evic·tion
evic·tor
ev·i·dence
ev·i·denced
ev·i·denc·ing
ev·i·dent
ev·i·dent·ly
ev·i·den·tial
evil
evil·do·er
evil·ly
evil·ness
evil·mind·ed
evince
evinced
evinc·ing
evin·ci·ble
evis·cer·ate
evis·cer·at·ed
evis·cer·at·ing
evis·cer·a·tion
evoke
evoked
evok·ing
ev·o·ca·tion
ev·o·lu·tion
ev·o·lu·tion·al
ev·o·lu·tion·ary
ev·o·lu·tion·ism
ev·o·lu·tion·ist
evolve
evolved

evolv·ing
evolve·ment
ew·er
ex·ac·er·bate
  ex·ac·er·bat·ed
  ex·ac·er·bat·ing
  ex·ac·er·ba·tion
ex·act
  ex·act·a·ble
ex·act·ing
  ex·act·ing·ly
ex·act·i·tude
ex·act·ly
ex·ag·ger·ate
  ex·ag·ger·at·ed
  ex·ag·ger·at·ing
  ex·ag·ger·a·tion
ex·alt
  ex·al·ta·tion
  ex·alt·ed
ex·am·ine
  ex·am·ined
  ex·am·in·ing
  ex·am·in·er
  ex·am·i·na·tion
ex·am·ple
  ex·am·pled
  ex·am·pling
ex·as·per·ate
  ex·as·per·at·ed
  ex·as·per·at·ing
  ex·as·per·a·tion
ex·ca·vate
  ex·ca·vat·ed
  ex·ca·vat·ing
  ex·ca·va·tion
  ex·ca·va·tor
ex·ceed
  ex·ceed·ed
  ex·ceed·ing
ex·cel
  ex·celled
  ex·cel·ling
ex·cel·lent
  ex·cel·lence
  ex·cel·len·cy
ex·cel·si·or
ex·cept

ex·cept·ing
ex·cep·tion
ex·cep·tion·al
ex·cerpt
  ex·cerp·tion
ex·cess
  ex·ces·sive
ex·change
  ex·changed
  ex·chang·ing
  ex·change·a·bil·i·ty
  ex·change·a·ble
ex·cheq·uer
ex·cise
  ex·cised
  ex·cis·ing
  ex·cis·a·ble
  ex·ci·sion
  ex·cit·a·ble
  ex·cit·a·bil·i·ty
ex·cite
  ex·cit·ed
  ex·cit·ing
  ex·ci·ta·tion
  ex·cit·ed·ly
  ex·cite·ment
ex·claim
  ex·cla·ma·tion
  ex·clam·a·to·ry
ex·clude
  ex·clud·ed
  ex·clud·ing
  ex·clud·a·ble
  ex·clu·sion
ex·clu·sive
  ex·clu·sive·ness
  ex·clu·siv·i·ty
ex·com·mu·ni·cate
  ex·com·mu·ni·cat·ed
  ex·com·mu·ni·cat·ing
  ex·com·mu·ni·cant
  ex·com·mu·ni·ca·ble
  ex·com·mu·ni·ca·tion
ex·co·ri·ate
  ex·co·ri·at·ed
  ex·co·ri·at·ing
  ex·co·ri·a·tion
ex·cre·ment

ex·cre·men·tal
ex·cres·cent
  ex·cres·cence
ex·cre·ta
  ex·cre·tal
ex·crete
  ex·cret·ed
  ex·cret·ing
  ex·cre·tion
ex·cru·ci·ate
  ex·cru·ci·at·ing
  ex·cru·ci·a·tion
ex·cul·pate
  ex·cul·pat·ed
  ex·cul·pat·ing
  ex·cul·pa·tion
  ex·cul·pa·to·ry
ex·cur·sion
  ex·cur·sion·al
  ex·cur·sion·ary
ex·cur·sive
ex·cuse
  ex·cused
  ex·cus·ing
  ex·cus·a·ble
  ex·cus·a·bly
  ex·cus·a·to·ry
ex·e·cra·ble
  ex·e·cra·bly
ex·e·crate
  ex·e·crat·ed
  ex·e·crat·ing
  ex·e·cra·tive
  ex·e·cra·tor
  ex·e·cra·tion
ex·e·cute
  ex·e·cut·ed
  ex·e·cut·ing
  ex·e·cut·er
  ex·e·cu·tion
  ex·e·cu·tion·er
ex·ec·u·tive
ex·ec·u·tor
  ex·ec·u·trix
ex·e·ge·sis
  ex·e·ge·ses
ex·em·plar
  ex·em·pla·ry

ex·em·pla·ri·ly
ex·em·pli·fy
  ex·em·pli·fied
  ex·em·pli·fy·ing
  ex·em·pli·fi·ca·tion
ex·empt
  ex·emp·tion
ex·er·cise
  ex·er·cised
  ex·er·cis·ing
  ex·er·cis·er
ex·ert
  ex·er·tion
ex·fo·li·ate
  ex·fo·li·at·ed
  ex·fo·li·at·ing
  ex·fo·li·a·tion
ex·hale
  ex·haled
  ex·hal·ing
  ex·ha·la·tion
ex·haust
  ex·haust·ed
  ex·haust·ing
  ex·haus·tion
ex·haus·tive
ex·hib·it
  ex·hib·i·tor
  ex·hi·bi·tion
  ex·hi·bi·tion·ism
  ex·hi·bi·tion·ist
ex·hil·a·rate
  ex·hil·a·rat·ed
  ex·hil·a·rat·ing
  ex·hil·a·ra·tion
  ex·hil·a·ra·tive
ex·hort
  ex·hor·ta·tive
  ex·hor·ta·tion
  ex·hor·ta·to·ry
  ex·hort·ing·ly
ex·hume
  ex·humed
  ex·hum·ing
  ex·hu·ma·tion
ex·i·gen·cy
  ex·i·gen·cies
ex·i·gent

ex·i·gent·ly
ex·ig·u·ous
ex·ile
  ex·iled
  ex·il·ing
ex·ist
  ex·ist·ence
  ex·ist·ent
ex·is·ten·tial
  ex·is·ten·tial·ism
ex li·bris
ex·o·dus
ex of·fi·cio
ex·og·a·my
  ex·og·a·mous
ex·og·e·nous
ex·on·er·ate
  ex·on·er·at·ed
  ex·on·er·at·ing
  ex·on·er·a·tion
  ex·on·er·a·tive
ex·or·bi·tant
  ex·or·bi·tance
  ex·or·bi·tant·ly
ex·or·cise
  ex·or·cised
  ex·or·cis·ing
  ex·or·cism
  ex·or·cist
ex·ot·ic
  ex·ot·i·cal·ly
  ex·ot·i·cism
ex·pand
  ex·pand·er
  ex·pand·able
ex·panse
ex·pan·si·ble
  ex·pan·si·bil·i·ty
ex·pan·sion
  ex·pan·sion·ism
  ex·pan·sion·ist
ex·pan·sive
  ex·pan·sive·ly
  ex·pan·sive·ness
ex·pa·ti·ate
  ex·pa·ti·at·ed
  ex·pa·ti·at·ing
  ex·pa·ti·a·tion

ex·pa·tri·ate
  ex·pa·tri·at·ed
  ex·pa·tri·at·ing
  ex·pa·tri·a·tion
ex·pect
  ex·pect·a·ble
  ex·pect·a·bly
  ex·pect·ing·ly
  ex·pect·an·cy
  ex·pect·ant
  ex·pec·ta·tion
ex·pec·to·rate
  ex·pec·to·rat·ed
  ex·pec·to·rat·ing
  ex·pec·to·ra·tion
ex·pe·di·ent
  ex·pe·di·en·cy
ex·pe·dite
  ex·pe·dit·ed
  ex·pe·dit·ing
  ex·pe·dit·er
  ex·pe·di·tious
ex·pe·di·tion
ex·pel
  ex·pelled
  ex·pel·ling
ex·pend
  ex·pend·a·ble
  ex·pend·a·bil·i·ty
ex·pend·i·ture
ex·pense
ex·pen·sive
ex·pe·ri·ence
  ex·pe·ri·enced
  ex·pe·ri·enc·ing
ex·pe·ri·en·tial
ex·per·i·ment
  ex·per·i·men·tal
  ex·per·i·men·ta·tion
ex·pert
  ex·pert·ly
  ex·pert·ness
ex·per·tise
ex·pi·ate
  ex·pi·at·ed
  ex·pi·at·ing
  ex·pi·a·tion
  ex·pi·a·to·ry

ex·pire
ex·pired
ex·pir·ing
ex·pi·ra·tion
ex·pir·a·to·ry
ex·plain
ex·plain·a·ble
ex·pla·na·tion
ex·plan·a·to·ry
ex·ple·tive
ex·pli·cate
ex·pli·cat·ed
ex·pli·cat·ing
ex·pli·ca·ble
ex·pli·ca·tion
ex·pli·ca·tive
ex·plic·it
ex·plic·it·ly
ex·plic·it·ness
ex·plode
ex·plod·ed
ex·plod·ing
ex·plo·sion
ex·plo·sive
ex·ploit
ex·ploit·a·ble
ex·ploi·ta·tion
ex·ploit·er
ex·ploit·ive
ex·plore
ex·plo·ra·tion
ex·plor·a·to·ry
ex·po·nent
ex·po·nen·tial
ex·port
ex·port·a·ble
ex·por·ta·tion
ex·port·er
ex·pose
ex·posed
ex·pos·ing
ex·pos·er
ex·po·sure
ex·po·se
ex·po·si·tion
ex·pos·i·tor
ex·pos·i·to·ry
ex·pos·tu·late

ex·pos·tu·lat·ed
ex·pos·tu·lat·ing
ex·pos·tu·la·tion
ex·pos·tu·la·to·ry
ex·po·sure
ex·pound
ex·press
ex·press·i·ble
ex·pres·sion
ex·pres·sive
ex·press·ly
ex·pres·sion·ism
ex·pres·sion·ist
ex·pro·pri·ate
ex·pro·pri·at·ed
ex·pro·pri·at·ing
ex·pro·pri·a·tion
ex·pul·sion
ex·pul·sive
ex·punge
ex·punged
ex·pung·ing
ex·pur·gate
ex·pur·gat·ed
ex·pur·gat·ing
ex·pur·ga·tion
ex·pur·ga·to·ry
ex·qui·site
ex·qui·site·ly
ex·qui·site·ness
ex·tant
ex·tem·po·re
ex·tem·po·rize
ex·tem·po·rized
ex·tem·po·riz·ing
ex·tem·po·ri·za·tion
ex·tem·po·ra·ne·ous
ex·tend
ex·tend·ed
ex·tend·i·ble
ex·ten·si·ble
ex·ten·sion
ex·ten·sive
ex·tent
ex·ten·u·ate
ex·ten·u·at·ed
ex·ten·u·at·ing
ex·ten·u·a·tion

ex·te·ri·or
ex·ter·mi·nate
ex·ter·mi·nat·ed
ex·ter·mi·nat·ing
ex·ter·mi·na·tion
ex·ter·nal
ex·ter·nal·ly
ex·ter·ri·to·ri·al
ex·tinct
ex·tinc·tion
ex·tin·guish
ex·tin·guish·a·ble
ex·tin·guish·er
ex·tin·guish·ment
ex·tir·pate
ex·tir·pat·ed
ex·tir·pat·ing
ex·tir·pa·tion
ex·tol
ex·tolled
ex·tol·ling
ex·tol·ment
ex·tort
ex·tor·ter
ex·tor·tive
ex·tor·tion
ex·tor·tion·ary
ex·tor·tion·ate
ex·tor·tion·er
ex·tor·tion·ist
ex·tra
ex·tract
ex·trac·tive
ex·trac·tor
ex·trac·tion
ex·tra·cur·ric·u·lar
ex·tra·dite
ex·tra·dit·ed
ex·tra·dit·ing
ex·tra·dit·a·ble
ex·tra·di·tion
ex·tra·ne·ous
ex·traor·di·nary
ex·trap·o·late
ex·trap·o·la·tion
ex·tra·sen·so·ry
ex·tra·ter·res·tri·al
ex·tra·ter·ri·to·ri·al

71

ex·trav·a·gant
  ex·trav·a·gance
  ex·trav·a·gan·cy
ex·trav·a·gan·za
ex·treme
  ex·treme·ly
ex·trem·ist
  ex·trem·ism
ex·trem·i·ty
  ex·trem·i·ties
ex·tri·cate
  ex·tri·cat·ed
  ex·tri·cat·ing
  ex·tri·ca·tion
ex·trin·sic
ex·tro·vert
  ex·tro·ver·sion
ex·trude
  ex·trud·ed
  ex·trud·ing
  ex·tru·sion
ex·u·ber·ant
  ex·u·ber·ance
ex·ude
  ex·ud·ed
  ex·ud·ing
  ex·u·da·tion
ex·ult
  ex·ult·ant
  ex·ul·ta·tion
  ex·ult·ing·ly
ex·ur·bia
  ex·ur·ban·ite
eye
  eyed
  eye·ing
eye·ball
  eye·glass·es
eye·o·pen·er
eye·wit·ness

F

fa·ble
  fa·bled
fab·ric
fab·ri·cate
  fab·ri·cat·ed

fab·ri·cat·ing
fab·ri·ca·tion
fab·ri·ca·tor
fab·u·lous
fa·cade
face
  faced
  fac·ing
fac·et
fa·ce·tious
fa·cial
  fa·cial·ly
fac·ile
  fac·ile·ly
fa·cil·i·tate
  fa·cil·i·tat·ed
  fa·cil·i·tat·ing
fa·cil·i·ty
  fa·cil·i·ties
fac·sim·i·le
fac·tion
  fac·tion·al
  fac·tion·al·ism
fac·ti·tious
fac·tor
fac·to·ry
  fac·to·ries
fac·to·tum
fac·tu·al
  fac·tu·al·ly
fac·ul·ty
fad·dist
fade
  fad·ed
  fad·ing
  fade·less
fag·
  fagged
  fag·ging
fag·got
Fahr·en·heit
fa·ience
fail·ing
fail·ure
faint·ly
faint·ness
faint·heart·ed
fair·ly

fair·mind·ed
fair·ness
fairy
  fair·ies
faith·ful
  faith·less
fake
  faked
  fak·ing
  fak·er
fa·kir
fal·con
fall
  fell
  fall·en
  fall·ing
fal·la·cious
fal·la·cy
fal·li·ble
  fal·li·bil·i·ty
Fal·lo·pi·an
fal·low
false
  false·ly
  false·ness
  false·hood
fal·si·fy
  fal·si·fied
  fal·si·fy·ing
  fal·si·fi·ca·tion
fal·si·ty
fal·ter
  fal·ter·ing
famed
fa·mil·ial
fa·mil·iar
  fa·mil·i·ar·i·ty
fa·mil·iarize
  fa·mil·iar·ized
  fa·mil·iar·iz·ing
  fa·mil·iari·za·tion
fam·i·ly
  fam·i·lies
  fa·mil·ial
fam·ine
fam·ish
fam·ished
fa·mous

fan
fanned
fan·ning
fa·nat·ic
fa·nat·i·cal
fa·nat·i·cism
fa·nat·i·cize
fan·ci·ful
fan·ci·ful·ly
fan·cy
fan·cies
fan·ci·er
fan·ci·est
fan·cied
fan·cy·ing
fan·ci·ly
fan·ci·ness
fan·dan·go
fang
fanged
fan·ta·sia
fan·tas·tic
fan·tas·ti·cal
fan·tas·ti·cal·ly
fan·tas·ti·cal·ness
fan·ta·sy
fan·ta·sies
far
far·ther
far·thest
far·ther·most
far·a·way
farce
farced
farc·ing
far·ci·cal
fare
fared
far·ing
fa·ri·na
farm·er
farm·ing
far·reach·ing
far·see·ing
far·sight·ed
far·sight·ed·ness
far·ther·most
fas·cia

fas·ci·cle
fas·ci·cled
fas·ci·nate
fas·ci·nat·ed
fas·ci·nat·ing
fas·ci·na·tion
fas·cism
fas·cist
fa·scis·tic
fash·ion
fash·ion·a·ble
fash·ion·a·ble·ness
fash·ion·a·bly
fas·ten
fas·ten·er
fas·ten·ing
fas·tid·i·ous
fat
fat·ter
fat·test
fat·ted
fat·ten
fat·ting
fat·ty
fat·ti·ness
fat·ness
fa·tal
fa·tal·ly
fa·tal·i·ty
fa·tal·i·ties
fa·tal·ism
fa·tal·ist
fa·tal·is·tic
fate
fat·ed
fat·ing
fate·ful
fa·ther
fa·ther·hood
fa·ther·li·ness
fa·ther·ly
fa·ther·land
fa·ther-in-law
fa·thers-in-law
fath·om
fath·om·a·ble
fath·om·less
fa·tigue

fa·tigued
fa·tig·uing
fat·i·ga·ble
fat·i·ga·bil·i·ty
fa·tu·i·ty
fa·tu·i·ties
fat·u·ous
fat·u·ous·ly
fau·cet
fault
fault·find·ing
fault·less·ly
faulty
fault·i·er
fault·i·ly
fault·i·ness
fau·na
fau·nas
fau·nae
faux pas
fa·vor
fa·vored
fa·vor·ing
fa·vor·a·ble
fa·vor·a·ble·ness
fa·vor·a·bly
fa·vored·ness
fa·vor·ite
fa·vor·it·ism
fawn
faze
fazed
faz·ing
fe·al·ty
fear·ful
fear·ful·ness
fear·less
fear·less·ness
fear·some
fear·some·ness
fea·si·ble
fea·si·bil·i·ty
fea·si·ble·ness
fea·si·bly
feath·er
feath·ered
feath·er·bed·ding
fea·ture

73

fea·tured
featur·ing
fea·ture·less
fe·brile
Feb·ru·ary
Feb·ru·ar·ies
fe·ces
fe·cal
fe·cund
fe·cun·di·ty
fe·cun·date
fe·cun·dat·ed
fe·cun·dat·ing
fe·cun·da·tion
fed·er·al
fed·er·al·ism
fed·er·al·ist
fed·er·al·ly
fed·er·al·ize
fed·er·al·ized
fed·er·al·iz·ing
fed·er·al·i·za·tion
fed·er·ate
fed·er·at·ed
fed·er·at·ing
fe·do·ra
fee·ble
fee·bler
fee·bly
fee·ble·mind·ed
feed
fed
feed·ing
feed·er
feel
felt
feel·ing
feel·er
feign
feigned
feign·ing
feign·er
feint
feisty
feist·i·est
fe·lic·i·tate
fe·lic·i·tat·ed

fe·lic·i·tat·ing
fe·lic·i·ta·tion
fe·lic·i·tous
fe·lic·i·ty
fe·lic·i·ties
fe·line
fe·lin·i·ty
fel·la·tio
fel·low·ship
fel·on
fel·o·ny
fel·o·nies
fe·lo·ni·ous
fe·male
fem·i·nine
fem·i·nine·ness
fem·i·nin·i·ty
fem·i·nism
fem·i·nist
fem·i·nis·tic
fem·i·nize
fem·i·nized
fem·i·niz·ing
fem·i·ni·za·tion
fe·mur
fence
fenced
fenc·ing
fenc·er
fen·der
fe·ra·cious
fe·ral
fer·ment
fer·men·ta·tion
fe·ro·cious
fe·ro·cious·ness
fe·ro·cious·ly
fe·ro·ci·ty
fer·ret
Fer·ris wheel
fer·ro·con·crete
fer·ro·mag·net·ic
fer·ru·gi·nous
fer·rule
fer·ry
fer·ries
fer·tile
fertile·ness

fer·til·i·ty
fer·ti·lize
fer·ti·lized
fer·ti·liz·ing
fer·ti·liz·er
fer·ti·li·za·tion
fer·ule
fer·vent
fer·ven·cy
fer·vent·ly
fer·vid
fer·vid·ness
fer·vor
fes·ter
fes·ti·val
fes·tive
fes·tive·ness
fes·tiv·i·ty
fes·toon
fe·tal
fetch
fetch·ing
fete
fet·id
fet·id·ness
fet·ish
fet·ish·ism
fet·ish·ist
fet·lock
fet·ter
fet·tle
fe·tus
feud
feud·ist
feu·dal
feu·dal·ism
feu·dal·is·tic
feu·dal·i·za·tion
feu·dal·ize
fe·ver
fe·ver·ish
fe·ver·ish·ness
fe·ver·ous
fez·zes
fi·an·ce
fi·an·cee
fi·as·co
fi·at

fib
  fibbed
  fib·ber
fi·ber
  fi·bered
fi·bril
fi·broid
fi·brous
fib·u·la
fick·le
  fick·le·ness
fic·tion
  fic·tion·al
fic·ti·tious
  fic·ti·tious·ness
fid·dle
  fid·dler
  fid·dled
  fid·dling
fi·del·i·ty
fidg·et
  fidg·ety
fi·du·ci·ary
fief
field·er
fiend
  fiend·ish
fierce
  fierce·ness
fiery
  fier·i·est
  fier·i·ly
  fier·i·ness
fif·teen
  fif·teenth
fif·ty
  fif·ti·eth
fight
  fought
  fight·ing
  fight·er
fig·ment
fig·ur·rate
  fig·u·ra·tion
fig·u·ra·tive
fig·ure
  fig·ured

fig·ur·ing
fig·ure·less
fig·ur·ine
fil·a·ment
  fil·a·men·ta·ry
  fil·a·ment·ed
  fil·a·men·tous
file
  filed
  fil·ing
fi·let
fi·let mi·gnon
fil·i·al
  fil·i·al·ly
fil·i·bus·ter
fil·i·gree
  fil·i·greed
  fil·i·gree·ing
Fil·i·pi·no
fill·er
fil·let
fill·ing
fil·lip
fil·ly
  fil·lies
filmy
  film·i·est
  film·i·ness
fil·ter
  fil·ter·able
fil·tra·tion
filth
  filth·i·ness
  filthy
  filth·i·est
fin
  finned
  fin·ning
  fin·less
fi·na·gle
  fi·na·gled
  fi·na·gling
  fi·na·gler
fi·nal
fi·na·le
fi·nal·ist
fi·nal·i·ty
  fi·nal·i·ties

fi·nal·ize
  fi·nal·ized
  fi·nal·iz·ing
fi·nal·ly
fi·nance
  fi·nanced
  fi·nanc·ing
fi·nan·cial
  fi·nan·cial·ly
fin·an·cier
finch
find
  found
  find·ing
fine
  fin·er
  fin·est
  fine·ness
fin·ery
  fin·er·ies
fi·nesse
  fi·nessed
  fi·nes·sing
fin·ger
  fin·ger·ing
  fin·ger·print
fin·i·cal
  fin·icky
fin·is
fin·ish
  fin·ished
  fin·ish·er
fi·nite
  fi·nite·ly
  fi·nite·ness
Fin·land
  Finn·ish
fire
  fired
  fir·ing
fire·arm
fire·crack·er
fire·fight·er
fire·fly
  fire·flies
fire·man
fire·place
fire·pow·er

fire·proof
fire·trap
firm
  firm·ly
fir·ma·ment
first·born
first·hand
first·rate
first·string
fis·cal
  fis·cal·ly
fish·er·man
  fish·er·men
fish·ery
  fish·er·ies
fish·ing
fishy
fis·sion
  fis·sion·able
fis·sure
  fis·sured
fis·sur·ing
fist·i·cuffs
fit
  fit·ter
  fit·test
  fit·ted
  fit·ting
  fit·ly
  fit·ness
fit·ful
  fit·ful·ness
fit·ting
  fit·ting·ly
five·fold
five-and-ten
fix
  fix·a·ble
  fixed
  fix·ed·ly
  fix·er
fix·a·tion
fix·a·tive
fix·ings
fix·i·ty
fix·ture
fiz·zle
  fiz·zled

fiz·zling
fiz·zy
fjord
flab·ber·gast
flab·by
  flab·bi·er
  flab·bi·est
  flab·bi·ly
  flab·bi·ness
flac·cid
fla·con
flag
  flagged
  flag·ging
flag·el·lant
flag·el·late
  flag·el·lat·ed
  flag·el·lat·ing
  flag·el·la·tion
fla·gi·tious
flag·on
fla·grant
  fla·grant·ly
flail
flair
flake
  flaked
  flak·ing
flaky
  flak·i·est
  flak·i·ness
flam·boy·ant
  flam·boy·ance
  flam·boy·an·cy
  flam·boy·ant·ly
flame
  flamed
  flam·ing
  flam·ing·ly
flam·ma·ble
fla·men·co
fla·min·go
flange
flank
  flank·er
flan·nel·ette
flap
  flapped

flap·ping
flap·per
flare
  flared
  flar·ing
flare-up
flash·back
flash·light
flashy
  flash·i·est
  flash·i·ness
flask
flat
  flat·ly
  flat·ted
  flat·ting
  flat·ness
  flat·ten
flat·foot·ed
flat·ter
  flat·ter·er
  flat·ter·ing·ly
flat·tery
  flat·ter·ies
flat·u·lent
  flat·u·lence
  flat·u·len·cy
fla·tus
flat·ware
flaunt
  flaunt·ed
  flaunt·ing·ly
  flaunty
fla·vor
  fla·vored
  fla·vor·less
  fla·vor·ing
flawed
flaw·less
flax·en
flea·bit·ten
flec·tion
fledge
  fledged
  fledg·ing
fledg·ling
flee
  fled

flee·ing
fleece
  fleeced
  fleec·ing
fleecy
  fleec·i·ness
fleet
  fleet·ly
  fleet·ness
fleet·ing
flesh·ly
  flesh·li·est
fleshy
  flesh·i·ness
fleur·de·lis
flex·i·ble
  flex·i·bil·i·ty
  flex·i·bly
flex·ure
flib·ber·ti·gib·bet
flick·er
  flick·er·ing
fli·er
flight
  flight·less
flighty
  flight·i·est
  flight·i·ly
  flight·i·ness
flim·flam
  flim·flammed
  flim·flam·ming
flim·sy
  flim·si·est
  flim·si·ly
  flim·si·ness
flinch
  flin·ch·ing
fling
  flung
  fling·ing
flinty
  flint·i·ness
flip
  flipped
  flip·ping
flip·flop
flip·pant

flip·pan·cy
flip·pant·ly
flip·per
flir·ta·tion
  flir·ta·tious
flit
  flit·ted
  flit·ting
  flit·ter
float·a·ble
float·a·tion
float·er
float·ing
floc·cu·lent
  floc·cu·lence
flocked
floe
flog
  flogged
  flog·ging
  flog·ger
flood·light
  flood·light·ed
  flood·lit
  flood·light·ing
floor·ing
floo·zy
  floo·zies
flop
  flopped
  flop·ping
  flop·per
flop·house
flop·py
  flop·pi·est
  flop·pi·ness
flo·ra
  flo·rae
flo·ral
flo·res·cence
  flo·res·cent
flo·ret
flo·ri·cul·ture
  flo·ri·cul·tur·ist
flor·id
  flo·rid·i·ty
  flor·id·ness
flo·rist

floss
  flossy
flo·ta·tion
flo·til·la
flot·sam
flounce
  flounced
  flounc·ing
floun·der
floury
flour·ish
  flour·ish·ing
flout·er
flow
flow·er
  flow·ered
  flow·er·ing
  flow·ery
flub
  flubbed
  flub·bing
fluc·tu·ate
  fluc·tu·at·ed
  fluc·tu·at·ing
  fluc·tu·a·tion
flue
flu·ent
  flu·en·cy
  flu·ent·ly
fluff
  fluff·i·ness
  fluffy
flu·id
  flu·id·i·ty
  flu·id·ness
fluke
  fluky
flun·ky
  flun·kies
flu·o·resce
  flu·o·resced
  flu·o·resc·ing
  flu·o·res·cence
  flu·o·res·cent
fluor·i·date
  fluor·i·da·tion
  fluor·i·dat·ed

fluor·i·dat·ing
fluor·o·scope
flur·ry
  flur·ries
  flur·ried
  flur·ry·ing
flus·ter
flute
  flut·ed
  flut·ing
  flut·ist
flut·ter
  flut·ter·ing
  flut·tery
flux·ion
fly
  flew
  flown
  flying
fly-by-night
fly·er
fly·leaf
fly·pa·per
fly·wheel
foal
foam
  foam·i·ness
  foamy
fo·cal
  fo·cal·ly
fo·cal·ize
  fo·cal·ized
  fo·cal·iz·ing
fo·cus
  fo·cus·es
  fo·cused
  fo·cus·ing
fod·der
foe·tus
  foe·tal
fog
  fogged
  fog·ging
fog·gy
  fog·gi·ly
  fog·gi·ness
fo·gy
  fo·gies

fo·gy·ish
foi·ble
fold·er
fol·de·rol
fo·li·a·ceous
fo·li·age
fo·li·ate
  fo·li·at·ed
  fo·li·at·ing
  fo·li·a·tion
fo·lio
folk·lore
folk·sy
folk·si·ness
fol·li·cle
  fol·lic·u·lar
fol·low
  fol·low·er
  fol·low·ing
fol·ly
  fol·lies
fo·ment
  fo·men·ta·tion
  fo·ment·er
fon·dant
fon·dle
  fon·dled
  fon·dling
  fond·ly
  fond·ness
fon·due
food·stuff
fool·ery
  fool·er·ies
fool·har·dy
  fool·har·di·ness
fool·ish
  fool·ish·ly
fool·proof
foot·age
foot·ball
foot·can·dle
foot·hold
foot·lights
foot·note
foot·path
foot·print
foot·step

fop
  fop·pery
  fop·pish
for·age
  for·aged
  for·ag·ing
for·ay
for·bear
  for·bore
  for·borne
  for·bear·ing
  for·bear·ance
for·bid
  for·bade
  for·bid·den
  for·bid·ding
  for·bid·dance
force
  forced
  forc·ing
  force·a·ble
  force·less
force·ful
  force·ful·ly
for·ceps
for·ci·ble
  for·ci·bly
ford·a·ble
fore·bode
  fore·bod·ed
  fore·bod·ing
fore·castle
fore·cast
  fore·cast·ed
  fore·cast·ing
  fore·cast·er
fore·close
  fore·closed
  fore·clos·ing
  fore·clo·sure
fore·fa·ther
fore·fin·ger
fore·gath·er
fore·go
  fore·went
  fore·gone
  fore·go·ing
fore·ground

fore·hand·ed
for·eign
  foreign·er
fore·know
  fore·knew
  fore·known
  fore·know·ing
  fore·knowl·edge
fore·man
fore·most
fore·name
fore·noon
fo·ren·sic
fore·or·dain
  fore·or·di·na·tion
fore·quarter
fore·run·ner
fore·see
  fore·saw
  fore·seen
  fore·see·ing
  fore·see·a·ble
fore·shad·ow
fore·short·en
fore·sight
fore·skin
for·est
  for·est·a·tion
  for·es·ter
  for·est·ry
fore·stall
fore·taste
fore·tell
  fore·told
  fore·tell·ing
  fore·tell·er
fore·thought
for·ev·er
for·ev·er·more
fore·warn
fore·woman
fore·word
for·feit
  for·fei·ture
for·gath·er
forge
  forged

forg·ing
forg·er
for·gery
  for·ger·ies
for·get
  for·got
  for·got·ten
  for·get·ting
  for·get·ta·ble
  for·get·ful
for·give
  for·gave
  for·giv·en
  for·giv·ing
  for·giv·a·ble
  for·give·ness
for·go
  for·went
  for·gone
  for·go·ing
forked
fork·lift
for·lorn
  for·lorn·ly
for·mal
  for·mal·ly
  for·mal·ism
  for·mal·i·ty
  for·mal·i·ties
  for·mal·ize
  for·mal·ized
  for·mal·iz·ing
  for·mal·i·za·tion
for·mat
for·ma·tion
form·a·tive
for·mer
  for·mer·ly
form·fit·ting
for·mi·da·ble
  for·mi·da·bly
form·less
  form·less·ness
for·mu·la
  for·mu·las
  for·mu·lary
  for·mu·lar·ies
  for·mu·late

for·mu·lat·ed
for·mu·lat·ing
for·mu·la·tion
for·mu·la·tor
for·ni·cate
  for·ni·cat·ed
  for·ni·cat·ing
  for·ni·cat·or
  for·ni·ca·tion
for·sake
  for·sook
  for·sak·en
  for·sak·ing
  for·sak·en
for·swear
  for·swore
  for·sworn
  for·swear·ing
fort
  for·ti·fi·cation
  for·ti·fy
  for·ti·fied
  for·ti·fy·ing
forte
for·te
forth·com·ing
forth·right
forth·with
for·tis·si·mo
for·ti·tude
fort·night
for·tress
for·tu·i·tous
  for·tu·i·tous·ness
for·tu·nate
  for·tu·nate·ly
for·tune
  for·tune·tell·er
for·ty
  for·ties
fo·rum
  fo·rums
for·ward
  for·ward·ness
fos·sil
  fos·sil·ized
  fos·sil·iz·ing
  fos·sil·i·za·tion

fos·ter
　fos·tered
　fos·ter·ing
fought
fou·lard
found
foun·da·tion
　foun·da·tion·al
found·er
found·ling
found·ry
　found·ries
foun·tain
four·flush·er
four·fold
four·post·er
four·score
four·some
four·teen
　four·teenth
fourth
　fourth·ly
foxy
　fox·i·ly
　fox·i·ness
foy·er
fra·cas
frac·tion
　frac·tion·al
frac·tious
frac·ture
　frac·tured
　frac·tur·ing
frag·ile
　fra·gil·i·ty
frag·ment
　frag·men·tal
　frag·men·tary
　frag·men·ta·tion
frag·ment·ize
fra·grance
　fra·grant
　fra·grant·ly
frail
　frail·ty
　frail·ness
frame
　framed

fram·ing
frame·work
franc
France
fran·chise
　fran·chised
　fran·chis·ing
　fran·chise·ment
Fran·cis·can
fran·gi·ble
fran·gi·pan·i
frank
　frank·ly
　frank·ness
frank·furt·er
frank·in·cense
fran·tic
　fran·ti·cal·ly
frap·pe
fra·ter·nal
　fra·ter·nal·ly
fra·ter·ni·ty
　fra·ter·ni·ties
frat·er·nize
　frat·er·nized
　frat·er·niz·ing
　frat·er·ni·za·tion
frat·ri·cide
　frat·ri·cid·al
fraud·u·lent
　fraud·u·lence
　fraud·u·lent·ly
fraught
fraz·zle
　fraz·zled
freak
　freak·ish
freaky
　freak·i·est
freck·le
　freck·led
　freck·ling
　freck·led
free
　fre·er
　fre·est
　free·ly

free·bie
free·boot·er
free·dom
free·lance
　free·lanced
　free·lanc·ing
Free·ma·son
free·stand·ing
free·spo·ken
free·think·er
freeze
　froze
　fro·zen
　freez·ing
freeze·dry
freez·er
freight·age
freight·er
fre·net·ic
　fre·net·i·cal·ly
fren·zy
　fren·zies
　fren·zied
　fren·zy·ing
fre·quen·cy
　fre·quen·cies
fre·quent
　fre·quent·ly
fres·co
　fres·coes
　fres·coed
　fres·co·ing
fresh
　fresh·en
　fresh·ness
fresh·man
fret
　fret·ted
　fret·ting
　fret·ful
　fret·ful·ly
Freud·i·an
fri·a·ble
fri·ar
fric·as·see
　fric·as·seed
　fric·as·see·ing
fric·tion

80

fric·tion·al
  fric·tion·less
friend
  friend·less
  friend·ship
friend·ly
  friend·li·est
  friend·li·ness
frieze
fright·en
  fright·en·ing
  fright·ful
frig·id
  fri·gid·i·ty
  frig·id·ness
frilly
  frill·i·est
fringe
  fringed
  fring·ing
frip·pery
frisky
  frisk·i·ness
frit·ter
friv·o·lous
  fri·vol·i·ty
  fri·vol·i·ties
  friv·o·lous·ly
frizz
  friz·zi·ness
  friz·zy
friz·zle
frog
  frogged
  frog·ging
frol·ic
  frol·icked
  frol·ick·ing
  frol·ic·some
front·age
fron·tal
fron·tier
  fron·tiers·man
fron·tis·piece
frost
  frost·ed
frost·bite
  frost·bit

frost·bit·ten
frost·bit·ing
frost·ing
frosty
  frost·i·ly
  frost·i·ness
froth
  froth·i·ness
  frothy
frou·frou
fro·ward
frown
frow·zy
fro·zen
  fro·zen·ness
fruc·ti·fy
  fruc·ti·fi·ca·tion
fruc·tose
fru·gal
  fru·gal·i·ty
  fru·gal·i·ties
  fru·gal·ly
fruit·ful
  fruit·ful·ly
  fruit·ful·ness
fru·i·tion
fruit·less
frump
  frump·ish
  frumpy
frus·trate
  frus·trat·ed
  frus·trat·ing
  frus·tra·tion
fry
  fried
  fry·ing
fuch·sia
fud·dle
fud·dy-dud·dy
fudge
  fudged
  fudg·ing
fu·el
  fu·eled
  fu·el·ing
fu·gi·tive
fugue
ful·crum

ful·fill
  ful·filled
  ful·fil·ling
  ful·fill·ment
full
  full·ness
  ful·ly
full·fledged
ful·mi·nate
  ful·mi·nat·ed
  ful·mi·nat·ing
  ful·mi·na·tion
ful·some
fum·ble
  fum·bled
  fum·bling
  fum·bler
fume
  fumed
  fum·ing
  fum·ing·ly
fu·mi·gate
  fu·mi·gat·ed
  fu·mi·gat·ing
  fu·mi·ga·tion
  fu·mi·ga·tor
func·tion
  func·tion·al
  func·tion·less
func·tion·ary
  func·tion·ar·ies
fun·da·men·tal
  fun·da·men·tal·ly
  fun·da·men·tal·ism
  fun·da·men·tal·ist
fu·ner·al
  fu·ne·re·al
fun·gi·cide
  fun·gi·cid·al
fun·gus
  fun·gi
fu·nic·u·lar
fun·nel
  fun·neled
  fun·nel·ing
fun·ny
  fun·ni·er
  fun·ni·est

fun·nies
fun·ni·ness
fur
  furred
  fur·ring
fur·be·low
fur·bish
fu·ri·ous
  fu·ri·ous·ly
fur·long
fur·lough
fur·nace
fur·nish
fur·nish·ings
fur·ni·ture
fu·ror
fu·rore
fur·ri·er
fur·row
fur·ry
fur·ther
fur·ther·ance
fur·ther·more
fur·ther·most
fur·thest
fur·tive
  fur·tive·ly
fu·ry
  fu·ries
fuse
  fused
  fus·ing
fu·se·lage
fu·si·ble
  fu·si·bil·i·ty
fu·sil·lade
  fu·sil·lad·ed
  fu·sil·lad·ing
fu·sion
fussy
  fuss·i·ness
fus·tian
fu·tile
fu·til·i·ty
  fu·til·i·ties
fu·ture
  fu·tu·ri·ty
  fu·tu·ri·ties

fu·tur·ism
fu·tur·is·tic
fuzzy
  fuzz·i·ness

G

gab
  gabbed
  gab·bing
gab·ar·dine
gab·ble
gab·by
ga·ble
  ga·bled
  ga·bling
gad
gad·ded
  gad·ding
gad·a·bout
gad·fly
gad·get
  gad·get·ry
gag
  gagged
  gag·ging
gai·e·ty
  gai·e·ties
gai·ly
gain·er
gain·ful
gain·say
  gain·said
gait
ga·la
gal·axy
  gal·ax·ies
  ga·lac·tic
gal·lant
  gal·lant·ry
  gal·lant·ries
gal·lery
  gal·ler·ies
gal·ley
gal·li·mau·fry
gall·ing
gal·li·vant
gal·lon

gal·lop
gal·lows
gall·stone
ga·lore
ga·losh·es
gal·van·ic
gal·va·nize
  gal·va·nized
  gal·va·niz·ing
gal·va·nom·e·ter
gam·bit
gam·ble
  gam·bled
  gam·bling
  gam·bler
gam·bol
game
  gam·ing
games·man·ship
gam·in
gam·ma
gam·ma glob·u·lin
gam·ut
gamy
  gam·i·ly
  gam·i·ness
gan·der
gang·land
gan·gling
gan·gly
gan·grene
  gan·gre·nous
gang·ster
gant·let
gan·try
gaol
gap
  gapped
  gap·ping
ga·rage
  ga·raged
  ga·rag·ing
gar·bage
gar·ble
  gar·bled
  gar·bling
gar·den
gar·gan·tu·an

gar·gle
  gar·gled
  gar·gling
gar·goyle
gar·ish
gar·land
gar·ment
gar·ner
gar·net
gar·nish
gar·nish·ee
  gar·nish·eed
  gar·nish·ee·ing
gar·nish·ment
gar·ni·ture
gar·ret
gar·ri·son
gar·rote
  gar·rot·ed
  gar·rot·ing
gar·ru·lous
gar·ter
gas
  gassed
  gas·sing
  gas·e·ous
gas·i·fy
  gas·i·fied
  gas·i·fy·ing
  gas·i·fi·ca·tion
gas·ket
gas·light
gas·o·line
gas·sy
  gas·si·ness
gas·tric
gas·tri·tis
gas·tro·en·ter·ol·o·gy
gas·tro·in·tes·ti·nal
gas·tron·o·my
  gas·tro·nom·ic
gath·er
  gath·er·ing
gauche
gau·che·rie
gau·cho
gaudy
  gaud·i·ly

gaud·i·ness
gauge
  gauged
  gaug·ing
gaunt
gaunt·let
gauze
  gauz·i·ness
  gauzy
gav·el
ga·votte
gawky
  gawk·i·ly
  gawk·i·ness
gay·e·ty
gay·ly
gaze
  gazed
  gaz·ing
ga·ze·bo
ga·zelle
ga·zette
gaz·et·teer
gear·shift
gear·wheel
Gei·ger count·er
gei·sha
gel
  gelled
  gel·ling
gel·a·tin
ge·la·ti·nize
ge·lat·i·nous
ge·la·tion
geld
  geld·ed
  gelt
  geld·ing
gel·id
ge·lid·i·ty
gem
  gemmed
  gem·ming
gem·i·nate
  gem·i·nat·ed
  gem·i·nat·ing
  gem·i·nate·ly
  gem·i·na·tion

Gem·i·ni
gem·ol·o·gy
  gem·o·log·i·cal
  gem·ol·o·gist
gen·darme
gen·der
gene
ge·ne·al·o·gy
  ge·ne·a·log·i·cal
  ge·ne·al·o·gist
gen·er·al
gen·er·al·is·si·mo
gen·er·al·ist
gen·er·al·i·ty
  gen·er·al·i·ties
gen·er·al·ize
  gen·er·al·ized
  gen·er·al·iz·ing
  gen·er·al·i·za·tion
gen·er·ate
  gen·er·at·ed
  gen·er·at·ing
  gen·er·a·tive
gen·er·a·tion
gen·er·a·tor
ge·ner·ic
  ge·ner·i·cal
gen·er·ous
  gen·er·os·i·ty
  gen·er·os·i·ties
gen·e·sis
  gen·e·ses
ge·net·ic
  ge·net·i·cal·ly
ge·net·ics
  ge·net·i·cist
gen·ial
ge·ni·al·i·ty
ge·nie
gen·i·tal
  gen·i·ta·lia
  gen·i·tals
gen·i·tive
gen·ius
  gen·ius·es
gen·o·cide
  gen·o·ci·dal

gen·re
gen·teel
gen·tian
gen·tile
gen·til·i·ty
gen·tle
    gen·tlest
    gen·tly
gen·tle·man
gen·tle·wom·an
gen·try
gen·u·flect
    gen·u·flec·tion
gen·u·ine
    gen·u·ine·ness
ge·nus
ge·o·cen·tric
    ge·o·cen·tri·cal·ly
ge·o·chem·is·try
    ge·o·chem·i·cal
    ge·o·chem·ist
ge·ode
ge·o·des·ic
geo·d·e·sy
geo·o·gra·phy
    ge·o·gra·phies
    ge·o·gra·pher
    ge·o·graph·ic
    ge·o·graph·i·cal
ge·ol·o·gy
    ge·ol·o·gies
    ge·o·log·ic
    ge·o·log·i·cal
    ge·o·log·i·cal·ly
    ge·ol·o·gist
ge·o·mag·net·ic
    geo·o·mag·ne·tism
ge·o·met·ric
ge·om·e·try
    ge·om·e·tries
ge·o·phys·ics
    ge·o·phys·i·cal
    ge·o·phys·i·cist
ge·o·pol·i·tics
    ge·o·po·lit·ic
    ge·o·po·lit·i·cal
    ge·o·po·lit·i·cal·ly
ge·o·ther·mal

ge·ra·ni·um
ger·bil
ger·i·at·rics
    geri·a·tric
    geri·a·tri·cian
    geri·a·trist
ger·mane
Ger·ma·ny
ger·mi·cide
    ger·mi·cid·al
ger·mi·nate
    ger·mi·nat·ed
    ger·mi·nat·ing
    ger·mi·na·tion
ger·on·tol·o·gy
    ger·on·tol·o·gist
ger·ry·man·der
ger·und
Ge·stalt
ge·sta·po
ges·tate
    ges·tat·ed
    ges·tat·ing
    ges·ta·tion
ges·tic·u·late
    ges·tic·u·lat·ed
    ges·tic·u·lat·ing
    ges·tic·u·la·tion
    ges·tic·u·la·to·ry
ges·ture
    ges·tured
    ges·tur·ing
ge·sund·heit
Geth·sem·a·ne
gew·gaw
gey·ser
ghast·ly
    ghast·li·er
    ghast·li·est
    ghast·li·ness
gher·kin
ghet·to
ghost·ly
    ghost·li·est
    ghost·li·ness
ghost·write
    ghost·writ·ten
ghoul

gi·ant
gib·ber·ish
gib·bon
gib·bous
gibe
    gib·ing·ly
gib·let
gid·dy
    gid·di·ly
    gid·di·ness
gift·ed
gi·gan·tic
    gi·gan·tism
gig·gle
    gig·gled
    gig·gling
    gig·gly
gig·o·lo
gild·ed
gilt-edged
gim·let
gim·mick
    gim·mick·y
gin·ger·bread
gin·ger·ly
    gin·ger·li·ness
ging·ham
gip·sy
    gip·sies
gi·raffe
gird·er
gir·dle
    gir·dled
    gir·dling
girl·hood
girl·ish
girth
gist
give
    gave
    giv·en
    giv·ing
giz·zard
gla·cial
gla·cier
glad
    glad·der
    glad·dest

84

glad·ly
glad·ness
glad·den
glad·i·a·tor
glad·i·a·to·ri·al
glad·i·o·lus
glad·i·o·lus·es
glad·i·o·la
glam·or·ize
glam·or·ized
glam·or·iz·ing
glam·or·i·za·tion
glam·or·ous
glam·or·ous·ness
glam·our
glance
glanced
glanc·ing
glan·du·lar
glare
glared
glar·ing
glar·i·ness
glary
glass·blow·ing
glass·ful
glass·ware
glassy
glass·i·er
glass·i·est
glass·i·ly
glass·i·ness
glau·co·ma
glaze
glazed
glaz·ing
gla·zier
gleam
gleam·ing
gleamy
glean
glean·er
glean·ing
glee
glee·ful
gleee·ful·ly
glee·ful·ness
glib

glib·best
glib·ly
glib·ness
glide
glid·ed
glid·ing
glim·mer
glimpse
glimpsed
glimps·ing
glis·san·do
glis·ten
glit·ter
glit·tery
gloam·ing
gloat
gloat·er
gloat·ing
glob·al
glob·al·ly
globe·trot·ter
globe·trot·ting
glob·u·lar
glob·ule
glock·en·spiel
gloomy
gloom·i·er
gloom·i·ly
gloom·i·ness
glo·ri·fy
glo·ri·fied
glo·ri·fy·ing
glo·ri·fi·ca·tion
glo·ri·ous
glo·ri·ous·ly
glo·ry
glo·ries
glo·ried
glo·ry·ing
glos·sa·ry
glossy
gloss·i·er
gloss·i·ly
gloss·i·ness
glot·tis
glove
glow
glow·er

glow·ing
glu·cose
glue
glued
glu·ing
glum
glum·mer
glum·mest
glut
glut·ted
glut·ting
glu·ten
glu·ten·ous
glu·ti·nous
glut·ton
glut·ton·ous
glut·tony
glyc·er·in
glyc·er·ine
gnarl
gnarled
gnash
gnat
gnaw
gnawed
gnaw·ing
gnome
gnu
go
went
gone
go·ing
goad·ed
goal·ie
goat·ee
goat·skin
gob·ble
gob·bled
gob·bling
gob·ble·dy·gook
gob·bler
gob·let
gob·lin
god·child
god·daugh·ter
god·son
god·dess
god·fa·ther

god·head
god·less
god·less·ness
god·ly
god·li·ness
god·moth·er
god·send
go·get·ter
gog·gle
gog·gled
gog·gling
go·ing
goi·ter
gold·en·rod
go·nad
gon·do·la
gon·do·lier
gon·or·rhea
good
better
best
good-by
good-bye
good-heart·ed
good·ish
good-look·ing
good·ly
good-na·tured
good·ness
good-tem·pered
goofy
goof·i·er
goof·i·est
goof·i·ness
goose·ber·ry
go·pher
gore
gored
gor·ing
gorge
gorged
gorg·ing
gor·geous
gor·geous·ness
gory
gor·i·er
gor·i·est
gos·ling

gos·pel
gos·sa·mer
gos·sip
gos·sip·ing
gos·sipy
Goth·ic
gouge
gouged
goug·ing
gou·lash
gourd
gour·mand
gour·met
gout
gouty
gov·ern
gov·ern·a·ble
gov·ern·ess
gov·ern·ment
gov·ern·men·tal
gov·er·nor
gowned
grab
grabbed
grab·bing
grab·ber
grace
graced
grac·ing
grace·ful
grace·ful·ly
grace·less
gra·cious
grack·le
gra·da·tion
grade
grad·ed
grad·ing
gra·di·ent
grad·u·al
grad·u·al·ly
grad·u·al·ness
grad·u·ate
grad·u·at·ed
grad·u·at·ing
grad·u·a·tion
graf·fi·ti
graft

graft·age
graft·er
graft·ing
gra·ham
grain
grainy
gran·i·ness
gram
gram·mar
gram·mar·i·an
gram·mat·i·cal
gra·na·ry
grand
grand·ly
grand·child
gran·dee
gran·deur
gran·dil·o·quence
gran·dil·o·quent
gran·di·ose
gran·di·ose·ly
grange
gran·ite
gran·ny
gran·u·lar
gran·u·lar·i·ty
gran·u·late
gran·u·lat·ed
gran·u·lat·ing
gran·u·la·tion
gran·ule
grape·fruit
graph·ic
graph·i·cal
graph·ite
graph·ol·o·gy
graph·ol·o·gist
grap·nel
grap·ple
grap·pled
grap·pling
grap·pler
grasp·ing
grass
grassy
grass·i·est
grass·hop·per
grass·land

grate
  grat·ed
  grat·ing
grate·ful
grat·i·fy
  grat·i·fied
  grat·i·fy·ing
  grat·i·fi·ca·tion
grat·ing
gra·tis
grat·i·tude
gra·tu·i·tous
gra·tu·i·ty
  gra·tu·i·ties
grave
  graved
  grav·en
  grav·ing
  grav·er
  grave·ly
  grave·ness
grav·el
  grav·eled
  grav·el·ing
  grav·el·ly
grav·i·tate
  grav·i·tat·ed
  grav·i·tat·ing
  grav·i·ta·tion
grav·i·ty
gra·vy
gray·ness
gray·ling
graze
  grazed
  graz·ing
grease
  greased
  greas·ing
greasy
  greas·i·ness
great
  great·ness
Great Brit·ain
Gre·cian
Greece
greedy
  greed·i·er

greed·i·est
greed·i·ly
greed·i·ness
green·house
green·ing
green·ish
greet
  greet·ing
gre·gar·i·ous
  gre·gar·i·ous·ly
  gre·gar·i·ous·ness
grem·lin
gre·nade
gren·a·dier
gren·a·dine
grey·ness
grid·dle
grid·i·ron
grief
griev·ance
grieve
  grieved
  griev·ing
  griev·ous
grill
gril·lage
grille
grim
  grim·ly
  grim·ness
grim·ace
  grim·aced
  grim·ac·ing
grime
  grimy
  grim·i·ness
grin
  grinned
  grin·ning
grind
  ground
  grind·ing
grin·go
grip
  gripped
  grip·ping
gripe
  griped

grip·ing
grip·er
grippe
gris·ly
  gris·li·ness
gris·tle
  gris·tly
grit
  grit·ted
  grit·ting
grit·ty
  grit·ti·ness
griz·zled
griz·zly
groan
gro·cer
gro·cery
  gro·cer·ies
grog·gy
  grog·gi·ly
  grog·gi·ness
groin
grom·met
groom
groove
  grooved
  groov·ing
  groov·er
grope
  groped
  grop·ing
gros·grain
gross
  gross·ly
  gross·ness
gro·tesque
  gro·tesque·ly
  gro·tesque·ness
grot·to
grouch
  grouchy
  grouch·i·ness
  grouch·i·ly
ground·less
ground·work
group
  group·ing

grouse
  groused
  grous·ing
grov·el
  grov·eled
  grov·el·ing
grow
  grew
  grown
  grow·ing
growl
  growl·er
  growl·ing
grown·up
growth
grub
  grubbed
  grub·bing
grub·by
  grub·bi·ness
grub·stake
grudge
  grudged
  grudg·ing
gru·el
  gru·el·ing
grue·some
gruff
  gruff·ly
  gruff·ness
grum·ble
  grum·bled
  grum·bling
grumpy
  grump·i·ly
  grump·i·ness
grunt
  grunt·ed
  grunt·ing
gua·no
guar·an·tee
  guar·an·teed
  guar·an·tee·ing
guar·an·tor
guar·an·ty
  guar·an·ties
  guar·an·tied
  guar·an·ty·ing

guard·ed
  guard·ed·ly
guard·house
guard·i·an
guards·man
gua·va
gu·ber·na·to·ri·al
gudg·eon
guern·sey
guer·ril·la
guess
  guess·ing
guess·work
guest
guf·faw
guid·ance
guide
  guid·ed
  guid·ing
gui·don
guild
guile
  guile·ful
  guile·less
guil·lo·tine
guilt
  guilt·less
guilty
  guilt·i·er
  guilt·i·ly
  guilt·i·ness
guin·ea
guise
gui·tar
  gui·tar·ist
gul·let
gul·li·ble
  gul·li·bil·i·ty
  gul·li·bly
gul·ly
  gul·lies
gum
  gummed
  gum·ming
  gum·my
  gum·mi·ness
gum·bo
gump·tion

gun
  gunned
  gun·ning
gun·ner
gun·nery
gun·ny
gun·wale
gup·py
  gup·pies
gur·gle
  gur·gled
  gur·gling
gu·ru
gush·er
gush·ing
gushy
  gush·i·er
  gush·i·est
  gush·i·ness
gus·set
gus·ta·to·ry
gus·to
gusty
  gust·i·er
  gust·i·est
  gust·i·ly
  gust·i·ness
gut
  gut·ted
  gut·ting
gut·less
gut·ter
gut·tur·al
  gut·tur·al·ly
guz·zle
  guz·zled
  guz·zling
gym·na·si·um
  gym·na·si·ums
gym·nast
gym·nas·tic
gy·ne·col·o·gy
  gy·ne·co·log·i·cal
  gy·ne·col·o·gist
gyp
  gypped
  gyp·ping
gyp·sum

gyp·sy
  gyp·sies
gy·rate
  gy·rat·ed
  gy·rat·ing
  gy·ra·tion
  gy·ra·tor
gy·ro·com·pass
gy·rom·e·ter
gy·ro·plane
gy·ro·scope
gy·rose
gy·ro·sta·bi·liz·er
gy·ro·sta·tics

H

ha·be·as· cor·pus
hab·er·dash·ery
ha·bil·i·ment
hab·it
hab·it·a·ble
hab·i·tat
hab·i·ta·tion
ha·bit·u·al
  ha·bit·u·al·ly
  ha·bit·u·al·ness
ha·bit·u·ate
  ha·bit·u·at·ed
  ha·bit·u·at·ing
  ha·bit·u·a·tion
ha·bit·ue
ha·ci·en·da
hack·le
  hack·led
  hack·ling
hack·ney
hack·neyed
hack·saw
had·dock
Ha·des
had·n't
hag·gard
  hag·gard·ness
hag·gis
hag·gle
  hag·gled
  hag·gling

hag·gler
ha·gi·og·ra·phy
hag·i·ol·o·gy
hail·storm
hair·breadth
hair·dress·er
hair·rais·ing
hairy
  hair·i·er
  hair·i·est
hale
  haled
  hal·ing
half
  halves
half·heart·ed
half·wit·ted
hal·i·but
hal·i·to·sis
hal·le·lu·jah
hall·mark
hal·lo
hal·low
  hal·lowed
Hal·low·een
hal·lu·ci·nate
  hal·lu·ci·nat·ed
  hal·lu·ci·nat·ing
  hal·lu·ci·na·tion
ha·lo
halt
  halt·ing
hal·ter
halve
  halved
  halv·ing
halves
hal·yard
ham·burg·er
ham·let
ham·mer
ham·mock
ham·per
ham·ster
ham·string
  ham·strung
hand·ed
hand·ful

hand·i·cap
  hand·i·capped
  hand·i·cap·ping
  hand·i·cap·per
hand·i·craft
hand·i·ly
  hand·i·ness
hand·i·work
hand·ker·chief
han·dle
  han·dled
  han·dling
hand·made
hand·picked
hand·some
  hand·som·est
  hand·some·ness
hand·writ·ing
handy
  hand·i·er
hand·y·man
hang
  hung
  hanged
  hang·ing
hang·ar
hang·er
hang·o·ver
hank·er
han·som
Ha·nuk·kah
hap·haz·ard
  hap·haz·ard·ly
hap·less
hap·pen
  hap·pen·ing
  hap·pen·stance
hap·py
  hap·pi·ly
  hap·pi·ness
ha·ra·ki·ri
ha·rangue
  ha·rangued
  ha·rang·uing
har·ass
  har·ass·ment
har·bin·ger
har·bor

hard·bit·ten
hard·boiled
hard·en
　hard·en·er
hardi·hood
hardi·ness
hard·ly
hard·ware
hard·wood
har·dy
　har·di·er
　har·di·est
　har·di·ly
hare·brained
hare·lip
har·em
har·ken
har·le·quin
har·lot
　har·lot·ry
harm·ful
　harm·ful·ly
　harm·ful·ness
harm·less
　harm·less·ly
　harm·less·ness
har·mon·ic
　har·mon·i·cal·ly
　har·mon·i·ca
　har·mon·ics
har·mo·ni·ous
har·mo·nize
　har·mo·nized
　har·mo·niz·ing
har·mo·ny
　har·mo·nies
har·ness
harp·ist
har·poon
harp·si·chord
har·ri·dan
har·row
har·ry
　har·ried
　har·ry·ing
harsh
　harsh·ly
　harsh·ness

har·um-scar·um
har·vest
har·ves·ter
hash·ish
　hash·eesh
has·n't
has·sle
　has·sled
　has·sling
has·sock
haste
has·ten
hast·y
　hast·i·ly
　hast·i·ness
hatch·ery
hatch·et
hate
　hat·ed
　hat·ing
hate·ful
　hate·ful·ly
　hate·ful·ness
ha·tred
haugh·ty
　haugh·ti·ly
　haugh·ti·ness
haul
　haul·age
haunch
　haunch·es
haunt·ed
haunt·ing
hau·teur
have
　had
　hav·ing
　has
ha·ven
have·n't
hav·er·sack
hav·oc
Ha·waii
hawk
　hawk·ish
haw·ser
haz·ard
　haz·ard·ous

haz·ard·ous·ness
haze
　hazed
　haz·ing
ha·zel·nut
ha·zy
　ha·zi·ly
　ha·zi·ness
head·ache
head·dress
head·first
　head·fore·most
head·hunt·er
head·ing
head·line
　head·lined
　head·lin·ing
head·long
head·quar·ters
heady
　head·i·ly
　head·i·ness
heal·er
health·ful
　health·ful·ly
healthy
　health·i·er
　health·i·est
　health·i·ly
　health·i·ness
heaped
hear
　heard
　hear·ing
heark·en
hear·say
hearse
heart·ache
heart·break
　heart·brok·en
heart·burn
heart·en
hearth·stone
heart·less
　heart·less·ly
　heart·less·ness
heart·rend·ing
heart·sick

hearty
  heart·i·ly
  heart·i·ness
heat·ed
heat·er
heath
hea·then
heath·er
heave
  heaved
  heav·ing
heav·en
  heav·en·ly
  heav·en·ward
heavy
  heav·i·ness
heav·y-hand·ed
heav·y-heart·ed
heav·y·weight
He·brew
  He·bra·ic
heck·le
  heck·led
  heck·ling
  heck·ler
hec·tare
hec·tic
  hec·ti·cal·ly
hec·to·gram
hec·to·li·ter
hec·to·me·ter
hedge
  hedged
  hedg·ing
  hedg·er
he·don·ism
  he·don·ist
  he·don·is·tic
heed·ful
heed·less
hefty
  heft·i·er
he·gem·o·ny
heif·er
height·en
hei·nous
  hei·nous·ness
heir·ess

heir·loom
heist
hel·i·cop·ter
he·li·um
he·lix
  he·lix·es
hel·i·cal
hel·lion
hell·ish
  hell·ish·ness
hel·lo
helm
  helm·less
hel·met
  hel·met·ed
helms·man
help·er
help·ful
  help·ful·ly
  help·ful·ness
help·ing
help·less
  help·less·ness
hel·ter-skel·ter
hem
  hemmed
  hem·ming
he·ma·tol·o·gy
hem·i·sphere
  hem·i·spher·i·cal
hem·lock
he·mo·glo·bin
he·mo·phil·ia
hem·or·rhage
  hem·or·rhag·ing
hem·or·rhoid
hem·stitch
hence·forth
hench·man
hen·na
hep·a·ti·tis
her·ald
  he·ral·dic
her·ald·ry
herb
  her·ba·ceous
her·bi·cide

her·biv·o·rous
her·cu·le·an
he·red·i·ty
  he·red·i·tary
  he·red·i·tari·ly
here·sy
  here·sies
here·tic
  he·ret·i·cal
her·it·a·ble
  her·it·a·bil·i·ty
her·it·age
her·maph·ro·dite
  her·maph·ro·dit·ism
her·met·ic
  her·met·i·cal·ly
her·mit
her·nia
  her·ni·al
he·ro
  he·roes
  her·o·ine
  her·o·ism
he·ro·ic
  he·ro·i·cal·ly
her·o·in
her·on
her·pes
her·pe·tol·o·gy
her·ring·bone
her·self
hes·i·tant
  hes·i·tan·cy
  hes·i·tance
  hes·i·tant·ly
hes·i·tate
  hes·i·tat·ed
  hes·i·tat·ing
  hes·i·ta·tion
het·er·o·dox
  het·er·o·doxy
het·er·o·ge·ne·ous
  het·er·o·ge·ne·i·ty
  het·er·o·ge·ne·ous·ness
het·er·o·sex·u·al
  het·er·o·sex·u·al·i·ty
hew

hewed
hewn
hew·ing
hex·a·gon
  hex·ag·o·nal
hexa·gram
hi·a·tus
hi·ba·chi
hi·ber·nate
  hi·ber·nat·ed
  hi·ber·nat·ing
  hi·ber·na·tion
hi·bis·cus
hic·cup
  hic·cuped
  hic·cup·ing
hick·o·ry
hid·den
hide
  hid
  hid·den
  hid·ing
hide·bound
hid·e·ous
  hid·e·ous·ness
hi·er·ar·chy
  hi·er·ar·chal
  hi·er·ar·chic
  hi·er·ar·chi·cal·ly
hi·ero·glyph
hi·ero·glyph·ic
high·grade
high·hand·ed
high·mind·ed
high·ness
high·pres·sure
  high-pres·sured
  high-pres·sur·ing
high-spir·it·ed
high-ten·sion
high-toned
high·way
hi·jack
  hi·jack·er
  hi·jack·ing
hike
  hiked

hik·ing
hi·lar·i·ous
  hi·lar·i·ous·ly
  hi·lar·i·ous·ness
  hi·lar·i·ty
hill·bil·ly
  hill·bil·lies
hill·ock
hilly
  hill·i·er
  hill·i·est
him·self
hin·der
  hind·er·er
hind·most
hind·quar·ter
hin·drance
hind·sight
Hin·du·ism
hinge
  hinged
  hing·ing
hin·ter·land
hipped
Hip·poc·ra·tes
Hip·po·crat·ic
hip·po·drome
hip·po·pot·a·mus
hire·ling
hir·sute
His·pan·ic
his·ta·mine
his·to·ri·an
his·tor·ic
his·tor·i·cal
  his·tor·i·cal·ly
  his·tor·i·cal·ness
his·to·ry
  his·to·ries
his·tri·on·ic
  his·tri·on·i·cal·ly
his·tri·on·ics
hit
  hit·ting
hitch·hike
  hitch·hiked
  hitch·hik·ing
  hitch·hik·er

hith·er
hith·er·to
hit·ter
hoard
  hoard·er
  hoard·ing
hoar·frost
hoarse
  hoarse·ly
  hoarse·ness
hoary
  hoar·i·ness
hoax
  hoax·er
hob·ble
  hob·bled
  hob·bling
hob·by
  hob·bies
  hob·by·ist
hob·gob·lin
hob·nail
hob·nob
  hob·nobbed
  hob·nob·bing
ho·bo
  ho·boes
hock·ey
ho·cus·-po·cus
hodge·podge
hoe
  hoed
  hoe·ing
hoe·down
hog
  hogged
  hog·ging
  hog·gish
hogs·head
hog·tie
hoi·poi·loi
hoist·ing
ho·kum
hold
  held
  hold·ing
hole
  holed

hol·ing
holey
hol·i·day
ho·li·ness
Hol·land
hol·low
  hol·low·ness
hol·ly
hol·ly·hock
hol·o·caust
hol·o·graph
Hol·stein
hol·ster
ho·ly
  ho·li·er
  ho·li·est
  ho·li·ness
hom·age
hom·bre
home·com·ing
home·less
home·ly
  home·li·ness
ho·me·op·a·thy
home·spun
home·stead
home·ward
homey
  hom·i·ness
hom·i·cide
  ho·mi·cid·al
hom·i·let·ics
hom·i·ly
hom·i·ny
ho·mo·ge·ne·ous
  ho·mo·ge·ne·i·ty
ho·mog·e·nize
  ho·mog·e·nized
  ho·mog·e·niz·ing
hom·o·graph
hom·o·nym
hom·o·phone
Ho·mo sa·pi·ens
ho·mo·sex·u·al
  ho·mo·sex·u·al·i·ty
hone
  honed

hon·ing
hon·est
  hon·est·ly
hon·es·ty
  hon·es·ties
hon·ey
hon·ey·moon·er
hon·ey·suck·le
honk·y·tonk
hon·or
hon·or·a·ble
  hon·or·a·bly
hon·o·rar·i·um
hon·or·ary
hon·or·if·ic
hood·ed
hood·lum
hoo·doo
hood·wink
hoof
  hoofs
  hooves
  hoofed
hooked
hook·er
hoo·li·gan
hoop
  hooped
hop
  hopped
  hop·ping
hope
  hoped
  hop·ing
hope·ful
  hope·ful·ness
hope·less
  hope·less·ness
hop·head
hop·per
hop·scotch
horde
  hord·ed
  hord·ing
ho·ri·zon
hor·i·zon·tal
  hor·i·zon·tal·ly
hor·mone

horn
  horned
  horny
hor·net
horn·swog·gle
ho·rol·o·gy
ho·rol·o·gist
hor·o·scope
hor·ren·dous
hor·ri·ble
  hor·ri·bly
hor·rid
  hor·rid·ly
  hor·rid·ness
hor·ri·fy
  hor·ri·fied
  hor·ri·fy·ing
  hor·ri·fi·ca·tion
hor·ror
hors d'oeu·vre
horse
  hors·es
  horsed
  hors·ing
horse·back
horse·man
horse op·era
horse·play
horse·pow·er
horse·rad·ish
horse·whipped
hors·ey
hor·ta·to·ry
hor·ti·cul·ture
  hor·ti·cul·tur·al
  hor·ti·cul·tur·ist
ho·san·na
hose
ho·siery
hos·pice
hos·pi·ta·ble
  hos·pi·ta·bly
hos·pi·tal
hos·pi·tal·i·ty
  hos·pi·tal·i·ties
hos·pi·tal·i·za·tion
hos·pi·tal·ize
  hos·pi·tal·ized

hos·pi·tal·iz·ing
hos·tage
hos·tel
  hos·tel·ry
host·ess
hos·tile
  hos·tile·ly
hos·til·i·ty
  hos·til·i·ties
hot
  hot·ter
  hot·test
  hot·ly
hot-blood·ed
ho·tel
hot·head·ed
hound
hour·glass
hour·ly
house
  hous·es
  housed
  hous·ing
house·bro·ken
house·hold
house·keep·er
house·warm·ing
house·wife
  house·wives
hov·el
hov·er
  hov·er·ing
how·ev·er
how·itz·er
howl·er
hoy·den
  hoy·den·ish
hub·bub
huck·le·ber·ry
huck·ster
hud·dle
  hud·dled
  hud·dling
huffy
  huff·i·ness
hug
  hugged

hug·ging
hug·ger
huge
  huge·ness
hulk·ing
hum
  hummed
  hum·ming
  hum·mer
hu·man
hu·mane
hu·man·ism
hu·man·i·tar·i·an
hu·man·i·ty
hu·man·ize
hum·ble
  hum·bled
  hum·bling
  hum·ble·ness
  hum·bly
hum·bug
hum·drum
hu·mer·us
hu·mid
hu·midi·fy
  hu·mid·i·fied
  hu·mid·i·fy·ing
  hu·mid·i·fi·er
hu·mid·i·ty
hu·mi·dor
hu·mil·i·ate
  hu·mil·i·at·ed
  hu·mil·i·at·ing
  hu·mil·i·a·tion
hu·mil·i·ty
hum·ming·bird
hum·mock
hu·mor
hu·mor·ist
hu·mor·ous
  hu·mor·ous·ness
hump
  humped
  humpy
hump·back
hu·mus
hunch·back
hun·dred

hun·dredth
hun·dred·weight
hun·ger
hun·gry
  hun·gri·ly
  hun·gri·ness
hunt
  hunt·er
  hunt·ing
  hunts·man
hur·dle
  hur·dled
  hur·dling
  hur·dler
hur·dy-gur·dy
hurl·er
hur·rah
hur·ri·cane
hur·ry
  hur·ried
  hur·ry·ing
hurt·ful
hurt·ing
hur·tle
  hur·tled
  hur·tling
hus·band
hus·band·ry
husk·er
husky
  husk·i·ly
  husk·i·ness
hus·sy
hus·tings
hus·tle
  hus·tled
  hus·tling
  hus·tler
hutch
huz·zah
hy·a·cinth
hy·brid
  hy·brid·ize
  hy·brid·ized
  hy·brid·iz·ing
  hy·brid·i·za·tion
hy·dran·gea
hy·drant

hy·drate
  hy·dra·ted
  hy·dra·ting
  hy·dra·tion
hy·drau·lic
  hy·drau·li·cal·ly
hy·drau·lics
hy·dro·car·bon
hy·dro·chlor·ic ac·id
hy·dro·dy·nam·ics
  hy·dro·dy·nam·ic
hy·dro·e·lec·tric
hy·dro·gen
  hy·drog·e·nous
hy·drol·y·sis
hy·drom·e·ter
hy·dro·pho·bia
hy·dro·plane
hy·dro·pon·ics
hy·dro·ther·a·py
  hy·dro·ther·a·pist
hy·drous
hy·drox·ide
hy·e·na
hy·giene
  hy·gi·en·ic
  hy·gi·en·i·cal·ly
  hy·gien·ist
hy·grom·e·ter
hy·men
hy·me·ne·al
  hy·me·ne·al·ly
hymn
  hym·nal
hy·per·bo·la
hy·per·bo·le
  hy·per·bo·lize
  hy·per·bo·lized
  hy·per·bo·liz·ing
hy·per·bol·ic
hy·per·crit·i·cal
hy·per·sen·si·tive
  hy·per·sen·si·tiv·i·ty
hy·per·ten·sion
hy·per·thy·roid·ism
hy·phen
hy·phen·ate
  hy·phen·at·ed

hy·phen·at·ing
hyp·no·sis
hyp·not·ic
hyp·no·tism
hyp·no·tist
hyp·no·tize
  hyp·no·tized
  hyp·no·tiz·ing
hy·po·chon·dria
  hy·po·chon·dri·ac
hy·poc·ri·sy
  hy·poc·ri·sies
hyp·o·crite
hy·po·der·mic
hy·po·gly·ce·mia
hy·po·sen·si·tize
hy·po·ten·sion
hy·pot·e·nuse
hy·poth·e·cate
  hy·poth·e·cat·ed
  hy·poth·e·cat·ing
  hy·poth·e·ca·tion
hy·poth·e·sis
  hy·poth·e·ses
  hy·poth·e·size
  hy·poth·e·sized
  hy·poth·e·siz·ing
hy·po·thet·i·cal
hys·ter·ec·to·my
hys·ter·e·sis
hys·te·ria
hys·ter·ic
hys·ter·i·cal
hys·ter·i·cal·ly
hys·ter·ics

I

iamb
  iam·bic
ibid
ibi·dem
ice
  iced
  ic·ing
  icy
  ici·ness
ice cream

ice-skate
  ice-skat·ed
  ice-skat·ing
ich·thy·ol·o·gy
  ich·thy·o·log·i·cal
  ich·thy·ol·o·gist
ici·cle
ici·ly
icon
icon·o·clast
  icon·o·clasm
  icon·o·clas·tic
idea
ide·al
  ide·al·ly
ide·al·ism
  ide·al·ist
  ide·al·is·tic
ide·al·ize
  ide·al·ized
  ide·al·iz·ing
  ide·al·i·za·tion
ide·ate
  ide·a·tion
iden·ti·cal
  iden·ti·cal·ly
  iden·ti·cal·ness
iden·ti·fi·a·ble
  iden·ti·fi·a·bly
iden·ti·fy
  iden·ti·fied
  iden·ti·fy·ing
  iden·ti·fi·ca·tion
iden·ti·ty
  iden·ti·ties
ide·ol·o·gist
ide·ol·o·gy
  ide·ol·o·gies
ides
id·i·o·cy
  id·i·o·cies
id·i·om
  id·i·o·mat·ic
  id·i·o·mat·i·cal·ly
id·i·o·syn·cra·sy
  id·i·o·syn·cra·sies
  id·i·o·syn·crat·ic
id·i·ot

idi·ot·ic
idi·ot·i·cal·ly
idle
  idler
  idlest
  idled
  idling
  idle·ness
  idly
idol
idol·a·try
  idol·a·tries
  idol·a·ter
  idol·a·trous
idol·ize
  idol·ized
  idol·iz·ing
  idol·i·za·tion
idyll
  idyl·lic
  idyl·lic·al·ly
ig·loo
ig·ne·ous
ig·nite
  ig·nit·ed
  ig·nit·ing
  ig·nit·er
  ig·nit·a·ble
  ig·nit·a·bil·i·ty
  ig·ni·tion
ig·no·ble
  ig·no·bil·i·ty
  ig·no·ble·ness
  ig·no·bly
ig·no·miny
  ig·no·min·ies
  ig·no·min·i·ous
ig·no·ra·mus
ig·no·rant
  ig·no·rance
  ig·no·rant·ly
ig·nore
  ig·nored
  ig·nor·ing
i·gua·na
ikon
ill
  worse

worst
ill-ad·vised
ill-bred
il·le·gal
  il·le·gal·i·ty
  il·le·gal·ly
il·leg·i·ble
  il·leg·i·bil·i·ty
  il·leg·i·ble·ness
  il·leg·i·bly
il·le·git·i·mate
  il·le·git·i·ma·cy
  il·le·git·i·ma·cies
  il·le·git·i·mate·ly
ill-fat·ed
ill-fa·vored
ill-got·ten
ill·lib·er·al
il·lic·it
il·lim·it·a·ble
il·lit·er·ate
  il·lit·er·a·cy
ill·ness
il·log·i·cal
ill-tempered
ill-timed
il·lu·mi·nate
  il·lu·mi·nat·ed
  il·lu·mi·nat·ing
  il·lu·mi·na·tor
  il·lu·mi·na·tion
il·lu·mine
  il·lu·mined
  il·lu·min·ing
ill-us·age
il·lu·sion
il·lu·sive
  il·lu·sive·ness
il·lu·so·ry
  il·lu·so·ri·ness
il·lus·trate
  il·lus·trat·ed
  il·lus·trat·ing
il·lus·tra·tion
  il·lus·tra·tive
  il·lus·tra·tor
il·lus·tri·ous
  il·lus·tri·ous·ness

im·age
  im·aged
  im·ag·ing
im·age·ry
  im·age·ries
  im·a·ge·ri·al
im·ag·ine
  im·ag·ined
  im·ag·in·ing
  im·ag·i·na·ble
  imag·i·na·bly
  im·ag·i·nary
  imag·i·nari·ly
  im·ag·i·na·tion
  im·ag·i·na·tive
im·bal·ance
im·be·cile
  im·be·cil·ic
  im·be·cil·i·ty
im·bed
  im·bed·ded
  im·bed·ding
im·bibe
  im·bibed
  im·bib·ing
im·bro·glio
im·bue
  im·bued
  im·bu·ing
im·i·tate
  im·i·tat·ed
  im·i·tat·ing
  im·i·ta·tor
  im·i·ta·tion
  im·i·ta·tive
im·mac·u·late
  im·mac·u·la·cy
  im·mac·u·late·ness
  im·mac·u·late·ly
im·ma·nent
  im·ma·nence
  im·ma·nen·cy
  im·ma·nent·ly
im·ma·te·ri·al
  im·ma·te·ri·al·ness
  im·ma·te·ri·al·i·ty
im·ma·ture
  im·ma·ture·ly

im·ma·ture·ness
im·ma·tu·ri·ty
im·meas·ur·a·ble
  im·meas·ur·a·bly
im·me·di·a·cy
  im·me·di·a·cies
im·me·di·ate
  im·me·di·ate·ly
im·me·mo·ri·al
im·mense
  im·mense·ness
  im·men·si·ty
im·merge
  im·merged
  im·merg·ing
  im·mer·gence
im·merse
  im·mersed
  im·mers·ing
  im·mer·sion
im·mi·grate
  im·mi·grat·ed
  im·mi·grat·ing
  im·mi·gra·tion
im·mi·grant
  im·mi·gra·tor
im·mi·nent
  im·mi·nence
im·mo·bile
  im·mo·bil·i·ty
  im·mo·bi·lize
  im·mo·bi·lized
  im·mo·bi·liz·ing
im·mod·er·ate
  im·mod·er·ate·ly
im·mod·est
  im·mod·est·ly
  im·mod·es·ty
im·mo·late
  im·mo·lat·ed
  im·mo·lat·ing
  im·mo·la·tion
  im·mo·la·tor
im·mor·al
  im·mor·al·i·ty
  im·mor·al·i·ties
  im·mor·al·ly
im·mor·tal

im·mor·tal·i·ty
im·mor·tal·ize
im·mor·tal·ized
im·mor·tal·iz·ing
im·mor·tal·ly
im·mov·a·ble
  im·mov·a·bil·i·ty
  im·mov·a·bly
im·mune
  im·mu·ni·ty
  im·mu·nize
  im·mu·nized
  im·mu·niz·ing
  im·mu·ni·za·tion
im·mu·nol·o·gy
im·mure
  im·mured
  im·mur·ing
im·mu·ta·ble
  im·mu·ta·bil·i·ty
  im·mu·ta·ble·ness
  im·mu·ta·bly
im·pact
  im·pac·tion
  im·pact·ed
im·pair
  im·pair·ment
impala
im·pale
  im·paled
  im·pal·ing
  im·pale·ment
im·pal·pa·ble
  im·pal·pa·bil·i·ty
im·pan·el
  im·pan·eled
  im·pan·el·ing
im·part
im·par·tial
  im·par·ti·al·i·ty
  im·par·tial·ness
  im·par·tial·ly
im·pass·a·ble
  im·pass·a·bil·i·ty
  im·pass·a·ble·ness
  im·pass·a·bly
im·passe
im·pas·si·ble

im·pas·si·bil·i·ty
im·pas·si·ble·ness
im·pas·sion
im·pas·sioned
im·pas·sioned·ness
im·pas·sive
  im·pas·sive·ly
  im·pas·sive·ness
  im·pas·siv·i·ty
im·pa·tient
  im·pa·tience
  im·pa·tient·ly
im·peach
  im·peach·a·ble
  im·peach·ment
im·pec·ca·ble
  im·pec·ca·bil·i·ty
  im·pec·ca·bly
im·pe·cu·ni·ous
  im·pe·cu·ni·ous·ness
im·pede
  im·ped·ed
  im·ped·ing
  im·ped·i·ment
im·pel
  im·pelled
  im·pel·ling
im·pend
  im·pend·ing
im·pen·e·tra·ble
  im·pen·e·tra·bil·i·ty
im·pen·i·tent
  im·pen·i·tence
im·per·a·tive
  im·per·a·tive·ness
im·per·cep·ti·ble
  im·per·cep·ti·bil·i·ty
  im·per·cep·ti·bly
  im·per·cep·tive
im·per·fect
  im·per·fect·ly
  im·per·fect·ness
  im·per·fec·tion
im·pe·ri·al
  im·pe·ri·al·ly
im·pe·ri·al·ism
  im·pe·ri·al·ist
  im·pe·ri·al·is·tic

im·pe·ri·al·is·ti·cal·ly
im·per·il
  im·per·iled
  im·per·il·ing
  im·per·il·ment
im·pe·ri·ous
  im·pe·ri·ous·ly
  im·pe·ri·ous·ness
im·per·ish·a·ble
  im·per·ish·a·bil·i·ty
im·per·ma·nent
  im·per·ma·nence
  im·per·ma·nen·cy
  im·per·ma·nent·ly
im·per·me·a·ble
  im·per·me·a·bil·i·ty
  im·per·me·a·ble·ness
im·per·son·al
  im·per·son·al·ly
im·per·son·ate
  im·per·son·at·ed
  im·per·son·at·ing
  im·per·son·a·tion
  im·per·son·a·tor
im·per·ti·nent
  im·per·ti·nence
  im·per·ti·nent·ly
im·per·turb·a·ble
  im·per·turb·a·bly
im·per·vi·ous
  im·per·vi·ous·ly
  im·per·vi·ous·ness
im·pe·ti·go
im·pet·u·ous
  im·pet·u·os·i·ty
  im·pet·u·ous·ly
  im·pet·u·ous·ness
im·pe·tus
im·pi·e·ty
  im·pi·e·ties
im·pinge
  im·pinged
  im·ping·ing
  im·pinge·ment
im·pi·ous
  im·pi·ous·ly
  im·pi·ous·ness
im·plac·a·ble

im·plac·a·bil·i·ty
im·plac·a·ble·ness
im·plac·a·bly
im·plant
  im·plan·ta·tion
im·plau·si·ble
  im·plau·si·bly
  im·plau·si·bil·i·ty
im·ple·ment
  im·ple·men·tal
  im·ple·men·ta·tion
im·pli·cate
  im·pli·cat·ed
  im·pli·cat·ing
  im·pli·ca·tion
im·plic·it
  im·plic·it·ly
  im·plic·it·ness
im·plode
  im·plod·ed
  im·plod·ing
  im·plo·sion
  im·plo·sive
im·plore
  im·plored
  im·plor·ing
  im·plo·ra·tion
im·ply
  im·plied
  im·ply·ing
im·po·lite
  im·po·lite·ly
  im·po·lite·ness
im·pol·i·tic
  im·pol·i·tic·ly
im·pon·der·a·ble
  im·pon·der·a·bil·i·ty
  im·pon·der·a·ble·ness
im·port
  im·port·a·ble
  im·port·er
  im·por·ta·tion
im·por·tance
  im·por·tant
  im·por·tant·ly
im·por·tu·nate
im·por·tune
  im·por·tuned

im·por·tun·ing
im·pose
  im·posed
  im·pos·ing
  im·po·si·tion
im·pos·si·ble
  im·pos·si·bil·i·ty
  im·pos·si·bil·i·ties
  im·pos·si·bly
im·pos·tor
  im·pos·ture
im·po·tent
  im·po·tence
  im·po·ten·cy
  im·po·tent·ly
im·pound
  im·pound·age
im·pov·er·ish
  im·pov·er·ish·ment
im·prac·ti·cal
  im·prac·ti·ca·ble
  im·prac·ti·ca·bil·i·ty
  im·prac·ti·ca·ble·ness
im·pre·cate
  im·pre·cat·ed
  im·pre·cat·ing
  im·pre·ca·tion
im·preg·na·ble
  im·preg·na·bil·i·ty
  im·preg·na·ble·ness
im·preg·nate
  im·preg·nat·ed
  im·preg·nat·ing
  im·preg·na·tion
  im·preg·na·tor
im·pre·sa·rio
  im·pre·sa·ri·os
im·press
  im·press·i·ble
  im·press·ment
im·pres·sion
  im·pres·sion·ist
im·pres·sion·a·ble
  im·pres·sion·a·bly
im·pres·sion·ism
  im·pres·sion·ist
  im·pres·sion·is·tic
im·pres·sive

im·pres·sive·ly
im·pres·sive·ness
im·pri·ma·tur
im·print
  im·prin·ter
im·pris·on
  im·pris·on·ment
im·prob·a·ble
  im·prob·a·bil·i·ty
  im·prob·a·ble·ness
  im·prob·a·bly
im·promp·tu
im·prop·er
  im·prop·er·ly
  im·prop·er·ness
im·pro·pri·e·ty
  im·pro·pri·e·ties
im·prove
  im·proved
  im·prov·ing
  im·prov·a·bil·i·ty
  im·prov·a·ble
  im·prove·ment
im·prov·i·dent
  im·prov·i·dence
  im·prov·i·dent·ly
im·prov·i·sa·tion
  im·prov·i·sa·tion·al
im·pro·vise
  im·pro·vised
  im·pro·vis·ing
im·pru·dent
  im·pru·dence
  im·pru·dent·ly
im·pu·dent
  im·pu·dence
im·pugn
  im·pugn·er
  im·pug·na·tion
im·pulse
  im·pul·sion
  im·pul·sive
im·pu·ni·ty
im·pure
  im·pure·ness
  im·pu·ri·ty
  im·pu·ri·ties
im·pute

im·put·ed
im·put·ing
im·pu·ta·tion
in·a·bil·i·ty
in ab·sen·tia
in·ac·ces·si·ble
in·ac·ces·si·bil·i·ty
in·ac·ces·si·bly
in·ac·cu·rate
  in·ac·cu·ra·cy
  in·ac·cu·ra·cies
in·ac·tion
in·ac·ti·vate
  in·ac·ti·va·tion
in·ac·tive
  in·ac·tive·ly
  in·ac·tiv·i·ty
in·ad·e·quate
  in·ad·e·qua·cy
  in·ad·e·qua·cies
in·ad·mis·si·ble
  in·ad·mis·si·bly
in·ad·ver·tent
  in·ad·ver·tence
  in·ad·ver·ten·cy
in·al·ien·a·ble
  in·al·ien·a·bil·i·ty
  in·al·ien·a·bly
in·al·ter·a·ble
in·ane
  in·ane·ness
  in·an·i·ty
in·an·i·mate
in·ap·pli·ca·ble
in·ap·pre·cia·bly
in·ap·pro·pri·ate
  in·ap·pro·pri·ate·ly
in·apt
  in·ap·ti·tude
  in·apt·ly
in·ar·tic·u·late
in·as·much as
in·at·ten·tion
  in·at·ten·tive
in·au·di·ble
  in·au·di·bly
in·au·gu·ral
in·au·gu·rate

in·au·gu·rat·ed
in·au·gu·rat·ing
in·au·gu·ra·tion
in·aus·pi·cious
in·bred
in·breed
  in·breed·ing
in·cal·cu·la·ble
  in·cal·cu·la·bil·i·ty
in·can·des·cent
  in·can·des·cence
in·can·ta·tion
in·ca·pa·ble
  in·ca·pa·bly
in·ca·pac·i·tate
  in·ca·pac·i·tat·ed
  in·ca·pac·i·tat·ing
in·ca·pac·i·ty
  in·ca·pac·i·ties
  in·ca·pac·i·ta·tion
in·car·cer·ate
  in·car·cer·at·ed
  in·car·cer·at·ing
  in·car·cer·a·tion
in·car·nate
  in·car·nat·ed
  in·car·nat·ing
  in·car·na·tion
in·cen·di·a·ry
in·cense
  in·censed
  in·cens·ing
in·cen·tive
in·cep·tion
in·cer·ti·tude
in·ces·sant
in·cest
  in·ces·tu·ous
in·cho·ate
in·ci·dence
in·ci·dent
  in·ci·den·tal
in·cin·er·ate
  in·cin·er·at·ed
  in·cin·er·at·ing
  in·cin·er·a·tion
  in·cin·er·a·tor
in·cip·i·ent

in·cise
in·cised
in·cis·ing
in·ci·sion
in·ci·sive
in·ci·sor
in·cite
in·cit·ed
in·cit·ing
in·cite·ment
in·ci·ta·tion
in·ci·vil·i·ty
in·clem·ent
in·clem·en·cy
in·cline
in·clined
in·clin·ing
in·cli·na·tion
in·clude
in·clud·ed
in·clud·ing
in·clu·sion
in·clu·sive
in·cog·ni·to
in·cog·ni·zant
in·co·her·ent
in·co·her·ence
in·com·bus·ti·ble
in·come
in·com·ing
in·com·men·su·rate
in·com·men·su·ra·ble
in·com·mode
in·com·mo·di·ous
in·com·mu·ni·ca·ble
in·com·mu·ni·ca·do
in·com·pa·ra·ble
in·com·pa·ra·bly
in·com·pat·i·ble
in·com·pat·i·bil·i·ty
in·com·pe·tent
in·com·pe·tence
in·com·pe·ten·cy
in·com·plete
in·com·ple·tion
in·com·pre·hen·si·ble
in·com·pre·hen·sion
in·con·ceiv·a·ble

in·con·ceiv·a·bly
in·con·clu·sive
in·con·gru·ous
in·con·gru·i·ty
in·con·se·quen·tial
in·con·sid·er·a·ble
in·con·sid·er·ate
in·con·sis·tent
in·con·sis·ten·cy
in·con·sol·a·ble
in·con·spic·u·ous
in·con·stant
in·con·stan·cy
in·con·test·a·ble
in·con·test·abil·i·ty
in·con·ti·nent
in·con·ti·nence
in·con·ti·nen·cy
in·con·trol·la·ble
in·con·ven·ient
in·con·ven·ience
in·con·ven·ienced
in·con·ven·ienc·ing
in·cor·po·rate
in·cor·po·rat·ed
in·cor·po·rat·ing
in·cor·po·ra·tion
in·cor·po·re·al
in·cor·rect
in·cor·ri·gi·ble
in·cor·ri·gi·bil·i·ty
in·cor·ri·gi·ble·ness
in·cor·rupt·i·ble
in·cor·rupt·i·bil·i·ty
in·cor·rupt·i·bly
in·crease
in·creased
in·creas·ing
in·creas·a·ble
in·cred·i·ble
in·cred·i·bil·i·ty
in·cred·i·bly
in·cred·u·lous
in·cre·du·li·ty
in·cre·ment
in·cre·men·tal
in·crim·i·nate
in·crim·i·nat·ed

in·crim·i·nat·ing
in·crim·i·na·tion
in·crust
in·crus·ta·tion
in·cu·bate
in·cu·bat·ed
in·cu·bat·ing
in·cu·ba·tion
in·cu·ba·tor
in·cul·cate
in·cul·cat·ed
in·cul·cat·ing
in·cul·ca·tion
in·cul·pate
in·cul·pat·ed
in·cul·pat·ing
in·cul·pa·tion
in·cum·bent
in·cum·ben·cy
in·cur
in·curred
in·cur·ring
in·cur·a·ble
in·cur·a·bly
in·cu·ri·ous
in·cur·sion
in·cur·sive
in·debt·ed
in·de·cent
in·de·cen·cy
in·de·ci·sion
in·de·ci·sive
in·de·co·rous
in·de·co·rum
in·deed
in·de·fat·i·ga·ble
in·de·fat·i·ga·bil·i·ty
in·de·fat·i·ga·bly
in·de·fea·si·ble
in·de·fen·si·ble
in·de·fen·si·bil·i·ty
in·de·fen·si·bly
in·de·fin·a·ble
in·def·i·nite
in·def·i·nite·ly
in·del·i·ble
in·del·i·bly
in·del·i·cate

in·del·i·ca·cy
in·dem·ni·fy
  in·dem·ni·fied
  in·dem·ni·fy·ing
  in·dem·ni·fi·ca·tion
  in·dem·ni·ty
in·dent
  in·den·ta·tion
  in·dent·ed
in·den·ture
  in·den·tur·ing
in·de·pend·ent
  in·de·pend·ence
  in·de·pend·en·cy
in·de·scrib·a·ble
  in·de·scrib·a·bil·i·ty
in·de·struct·i·ble
  in·de·struct·i·bil·i·ty
in·de·ter·mi·nate
  in·de·ter·mi·na·cy
  in·de·ter·mi·na·tion
in·dex
in·di·cate
  in·di·cat·ed
  in·di·cat·ing
  in·di·ca·tion
  in·dic·a·tive
  in·di·ca·tor
in·dict
  in·dict·a·ble
  in·dict·ment
in·dif·fer·ent
  in·dif·fer·ence
  in·dif·fer·ent·ly
in·dig·e·nous
in·di·gent
  in·di·gence
in·di·ges·tion
  in·di·gest·i·ble
  in·di·gest·i·bil·i·ty
  in·di·gest·i·ble·ness
in·dig·nant
  in·dig·nant·ly
  in·dig·na·tion
in·dig·ni·ty
in·di·go
in·di·rect
  in·di·rec·tion

in·dis·creet
  in·dis·cre·tion
in·dis·crete
in·dis·crim·i·nate
  in·dis·crim·i·nat·ing
  in·dis·crim·i·na·tion
in·dis·pen·sa·ble
  in·dis·pen·sa·bil·i·ty
  in·dis·pen·sa·ble·ness
in·dis·posed
  in·dis·po·si·tion
in·dis·put·a·ble
in·dis·sol·u·ble
  in·dis·sol·u·bil·i·ty
in·dis·tinct
in·dis·tin·guish·a·ble
in·di·vid·u·al
  in·di·vid·u·al·ly
  in·di·vid·u·al·is·tic
  in·di·vid·u·al·i·ty
  in·di·vid·u·al·ize
in·di·vis·i·ble
in·doc·tri·nate
  in·doc·tri·nat·ed
  in·doc·tri·nat·ing
  in·doc·tri·na·tion
in·do·lent
  in·do·lence
in·dom·i·ta·ble
  in·dom·i·ta·bil·i·ty
  in·dom·i·ta·bly
in·du·bi·ta·ble
  in·du·bi·ta·bil·i·ty
  in·du·bi·ta·bly
in·duce
  in·duced
  in·duc·ing
  in·duce·ment
in·duct
  in·duct·ee
in·duc·tion
  in·duct·ance
  in·duc·tive
in·dulge
  in·dulged
  in·dulg·ing
  in·dul·gence
  in·dul·gent

in·dus·try
  in·dus·tries
  in·dus·tri·al
in·dus·tri·al·ize
  in·dus·tri·al·i·za·tion
  in·dus·tri·al·ist
in·dus·tri·ous
in·e·bri·ate
  in·e·bri·at·ed
  in·e·bri·at·ing
  in·e·bri·a·tion
in·ed·i·ble
in·ef·fa·ble
  in·ef·fa·bil·i·ty
  in·ef·fa·bly
in·ef·fec·tive
in·ef·fec·tu·al
in·ef·fi·ca·cy
in·ef·fi·cient
  in·ef·fi·cien·cy
in·el·e·gant
in·el·i·gi·ble
  in·el·i·gi·bil·i·ty
in·ept
  in·ept·i·tude
in·e·qual·i·ty
in·e·rad·i·ca·ble
in·er·rant
in·ert
in·er·tia
  in·er·tial
in·es·cap·a·ble
in·es·sen·tial
in·es·ti·ma·ble
  in·es·ti·ma·bly
in·ev·i·ta·ble
  in·ev·i·ta·bil·i·ty
  in·ev·i·ta·bly
in·ex·act
in·ex·cus·a·ble
in·ex·haust·i·ble
  in·ex·haust·i·bil·i·ty
in·ex·o·ra·ble
  in·ex·o·ra·bil·i·ty
  in·ex·o·ra·bly
in·ex·pe·ri·ence
  in·ex·pe·ri·enced
in·ex·pert

in·ex·pi·a·ble
in·ex·pi·a·bly
in·ex·pli·ca·ble
in·ex·pli·ca·bil·i·ty
in·ex·pli·ca·bly
in·ex·press·i·ble
in·ex·press·i·bil·i·ty
in·ex·press·i·bly
in·ex·pres·sive
in·ex·tin·guish·a·ble
in·ex·tri·ca·ble
in·ex·tri·ca·bil·i·ty
in·ex·tri·ca·bly
in·fal·li·ble
in·fal·li·bil·i·ty
in·fal·li·bly
in·fa·mous
in·fa·my
in·fa·mies
in·fan·cy
in·fan·cies
in·fant
in·fant·hood
in·fan·ti·cide
in·fan·tile
in·fan·tine
in·fan·try
in·fan·tries
in·fat·u·ate
in·fat·u·at·ed
in·fat·u·at·ing
in·fat·u·a·tion
in·fect
in·fec·tion
in·fec·tious
in·fec·tive
in·fe·lic·i·ty
in·fer
in·ferred
in·fer·ring
in·fer·a·ble
in·fer·ence
in·fer·en·tial
in·fe·ri·or
in·fe·ri·or·i·ty
in·fer·nal
in·fer·no
in·fer·nos

in·fest
in·fes·ta·tion
in·fi·del
in·fi·del·i·ty
in·fi·del·i·ties
in·field
in·field·er
in·fight·ing
in·fight·er
in·fil·trate
in·fil·trat·ed
in·fil·trat·ing
in·fil·tra·tion
in·fil·tra·tor
in·fi·nite
in·fi·nite·ness
in·fin·i·tes·i·mal
in·fin·i·tive
in·fin·i·tive·ly
in·fin·i·ty
in·fin·i·ties
in·firm
in·fir·ma·ry
in·fir·ma·ries
in·fir·mi·ty
in·fir·mi·ties
in·flame
in·flamed
in·flam·ing
in·flam·ma·ble
in·flam·ma·bil·i·ty
in·flam·ma·ble·ness
in·flam·ma·tion
in·flam·ma·to·ry
in·flate
in·flat·ed
in·flat·ing
in·flat·a·ble
in·fla·tion
in·fla·tion·ary
in·flect
in·flec·tion
in·flec·tion·less
in·flec·tive
in·flex·i·ble
in·flex·i·bil·i·ty
in·flex·i·bly
in·flict

in·flict·a·ble
in·flic·tion
in·flo·res·cence
in·flu·ence
in·flu·enced
in·flu·enc·ing
in·flu·en·tial
in·flu·en·za
in·flux
in·form
in·formed
in·form·er
in·for·mal
in·for·mal·i·ty
in·for·mal·ly
in·form·ant
in·for·ma·tion
in·for·ma·tion·al
in·for·ma·tive
in·for·ma·to·ry
in·frac·tion
in·fran·gi·ble
in·fran·gi·bil·i·ty
in·fran·gi·bly
in·fra·red
in·fra·son·ic
in·fra·struc·ture
in·fre·quent
in·fre·quen·cy
in·fringe
in·fringed
in·fring·ing
in·fringe·ment
in·fu·ri·ate
in·fu·ri·at·ed
in·fu·ri·at·ing
in·fu·ri·a·tion
in·fuse
in·fused
in·fus·ing
in·fus·i·ble
in·fu·sion
in·gen·ious
in·gé·nue
in·ge·nu·i·ty
in·gen·u·ous
in·gest
in·ges·tion

in·glo·ri·ous
in·got
in·grain
in·grate
in·gra·ti·ate
  in·gra·ti·at·ed
  in·gra·ti·at·ing
  in·gra·ti·a·tion
in·grat·i·tude
in·gre·di·ent
in·gress
in·grow·ing
  in·grown
in·hab·it
  in·hab·it·a·ble
  in·hab·i·ta·tion
  in·hab·it·ed
  in·hab·it·ant
in·hal·ant
  in·ha·la·tion
  in·ha·la·tor
in·hale
  in·haled
  in·hal·ing
in·har·mo·ny
  in·har·mon·ic
in·here
  in·hered
  in·her·ing
  in·her·ence
  in·her·ent
in·her·it
  in·her·i·tor
  in·her·i·tance
in·hib·it
  in·hib·i·tive
  in·hib·i·to·ry
  in·hib·i·ter
  in·hi·bi·tion
in·hos·pi·ta·ble
  in·hos·pi·tal·i·ty
in·hu·man
  in·hu·man·i·ty
in·hu·mane
in·hu·ma·tion
in·im·i·cal
in·im·i·ta·ble
  in·im·i·ta·bly

in·iq·ui·ty
  in·iq·ui·ties
  in·iq·ui·tous
in·i·tial
  in·i·tialed
  in·i·tial·ing
  in·i·tial·ly
in·i·ti·ate
  in·i·ti·at·ed
  in·i·ti·at·ing
  in·i·ti·a·tion
  in·i·ti·a·tor
in·i·ti·a·tive
in·ject
  in·jec·tion
  in·jec·tor
in·ju·di·cious
in·junc·tion
in·jure
  in·jured
  in·jur·ing
  in·ju·ri·ous
in·ju·ry
  in·ju·ries
in·jus·tice
ink·blot
ink·ling
inky
  ink·i·er
in·law
in·lay
  in·laid
  in·lay·ing
in·let
in·mate
in me·mo·ri·am
in·most
in·nards
in·nate
in·ner
in·ner·most
in·ner·sole
in·ner·vate
  in·ner·vat·ed
  in·ner·vat·ing
  in·ner·va·tion
in·ning
inn·keep·er

in·no·cent
  in·no·cence
in·noc·u·ous
in·no·vate
  in·no·vat·ed
  in·no·vat·ing
  in·no·va·tion
  in·no·va·tive
  in·no·va·tor
in·nu·en·do
  in·nu·en·dos
  in·nu·en·does
in·nu·mer·a·ble
  in·nu·mer·ous
  in·nu·mer·a·bly
in·nu·tri·tion
in·ob·serv·ance
  in·ob·serv·ant
in·oc·u·late
  in·oc·u·lat·ed
  in·oc·u·lat·ing
  in·oc·u·lant
  in·oc·u·la·tion
in·of·fen·sive
in·op·er·a·ble
  in·op·er·a·tive
in·op·por·tune
  in·op·por·tu·ni·ty
in·or·di·nate
in·or·gan·ic
in·pa·tient
in·pour
in·put
in·quest
in·qui·e·tude
in·quire
  in·quired
  in·quir·ing
  in·quir·er
in·quiry
  in·quir·ies
in·qui·si·tion
in·quis·i·tive
in·quis·i·tor
in·road
in·sa·lu·bri·ous
in·sane
  in·san·i·ty

103

in·san·i·ties
in·san·i·tary
in·sa·ti·ate
  in·sa·tia·ble
  in·sa·tia·bil·i·ty
  in·sa·tia·bly
in·scribe
  in·scribed
  in·scrib·ing
  in·scrip·tion
  in·scrip·tive
in·scru·ta·ble
  in·scru·ta·bil·i·ty
  in·scru·ta·bly
in·seam
in·sect
  in·sec·ti·cide
  in·sec·ti·cid·al
in·se·cure
  in·se·cu·ri·ty
in·sem·i·nate
  in·sem·i·nat·ed
  in·sem·i·nat·ing
  in·sem·i·na·tion
in·sen·sate
in·sen·si·ble
  in·sen·si·bil·i·ty
in·sen·si·tive
  in·sen·si·tiv·i·ty
in·sen·ti·ent
in·sep·a·ra·ble
  in·sep·a·ra·bil·i·ty
  in·sep·a·ra·bly
in·sert
  in·sert·er
  in·ser·tion
in·set
  in·set·ting
in·shore
in·side
in·sid·er
in·sid·i·ous
in·sight
in·sig·nia
in·sig·nif·i·cant
  in·sig·nif·i·cance
in·sin·cere
  in·sin·cer·i·ty

in·sin·cer·i·ties
in·sin·u·ate
  in·sin·u·at·ed
  in·sin·u·at·ing
  in·sin·u·a·tor
  in·sin·u·a·tion
in·sip·id
  in·si·pid·i·ty
  in·sip·id·ness
in·sist
  in·sist·ence
  in·sist·ent
in·so·bri·e·ty
in·so·cia·ble
  in·so·cia·bil·i·ty
  in·so·cia·bly
in·so·far
in·so·lent
  in·so·lence
in·sol·u·ble
  in·sol·u·bil·i·ty
  in·sol·u·bly
in·solv·a·ble
in·sol·vent
  in·sol·ven·cy
in·som·nia
  in·som·ni·ac
in·so·much
in·sou·ci·ant
  in·sou·ci·ance
in·spect
  in·spec·tion
  in·spec·tor
in·spire
  in·spired
  in·spir·ing
  in·spi·ra·tion
in·spir·it
in·sta·ble
  in·sta·bil·i·ty
in·stall
  in·stalled
  in·stall·ing
  in·stal·la·tion
in·stall·ment
in·stance
in·stant
  in·stan·ta·ne·ous

in·state
  in·stat·ed
  in·stat·ing
  in·state·ment
in·stead
in·step
in·sti·gate
  in·sti·gat·ed
  in·sti·gat·ing
  in·sti·ga·tion
  in·sti·ga·tor
in·still
  in·stilled
  in·stil·ling
  in·stil·la·tion
in·stinct
  in·stinc·tive
  in·stinc·tu·al
in·sti·tute
  in·sti·tut·ed
  in·sti·tut·ing
in·sti·tu·tion
  in·sti·tu·tion·al
  in·sti·tu·tion·al·ism
  in·sti·tu·tion·al·ize
  in·sti·tu·tion·al·ized
  in·sti·tu·tion·al·iz·ing
in·struct
  in·struc·tion
  in·struc·tive
  in·struc·tor
in·stru·ment
  in·stru·men·tal
  in·stru·men·ta·list
  in·stru·men·ta·tion
in·sub·or·di·nate
  in·sub·or·di·na·tion
in·sub·stan·tial
  in·sub·stan·ti·al·i·ty
in·suf·fer·a·ble
in·suf·fer·a·bly
in·suf·fi·cient
  in·suf·fi·cience
  in·suf·fi·cien·cy
in·su·lar
  in·su·lar·i·ty
in·su·late
  in·su·lat·ed

in·su·lat·ing
in·su·la·tion
in·su·la·tor
in·su·lin
in·sult
in·sup·port·a·ble
in·sup·press·i·ble
in·sure
  in·sured
  in·sur·ing
  in·sur·a·ble
  in·sur·a·bil·i·ty
  in·sur·ance
in·sur·gent
  in·sur·gence
  in·sur·gen·cy
in·sur·mount·a·ble
in·sur·rec·tion
in·sus·cep·ti·ble
in·tact
in·ta·glio
in·take
in·tan·gi·ble
  in·tan·gi·bil·i·ty
  in·tan·gi·ble·ness
  in·tan·gi·bly
in·te·ger
in·te·gral
in·te·grate
  in·te·grat·ed
  in·te·grat·ing
  in·te·grant
  in·te·gra·tion
in·teg·ri·ty
in·tel·lect
in·tel·lec·tu·al
  in·tel·lec·tu·al·ism
  in·tel·lec·tu·al·ize
  in·tel·lec·tu·al·ly
in·tel·li·gent
  in·tel·li·gence
  in·tel·li·gent·sia
in·tel·li·gi·ble
  in·tel·li·gi·bil·i·ty
  in·tel·li·gi·bly
in·tem·per·ate
  in·tem·per·ance
in·tend

in·tend·ant
in·tense
  in·tense·ness
in·ten·si·fy
  in·ten·si·fied
  in·ten·si·fy·ing
  in·ten·si·fi·ca·tion
  in·ten·sion
in·ten·si·ty
  in·ten·si·ties
in·ten·sive
in·tent
  in·ten·tion
  in·ten·tion·al·ly
in·ter
  in·terred
  in·ter·ring
  in·ter·ment
in·ter·act
  in·ter·ac·tion
  in·ter·ac·tive
in·ter·breed
  in·ter·bred
  in·ter·breed·ing
in·ter·ca·late
in·ter·cede
  in·ter·ced·ed
  in·ter·ced·ing
in·ter·cept
  in·ter·cept·or
  in·ter·cep·tion
in·ter·ces·sion
  in·ter·ces·sor
in·ter·change
  in·ter·changed
  in·ter·chang·ing
  in·ter·change·a·ble
  in·ter·change·a·bil·i·ty
in·ter·col·le·gi·ate
in·ter·com
in·ter·com·mu·ni·cate
  in·ter·com·mu·ni·cat·ed
  in·ter·com·mu·ni·cat·ing
  in·ter·com·mu·ni·ca·tion
in·ter·con·nect
  in·ter·con·nec·tion
in·ter·con·ti·nen·tal
in·ter·course

in·ter·cul·tur·al
in·ter·de·nom·i·na·tion·al
in·ter·de·part·men·tal
in·ter·de·pend·ent
  in·ter·de·pend·ence
in·ter·dict
  in·ter·dic·tion
in·ter·dis·ci·pli·nary
in·ter·est
  in·ter·est·ed
  in·ter·est·ing
in·ter·face
in·ter·faith
in·ter·fere
  in·ter·fered
  in·ter·fer·ing
  in·ter·fer·ence
in·ter·fer·on
in·ter·ga·lac·tic
in·ter·im
in·te·ri·or
in·ter·ject
  in·ter·jec·tion
  in·ter·jec·to·ry
in·ter·lay·er
in·ter·leaf
  in·ter·leave
in·ter·line
in·ter·link
in·ter·lock
in·ter·lo·cu·tion
  in·ter·loc·u·tor
  in·ter·loc·u·to·ry
in·ter·lope
  in·ter·loped
  in·ter·lop·ing
  in·ter·lop·er
in·ter·lude
in·ter·lu·nar
  in·ter·lu·na·ry
in·ter·marry
  in·ter·marriage
in·ter·me·di·ate
  in·ter·me·di·at·ing
  in·ter·me·di·a·tion
  in·ter·me·di·ary
  in·ter·me·di·a·tor
in·ter·mi·na·ble

in·ter·min·gle
  in·ter·min·gled
  in·ter·min·gling
in·ter·mis·sion
in·ter·mit
  in·ter·mit·ted
  in·ter·mit·ting
  in·ter·mit·tence
  in·ter·mit·ten·cy
  in·ter·mit·tent
in·ter·mix
  in·ter·mix·ture
in·tern
  in·terne
in·ter·nal
  in·ter·nal·ize
  in·ter·nal·i·za·tion
in·ter·na·tion·al
  in·ter·na·tion·al·i·ty
  in·ter·na·tion·al·ly
  in·ter·na·tion·al·ize
  in·ter·na·tion·al·ized
  in·ter·na·tion·al·iz·ing
  in·ter·na·tion·al·i·za·tion
  in·ter·na·tion·al·ism
in·tern·ee
in·tern·ist
in·tern·ment
in·ter·nun·cio
in·ter·of·fice
in·ter·pen·e·trate
  in·ter·pen·e·tra·tion
in·ter·plan·e·tary
in·ter·play
in·ter·po·late
  in·ter·po·la·tion
  in·ter·po·la·tor
in·ter·pose
  in·ter·posed
  in·ter·pos·ing
  in·ter·po·si·tion
in·ter·pret
  in·ter·pret·er
  in·ter·pre·tive
  in·ter·pre·ta·tion
in·ter·ra·cial
in·ter·re·late
  in·ter·re·lat·ed

in·ter·re·lat·ing
in·ter·ro·gate
  in·ter·ro·gat·ed
  in·ter·ro·gat·ing
  in·ter·ro·ga·tion
  in·ter·rog·a·tive
in·ter·rupt
  in·ter·rup·tion
in·ter·scho·las·tic
in·ter·sect
  in·ter·sec·tion
in·ter·space
in·ter·sperse
  in·er·spersed
  in·ter·spers·ing
  in·ter·sper·sion
in·ter·state
in·ter·stel·lar
in·ter·tid·al
in·ter·twine
in·ter·ur·ban
in·ter·val
in·ter·vene
  in·ter·vened
  in·ter·ven·ing
  in·ter·ven·tion
in·ter·view
in·ter·weave
  in·ter·wove
  in·ter·weav·ing
  in·ter·wo·ven
in·tes·tate
in·tes·tine
  in·tes·ti·nal
in·ti·mate
  in·ti·mat·ed
  in·ti·mat·ing
  in·ti·ma·tion
in·ti·mate
  in·ti·mate·ness
  in·ti·mate·ly
in·tim·i·date
  in·tim·i·dat·ed
  in·tim·i·dat·ing
  in·tim·i·da·tion
in·to
in·tol·er·ant
  in·tol·er·a·ble

in·tol·er·ance
in·tomb
in·to·nate
  in·to·nat·ed
  in·to·nat·ing
  in·to·na·tion
in·tone
  in·toned
  in·ton·ing
in·tox·i·cate
  in·tox·i·cat·ed
  in·tox·i·cat·ing
  in·tox·i·ca·tion
in·trac·ta·ble
  in·trac·ta·bil·i·ty
in·tra·mu·ral
  in·tra·mu·ral·ly
in·tran·si·gent
  in·tran·si·gence
  in·tran·si·gen·cy
in·tran·si·tive
in·tra·state
in·tra·u·ter·ine
in·tra·ve·nous
in·trench
in·trep·id
  in·tre·pid·i·ty
in·tri·cate
  in·tri·ca·cy
  in·tri·ca·cies
in·trigue
  in·trigued
  in·tri·guing
in·trin·sic
  in·trin·si·cal·ly
in·tro·duce
  in·tro·duced
  in·tro·duc·ing
  in·tro·duc·tion
  in·tro·duc·to·ry
in·tro·spect
  in·tro·spec·tion
  in·tro·spec·tive
in·tro·ver·sion
in·tro·vert
in·trude
  in·trud·ed
  in·trud·ing

in·trud·er
in·tru·sion
in·tu·i·tion
  in·tu·i·tive
in·tu·mes·cent
  in·tu·mes·cence
in·un·date
  in·un·dat·ed
  in·un·dat·ing
  in·un·da·tion
in·ure
  in·ured
  in·ur·ing
in·vade
  in·vad·ed
  in·vad·ing
  in·vad·er
in·va·lid
  in·va·lid·ism
in·val·id
in·val·u·a·ble
in·var·i·a·ble
  in·var·i·a·bil·i·ty
in·var·i·ant
in·va·sion
in·vec·tive
in·veigh
  in·vei·gle
in·vent
  in·ven·tion
  in·ven·tive
  in·ven·tor
in·ven·to·ry
  in·ven·to·ries
  in·ven·to·ried
  in·ven·to·ry·ing
in·verse
  in·ver·sion
  in·vert·ed
  in·vert
in·ver·te·brate
in·vest
  in·ves·tor
in·ves·ti·gate
  in·ves·ti·gat·ed
  in·ves·ti·gat·ing
  in·ves·ti·ga·tion
in·ves·ti·ture

in·vest·ment
in·vet·er·ate
in·vid·i·ous
in·vig·or·ate
  in·vig·or·at·ed
  in·vig·or·at·ing
  in·vig·or·a·tion
in·vin·ci·ble
  in·vin·ci·bil·i·ty
  in·vin·ci·bly
in·vi·o·la·ble
  in·vi·o·la·bil·i·ty
  in·vi·o·la·bly
in·vi·o·late
in·vis·i·ble
  in·vis·i·bil·i·ty
in·vite
  in·vit·ed
  in·vit·ing
  in·vi·ta·tion
in·vo·ca·tion
in·voice
in·voke
  in·voked
  in·vok·ing
in·vol·un·tary
  in·vol·un·tar·i·ly
in·vo·lute
  in·vo·lu·tion
in·volve
  in·volved
  in·volv·ing
  in·volve·ment
in·vul·ner·a·ble
  in·vul·ner·a·bil·i·ty
in·ward
  in·ward·ly
in·weave
  in·wove
  in·weaved
  in·wov·en
  in·weav·ing
in·wrought
io·dine
ion
  ion·ic
  ion·ize
  ion·i·za·tion

ion·o·sphere
io·ta
ip·so fac·to
iras·ci·ble
  iras·ci·bil·i·ty
irate
Ire·land
ir·i·des·cent
  ir·i·des·cence
iris
  iris·es
Irish·man
irk·some
iron
  iron·er
iron·clad
iron·hand·ed
iron·heart·ed
iron·ic
  iron·i·cal
iron·stone
iron·ware
iron·work
ir·ra·di·ate
  ir·ra·di·at·ed
  ir·ra·di·at·ing
  ir·ra·di·a·tion
ir·rad·i·ca·ble
ir·ra·tion·al
  ir·ra·tion·al·i·ty
ir·re·claim·a·ble
ir·rec·on·cil·a·ble
  ir·rec·on·cil·a·bil·i·ty
ir·re·cov·er·a·ble
ir·re·deem·a·ble
ir·re·duc·i·ble
ir·ref·u·ta·ble
ir·reg·u·lar
  ir·reg·u·lar·i·ty
ir·rel·e·vant
  ir·rel·e·vance
  ir·rel·e·van·cy
ir·re·li·gious
ir·re·me·di·a·ble
ir·re·mis·si·ble
ir·re·mov·a·ble
ir·rep·a·ra·ble
ir·re·place·a·ble

irre·press·i·ble
irre·proach·a·ble
irre·sist·i·ble
   ir·re·sist·i·bil·i·ty
irres·o·lute
   ir·res·o·lu·tion
ir·re·spec·tive
ir·re·spon·si·ble
   ir·re·spon·si·bil·i·ty
ir·re·spon·sive
ir·re·triev·a·ble
   ir·re·triev·a·bil·i·ty
ir·rev·er·ence
   ir·rev·er·ent
ir·re·vers·i·ble
   ir·re·vers·i·bil·i·ty
ir·rev·o·ca·ble
   ir·rev·o·ca·bil·i·ty
ir·ri·gate
   ir·ri·gat·ed
   ir·ri·gat·ing
   ir·ri·ga·tion
ir·ri·ta·ble
   ir·ri·ta·bil·i·ty
ir·ri·tant
ir·ri·tate
   ir·ri·tat·ed
   ir·ri·tat·ing
   ir·ri·ta·tion
ir·rupt
Is·lam
   Is·lam·ic
   Is·lam·ism
is·land
isle
   is·let
iso·bar
iso·late
   iso·lat·ed
   iso·lat·ing
   iso·la·tion
iso·la·tion·ist
iso·met·ric
   iso·met·ri·cal
isos·ce·les
iso·therm
   iso·ther·mal
iso·ton·ic

iso·tope
   iso·top·ic
Is·ra·el
   Is·rae·li
is·sue
   is·sued
   is·su·ing
   is·su·ance
isth·mus
Ital·ian
ital·ic
   ital·i·cize
   ital·i·cized
   ital·i·ciz·ing
   ital·i·ci·za·tion
It·a·ly
itch
   itch·i·ness
   itchy
item
   item·ize
   item·ized
   item·iz·ing
it·er·ate
   it·er·a·tion
itin·er·ant
   itin·er·ate
   itin·er·a·tion
   itin·er·ary
   itin·er·ar·ies
ivo·ry
ivy
   ivied
   ivies

J

jab
   jabbed
   jab·bing
jab·ber
jack·al
jack·ass
jack·et
   jack·et·ed
jack·ham·mer
jack-in-the-box
jack·knife

jack-of-all-trades
jack-o'-lan·tern
jack rab·bit
jade
   jad·ed
   jad·ing
jag
   jagged
   jag·ging
jag·uar
jail·bird
jail·break
ja·lopy
   ja·lop·ies
jal·ou·sie
jam
   jammed
   jam·ming
   jam·mer
jamb
jam·bo·ree
jan·gle
   jan·gled
   jan·gling
jan·i·tor
   jan·i·to·ri·al
Jan·u·ary
Ja·pan
Jap·a·nese
jar
   jarred
   jar·ring
   jar·ful
jar·di·niere
jar·gon
jas·mine
jaun·dice
   jaun·diced
jaunt
jaun·ty
   jaun·ti·ly
   jaun·ti·ness
jave·lin
jaw·bone
jaw·break·er
jay·walk
jazz
jazzy

jazz·i·ly
jazz·i·ness
jeal·ous
  jeal·ousy
  jeal·ous·ies
jeer·er
Jef·fer·son
Je·ho·vah
Jek·yll
jel·li·fy
jel·ly
jel·ly·fish
jen·ny
jeop·ar·dy
  jeop·ar·dize
  jeop·ar·dized
  jeop·ar·diz·ing
jerk
  jerk·i·ly
  jerk·i·ness
  jerky
jer·kin
jer·ry·build
  jer·ry·built
jer·sey
Je·ru·sa·lem
jes·sa·mine
jest·er
Jes·u·it
Je·sus
jet
  jet·ted
  jet·ting
jet·lin·er
jet-pro·pelled
jet·sam
jet·ti·son
jet·ty
jew·el
jew·el·er
jew·el·ry
Jew·ish
Jew·ry
jew's-harp
Jez·e·bel
jibe
jif·fy
jig

jigged
jig·ging
jig·gle
  jig·gled
  jig·gling
  jig·gly
jilt·er
Jim Crow·ism
jim-dan·dy
jim·my
  jim·mied
  jim·my·ing
jin·gle
  jin·gled
  jin·gling
jin·go·ism
jin·rik·i·sha
jinx
jit·ney
jit·ter
  jit·ters
  jit·tery
jit·ter·bug
  jit·ter·bug·ging
job
  jobbed
  job·bing
job·ber
job·hold·er
jock·ey
  jock·ey·ing
jock·strap
jo·cose
jo·cos·i·ty
joc·u·lar
  joc·u·lar·i·ty
joc·und
  jo·cun·di·ty
jodh·pur
jog
  jogged
  jog·ging
  jog·ger
jog·gle
  jog·gled
  jog·gling
join·er
joint

joint·ed
joint·ly
joist
joke
  joked
  jok·ing
  joke·ster
jol·ly
jolt
  jolt·ing·ly
  jolty
jon·quil
jos·tle
  jos·tled
  jos·tling
jot
  jot·ted
  jot·ting
joule
jour·nal·ism
jour·nal·ist
  jour·nal·is·tic
jour·ney
joust
jo·vi·al
  jo·vi·al·i·ty
jowl
joy·ful
joy·less
joy·ous
joy·ride
ju·bi·lant
  ju·bi·lance
  ju·bi·la·tion
ju·bi·lee
Ju·da·ism
  Ju·da·ic
  Ju·da·i·cal
judge
  judged
  judg·ing
judg·ment
ju·di·cial
ju·di·ci·ary
ju·di·cious
ju·do
jug·ger·naut
jug·gle

jug·gled
jug·gling
jug·gler
jug·u·lar
juice
juic·er
juicy
　juic·i·er
　juic·i·ness
ju·jit·su
ju·jube
juke·box
ju·lep
ju·li·enne
jum·ble
　jum·bled
　jum·bling
jum·bo
jump
　jump·ing
　jump·i·ness
　jumpy
junc·tion
junc·ture
jun·gle
jun·ior
ju·ni·per
junk
　junky
jun·ket
junk·ie
jun·ta
Ju·pi·ter
ju·ris·dic·tion
　ju·ris·dic·tion·al
ju·ris·pru·dence
　ju·ris·pru·dent
　ju·ris·pru·den·tial
ju·rist
ju·ror
ju·ry
　ju·ries
just
　just·ness
jus·tice
　jus·tice·less
jus·ti·fy
　jus·ti·fied

jus·ti·fy·ing
jus·ti·fi·a·ble
jus·ti·fi·ca·to·ry
jus·ti·fi·ca·tion
jut
　jut·ted
　jut·ting
jute
ju·ve·nes·cent
ju·ve·nile
　ju·ve·nil·i·ty
jux·ta·pose
　jux·ta·posed
　jux·ta·pos·ing
　jux·ta·po·si·tion

K

ka·bob
kai·ser
ka·lei·do·scope
　ka·lei·do·scop·ic
ka·mi·ka·ze
kan·ga·roo
ka·o·lin
　ka·o·line
ka·pok
ka·put
kar·a·kul
karat
ka·ra·te
kar·ma
ka·ty·did
kay·ak
kayo
kedge
　kedged
　kedg·ing
keel·haul
keel·son
keen·ly
　keen·ness
keep
　kept
　keep·ing
keep·sake
keg·ler
kelp

ken·nel
　ken·neled
ke·no
ker·a·tin
ker·chief
ker·nel
ker·o·sene
kes·trel
ketch·up
ke·tone
ket·tle·drum
key
　keyed
key·board
key·hole
　key·note
　key·not·ing
key·stone
khaki
kha·lif
khan
kib·butz
　kib·but·zim
kib·itz·er
kick·back
kick·off
kid
　kid·dish
　kid·dish·ness
　kid·ded
　kid·ding
kid·nap
　kid·naped
　kid·napped
　kid·nap·ing
　kid·nap·ping
　kid·nap·er
　kid·nap·per
kid·ney
kill·deer
kill·ing
kill·joy
kiln
kilo
kil·o·cy·cle
kil·o·gram
kil·o·li·ter
kil·o·me·ter

kil·o·volt
kil·o·watt
kilt
kilt·er
ki·mo·no
kin·der·gar·ten
kind·heart·ed
kin·dle
kin·dled
kin·dling
kind·ly
kind·li·est
kind·li·ness
kin·dred
kin·e·mat·ics
kin·e·mat·ic
kin·e·mat·i·cal
kin·e·scope
ki·net·ic
ki·net·ics
kin·folk
king·bolt
king·dom
king·fish·er
king·ly
king·li·ness
king·pin
king-size
king-sized
kinky
kink·i·est
kins·folk
kin·ship
kins·man
kins·wom·an
ki·osk
kip·per
kis·met
kiss·a·ble
kitch·en
kitch·en·ette
kitch·en·ware
kite
kit·ed
kit·ing
kit·ten
kit·ten·ish
kit·ty

kit·ties
kit·ty-cor·ner
ki·wi
klatch
klep·to·ma·nia
klep·to·ma·ni·ac
knack
knap·sack
knave
knav·ish
knead
knee
kneed
knee·ing
knee·cap
knee·deep
kneel
knelt
kneeled
kneel·ing
knell
knick·ers
knick·er·bock·ers
knick·knack
knife
knives
knifed
knif·ing
knight
knight·hood
knight·ly
knight-er·rant
knit
knit·ted
knit·ting
knob
knobbed
knob·by
knob·bi·er
knock
knock·down
knock·er
knock-kneed
knock·out
knoll
knot
knot·ted
knot·ting

knot·less
knot·ty
knot·hole
knout
know
knew
known
know·ing
know·a·ble
know·ing·ly
know-how
knowl·edge
knowl·edge·a·ble
know-noth·ing
knuck·le
knuck·led
knuck·ling
knurl
knurled
knurly
ko·a·la
kohl·ra·bi
ko·la
ko·lin·sky
kook
kooky
kook·i·er
kook·a·bur·ra
Ko·ran
Ko·rea
ko·sher
Krem·lin
krim·mer
Krish·na
kryp·ton
Ku·blai Khan
ku·dos
ku·miss
küm·mel
kum·mer·bund
kum·quat

L

la·bel
la·beled
la·bel·ing
la·bel·er

la·bi·al
la·bi·ate
la·bile
la·bi·o·den·tal
la·bi·um
la·bor
  la·bor·er
lab·o·ra·to·ry
la·bored
la·bo·ri·ous
  la·bo·ri·ous·ly
la·bor-sav·ing
la·bur·num
lab·y·rinth
  lab·y·rin·thine
  lab·y·rin·thi·an
lace
  laced
  lac·ing
  lacy
  lac·i·est
lac·er·ate
  lac·er·at·ed
  lac·er·at·ing
  lac·er·a·tion
lach·ry·mal
lach·ry·mose
  lach·ry·mose·ly
lack·a·dai·si·cal
lack·ey
lack·lus·ter
la·con·ic
  la·con·i·cal·ly
lac·quer
la·crosse
lac·tate
  lac·tat·ed
  lac·tat·ing
  lac·ta·tion
lac·te·al
lac·tic
lac·tose
la·cu·na
la·cus·trine
lad·der
lad·die
lade
  lad·ed

lad·en
lad·ing
la·dle
  la·dled
  la·dling
la·dy·bug
la·dy·fin·ger
la·dy-in-wait·ing
la·dy-kil·ler
la·dy's-slip·per
lag
  lagged
  lag·ging
  lag·gard
la·ger
la·gniappe
la·goon
La Guar·dia
lair
lais·sez faire
la·i·ty
lake·side
lal·la·tion
lam
  lammed
  lam·ming
la·ma
  la·ma·sery
La·ma·ism
  La·ma·ist
lam·baste
  lam·bast·ed
  lam·bast·ing
lam·bent
  lam·bent·ly
lam·bre·quin
lamb·skin
lame
  lamed
  lam·ing
  lame·ness
la·mé
la·ment
  lam·en·ta·ble
  lam·en·ta·bly
  lam·en·ta·tion
lam·i·nate
  lam·i·nat·ed

lam·i·nat·ing
lam·i·na·tion
lamp·black
lam·poon
lam·prey
lance
  lanced
  lanc·ing
lan·ce·o·late
lan·cet
lan·dau
land·ed
land·fall
land·hold·er
land·ing
land·la·dy
land·locked
land·lord
land·lub·ber
land·mark
land·own·er
land·scape
  land·scap·ing
  land·scap·er
land·slide
land·ward
lang·syne
lan·guage
lan·guid
lan·guish
  lan·guish·ing
lan·guor
  lan·guor·ous
lank·ness
lanky
  lank·i·ness
lan·o·lin
lan·tern
lan·yard
lap
  lapped
  lap·ping
la·pel
lap·ful
lap·i·dary
lap·in
lap·is laz·u·li
lap·pet

lapse
  lapsed
  laps·ing
lar·board
lar·ce·ny
  lar·ce·nous
larch
lar·der
large
  larg·er
  larg·est
  large·ness
  large·ly
large-scale
lar·gess
lar·ghet·to
lar·go
lar·i·at
lark·spur
lar·va
lar·ynx
  la·ryn·ge·al
  la·ryn·gi·tis
las·civ·i·ous
  las·civ·i·ous·ly
la·ser
lash
  lash·ing
las·si·tude
las·so
last·ing
last·ly
latch·key
late
  lat·er
  lat·est
  late·ness
  late·ly
la·teen
la·tent
  la·ten·cy
  la·tent·ly
lat·er·al
  lat·er·al·ly
la·tex
lath
  lath·ing
lathe

lath·er
  lath·ery
Lat·in-A·mer·i·can
lat·i·tude
  lat·i·tu·di·nal
  lat·i·tu·di·nar·i·an
la·trine
lat·ter
Lat·ter-day Saint
lat·tice
  lat·ticed
  lat·tic·ing
lat·tice·work
laud·a·ble
  laud·a·bly
lau·da·num
laud·a·to·ry
  laud·a·tive
laugh
  laugh·ing
  laugh·a·ble
  laugh·a·bly
  laugh·ter
launch
  launch·er
laun·der
  laun·dress
Laun·dro·mat
laun·dry
lau·re·ate
lau·rel
la·va
lav·a·liere
lav·a·to·ry
  lav·a·to·ries
lav·en·der
lav·ish
  lav·ish·ness
law-a·bid·ing
law·break·er
law·ful
  law·ful·ly
  law·ful·ness
law·less
  law·less·ness
law·mak·er
  law·mak·ing
lawn

law·suit
law·yer
lax
  lax·i·ty
  lax·ness
lax·a·tive
lay
  laid
  laying
lay·er
lay·ette
lay·man
lay·off
lay·out
lay·o·ver
la·zy
  la·zi·est
  la·zi·ly
  la·zi·ness
leach
lead
  led
  lead·ing
lead·en
lead·er
  lead·er·ship
leaf·age
leaf·less
leaf·let
leaf·stalk
leafy
  leaf·i·ness
league
leak
  leak·age
  leak·i·ness
  leaky
lean
  lean·ness
  lean·ing
  lean-to
leap
  leaped
  leapt
  leap·ing
learn
  learned
  learnt

113

learn·ing
learn·er
lease
  leased
  leas·ing
leash
least·wise
  least·ways
leath·er
leath·er·neck
leath·ery
leave
  left
  leav·ing
leav·en
leaves
leave-tak·ing
Leb·a·nese
Leb·a·non
lech·er
  lech·er·ous
  lech·ery
lec·tern
lec·ture
  lec·tured
  lec·tur·ing
  lec·tur·er
ledge
ledg·er
leech
leek
leer·ing·ly
leery
lee·ward
lee·way
left-hand·ed
left·ist
left·o·ver
left-wing
leg
  legged
  leg·ging
leg·a·cy
  leg·a·cies
le·gal
  le·gal·ly
le·gal·ism
  le·gal·ist

le·gal·is·tic
le·gal·i·ty
  le·gal·i·ties
le·gal·ize
  le·gal·ized
  le·gal·iz·ing
  le·gal·i·za·tion
leg·ate
leg·a·tee
le·ga·tion
le·ga·to
leg·end
  leg·end·ary
leg·er·de·main
leg·gy
leg·horn
leg·i·ble
  leg·i·bil·i·ty
  leg·i·bly
le·gion
  le·gion·ary
  le·gion·naire
leg·is·late
  leg·is·lat·ed
  leg·is·lat·ing
  leg·is·la·tive
  leg·is·la·tor
  leg·is·la·tion
  leg·is·la·ture
le·git·i·mate
  le·git·i·mat·ed
  le·git·i·mat·ing
  le·git·i·ma·cy
  le·git·i·mate·ly
le·git·i·mize
  le·git·i·mized
  le·git·i·miz·ing
leg·ume
  le·gu·mi·nous
lei
  leis
lei·sure
lei·sure·ly
  lei·sure·li·ness
leit·mo·tif
lem·ming
lem·on
lem·on·ade

le·mur
lend
lent
lend·ing
length
  length·en
length·wise
lengthy
  length·i·ly
  length·i·ness
le·ni·ent
  le·ni·ence
  le·ni·en·cy
len·i·tive
len·i·ty
lens
Lent·en
len·til
le·o·nine
leop·ard
le·o·tard
lep·er
  lep·ro·sy
  lep·rous
lep·re·chaun
les·bi·an
  les·bi·an·ism
le·sion
les·see
less·en
less·er
les·son
les·sor
least
let
  let·ting
le·thal
  le·thal·ly
leth·ar·gy
  le·thar·gic
  le·thar·gi·cal
let·ter
  let·ter·er
  let·tered
  let·ter·head
  let·ter·ing
  let·ter-per·fect
  let·ter·press

let·tuce
leu·ke·mia
leu·ko·cyte
lev·ee
lev·el
  lev·eled
  lev·el·ing
  lev·el·ness
lev·el-head·ed
lev·er
  lev·er·age
le·vi·a·than
lev·i·tate
  lev·i·tat·ed
  lev·i·tat·ing
  lev·i·ta·tion
lev·i·ty
levy
  lev·ies
lewd
  lewd·ly
  lewd·ness
lex·i·cog·ra·phy
  lex·i·cog·ra·pher
  lex·i·co·graph·ic
lex·i·con
li·a·bil·i·ty
  li·a·bil·i·ties
li·a·ble
li·ai·son
li·ar
li·ba·tion
li·bel
  li·beled
  li·bel·ing
  li·bel·er
  li·bel·ous
lib·er·al
  lib·er·al·ly
  lib·er·al·i·ty
  lib·er·al·ism
lib·er·al·ize
  lib·er·al·ized
  lib·er·al·iz·ing
  lib·er·al·i·za·tion
lib·er·ate
  lb·er·at·ed
  lib·er·at·ing

lib·er·a·tion
lib·er·a·tor
lib·er·tine
lib·er·tin·ism
lib·er·ty
  lib·er·ties
li·bid·i·nous
  li·bid·i·nous·ness
li·bi·do
  li·bid·in·al
li·brary
  li·brar·ies
  li·brar·i·an
li·bret·to
lice
  louse
li·cense
  li·censed
  li·cens·ing
  li·cen·see
  li·cens·er
li·cen·ti·ate
  li·cen·tious·ness
li·chen
lic·it
lick·e·ty-split
lic·o·rice
lid·ded
lie
  lay
  lain
  lay·ing
lie
  lied
  ly·ing
Lieb·frau·milch
Lie·der·kranz
lien
lieu
lieu·ten·ant
  lieu·ten·an·cy
life·blood
life·boat
life·guard
life·less
life·like
life·line
life·sav·er

life-size
life-style
life·time
life·work
lift-off
lig·a·ment
lig·a·ture
light·en
light·er
light-fin·gered
light·foot·ed
light-head·ed
light·heart·ed
light·house
light·ing
light·ly
light-mind·ed
light·ning
light·weight
light-year
lig·nite
like
  liked
  lik·ing
  like·a·ble
like·li·hood
like·ly
  like·li·est
lik·en
like·ness
like·wise
li·lac
lilt·ing
lily
limb
lim·ber
lim·bo
Lim·burg·er
lime
  limed
  lim·ing
  limy
lime·light
lim·er·ick
lime·stone
lim·it
  lim·it·a·ble
  lim·i·ta·tive

lim·i·ta·tion
lim·it·ed
lim·it·less
lim·ou·sine
limp
  limp·ing·ly
  limp·ly
lim·pet
lim·pid
  lim·pid·ness
Lin·coln
lin·den
line
  lined
  lin·ing
  lin·age
  lin·er
lin·e·age
  lin·e·al
lin·e·a·ment
lin·e·ar
line·back·er
line·man
lin·en
lin·ger
  lin·ger·ing·ly
lin·ge·rie
lin·go
lin·gua fran·ca
lin·gual
  lin·guist
  lin·guis·tics
  lin·guis·tic
lin·i·ment
link
  linked
  link·er
link·age
lin·net
li·no·le·um
lin·seed
lint
  linty
  lint·i·er
lin·tel
li·on
  li·on·ess
  li·on·heart·ed

li·on·ize
li·on·ized
li·on·iz·ing
li·on·i·za·tion
lip·py
lip·stick
liq·ue·fy
  liq·ue·fied
  liq·ue·fy·ing
  liq·ue·fac·tion
  liq·ue·fi·a·ble
li·queur
liq·uid
  li·quid·i·ty
  liq·uid·ness
liq·ui·date
  liq·ui·dat·ed
  liq·ui·dat·ing
  liq·ui·da·tion
  liq·ui·da·tor
liq·uor
lisle
lisp
lis·some
  lis·some·ness
list
  list·ing
lis·ten
  lis·ten·er
list·less
lit·a·ny
  lit·a·nies
li·tchi
li·ter
lit·er·al
  lit·er·al·i·ty
  lit·er·al·ly
  lit·er·al·ism
lit·er·ary
  lit·er·ari·ness
lit·er·ate
  lit·er·a·cy
lit·e·ra·ti
lit·er·a·ture
lithe
  lithe·some
li·thog·ra·phy
  li·thog·ra·pher

lith·o·graph·ic
lit·i·gate
  lit·i·gat·ed
  lit·i·gat·ing
  lit·i·ga·tion
lit·mus
lit·ter
  lit·ter·bug
lit·tle
lit·to·ral
lit·ur·gy
  lit·ur·gist
  li·tur·gic
  li·tur·gi·cal
liv·a·ble
  live·a·ble
live·li·hood
live·ly
  live·li·est
  live·li·ness
liv·en
liv·er
liv·er·wurst
liv·ery
  liv·er·ied
live·stock
liv·id
  li·vid·i·ty
  liv·id·ly
liv·ing
liz·ard
lla·ma
lla·no
load
  load·ed
loaf
  loaves
loamy
loath
loathe
  loathed
  loath·ing
  loath·some
lob
  lobbed
  lob·bing
lob·by
  lob·bies

lob·by·ist
lobe
  lo·bar
  lobed
lob·ster
lo·cal
  lo·cal·ly
lo·cale
  lo·cal·i·ty
  lo·cal·i·ties
lo·cal·ize
  lo·cal·ized
  lo·cal·iz·ing
  lo·cal·i·za·tion
lo·cate
  lo·cat·ed
  lo·cat·ing
  lo·ca·tion
  lo·ca·tor
lock·a·ble
lock·er
lock·et
lock·jaw
lock·out
lock·smith
lock·up
lo·co·mo·tion
lo·co·mo·tive
lo·cus
  lo·ci
lo·cust
lo·cu·tion
lode·star
lode·stone
lodge
  lodged
  lodg·ing
  lodg·er
  lodg·ment
lofty
  loft·i·est
  loft·i·ly
  loft·i·ness
lo·gan·ber·ry
log·a·rithm
  log·a·rith·mic
loge
log·ger

log·ger·head
log·ic
  lo·gi·cian
log·i·cal
  log·i·cal·ly
  log·i·cal·ness
lo·gis·tics
  lo·gis·tic
  lo·gis·ti·cal
log·roll·ing
lo·gy
loin·cloth
loi·ter
  loi·ter·er
lone·ly
lone·li·ness
  lone·some
lon·er
lon·gev·i·ty
long·hair
long·hand
long·ing
lon·gi·tude
  lon·gi·tu·di·nal
long-lived
long-play·ing
long-range
long·shore·man
long-suf·fer·ing
long-term
long-wind·ed
look·out
loony
  loon·ies
  loon·i·est
  loon·i·ness
loop·hole
loose
  loosed
  loos·ing
  loos·er
  loos·est
  loose·ness
  loos·en
loot·er
lop
  lopped
  lop·ping

lope
  loped
  lop·ing
  lop·er
lop·sid·ed
lo·qua·cious
  lo·qua·cious·ness
  lo·quac·i·ty
lord·ly
  lord·li·est
  lord·li·ness
lor·gnette
lor·ry
lose
  lost
  los·ing
  los·a·ble
  los·er
lot
  lot·ted
  lot·ting
lo·tion
lot·tery
lo·tus
loud
  loud·ness
loud-mouthed
loud·speak·er
lounge
  lounged
  loung·ing
lousy
  lous·i·ness
lout
  lout·ish·ness
lou·ver
love
  loved
  lov·ing
  lov·a·ble
  lov·a·bil·i·ty
  lov·a·ble·ness
  lov·a·bly
  love·less
love·ly
  love·li·er
  love·li·est
lov·er

lov·ing
  lov·ing·ness
low·born
low·boy
low·brow
low-down
low·er
low·er-case
low·er·ing
low·keyed
low·land
low-lev·el
low·ly
  low·li·est
  low·li·ness
low-mind·ed
low-pres·sure
low-ten·sion
loy·al
  loy·al·ist
  loy·al·ly
  loy·al·ty
  loy·al·ties
loz·enge
lu·au
lub·ber
lu·bri·cate
  lu·bri·cat·ed
  lu·bri·cat·ing
  lu·bri·cant
  lu·bri·ca·tion
  lu·bri·ca·tor
lu·bri·cious
lu·cid
  lu·cid·i·ty
  lu·cid·ness
luck
  luck·i·est
  luck·i·ly
  luck·i·ness
  lucky
lu·cra·tive
  lu·cra·tive·ness
lu·cre
lu·cu·brate
  lu·cu·bra·tion
lu·di·crous
  lu·di·crous·ness

lug
  lugged
  lug·ging
lug·gage
lug·ger
lu·gu·bri·ous
luke·warm
lull·a·by
  lull·a·bies
lum·ba·go
lum·bar
lum·ber
  lum·ber·ing
  lum·ber·jack
lu·men
lu·mi·nary
  lu·mi·naries
lu·mi·nous
  lu·mi·nous·ness
lu·mi·nes·cence
  lu·mi·nes·cent
lum·mox
lumpy
  lump·i·est
  lump·i·ness
lu·nar
lu·nate
lu·na·tic
  lu·na·cy
  lu·na·cies
lunch
  lunch·eon
lunge
  lunged
  lung·ing
lunk·head
lu·pine
lurch
lure
  lured
  lur·ing
lu·rid
  lu·rid·ly
  lu·rid·ness
lurk
  lurk·er
lus·cious
  lus·cious·ly

  lus·cious·ness
lush
  lush·ness
lust
  lust·ful·ness
lus·ter
  lus·ter·less
  lus·trous
lusty
  lust·i·ly
  lust·i·ness
Lu·ther·an
lux·u·ri·ate
  lux·u·ri·at·ed
  lux·u·ri·at·ing
  lux·u·ri·a·tion
lux·u·ry
  lux·u·ries
  lux·u·ri·ous
  lux·u·ri·ant
  lux·u·ri·ance
ly·ce·um
ly·ing
lymph
  lym·phat·ic
lynch
  lynch·ing
lynx
lyre
lyr·ic
  lyr·i·cal
  lyr·i·cism
  lyr·i·cist

M

ma·ca·bre
mac·ad·am
  mac·ad·am·ize
ma·caque
mac·a·ro·ni
mac·a·roon
ma·caw
mace
  maced
  mac·ing
mac·er·ate
  mac·er·at·ed

mac·er·at·ing
mac·er·a·tion
Mach
ma·chete
Mach·i·a·vel·li·an
mach·i·nate
mach·i·nat·ed
mach·i·nat·ing
mach·i·na·tion
ma·chine
ma·chined
ma·chin·ing
ma·chin·ery
ma·chin·ist
mack·er·el
mack·i·naw
mack·in·tosh
mac·ra·mé
mac·ro·cosm
ma·cron
mac·ro·scop·ic
mad
mad·den
mad·dest
mad·ly
mad·ness
mad·am
mad·ame
mes·dames
Ma·dei·ra
made·moi·selle
Ma·don·na
mad·ras
mad·ri·gal
mael·strom
maes·tro
Ma·fia
mag·a·zine
ma·gen·ta
mag·got
mag·goty
mag·ic
mag·i·cal
ma·gi·cian
mag·is·trate
mag·is·te·ri·al
mag·is·tra·cy
mag·is·tra·cies

mag·ma
Mag·na Car·ta
mag·nan·i·mous
mag·na·nim·i·ty
mag·nate
mag·ne·sia
mag·ne·si·um
mag·net
mag·net·ic
mag·net·i·cal·ly
mag·net·ism
mag·net·ize
mag·net·ized
mag·net·iz·ing
mag·ne·to
mag·ne·tom·e·ter
mag·nif·i·cent
mag·nif·i·cence
mag·nif·i·cent·ly
mag·ni·fy
mag·ni·fied
mag·ni·fy·ing
mag·ni·fi·ca·tion
mag·ni·fi·er
mag·nil·o·quent
mag·ni·tude
mag·no·lia
mag·num
mag·pie
ma·ha·ra·jah
ma·ha·ra·ni
ma·hat·ma
mah-jongg
ma·hog·a·ny
ma·hout
maid·en
maid·en·hair
maid·en·head
mail·a·ble
mail·box
mail·man
maim
main·land
main·ly
main·mast
main·sail
main·spring
main·stream

main·tain
main·tain·a·ble
main·te·nance
maî·tre d'hô·tel
maize
ma·jes·tic
ma·jes·ti·cal
maj·es·ty
ma·jol·i·ca
ma·jor
ma·jor-do·mo
ma·jor-do·mos
ma·jor·i·ty
ma·jor·i·ties
make
mak·a·ble
ma·ker
mak·ing
make-be·lieve
make·shift
make-up
mal·a·dapt·ed
mal·ad·ap·ta·tion
mal·ad·just·ment
mal·ad·just·ed
mal·ad·min·is·ter
mal·ad·min·is·tra·tion
mal·a·droit
mal·a·droit·ness
mal·a·dy
mal·a·dies
ma·laise
mal·a·prop
mal·a·prop·ism
ma·lar·ia
ma·lar·i·al
ma·lar·key
mal·con·tent
mal de mer
mal·e·dic·tion
mal·e·dic·to·ry
mal·e·fac·tion
mal·e·fac·tor
ma·lef·ic
ma·lef·i·cent
ma·lev·o·lent
ma·lev·o·lence
ma·lev·o·lent·ly

mal·fea·sance
mal·fea·sant
mal·for·ma·tion
mal·formed
mal·func·tion
mal·ice
ma·li·cious
ma·li·cious·ly
ma·lign
ma·lign·ly
ma·lig·nant
ma·lig·nan·cy
ma·lig·nan·cies
ma·lig·nant·ly
ma·lin·ger
ma·lin·ger·er
mal·lard
mal·le·a·ble
mal·le·a·bil·i·ty
mal·le·a·ble·ness
mal·let
mal·low
mal·nour·ished
mal·nu·tri·tion
mal·oc·clu·sion
mal·o·dor
mal·o·dor·ous
mal·prac·tice
mal·prac·ti·tion·er
malt
malty
mal·tose
mal·treat
mal·treat·ment
mam·bo
mam·ma
ma·ma
mam·mal
mam·ma·li·an
mam·ma·ry
mam·ma·ries
mam·mon
mam·moth
mam·my
man
manned
man·ning
man·a·cle

man·a·cled
man·a·cling
man·age
man·aged
man·ag·ing
man·age·a·ble
man·age·a·bil·i·ty
man·age·a·ble·ness
man·age·a·bly
man·age·ment
man·ag·er
man·ag·er·ship
man·a·ge·ri·al
ma·ña·na
man·a·tee
man·da·mus
man·da·rin
man·date
man·dat·ed
man·dat·ing
man·da·to·ry
man·da·to·ri·ly
man·di·ble
man·do·lin
man·drake
man·drel
man·drill
man-eat·er
man-eat·ing
ma·nege
ma·neu·ver
ma·neu·ver·a·bil·i·ty
ma·neu·ver·a·ble
man·ful
man·ful·ly
man·ga·nese
mange
man·gy
man·gi·ness
man·ger
man·gle
man·gled
man·gling
man·go
man·grove
man·han·dle
Man·hat·tan
man·hole

man·hood
man·hour
man·hunt
ma·nia
man·ic
ma·ni·ac
ma·ni·a·cal
man·ic-de·pres·sive
man·i·cure
man·i·cured
man·i·cur·ing
man·i·cur·ist
man·i·fest
man·i·fest·ly
man·i·fes·ta·tion
man·i·fes·to
man·i·fold
man·i·kin
man·a·kin
man·ni·kin
ma·nil·la
ma·nip·u·late
ma·nip·u·lat·ed
ma·nip·u·lat·ing
ma·nip·u·la·ble
ma·nip·u·la·tion
ma·nip·u·la·tive
ma·nip·u·la·tor
ma·nip·u·la·to·ry
man·kind
man·like
man·ly
man·li·er
man·li·ness
man-made
man·na
manned
man·ne·quin
man·ner
man·nered
man·ner·ism
man·ner·ly
man·nish
man-of-war
men-of-war
ma·nom·e·ter
man·or
ma·no·ri·al

man·pow·er
man·sard
man·sion
man·sized
man·slaugh·ter
man·slay·er
man·tel
  man·tle
man·til·la
man·tis
man·tle
man·u·al
  man·u·al·ly
man·u·fac·ture
  man·u·fac·tured
  man·u·fac·tur·ing
  man·u·fac·tur·er
man·u·mis·sion
ma·nure
man·u·script
many
  more
  most
man·y-sid·ed
map
  mapped
  map·ping
ma·ple
mar
  marred
  mar·ring
ma·ra·ca
mar·a·schi·no
mar·a·thon
ma·raud
  ma·raud·er
mar·ble
  mar·bled
  mar·bling
  mar·ble·ize
mar·cel
  mar·celled
  mar·cel·ling
march·er
mar·chion·ess
mar·ga·rine
mar·ga·ri·ta
mar·gin

mar·gin·al
  mar·gin·al·ly
mar·gue·rite
mar·i·gold
ma·ri·jua·na
ma·rim·ba
ma·ri·na
mar·i·nade
mar·i·nate
  mar·i·nat·ing
ma·rine
mar·i·ner
mar·i·on·ette
mar·i·tal
mar·i·time
mar·jo·ram
marked
  mark·ed·ly
mark·er
mar·ket
  mar·ket·a·ble
  mar·ket·a·bil·i·ty
  mar·ket·ing
  mar·ket·place
mark·ing
marks·man
  marks·man·ship
mar·lin
  mar·line
mar·ma·lade
mar·mo·set
mar·mot
ma·roon
mar·que·try
mar·quis
  mar·quess
  mar·quise
  mar·qui·sette
mar·riage
  mar·riage·a·ble
mar·row
  mar·row·y
  mar·row·bone
mar·ry
  mar·ried
  mar·ry·ing
mar·shal
  mar·shaled

mar·shal·ing
marsh·mal·low
marshy
  marsh·i·ness
mar·su·pi·al
mar·tial
Mar·tian
mar·ten
mar·tin
mar·ti·ni
mar·tyr
  mar·tyr·dom
mar·vel
  mar·veled
  mar·vel·ing
  mar·vel·ous
Marx·ism
  Marx·ist
mar·zi·pan
mas·ca·ra
mas·cot
mas·cu·line
  mas·cu·lin·i·ty
  mas·cu·lin·ize
mask
  masked
mas·och·ism
  mas·och·ist
  mas·och·is·tic
ma·son
  ma·son·ic
ma·son·ry
masque
mas·quer·ade
  mas·quer·ad·ing
Mas·sa·chu·setts
mas·sa·cre
  mas·sa·cred
  mas·sa·cring
mas·sage
  mas·saged
  mas·sag·ing
mas·seur
  mas·seuse
mas·sive
mass-pro·duce
  mass-pro·duc·tion
mas·tec·to·my

mas·ter
mas·ter·ful
mas·ter·mind
mas·ter·piece
mas·tery
mast·head
mas·ti·cate
  mas·ti·ca·ting
  mas·ti·ca·tion
mas·tiff
mas·to·don
mas·toid
mas·tur·bate
  mas·tur·ba·tion
mat
  mat·ted
  mat·ting
mat·a·dor
match·mak·ing
mate
  mat·ed
  mat·ing
ma·te·ri·al
  ma·te·ri·al·ly
  ma·te·ri·al·ism
  ma·te·ri·al·ist
  ma·te·ri·al·is·tic
  ma·te·ri·al·is·ti·cal·ly
  ma·te·ri·al·ize
  ma·te·ri·al·ized
  ma·te·ri·al·iz·ing
  ma·te·ri·al·iza·tion
ma·te·ri·el
ma·ter·nal
  ma·ter·nal·is·tic
  ma·ter·nal·ly
ma·ter·ni·ty
math·e·mat·ics
math·e·mat·i·cal
  math·e·ma·ti·cian
mat·i·nee
ma·tri·arch
  ma·tri·ar·chal·ism
  ma·tri·ar·chy
mat·ri·cide
ma·tric·u·late
  ma·tric·u·lat·ed
  ma·tric·u·lat·ing

ma·tric·u·lant
ma·tric·u·la·tion
ma·tri·lin·e·al
mat·ri·mo·ny
  mat·ri·mo·ni·al
ma·trix
  ma·tri·ces
ma·tron
  ma·tron·ly
mat·ter
mat·ter-of-course
mat·ter-of-fact
mat·ting
mat·tress
ma·ture
  mat·u·rate
  mat·u·rat·ing
  mat·u·ra·tion
  ma·tu·ri·ty
mat·zo
maud·lin
maul
mau·so·le·um
mauve
mav·er·ick
mawk·ish
max·im
max·i·mal
max·i·mize
  max·i·mized
  max·i·miz·ing
max·i·mum
may·be
may·flow·er
may·hem
may·on·naise
may·or
  may·or·al
  may·or·al·ty
maze
  mazed
  maz·ing
  ma·zy
mead·ow
mead·ow·lark
mea·ger
  mea·ger·ness
mealy

meal·i·ness
meal·y-mouthed
mean
meant
mean·ing
mean·ing·ful
mean·ing·ful·ly
mean·ing·less
mean·ly
mean·ness
me·an·der
mean·time
mean·while
mea·sles
mea·sly
  mea·sli·est
meas·ur·a·ble
  meas·ur·a·bil·i·ty
  meas·ur·a·bly
meas·ure
  meas·ur·er
  meas·ured
  meas·ure·ment
meat
  meaty
  meat·i·ness
mec·ca
me·chan·ic
me·chan·i·cal
me·chan·ics
mech·an·ism
mech·a·nis·tic
mech·a·nize
  mech·a·nized
  mech·a·niz·ing
  mech·a·ni·za·tion
med·al
  med·aled
  med·al·ist
me·dal·lion
med·dle
  med·dled
  med·dling
  med·dler
med·dle·some
me·dia
me·di·al
me·di·an

me·di·ate
  me·di·at·ed
  me·di·at·ing
  me·di·a·tion
  me·di·a·to·ry
  me·di·a·tor
med·ic
med·i·ca·ble
Med·i·caid
med·i·cal
  med·i·cal·ly
Med·i·care
med·i·cate
  med·i·cat·ed
  med·i·cat·ing
med·i·ca·tion
me·dic·i·nal
med·i·cine
me·di·e·val
  me·di·e·val·ism
me·di·o·cre
  me·di·oc·ri·ty
med·i·tate
  med·i·tat·ed
  med·i·tat·ing
  med·i·ta·tor
  med·i·ta·tion
  med·i·ta·tive
Med·i·ter·ra·ne·an
me·di·um
  me·dia
  me·di·ums
med·ley
meet
  met
  meet·ing
meet·ing·house
meg·a·cy·cle
meg·a·lo·ma·nia
  meg·a·lo·ma·ni·ac
meg·a·lop·o·lis
meg·a·phone
meg·a·ton
meg·a·watt
mel·an·choly
  mel·an·cho·lia
  mel·an·chol·ic
  mel·an·chol·i·ness

mé·lange
mel·a·no·ma
me·lee
mel·io·rate
  mel·io·rat·ed
  mel·io·rat·ing
  mel·io·ra·ble
  mel·io·ra·tion
  mel·io·ra·tor
mel·lif·lu·ous
  mel·lif·lu·ent
mel·low
me·lo·de·on
mel·o·dra·ma
  mel·o·dra·mat·ic
  mel·o·dra·mat·i·cal·ly
mel·o·dy
  mel·o·dies
  me·lod·ic
  me·lod·i·cal·ly
  me·lo·di·ous
  me·lo·di·ous·ness
mel·on
melt
  melt·ed or mol·ten
  melt·ing
  melt·a·ble
mem·ber
  mem·ber·less
  mem·ber·ship
mem·brane
  mem·bra·nous
me·men·to
memo
mem·oir
mem·o·ra·bil·ia
mem·o·ra·ble
  mem·o·ra·bly
mem·o·ran·dum
me·mo·ri·al
  me·mo·ri·al·ly
  me·mo·ri·al·ize
  me·mo·ri·al·ized
  me·mo·ri·al·iz·ing
  me·mo·ri·al·i·za·tion
  me·mo·ri·al·ly
mem·o·rize
  mem·o·rized

mem·o·riz·ing
  mem·o·ri·za·tion
mem·o·ry
  mem·o·ries
men·ace
  men·aced
  men·ac·ing
mé·nage
me·nag·er·ie
mend
  mend·a·ble
men·da·cious
  men·dac·i·ty
men·di·cant
me·ni·al
  me·ni·al·ly
men·in·gi·tis
me·nis·cus
Men·no·nite
men·o·pause
  men·o·pau·sal
men·sal
men·ses
men·stru·al
men·stru·a·tion
  men·stru·ate
  men·stru·at·ed
  men·stru·at·ing
men·sur·a·ble
men·su·ra·tion
men·tal
  men·tal·ly
men·tal·i·ty
  men·tal·i·ties
men·thol
  men·tho·lat·ed
men·tion
  men·tion·a·ble
men·tor
menu
me·phit·ic
mer·can·tile
  mer·can·til·ism
mer·ce·nary
  mer·ce·nar·ies
mer·cer·ize
  mer·cer·ized
mer·chan·dise

merchandised
merchandising
merchandiser
merchant
mercurial
mercurochrome
mercury
mercy
mercies
merciful
mercifully
merciless
merely
meretricious
meretriciousness
merge
merged
merging
mergence
merger
meridian
meringue
merit
merited
meritedly
meritless
meritorious
mermaid
merry
merriest
merriness
merriment
merry-go-round
merrymaker
merrymaking
mesa
mescal
mesdames
mesdemoiselles
meshwork
mesmerism
mesmeric
mesmerically
mesmerize
mesmerized
mesmerizing
mesmerization
Mesozoic

mesquite
mess
messily
messiness
messy
message
messenger
Messiah
Messianic
messieurs
mestizo
metabolism
metabolic
metabolical
metabolize
metabolized
metabolizing
metal
metaled
metaling
metalize
metalized
metalizing
metallic
metalloid
metallurgy
metallurgic
metallurgical
metallurgist
metalwork
metamorphism
metamorphic
metamorphose
metamorphosed
metamorphosing
metamorphosis
metaphor
metaphoric
metaphorical
metaphysic
metaphysics
metaphysical
metatarsus
Metazoa
mete
meted
meting
meteor

meteoric
meteorite
meteoroid
meteorology
meteorological
meteorologist
meter
metre
meter-kilogram-second
methadone
methane
methanol
method
methodical
Methodist
methodize
methodology
methodological
methodologist
meticulous
meticulosity
meticulously
métier
metric
metrical
metrically
metro
metronome
metronomic
metropolis
metropolitan
mettle
mettlesome
Mexican
Mexico
mezzanine
mezzo
miasma
mica
Michelangelo
microanalysis
microbe
microbial
microbiology
microcopy
microcosm
microfiche
microfilm

124

mi·cro·gram
mi·cro·groove
mi·crom·e·ter
mi·cro·mi·cron
mi·cro·mil·li·me·ter
mi·cron
mi·cro·or·gan·ism
mi·cro·phone
mi·cro·pho·to·graph
mi·cro·read·er
mi·cro·scope
mi·cro·scop·ic
  mi·cro·scop·i·cal·ly
mi·cros·co·py
mi·cro·sec·ond
mi·cro·wave
mid·day
mid·dle
mid·dle-aged
mid·dle·man
mid·dle·weight
mid·dling
mid·dy
  mid·dies
midg·et
mid·land
mid·most
mid·night
mid·point
mid·riff
mid·sec·tion
mid·ship·man
midst
mid·sum·mer
mid·term
mid·way
mid·wife
mid·year
mien
mighty
  might·i·er
  might·i·est
  might·i·ly
  might·i·ness
mi·graine
mi·grant
mi·grate
  mi·grat·ed

mi·grat·ing
mi·gra·tion
mi·gra·tor
mi·gra·to·ry
mi·ka·do
mi·la·dy
mi·la·dies
mild
mild·ly
mild·ness
mil·dew
mil·dewy
mile·age
mil·er
mile·stone
mi·lieu
mil·i·tant
mil·i·tan·cy
mil·i·tant·ness
mil·i·ta·rism
mil·i·ta·ris·tic
mil·i·ta·ris·ti·cal·ly
mil·i·ta·rize
mil·i·ta·ri·za·tion
mil·i·tary
mil·i·tar·i·ly
mi·li·tia
milk
milk·er
milky
milk·i·ness
milk·maid
milk·man
milk·weed
mil·len·ni·um
mil·len·nia
mil·len·ni·al
mill·er
mil·let
mil·li·gram
mil·li·li·ter
mil·li·me·ter
mil·li·ner
mil·li·nery
mill·ing
mil·lion
mil·lionth
mil·lion·aire

mil·li·sec·ond
mill·pond
mime
mimed
mim·ing
mim·er
mim·ic
mim·icked
mim·ick·ing
mim·i·cal
mim·ick·er
mim·ic·ry
mim·ic·ries
mi·mo·sa
min·a·ret
mi·na·to·ry
mince
minced
minc·ing
minc·er
minc·ing·ly
mince·meat
mind·ed
mind·less
min·er
mine·field
min·er·al
min·er·al·ize
min·er·al·ized
min·er·al·iz·ing
min·er·al·i·za·tion
min·er·al·o·gy
min·er·al·og·i·cal
min·er·al·o·gist
min·e·stro·ne
mine·sweep·er
min·gle
min·gled
min·gling
min·i·a·ture
min·i·a·tur·ize
min·i·a·tur·ized
min·i·a·tur·iz·ing
min·i·a·tur·i·za·tion
min·im
min·i·mal
min·i·mal·ly
min·i·mize

min·i·mized
min·i·miz·ing
min·i·mi·za·tion
min·i·mum
min·ing
min·ion
min·is·cule
min·is·ter
min·is·te·ri·al
min·is·trant
min·is·tra·tion
min·is·try
min·is·tries
min·now
mi·nor
mi·nor·i·ty
mi·nor·i·ties
min·strel
mint·age
min·u·end
mi·nus
mi·nus·cule
min·ute
mi·nute
mi·nut·est
min·ute·man
mi·nu·tia
minx
mir·a·cle
mi·rac·u·lous
mi·rage
mire
mired
mir·ing
miry
mir·ror
mirth
mirth·ful·ly
mirth·ful·ness
mirth·less
mis·ad·ven·ture
mis·ad·vise
mis·al·li·ance
mis·an·thrope
mis·an·throp·ic
mis·an·thro·py
mis·ap·ply
mis·ap·plied

mis·ap·ply·ing
mis·ap·pli·ca·tion
mis·ap·pre·hend
mis·ap·pre·hen·sion
mis·ap·pro·pri·ate
mis·ap·pro·pri·at·ed
mis·ap·pro·pri·at·ing
mis·ap·pro·pri·a·tion
mis·be·have
mis·be·haved
mis·be·hav·ing
mis·be·ha·vior
mis·belief
mis·believ·er
mis·cal·cu·late
mis·cal·cu·lat·ed
mis·cal·cu·lat·ing
mis·cal·cu·la·tion
mis·cal·cu·la·tor
mis·call
mis·car·ry
mis·car·ried
mis·car·ry·ing
mis·car·rige
mis·ce·ge·na·tion
mis·cel·la·ne·ous
mis·cel·la·ny
mis·chance
mis·chief
mis·chie·vous
mis·ci·ble
mis·ci·bil·i·ty
mis·con·ceive
mis·con·ceived
mis·con·ceiv·ing
mis·con·cep·tion
mis·con·duct
mis·con·strue
mis·con·strued
mis·con·stru·ing
mis·con·struc·tion
mis·count
mis·cre·ant
mis·cue
mis·cued
mis·cu·ing
mis·deal
mis·dealt

mis·deal·ing
mis·deed
mis·de·mean·or
mis·di·rect
mis·di·rec·tion
mis·do
mis·did
mis·done
mis·do·ing
mis·em·ploy
mis·em·ploy·ment
mi·ser
mi·ser·li·ness
mi·ser·ly
mis·er·a·ble
mis·er·a·ble·ness
mis·er·a·bly
mis·ery
mis·er·ies
mis·es·ti·mate
mis·fea·sance
mis·fire
mis·fired
mis·fit
mis·fit·ted
mis·fit·ting
mis·for·tune
mis·giv·ing
mis·gov·ern
mis·gov·ern·ment
mis·guide
mis·guid·ed
mis·guid·ing
mis·guid·ance
mis·han·dle
mis·han·dled
mis·han·dling
mis·hap
mish·mash
mis·in·form
mis·in·orm·ant
mis·in·form·er
mis·in·for·ma·tion
mis·in·ter·pret
mis·in·ter·pre·ta·tion
mis·in·ter·pret·er
mis·judge
mis·judged

mis·judg·ing
mis·judg·ment
mis·lay
  mis·laid
  mis·lay·ing
mis·lead
  mis·lead·ing
  mis·lead·er
mis·man·age
  mis·man·aged
  mis·man·ag·ing
  mis·man·age·ment
mis·match
mis·mate
  mis·mat·ed
  mis·mat·ing
mis·name
  mis·named
  mis·nam·ing
mis·no·mer
mi·sog·a·my
mi·sog·y·ny
  mi·sog·y·nist
  mi·sog·y·nous
mis·place
  mis·placed
  mis·plac·ing
  mis·place·ment
mis·play
mis·print
mis·pri·sion
mis·prize
mis·pro·nounce
  mis·pro·nounced
  mis·pro·nounc·ing
  mis·pro·nun·ci·a·tion
mis·quote
  mis·quot·ed
  mis·quot·ing
  mis·quo·ta·tion
mis·read
  mis·read·ing
mis·rep·re·sent
  mis·rep·re·sen·ta·tion
  mis·rep·re·sen·ta·tive
mis·rule
  mis·ruled
  mis·rul·ing

mis·sal
mis·shape
  mis·shaped
  mis·shap·ing
  mis·shap·en
mis·sile
miss·ing
mis·sion
  mis·sion·ary
  mis·sion·ar·ies
mis·sive
mis·spell
  mis·spelled
  mis·spelt
  mis·spel·ling
mis·spend
  mis·spent
  mis·spend·ing
mis·state
  mis·stat·ed
  mis·stat·ing
  mis·state·ment
mis·step
mist
  mist·i·ly
  mist·i·ness
mis·tak·a·ble
mis·take
  mis·took
  mis·tak·en
  mis·tak·ing
  mis·tak·en·ly
  mis·tak·en·ness
Mis·ter
mis·tle·toe
mis·treat
  mis·treat·ment
mis·tress
mis·tri·al
mis·trust
  mis·trust·ful
  mis·trust·ful·ly
  mis·trust·ing·ly
misty
  mist·i·er
  mist·i·ness
mis·un·der·stand
  mis·un·der·stood

mis·un·der·stand·ing
mis·use
  mis·used
  mis·us·ing
  mis·us·age
mis·val·ue
mi·ter
mi·tre
mit·i·gate
  mit·i·gat·ed
  mit·i·gat·ing
  mit·i·ga·tion
  mit·i·ga·tive
  mit·i·ga·tor
  mit·i·ga·to·ry
mi·to·sis
mitt
  mit·ten
mix
  mixed
  mix·ing
  mix·er
  mix·ture
miz·zen
mne·mon·ic
  mne·mon·ics
mob
  mobbed
  mob·bing
  mob·bish
mo·bile
  mo·bil·i·ty
mo·bi·lize
  mo·bi·lized
  mo·bi·liz·ing
  mo·bi·li·za·tion
mob·ster
moc·ca·sin
mo·cha
mock
  mock·er
  mock·ing·ly
  mock·ery
  mock·ing·bird
  mock-up
mod·al
  mo·dal·i·ty
  mod·al·ly

mod·el
  mod·eled
  mod·el·ing
mod·er·ate
  mod·er·at·ed
  mod·er·at·ing
  mod·er·ate·ness
  mod·er·a·tion
mod·er·a·tor
mod·ern
  mod·ern·ism
  mod·ern·ist
  mod·ern·is·tic
mod·ern·ize
  mod·ern·ized
  mod·ern·iz·ing
  mod·ern·i·za·tion
mod·est
  mod·est·ly
  mod·es·ty
mod·i·cum
mod·i·fi·ca·tion
mod·i·fy
  mod·i·fied
  mod·i·fy·ing
  mod·i·fi·a·ble
  mod·i·fi·er
mod·ish
  mod·ish·ly
  mod·ish·ness
mo·diste
mod·u·late
  mod·u·lat·ed
  mod·u·lat·ing
  mod·u·la·tion
  mod·u·la·to·ry
mod·ule
  mod·u·lar
mo·dus o·pe·ran·di
mo·dus vi·ven·di
mo·gul
mo·hair
Mo·ham·med
moi·e·ty
moi·ré
mois·ten
  moist·en·er
mois·ture

mois·tur·ize
mois·tur·ized
mois·tur·iz·ing
mois·tur·iz·er
mo·lar
mo·las·ses
mold
  mold·a·ble
  mold·er
mold·ing
moldy
  mold·i·er
  mold·i·ness
mol·e·cule
  mo·lec·u·lar
mole·skin
mo·lest
  mo·les·ta·tion
  mo·lest·er
mol·li·fy
  mol·li·fied
  mol·li·fy·ing
  mol·li·fi·ca·tion
  mol·li·fi·er
mol·lusk
mol·ly·cod·dle
molt
  molt·er
mol·ten
mo·lyb·de·num
mo·ment
mo·men·tary
  mo·men·tar·i·ly
mo·men·tous
  mo·men·tous·ness
mo·men·tum
mon·ad
  mo·nad·ic
  mo·nad·i·cal
mon·arch
  mo·nar·chal
  mo·nar·chic
  mo·nar·chi·cal·ly
mon·ar·chism
  mon·ar·chist
mon·ar·chy
  mon·ar·chies
mon·as·tery

mon·as·te·ri·al
mo·nas·tic
  mo·nas·ti·cal
  mo·nas·ti·cism
mon·au·ral
  mon·au·ral·ly
mon·e·tary
  mon·e·tar·i·ly
mon·e·tize
  mon·e·tized
  mon·e·tiz·ing
  mon·e·ti·za·tion
mon·ey
mon·eyed
  mon·ied
mon·ger
Mon·gol·ism
  mon·gol·oid
mon·goose
mon·grel
mon·i·ker
mon·ism
  mo·nis·tic
  mo·nis·ti·cal·ly
mo·ni·tion
mon·i·tor
  mon·i·to·ri·al
monk
  monk·ish
mon·key
  mon·keys
  mon·keyed
  mon·key·ing
mon·key·shines
mon·o·chro·mat·ic
  mon·o·chro·mat·i·cal·ly
mon·o·chrome
  mon·o·chro·mic
  mon·o·chro·mi·cal
  mon·o·chro·mi·cal·ly
mon·o·cle
mon·o·dist
mon·o·dy
  mo·nod·ic
mo·nog·a·my
  mo·nog·a·mist
  mo·nog·a·mous
mon·o·gram

mon·o·grammed
mon·o·gram·ming
mon·o·gram·mat·ic
mon·o·graph
mo·nog·ra·pher
mon·o·graph·ic
mon·o·lith
mon·o·logue
mon·o·log
mon·o·logu·ist
mon·o·log·ist
mon·o·ma·nia
mon·o·ma·ni·ac
mon·o·met·al·lism
mon·o·me·tal·lic
mo·no·mi·al
mon·o·nu·cle·o·sis
mon·o·plane
mo·nop·o·lize
mo·nop·o·lized
mo·nop·o·liz·ing
mo·nop·o·li·za·tion
mo·nop·o·liz·er
mo·nop·o·ly
mo·nop·o·lies
mon·o·rail
mon·o·so·di·um glu·ta·mate
mon·o·syl·lab·ic
mon·o·the·ism
mon·o·the·ist
mon·o·the·is·tic
mon·o·tone
mo·not·o·ny
mo·not·o·nous
mon·o·type
mon·ox·ide
mon·sei·gneur
mon·sieur
mes·sieurs
Mon·si·gnor
mon·soon
mon·ster
mon·stros·i·ty
mon·strous
mon·tage
Mon·tes·so·ri
month·ly
month·lies

mon·u·ment
mon·u·men·tal
mon·u·men·tal·ly
mooch
mooch·er
moody
mood·i·er
mood·i·ly
mood·i·ness
moon·beam
moon·light·ing
moon·scape
moon·shine
moor·ing
moot·ness
mop
mopped
mop·ping
mope
moped
mop·ing
mop·pet
mo·raine
mor·al
mor·al·ly
mo·rale
mor·al·ist
mor·al·is·tic
mo·ral·i·ty
mor·al·ize
mor·al·ized
mor·al·iz·ing
mor·al·i·za·tion
mor·al·iz·er
mo·rass
mor·a·to·ri·um
mo·ray
mor·bid
mor·bid·ly
mor·bid·i·ty
mor·bid·ness
mor·dant
mor·dan·cy
more·o·ver
mo·res
mor·ga·nat·ic
morgue
mor·i·bund

Mor·mon·ism
morn·ing
morn·ing-glo·ry
mo·roc·co
mo·ron
mo·ron·ic
mo·ron·i·cal·ly
mo·rose
mo·rose·ly
mo·rose·ness
mor·pheme
mor·phine
mor·phol·o·gy
mor·pho·log·ic
mor·pho·log·i·cal
mor·phol·o·gist
mor·row
mor·sel
mor·tal
mor·tal·ly
mor·tal·i·ty
mor·tal·i·ties
mor·tar
mor·tar·board
mort·gage
mort·gaged
mort·gag·ing
mort·ga·gee
mort·ga·ger
mor·ti·cian
mor·ti·fy
mor·ti·fied
mor·ti·fy·ing
mor·ti·fi·ca·tion
mor·tise
mor·tised
mor·tis·ing
mor·tu·ary
mor·tu·ar·ies
mo·sa·ic
mo·sey
mo·seyed
mo·sey·ing
Mos·lem
mosque
mos·qui·to
mos·qui·toes
mos·qui·tos

moss
  moss·like
  mossy
  moss·i·er
moss·back
most·ly
mo·tel
mo·tet
moth·ball
moth-eat·en
moth·er
  moth·er·less
  moth·er·hood
  moth·er·ly
  moth·er·li·ness
moth·er-in-law
  moth·ers-in-law
moth·er·land
moth·er-of-pearl
mo·tif
mo·tile
  mo·til·i·ty
mo·tion
  mo·tion·less·ness
mo·ti·vate
  mo·ti·vat·ed
  mo·ti·vat·ing
  mo·ti·va·tion
  mo·ti·va·tion·al
mo·tive
mot·ley
mo·tor
mo·tor·bike
mo·tor·boat
mo·tor·bus
mo·tor·cade
mo·tor·car
mo·tor court
mo·tor·cy·cle
  mo·tor·cy·cled
  mo·tor·cy·cling
  mo·tor·cy·clist
mo·tor·ist
mo·tor·ize
  mo·tor·ized
  mo·tor·iz·ing
  mo·tor·i·za·tion
mo·tor·man

mot·tle
  mot·tled
  mot·tling
mound
mount
  mount·a·ble
moun·tain
moun·tain·eer
moun·tain·ous
moun·te·bank
mount·ing
mourn
  mourn·er
  mourn·ful
  mourn·ful·ly
mourn·ing
mouse
  mous·er
mousse
mous·tache
mousy
  mous·i·er
mouth
  mouthed
mouth·ful
mouth·piece
mouthy
  mouth·i·ness
mou·ton
mov·a·ble
  mov·a·bil·i·ty
  mov·a·bly
move
  moved
  mov·ing
move·ment
mov·ie
mow
  mowed or mown
  mow·ing
  mow·er
mox·ie
mu·ci·lage
  mu·ci·lag·i·nous
muck
  mucky
muck·rake
  muck·raked

muck·rak·ing
muck·rak·er
mu·cous
  mu·cos·i·ty
mu·cus
mud
  mud·ded
  mud·ding
mud·dle
  mud·dled
  mud·dling
  mud·dler
mud·dy
  mud·di·er
  mud·di·ness
mu·ez·zin
muf·fin
muf·fle
  muf·fled
  muf·fling
  muf·fler
muf·ti
mug
  mugged
  mug·ging
  mug·ger
mug·gy
  mug·gi·ness
mu·lat·to
  mu·lat·toes
mul·berry
mulch
mulct
mu·le·teer
mul·ish
  mul·ish·ness
mul·let
mul·li·gan
mul·li·ga·taw·ny
mul·lion
  mul·lioned
mul·ti·col·ored
mul·ti·far·i·ous
  mul·ti·far·i·ous·ness
mul·ti·lat·er·al
mul·ti·lev·el
mul·ti·mil·lion·aire
mul·ti·par·tite

mul·ti·ple
mul·ti·ple-choice
mul·ti·ple scle·ro·sis
mul·ti·pli·cand
mul·ti·pli·ca·tion
mul·ti·plic·i·ty
mul·ti·pli·er
mul·ti·ply
  mul·ti·plied
  mul·ti·ply·ing
  mul·ti·pli·a·ble
mul·ti·tude
  mul·ti·tu·di·nous
mum·ble
  mum·bled
  mum·bling
  mum·bler
mum·bo jum·bo
mum·mer
mum·mi·fy
  mum·mi·fied
  mum·mi·fy·ing
  mum·mi·fi·ca·tion
mum·my
  mum·mies
munch
mun·dane
mu·nic·i·pal
  mu·nic·i·pal·ly
  mu·nic·i·pal·i·ty
mu·nif·i·cent
  mu·nif·i·cence
  mu·nif·i·cent·ly
mu·ni·tion
mu·ral
  mu·ral·ist
mur·der
  mur·der·er
  mur·der·ess
  mur·der·ous
  mur·der·ous·ly
mu·ri·at·ic ac·id
murky
  murk·i·er
  murk·i·ness
mur·mur
  mur·mur·er
  mur·mur·ing

mur·rain
mus·cat
  mus·ca·tel
mus·cle
  mus·cled
  mus·cling
mus·cle-bound
mus·cu·lar
  mus·cu·lar·i·ty
  mus·cu·lar dys·tro·phy
  mus·cu·la·ture
muse
  mused
  mus·ing
mu·se·um
mush
  mushy
  mush·i·ness
mush·room
mu·sic
mu·si·cal
  mu·si·cal·ly
  mu·si·cal·ness
mu·si·cale
mu·si·cian
musk
  musky
  musk·i·ness
mus·kel·lunge
mus·ket
  mus·ket·eer
  mus·ket·ry
musk·mel·on
musk·rat
Mus·lim
mus·lin
muss
  mussy
mus·sel
mus·tache
mus·tang
mus·tard
mus·ter
mus·ty
  mus·ti·ly
  mus·ti·ness
mu·ta·ble
  mu·ta·bil·i·ty

mu·ta·ble·ness
mu·ta·bly
mu·tant
mu·ta·tion
mu·tate
mu·tat·ed
mu·tat·ing
mu·ta·tion·al
mute
  mut·ed
  mut·ing
  mute·ly
  mute·ness
mu·ti·late
  mu·ti·lat·ed
  mu·ti·lat·ing
  mu·ti·la·tion
  mu·ti·la·tor
mu·ti·neer
mu·ti·ny
  mu·ti·nied
  mu·ti·ny·ing
  mu·ti·nous
mut·ter
  mut·tered
  mut·ter·ing
mut·ton
mu·tu·al
  mu·tu·al·i·ty
  mu·tu·al·ly
muu·muu
muz·zle
  muz·zled
  muz·zling
my·col·o·gy
  my·col·o·gist
my·na
my·o·pia
  my·op·ic
myr·i·ad
myrrh
myr·tle
my·self
mys·te·ri·ous
  mys·te·ri·ous·ly
mys·tery
  mys·ter·ies
mys·tic

mys·ti·cal
  mys·ti·cal·ly
  mys·ti·cism
mys·ti·fy
  mys·ti·fied
  mys·ti·fy·ing
  mys·ti·fi·ca·tion
mys·tique
myth
  myth·i·cal
  myth·i·cal·ly
my·thol·o·gy
  myth·o·log·ic
  myth·o·log·i·cal
  my·thol·o·gist

N

nab
  nabbed
  nab·bing
na·bob
na·celle
na·cre
  na·cre·ous
na·dir
nag
  nagged
  nag·ging
  nag·ger
nain·sook
na·ive
  na·ive·ly
  na·ive·ness
na·ive·te
na·ked
na·ked·ness
nam·by-pam·by
name
  named
  nam·ing
  name·less
name·ly
name·sake
nan·keen
nan·ny
nap
  napped

nap·ping
na·palm
nape
naph·tha
naph·tha·lene
nap·kin
Na·po·leon
nar·cis·sism
  nar·cism
  nar·cis·sist
  nar·cis·sis·tic
nar·cis·sus
nar·co·sis
nar·cot·ic
  nar·co·tize
  nar·co·tized
  nar·co·tiz·ing
  nar·cot·ism
nar·rate
  nar·ra·ted
  nar·ra·ting
  nar·ra·tor
  nar·ra·tion
  nar·ra·tive
nar·row
  nar·row·ly
nar·row-mind·ed
na·sal
  na·sal·i·ty
  na·sal·ize
  na·sal·ized
  na·sal·iz·ing
  na·sal·ly
nas·cent
  nas·cence
  nas·cen·cy
na·stur·tium
nas·ty
  nas·ti·er
  nas·ti·ly
  nas·ti·ness
na·tal
  na·tal·i·ty
na·tant
  na·ta·to·ri·al
  na·ta·to·ri·um
na·tion
  na·tion·hood

na·tion·al
  na·tion·al·ly
  na·tion·al·ism
  na·tion·al·ist
  na·tion·al·is·tic
  na·tion·al·i·ty
  na·tion·al·i·ties
  na·tion·al·ize
  na·tion·al·ized
  na·tion·al·iz·ing
  na·tion·al·i·za·tion
na·tion-wide
na·tive
  na·tive·ly
  na·tive·ness
na·tiv·ism
  na·tiv·ist
na·tiv·i·ty
  na·tiv·i·ties
nat·ty
  nat·ti·ly
  nat·ti·ness
nat·u·ral
  nat·u·ral·ly
  nat·u·ral·ness
nat·u·ral·ism
  nat·u·ral·ist
  nat·u·ral·is·tic
nat·u·ral·ize
  nat·u·ral·ized
  nat·u·ral·iz·ing
  nat·u·ral·i·za·tion
na·ture
naught
naugh·ty
  naugh·ti·est
  naugh·ti·ly
  naugh·ti·ness
nau·sea
nau·se·ate
  nau·se·at·ed
  nau·se·at·ing
nau·seous
  nau·seous·ness
nau·ti·cal
  nau·ti·cal·ly
nau·ti·lus
  nau·ti·lus·es

Nav·a·ho
na·vel
nav·i·ga·ble
  nav·i·ga·bil·i·ty
  nav·i·ga·ble·ness
nav·i·gate
  nav·i·gat·ed
  nav·i·gat·ing
  nav·i·ga·tion
  nav·i·ga·tor
na·vy
  na·vies
  na·val
Naz·a·reth
Na·zi
  Na·zism
  Na·si·ism
Ne·an·der·thal
near
  near·ly
  near·ness
near·by
near-sight·ed
neat
  neat·ly
  neat·ness
Neb·u·chad·nez·zar
neb·u·la
  neb·u·lae
neb·u·lous
  neb·u·lar
  neb·u·lous·ness
  neb·u·los·i·ty
nec·es·sary
  nec·es·sar·ies
  nec·es·sar·i·ly
ne·ces·si·tate
  ne·ces·si·ta·ted
  ne·ces·si·ta·ting
ne·ces·si·ty
  ne·ces·si·ites
neck·er·chief
neck·lace
neck·tie
ne·crol·o·gy
  ne·crol·o·gies
nec·ro·man·cy
nec·ro·man·cer

ne·crop·o·lis
nec·tar
nec·tar·ine
need·ful
  need·ful·ly
nee·dle
nee·dled
  nee·dling
nee·dle·point
need·less
  need·less·ly
nee·dle·work
needy
  need·i·est
  need·i·ness
ne'er-do-well
ne·far·i·ous
  ne·far·i·ous·ness
ne·gate
  ne·gat·ed
  ne·gat·ing
  ne·ga·tion
neg·a·tive
  neg·a·tive·ness
  neg·a·tiv·i·ty
  neg·a·tiv·ism
ne·glect
  ne·glect·ful
  ne·glect·ful·ly
neg·li·gee
neg·li·gent
  neg·li·gence
  neg·li·gent·ly
neg·li·gi·ble
  neg·li·gi·bly
  neg·li·gi·bil·i·ty
ne·go·ti·a·ble
  ne·go·ti·a·bil·i·ty
ne·go·ti·ate
  ne·go·ti·at·ed
  ne·go·ti·at·ing
  ne·go·ti·a·tion
  ne·go·ti·a·tor
e·gro
  Ne·groes
Ne·groid
neigh
neigh·bor

neigh·bor·ing
neigh·bor·ly
neigh·bor·li·ness
neigh·bor·hood
nei·ther
nem·a·tode
nem·e·sis
ne·o·clas·sic
  ne·o·clas·si·cal
  ne·o·clas·si·cism
ne·o·lith·ic
ne·ol·o·gism
  ne·ol·o·gy
ne·on
ne·o·phyte
neo·prene
neph·ew
ne·phri·tis
nep·o·tism
  nep·o·tist
nerve
nerve·less
nerve·rack·ing
  nerve·wrack·ing
nerv·ous
  nerv·ous·ness
nervy
  nerv·i·ness
nes·tle
  nes·tled
  nes·tling
net
  net·ted
  net·ting
neth·er
Neth·er·lands
neth·er·most
net·tle
  net·tled
  net·tling
  net·tle·some
net·work
neu·ral
neu·ral·gia
neu·ras·the·nia
neu·ri·tis
  neu·riti·c
neu·rol·o·gy

neu·ro·log·i·cal
neu·rol·o·gist
neu·ron
neu·ro·sis
neu·ro·ses
neu·rot·ic
neu·rot·i·cal·ly
neu·ter
neu·tral
neu·tral·i·ty
neu·tral·ly
neu·tral·ism
neu·tral·ist
neu·tral·ize
neu·tral·ized
neu·tral·iz·ing
neu·tral·i·za·tion
neu·tral·iz·er
neu·tron
nev·er
nev·er·more
nev·er·the·less
new
new·ish
new·ness
new·born
new·com·er
new·el
new·fan·gled
new·ly·wed
news·cast·er
news·pa·per
news·print
news·reel
news·stand
New Test·a·ment
New Zea·land
nex·us
ni·a·cin
Ni·ag·a·ra
nib·ble
nib·bled
nib·bling
Nic·a·ra·gua
nice
nice·ly
nice·ness
ni·ce·ty

ni·ce·ties
niche
nick·el·o·de·on
nick·name
nic·o·tine
nic·o·tin·ic
niece
nif·ty
nif·ti·est
Ni·ge·ria
nig·gard
nig·gard·li·ness
nig·gard·ly
nig·gling
night·fall
night·gown
night·in·gale
night·ly
night·mare
night·mar·ish
night·time
ni·hil·ism
ni·hil·ist
ni·hil·is·tic
nim·ble
nim·ble·ness
nim·bly
nim·bus
nim·rod
nin·com·poop
nine·teen
nine·teenth
nine·ty
nine·ties
nine·ti·eth
nin·ny
ninth
nip
nipped
nip·ping
nip·per
nip·ple
Nip·pon
nip·py
nir·va·na
Ni·sei
nit·pick
ni·trate

ni·tra·tion
ni·tric
ni·tro·gen
ni·trog·e·nous
ni·tro·glyc·er·in
nit·ty-grit·ty
nit·wit
no·bil·i·ty
no·ble
no·bler
no·blest
no·ble·man
no·ble·ness
no·bly
no·blesse oblige
no·body
noc·tur·nal
noc·turne
nod
nod·ded
nod·ding
node
nod·al
nod·ule
nod·u·lar
no·el
nog·gin
noise
noised
nois·ing
noise·less
noi·some
noisy
nois·i·ly
nois·i·ness
no·lo con·ten·de·re
no·mad
no·mad·ic
no·mad·i·cal·ly
no·mad·ism
nom de plume
no·men·cla·ture
nom·i·nal
nom·i·nal·ly
nom·i·nate
nom·i·nat·ed
nom·i·nat·ing
nom·i·na·tion

nom·i·na·tive
nom·i·nee
non·age
non·align·ment
non·cha·lant
  non·cha·lance
  non·cha·lant·ly
non·com
non·com·bat·ant
non·com·mis·sioned
non·com·mit·tal
non·con·duc·tor
non·con·form·ist
  non·con·form·i·ty
non·de·script
non·en·ti·ty
none·the·less
non·in·ter·ven·tion
non·met·al
  non·me·tal·lic
non·pa·reil
non·par·ti·san
non·plus
  non·plused
  non·plus·ing
non·prof·it
non·res·i·dent
  non·res·i·dence
  non·res·i·den·cy
non·re·sis·tance
non·re·stric·tive
non·sched·uled
non·sec·tar·i·an
non·sense
  non·sen·si·cal
  non·sen·si·cal·ly
non se·qui·tur
non·stop
non·sup·port
non·un·ion
non·vi·o·lence
  non·vi·o·lent·ly
noo·dle
noon
  noon·day
  noon·time
noose
normal

nor·mal·cy
nor·mal·i·ty
nor·mal·ly
nor·mal·ize
  nor·mal·ized
  nor·mal·iz·ing
  nor·mal·i·za·tion
Norse·man
North Amer·i·ca
north·east
  north·east·ern
north·east·ern
north·east·er
north·east·er·ly
north·east·ward
north·er
nor·ther·ly
  north·er·li·ness
north·ern
  north·ern·most
north·ern·er
north·ward
  north·wards
  north·ward·ly
north·west
  north·west·ern
  north·west·ward
Nor·we·gian
nose
  nosed
  nos·ing
nose·gay
nos·tal·gia
  nos·tal·gic
nos·tril
nos·trum
nosy
  nos·i·ly
  nos·i·ness
no·ta·ble
  no·ta·ble·ness
  no·ta·bil·i·ty
  no·ta·bly
no·ta·rize
  no·ta·rized
  no·ta·riz·ing
  no·ta·ri·za·tion
no·ta·ry

no·ta·tion
  no·ta·tion·al
notch
  notched
note
  not·ed
  not·ing
not·ed
  not·ed·ness
note·wor·thy
  note·wor·thi·ness
noth·ing
  noth·ing·ness
no·tice
  no·ticed
  no·tic·ing
  no·tice·a·ble
  no·tice·a·bly
no·ti·fy
  no·ti·fied
  no·ti·fy·ing
  no·ti·fi·ca·tion
no·tion
no·to·ri·ous
  no·to·ri·ous·ness
  no·to·ri·e·ty
no-trump
nought
nour·ish
  nour·ish·ing
  nour·ish·ment
no·va
No·va Sco·tia
nov·el
  nov·el·ist
  nov·el·is·tic
  nov·el·ette
nov·el·ty
  nov·el·ties
no·ve·na
nov·ice
no·vi·ti·ate
no·vo·cain
now·a·days
no·where
no·wise
nox·ious
noz·zle

nu·ance
nub·bin
nu·bile
nu·cle·ar
nu·cle·ate
nu·cle·on
nu·cle·onics
nu·cle·us
  nu·clei
nude
nude·ness
  nu·di·ty
  nud·ism
  nud·ist
nudge
  nudged
  nudg·ing
nu·ga·to·ry
nug·get
nui·sance
null
  nul·li·ty
nul·li·fy
  nul·li·fied
  nul·li·fy·ing
  nul·li·fi·ca·tion
  nul·li·fi·er
numb
  numb·ly
  numb·ness
num·ber
  num·ber·less
nu·mer·al
  num·er·al·ly
nu·mer·a·ble
nu·mer·ate
  nu·mer·at·ed
  nu·mer·at·ing
  nu·mer·a·tion
nu·mer·a·tor
nu·mer·i·cal
nu·mer·ous
nu·mis·mat·ics
  nu·mis·mat·ic
  nu·mis·ma·tist
num·skull
  numb·skull
nun·cio

nun·nery
  nun·ner·ies
nup·tial
  nup·tial·ly
nurse
  nursed
  nurs·ing
nurse·maid
nurs·ery
  nurs·er·ies
nur·ture
  nur·tured
  nur·tur·ing
nut
  nut·ty
nut·crack·er
nut·hatch
nut·meg
nu·tri·ent
  nu·tri·ment
nu·tri·tion
  nu·tri·tion·al
  nu·tri·tion·al·ly
  nu·tri·tion·ist
nu·tri·tious
nu·tri·tive
nut·shell
nut·ty
nuz·zle
  nuz·zled
  nuz·zling
ny·lon
nymph
nym·pho·ma·nia
  nym·pho·ma·ni·ac

O

oaf
  oaf·ish
oak·en
oa·kum
oar·lock
oars·man
oa·sis
oath
oat·meal
ob·bli·ga·to

ob·du·rate
  ob·du·ra·cy
  ob·du·rate·ness
obe·di·ence
  obe·di·ent
obei·sance
  obei·sant
ob·e·lisk
obese
obese·ness
  obes·i·ty
obey
ob·fus·cate
  ob·fus·ca·ted
  ob·fus·ca·ting
  ob·fus·ca·tion
obit·u·ary
  obit·u·ar·ies
ob·ject
  ob·ject·less
  ob·ject·or
ob·jec·tion
  ob·jec·tion·a·ble
  ob·jec·tion·a·bly
ob·jec·tive
  ob·jec·tive·ly
  ob·jec·tive·ness
  ob·jec·tiv·i·ty
ob·jet d'art
ob·jur·gate
  ob·jur·gat·ed
  ob·jur·gat·ing
  ob·jur·ga·tion
  ob·jur·ga·to·ry
ob·late
  ob·la·tion
ob·li·gate
  ob·li·gat·ed
  ob·li·gat·ing
  ob·li·ga·tion
  ob·lig·a·to·ry
oblige
  obliged
  oblig·ing
ob·lique
  ob·lique·ly
  ob·liq·ui·ty
ob·lit·er·ate

ob·lit·er·at·ed
ob·lit·er·at·ing
ob·lit·er·a·tion
ob·lit·er·a·tive
ob·liv·i·on
ob·liv·i·ous
ob·long
ob·lo·quy
ob·nox·ious
oboe
  obo·ist
ob·scene
  ob·scene·ly
  ob·scene·ness
  ob·scen·i·ty
ob·scure
  ob·scured
  ob·scur·ing
  ob·scure·ness
  ob·scu·ri·ty
ob·se·qui·ous
ob·se·quy
ob·ser·va·to·ry
ob·serve
  ob·served
  ob·serv·ing
  ob·serv·er
  ob·serv·a·ble
  ob·serv·a·bly
  ob·ser·vance
  ob·ser·vant
  ob·ser·va·tion
ob·sess
  ob·ses·sive
  ob·ses·sion
ob·sid·i·an
ob·so·les·cent
  ob·so·les·cence
ob·so·lete
  ob·so·lete·ness
ob·sta·cle
ob·stet·rics
  ob·stet·ric
  ob·stet·ri·cal
ob·ste·tri·cian
ob·sti·nate
  ob·sti·na·cy
  ob·sti·nate·ly

ob·sti·nate·ness
ob·strep·er·ous
  ob·strep·er·ous·ness
ob·struct
  ob·struc·tive
  ob·struc·tor
  ob·struc·tion
  ob·struc·tion·ism
  ob·struc·tion·ist
ob·tain
  ob·tain·a·ble
  ob·tain·ment
ob·trude
  ob·trud·ed
  ob·trud·ing
  ob·tru·sion
  ob·tru·sive
ob·tuse
  ob·tuse·ness
ob·verse
  ob·verse·ly
ob·vert
ob·vi·ate
  ob·vi·at·ed
  ob·vi·at·ing
  ob·vi·a·tion
ob·vi·ous
  ob·vi·ous·ness
ob·vo·lute
oc·a·ri·na
oc·ca·sion
  oc·ca·sion·al
  oc·ca·sion·al·ly
oc·ci·dent
  oc·ci·den·tal
oc·clude
  oc·clud·ed
  oc·clud·ing
  oc·clu·sive
  oc·clu·sion
oc·cult
  oc·cult·ism
  oc·cult·ist
oc·cu·pa·tion
  oc·cu·pa·tion·al
  oc·cu·pa·tion·al·ly
oc·cu·py
  oc·cu·pied

oc·cu·py·ing
oc·cu·pi·er
oc·cu·pan·cy
oc·cu·pant
oc·cur
  oc·curred
  oc·cur·ring
  oc·cur·rence
  oc·cur·rent
ocean
  oce·an·ic
oce·a·nog·ra·phy
  oce·a·nog·ra·pher
  oce·a·no·graph·ic
  oce·a·no·graph·i·cal
oce·lot
ocher
  ochery
o'clock
oc·ta·gon
  oc·tag·o·nal·ly
oc·ta·he·dron
  oc·ta·he·dra
  oc·ta·he·dral
oc·tane
oc·tave
oc·ta·vo
oc·tet
oc·to·ge·nar·i·an
oc·to·pus
oc·to·roon
oc·u·lar
oc·u·list
odd
  odd·ness
odd·ball
odd·i·ty
  odd·i·ties
odi·ous
  odi·ous·ness
odi·um
odom·e·ter
odor
  odored
  odorless
  odorous
  odorif·er·ous
od·ys·sey

Oed·i·pus
of·fal
off·beat
off·col·or
of·fend
  of·fend·er
of·fense
  of·fense·less
of·fen·sive
  of·fen·sive·ly
of·fer
of·fer·er
of·fer·ing
of·fer·to·ry
  of·fer·to·ries
  of·fer·to·ri·al
off·hand
  off·hand·ed·ness
of·fice
of·fice·hold·er
of·fic·er
of·fi·cial
  of·fi·cial·ly
  of·fi·cial·dom
of·fi·ci·ate
  of·fi·ci·at·ed
  of·fi·ci·at·ing
  of·fi·ci·a·tion
  of·fi·ci·a·tor
of·fi·cious
  of·fi·cious·ly
off·ing
off·set
  off·set·ting
off·shoot
off·shore
off·side
off·spring
off·stage
off-the-record
of·ten
of·ten·times
ogle
  ogled
  ogling
  ogler
ogre
  ogre·ish

ohm
  ohm·age
  ohm·ic
ohm·me·ter
oil·cloth
oil·skin
oily
  oil·i·ness
oint·ment
okra
old
old·er
  old·est
  old·en
  old·ish
  old·ness
old-fash·ioned
old·ster
Old Test·a·ment
old-tim·er
old-world
ole·ag·i·nous
ole·o·mar·ga·rine
ol·fac·tion
  ol·fac·to·ry
ol·i·gar·chy
  ol·i·gar·chic
  oli·gar·chi·cal
  ol·i·garch
ol·i·gop·o·ly
ol·ive
Olym·pi·an
O·lym·pic
om·buds·man
ome·ga
om·e·let
omen
om·i·nous
  om·i·nous·ly
omis·sion
omit
  omit·ted
  omit·ting
om·ni·bus
om·nip·o·tence
  om·nip·o·tent·ly
om·ni·pres·ent
  om·ni·pres·ence

om·nis·cience
  om·nis·cient
om·niv·or·ous
on·com·ing
on·er·ous
one·self
one-sid·ed
one-up·man·ship
one-way
on·go·ing
on·ion
  on·iony
on·look·er
on·ly
on·o·mat·o·poe·ia
  on·o·mat·o·poe·ic
  on·o·mat·o·poe·i·cal·ly
on·rush·ing
on·set
on·shore
on·slaught
on·to
onus
on·ward
on·yx
oo·dles
ooze
  oozed
  ooz·ing
  oo·zi·ness
  oo·zy
opac·i·ty
opal
opal·es·cence
  opal·es·cent
opaque
  opaque·ly
open
  open·ly
  open·ness
open·hand·ed
open house
open·ing
open-mind·ed
open-mouthed
open ses·a·me
open·work
opera

138

op·er·at·ic
op·er·a·ble
  op·er·a·bil·i·ty
  op·er·a·bly
op·er·ate
  op·er·at·ed
  op·er·at·ing
  op·er·a·tion
  op·er·a·tive
  op·er·a·tor
op·er·et·ta
oph·thal·mic
oph·thal·mol·o·gist
oph·thal·mol·o·gy
opi·ate
opin·ion
opin·ion·at·ed
opi·um
opos·sum
op·po·nent
op·por·tune
  op·por·tune·ly
op·por·tun·ism
  op·por·tun·ist
  op·por·tun·is·tic
op·por·tu·ni·ty
  op·por·tu·ni·ties
op·pose
  op·posed
  op·pos·ing
  op·pos·er
op·po·site
  op·po·site·ness
  op·po·si·tion
op·press
  op·pres·sor
  op·pres·sion
  op·pres·sive
op·pro·bri·um
op·pro·bri·ous
op·tic
  op·ti·cal
  op·ti·cal
  op·ti·cian
  op·tics
op·ti·mal
op·ti·mism
  op·ti·mist

op·ti·mis·tic
  op·ti·mis·ti·cal·ly
op·ti·mize
  op·ti·mized
  op·ti·miz·ing
  op·ti·mi·za·tion
op·ti·mum
op·tion
  op·tion·al
op·tom·e·try
  op·to·met·ric
  op·tom·e·trist
op·u·lent
  op·u·lence
  op·u·lent·ly
opus
  opus·es
ora·cle
  orac·u·lar
oral
  oral·ly
or·ange
orang·u·tan
orate
  orat·ed
  orat·ing
  ora·tion
  ora·tor
  ora·tor·i·cal
  ora·to·ry
ora·to·rio
or·bic·u·lar
or·bit
  or·bit·al
or·chard
or·ches·tra
  or·ches·tral
or·ches·trate
  or·ches·trat·ed
  or·ches·trat·ing
  or·ches·tra·tion
or·chid
or·dain
  or·dain·er
  or·dain·ment
or·deal
or·der
  or·dered

or·der·ly
  or·der·li·ness
or·di·nal
or·di·nance
or·di·nar·i·ly
or·di·nary
  or·di·nar·i·ness
or·di·na·tion
ord·nance
oreg·a·no
or·gan
or·gan·dy
or·gan·ic
  or·gan·i·cal·ly
or·gan·ism
or·gan·ist
or·gan·i·za·tion
  or·gan·i·za·tion·al
or·gan·ize
  or·gan·ized
  or·gan·iz·ing
  or·gan·iz·a·ble
  or·gan·iz·er
or·gasm
  or·gas·mic
or·gi·as·tic
  or·gi·as·ti·cal·ly
or·gy
  or·gies
ori·ent
Ori·en·tal
ori·en·tate
  ori·en·tat·ed
  ori·en·tat·ing
  ori·en·ta·tion
or·i·fice
orig·i·nal
  orig·i·nal·i·ty
  orig·i·nal·ly
orig·i·nate
  orig·i·nat·ed
  orig·i·nat·ing
  orig·i·na·tion
  orig·i·na·tor
  orig·i·na·tive
ori·son
or·mo·lu
or·na·ment

or·na·men·tal
or·na·men·ta·tion
or·nate
  or·nate·ness
or·nery
  or·ner·i·ness
or·ni·thol·o·gy
  or·ni·tho·log·ic
  or·ni·thol·o·gist
oro·tund
  oro·tun·di·ty
or·phan
or·phan·age
or·tho·don·tics
  or·tho·don·tic
  or·tho·don·tist
or·tho·dox
  or·tho·dox·ly
  or·tho·dox·ness
  or·tho·doxy
or·thog·o·nal
or·thog·ra·phy
  or·tho·graph·ic
or·tho·pe·dics
  or·tho·pe·dic
  or·tho·pe·dist
os·cil·late
  os·cil·lat·ed
  os·cil·lat·ing
  os·cil·la·tion
  os·cil·la·tor
  os·cil·la·to·ry
os·cil·lo·scope
os·cu·late
  os·cu·la·tion
os·mo·sis
  os·mot·ic
os·prey
os·si·fy
  os·si·fied
  os·si·fy·ing
  os·si·fi·ca·tion
os·ten·sive
  os·ten·si·ble
  os·ten·si·bly
  os·ten·sive·ly
os·ten·ta·tion
  os·ten·ta·tious

os·te·op·a·thy
os·te·o·path
os·te·o·path·ic
os·tra·cize
  os·tra·cized
  os·tra·ciz·ing
  os·tra·cism
os·trich
oth·er
oth·er·ness
oth·er·wise
oti·ose
ot·ter
ot·to·man
ought
ounce
our·self
  our·selves
oust·er
out·bid
  out·bid·ding
out·board
out·bound
out·brave
out·break
out·build·ing
out·burst
out·cast
out·come
out·cry
  out·cries
out·dat·ed
out·dis·tance
out·do
out·door
out·er
out·er·most
out·er space
out·face
out·field
out·flank
out·grow
out·growth
out·land·ish
out·last
out·law
out·let
out·ly·ing

out·mod·ed
out·num·ber
out-of-date
out·post
out·rage
out·ra·geous
out·range
out·rank
out·right
out·sid·er
out·skirts
out·spo·ken
out·stand·ing
out·strip
out·ward
out·wear
out·weigh
ova
oval
  oval·ness
ova·ry
  ova·ries
ovar·i·an
ovate
ova·tion
ov·en
over
over·act
over·age
over·bear·ing
over·board
over·charge
  over·charged
  over·charg·ing
over·come
over·com·pen·sa·tion
over·con·fi·dence
over·dose
over·drawn
over·em·pha·sis
over·es·ti·mate
over·flow·ing
over·gen·er·ous
over·growth
over·hand
over·hang·ing
over·haul·ing
over·in·dul·gence

over·joyed
over·much
over·night
over·pass
over·pow·er
over·rat·ed
over·reach
over·ride
over·rule
over·sexed
over·shad·ow
over·shoot
over·sight
over·sim·pli·fy
over·state·ment
over·stepped
overt
  overt·ly
over·take
over-the-coun·ter
over·throw
over·time
over·ture
over·weight
over·whelm
over·worked
ovip·a·rous
ovoid
ovu·late
  ovu·la·tion
ovum
  ova
owe
  owed
  ow·ing
owl·ish
own·er
ox·en
ox·ford
ox·i·da·tion
ox·ide
ox·i·dize
  ox·i·dized
  ox·i·diz·ing
ox·y·a·cet·y·lene
ox·y·gen
ox·y·gen·ate
  ox·y·gen·at·ed

ox·y·gen·at·ing
ox·y·gen·a·tion
oys·ter
ozone

P

pab·u·lum
pace
  paced
  pac·ing
  pac·er
pace·mak·er
pachy·derm
pa·cif·ic
pa·cif·i·ca·tion
  pa·cif·i·ca·tor
  pa·cif·i·ca·to·ry
pac·i·fi·er
pac·i·fism
  pac·i·fist
pac·i·fy
  pac·i·fied
  pac·i·fy·ing
pack·age
  pack·ag·er
pack·er
pack·et
pack·ing
pack·sad·dle
pad
pad·ded
  pad·ding
pad·dle
  pad·dled
  pad·dling
pad·dock
pad·dy
pad·lock
pa·dre
pae·an
pa·gan
  pa·gan·ism
page
  paged
  pag·ing
pag·eant
  pag·eant·ry

pag·i·nate
  pag·i·na·tion
pa·go·da
pail·ful
pain
  pain·ful·ly
  pain·less
pains·tak·ing
paint·er
paint·ing
pais·ley
pa·jam·as
pal·ace
pa·lan·quin
pal·at·a·ble
  pal·at·a·bil·i·ty
  pal·at·a·bly
pal·ate
pa·la·tial
  pa·la·tial·ly
pal·a·tine
pa·lav·er
pale
  paled
  pal·ing
  pale·ly
  pale·ness
pa·le·og·ra·phy
Pa·le·o·lith·ic
pa·le·on·tol·o·gy
  pa·le·on·tol·o·gist
Pa·le·o·zo·ic
pal·ette
pal·ing
pal·i·sade
  pal·i·sad·ed
  pal·i·sad·ing
pal·la·di·um
pall·bear·er
pal·let
pal·li·ate
  pal·li·at·ed
  pal·li·at·ing
  pal·li·a·tion
  pal·li·a·tive
pal·lid
pal·lor
palm

pal·mate
pal·met·to
palm·is·try
  palm·ist
pal·o·mi·no
pal·pa·ble
  pal·pa·bil·i·ty
  pal·pa·bly
pal·pate
  pal·pat·ed
  pal·pat·ing
  pal·pa·tion
pal·pi·tate
  pal·pi·tat·ed
  pal·pi·tat·ing
  pal·pi·ta·tion
pal·sy
  pal·sied
pal·try
  pal·tri·ness
pam·pas
pam·per
pam·phlet
  pam·phle·teer
pan
  panned
  pan·ning
pan·a·ce·a
pa·nache
Pan-Ameri·can
pan·cake
  pan·caked
  pan·cak·ing
pan·chro·mat·ic
pan·cre·as
  pan·cre·at·ic
pan·da
pan·dem·ic
pan·de·mo·ni·um
pan·der
  pan·der·er
pan·el
  pan·eled
  pan·el·ing
pan·el·ist
pang
pan·han·dler
pan·ic

pan·icked
  pan·ick·ing
pan·nier
pan·o·ply
pan·o·rama
  pan·o·ram·ic
  pan·o·ram·i·cal·ly
pan·sy
  pan·sies
pan·ta·loon
pan·the·ism
  pan·the·ist
  pan·the·is·tic
pan·the·on
pan·ther
pan·tie
  pan·ty
pan·to·mime
  pan·to·mimed
  pan·to·mim·ing
  pan·to·mim·ic
  pan·to·mim·ist
pan·try
  pan·tries
pant·y·hose
pa·pa
pa·pa·cy
pa·pal
pa·pau
pa·pa·ya
pa·per
  pa·per·er
  pa·pery
pa·per·back
pa·per·weight
pa·per·work
pa·pier·ma·che
pa·pil·la
pa·poose
pap·ri·ka
pa·py·rus
pa·ra·ble
pa·rab·o·la
par·a·chute
  par·a·chut·ed
  par·a·chut·ing
  par·a·chut·ist
pa·rade

pa·rad·ed
pa·rad·ing
par·a·digm
par·a·dise
  par·a·di·si·a·cal
par·a·dox
  par·a·dox·i·cal
par·a·dox
  par·a·dox·i·cal
par·af·fin
par·a·gon
par·a·graph
Par·a·guay
par·a·keet
par·al·lax
  par·al·lac·tic
par·al·lel
  par·al·leled
  par·a·lel·ing
par·al·lel·o·gram
pa·ral·y·sis
  par·a·lyt·ic
par·a·lyze
  par·a·lyzed
  par·a·lyz·ing
  par·a·ly·za·tion
par·a·med·ic
pa·ram·e·ter
par·a·mount
  par·a·mount·cy
par·a·mour
par·a·noia
  par·a·noi·ac
  par·a·noid
par·a·pet
par·a·pher·nal·ia
par·a·phrase
  par·a·phrased
  par·a·phras·ing
par·a·ple·gia
  par·a·ple·gic
par·a·psy·chol·o·gy
par·a·site
  par·a·sit·ic
  par·a·sit·i·cal·ly
  par·a·sit·ism
par·a·sol
par·a·troop·er

par·boil
par·cel
  parceled
  parcel·ling
parch·ment
pardon
  pardon·a·ble
  pardon·a·bly
pare
  pared
  paring
par·e·gor·ic
parent
  pa·ren·tal
parent·age
pa·ren·the·sis
  pa·ren·the·ses
  par·en·thet·ic
  par·en·thet·i·cal
pa·re·sis
parfait
pa·ri·ah
pa·ri·mu·tu·el
par·ish
  pa·rish·ion·er
par·i·ty
par·ka
par·lance
par·lay
  par·layed
  par·lay·ing
par·ley
  par·leyed
  par·ley·ing
par·lia·ment
  par·lia·men·tari·an
  par·lia·men·ta·ry
par·lor
pa·ro·chi·al
par·o·dy
  par·o·died
  par·o·dy·ing
  par·o·dist
pa·role
  pa·roled
  pa·rol·ing
  pa·rol·ee
par·ox·ysm

par·ox·ys·mal
par·quet
  par·queted
  par·quet·ing
  par·quet·ry
par·ra·keet
par·ri·cide
parry
  parried
  parry·ing
parse
par·si·mo·ny
  par·si·mo·ni·ous
  par·si·mo·ni·ous·ness
pars·ley
pars·nip
par·son
  par·son·age
par·take
  par·took
  par·tak·en
  par·tak·ing
  par·ta·ker
part·ed
par·the·no·gen·e·sis
par·tial
  par·tial·ly
  par·ti·al·i·ty
par·tic·i·pate
  par·tic·i·pat·ed
  par·tic·i·pat·ing
  par·tic·i·pant
  par·tic·i·pa·tion
  par·tic·i·pa·tive
  par·tic·i·pa·tor
par·ti·ci·ple
  par·ti·cip·i·al
par·ti·cle
par·ti·col·ored
par·tic·u·lar
  par·tic·u·lar·i·ty
  par·tic·u·lar·ize
par·tic·u·late
part·ing
par·ti·san
  par·ti·san·ship
par·tite
  par·ti·tion

par·ti·tive
part·ly
part·ner
  part·ner·ship
par·tridge
par·tu·ri·ent
par·tu·ri·tion
party
  par·ties
par·ve·nu
pas·chal
pa·sha
pass·a·ble
  pass·a·bly
pass·sage
  pas·sage·way
pas·se
pas·sen·ger
pass·er·by
pass·ing
pas·sion
  pas·sion·less
pas·sion·ate
  pas·sion·ate·ly
  pas·sion·ate·ness
pas·sive
  pas·siv·i·ty
Pass·over
pass·word
pas·ta
paste
  pas·ted
  pas·ting
paste·board
pas·tel
pas·teur·ize
  pas·teur·ized
  pas·teur·iz·ing
  pas·teur·i·za·tion
pas·tille
pas·time
pas·tor
pas·tor·ate
pas·to·ral
pas·tra·mi
pas·try
  pas·tries
pas·ture

pas·tured
pas·tur·ing
pas·tur·age
pasty
past·i·ness
pat
pat·ted
pat·ting
patchy
patch·i·est
pâ·té
pat·ent
pa·ten·cy
pat·ent·ly
pat·ent·ee
pat·er·nal
pat·ter·nal·ly
pa·ter·nal·ism
pa·ter·nal·is·tic
pa·ter·ni·ty
pa·ter·noster
pa·thet·ic
pa·thet·i·cal·ly
patho·gen·ic
pa·thol·o·gy
path·o·log·ic
path·o·log·i·cal
pa·thol·o·gist
pa·thos
pa·tient
pa·tience
pa·tient·ly
pat·i·na
pa·tio
pat·ois
pa·tri·arch
pa·tri·archy
pa·tri·ar·chal
pa·tri·cian
pat·ri·cide
pat·ri·mo·ny
pa·tri·ot
pa·tri·ot·ic
pa·tri·ot·i·cal·ly
pa·tri·ot·ism
pa·trol
pa·trolled
pa·trol·ling

pa·trol·ler
pa·trol·man
pa·tron
pa·tron·ess
pa·tron·age
pa·tron·ize
pa·tron·ized
pa·tron·iz·ing
pat·ro·nym·ic
pat·sy
pat·sies
pat·ter
pat·tern
pat·terned
pat·ty
pat·ties
pau·ci·ty
paunch
paunch·i·ness
paunchy
pau·per
pau·per·ism
pau·per·ize
pause
paused
paus·ing
pave
paved
pav·ing
pave·ment
pa·vil·ion
Pav·lov
pawn
pawn·bro·ker
pay
paid
pay·ing
pay·ee
pay·ment
pay·a·ble
peace
peace·a·ble
peace·a·bly
peace·ful
peace·ful·ly
peach
pea·cock
peak·ed

peal
pea·nut
pearl
pearly
peas·ant
peas·ant·ry
peaty
peb·ble
peb·bled
peb·bling
peb·bly
pe·can
pec·ca·dil·lo
pec·tin
pec·to·ral
pec·u·late
pec·u·la·tion
pe·cu·liar
pe·cu·liar·ly
pe·cu·li·ar·i·ty
pe·cu·li·ar·i·ties
pe·cu·ni·ary
ped·a·gogue
ped·a·gog·ic
ped·a·gog·i·cal
ped·a·go·gy
ped·al
ped·aled
ped·al·ing
ped·ant
pe·dan·tic
pe·dan·ti·cal·ly
ped·ant·ry
ped·dle
ped·dler
ped·es·tal
pe·des·tri·an
pe·di·at·rics
pe·di·at·ric
pe·di·a·tri·cian
pe·di·at·rist
ped·i·cure
ped·i·cur·ist
ped·i·gree
ped·i·greed
ped·i·ment
pe·dol·o·gy
pe·dom·e·ter

peel·ing
peer
peer·age
  peer·ess
peer·less
peeve
  peeved
  peev·ing
  peev·ish
peg
  pegged
  peg·ging
pei·gnoir
pe·jo·ra·tive
Pe·king·ese
pe·koe
pel·age
pe·lag·ic
pel·i·can
pel·la·gra
pel·let
pell-mell
pel·vis
  pel·vic
pem·mi·can
pen
  penned
  pen·ning
pe·nal
pe·nal·ize
  pe·nal·ized
  pe·nal·iz·ing
  pe·nal·i·za·tion
pen·al·ty
  pen·al·ties
pen·ance
pen·chant
pen·cil
  pen·ciled
  pen·cil·ing
pend·ant
pend·ent
  pend·en·cy
  pend·ent·ly
pend·ing
pen·du·lous
pen·e·trate
  pen·e·trat·ed

pen·e·trat·ing
pen·e·tra·tive
pen·e·tra·ble
pen·e·tra·bil·i·ty
pen·e·tra·ble·ness
pen·e·tra·bly
pen·e·tra·tion
pen·guin
pen·i·cil·lin
pen·in·su·la
  pen·in·su·lar
pe·nis
pen·i·tent
  pen·i·tence
  pen·i·ten·tial
  pen·i·tent·ly
pen·i·ten·tia·ry
  pen·i·ten·tia·ries
pen·knife
pen·man·ship
pen·nant
Penn·syl·va·nia
pen·ny
  pen·nies
  pen·ni·less
pen·ny an·te
pen·ny pinch·er
pe·nol·o·gy
  pe·no·log·i·cal
  pen·nol·o·gist
pen·sion
  pen·sion·a·ble
  pen·sion·er
pen·sive
  pen·sive·ness
pen·ta·cle
pen·ta·gon
  pen·tag·o·nal
pen·tam·e·ter
pen·tath·lon
Pen·te·cost
  Pen·te·cos·tal
pent·house
pen·tom·ic
pe·nult
pe·num·bra
pe·nu·ri·ous
pen·u·ry

pe·on
  pe·on·age
pe·o·ny
peo·ple
  peo·pled
  peo·pling
pep
  pepped
  pep·ping
pep·lum
pep·per
pep·per·corn
pep·per·mint
pep·per·y
  pep·per·i·ness
pep·py
  pep·pi·er
  pep·pi·ness
pep·sin
pep·tic
per·am·bu·late
  per·am·bu·lat·ed
  per·am·bu·lat·ing
  per·am·bu·la·tion
  per·am·bu·la·to·ry
per an·num
per·cale
per cap·i·ta
per·ceive
  per·ceived
  per·ceiv·ing
  per·ceiv·a·ble
  per·ceiv·a·bly
per·cent
  per·cent·age
  per·cen·tile
per·cept
  per·cep·ti·ble
  per·cep·ti·bil·i·ty
  per·cep·ti·bly
  per·cep·tion
  per·cep·tive
  per·cep·tu·al
per·chance
Per·che·ron
per·cip·i·ent
  per·cip·i·ence
per·co·late

per·co·lat·ed
per·co·lat·ing
per·co·la·tion
per·co·la·tor
per·cus·sion
per·cus·sive
per di·em
per·di·tion
per·du·ra·ble
pere·grine
  pere·gri·na·tion
per·emp·to·ry
  per·emp·to·ri·ly
  per·emp·to·ri·ness
per·en·ni·al
  per·en·ni·al·ly
perfect
  perfect·er
  perfect·ness
  perfect·i·ble
  perfect·i·bil·i·ty
  perfec·tive
  perfec·tion
  perfect·ly
per·fi·dy
  perfid·i·ous
perfo·rate
  perfo·rat·ed
  perfo·rat·ing
  perfo·ra·tor
  perfo·ra·tion
per·force
per·form
  perform·a·ble
  perform·er
  performance
per·fume
  perfumed
  perfum·ing
  perfum·ery
perfunc·to·ry
  perfunc·to·ri·ly
  perfunc·to·ri·ness
per·haps
per·go·la
peri·gee
peril
  periled

peril·ing
peril·ous
peril·ous·ly
pe·rim·e·ter
peri·met·ric
peri·met·ri·cal
pe·ri·od
pe·ri·od·ic
  pe·ri·o·dic·i·ty
pe·ri·od·i·cal
  pe·ri·od·i·cal·ly
peri·pa·tet·ic
pe·riph·ery
  pe·riph·er·al
  pe·riph·er·al·ly
peri·phrase
peri·scope
  peri·scopic
perish
  perish·a·ble
  perish·a·bil·i·ty
  perish·a·ble·ness
  perish·a·bly
peri·stal·sis
  peri·stal·tic
peri·style
peri·to·ni·tis
peri·win·kle
per·jure
  per·jured
  per·juring
  per·jurer
  per·ju·ri·ous
  per·ju·ry
perky
  perk·i·est
perma·frost
perma·nent
  perma·nen·cy
perme·ate
  perme·at·ed
  perme·at·ing
  perme·a·ble
  perme·a·bil·i·ty
  perme·a·bly
  perme·a·tion
  perme·a·tive
per·mis·si·ble

per·mis·si·bil·i·ty
per·mis·si·bly
per·mis·sion
per·mis·sive
permit
  permit·ted
  permit·ting
permute
  permu·ta·tion
per·ni·cious
pero·rate
  pero·ra·tion
perox·ide
perpen·dic·u·lar
perpe·trate
  perpe·trat·ed
  perpe·trat·ing
  perpe·tra·tion
  perpe·tra·tor
perpet·u·al
  perpet·u·al·ly
perpet·u·ate
  perpet·u·at·ed
  perpet·u·at·ing
  perpet·u·a·tor
perpe·tu·i·ty
perplex
  perplexed
  perplex·ing
  perplex·i·ty
perqui·site
per se
perse·cute
  perse·cut·ed
  perse·cut·ing
  perse·cu·tive
  perse·cu·tor
  perse·cu·tion
perse·vere
  perse·vered
  perse·vering
  perse·ver·ance
per·si·flage
per·sim·mon
per·sist
  per·sist·ence
  per·sis·ten·cy
  per·sist·ent

per·snick·et·y
per·son
per·son·a·ble
per·son·age
per·son·al
per·son·al·i·ty
per·son·al·ize
  per·son·al·ized
  per·son·al·iz·ing
per·son·al·ly
per·so·na non gra·ta
per·son·ate
  per·son·at·ed
  per·son·at·ing
  per·son·a·tion
  per·son·a·tor
per·son·i·fy
  per·son·i·fied
  per·son·i·fy·ing
  per·son·i·fi·ca·tion
per·son·nel
per·spec·tive
per·spi·ca·cious
  per·spi·cac·i·ty
per·spi·cu·i·ty
  per·spic·u·ous
per·spire
  per·spired
  per·spir·ing
  per·spi·ra·tion
per·suade
  per·suad·ed
  per·suad·ing
  per·suad·a·ble
  per·sua·sion
  per·sua·sive
pert
  pert·ly
  pert·ness
per·tain
per·ti·na·cious
  per·ti·nac·i·ty
per·ti·nent
  per·ti·nence
  per·ti·nent·ly
per·turb
  per·turb·a·ble
  per·tur·ba·tion

pe·ruse
  pe·rused
  pe·rus·ing
  pe·rus·al
per·vade
  per·vad·ed
  per·vad·ing
  per·vad·er
  per·va·sion
  per·va·sive
per·verse
  per·verse·ness
  per·ver·si·ty
  per·ver·sion
per·vert
  per·vert·ed
per·vi·ous
pes·ky
  pesk·i·ness
pes·si·mism
  pes·si·mist
  pes·si·mis·tic
  pes·si·mis·ti·cal·ly
pes·ter
pest·i·cide
pes·tif·er·ous
pes·ti·lent
  pes·ti·lence
  pes·ti·len·tial
pes·tle
pet
  pet·ted
  pet·ting
pet·al
  pet·aled
pet·i·ole
pe·tite
  pe·tite·ness
pet·it four
pe·ti·tion
  pe·ti·tion·ary
  pe·ti·tion·er
pet·rel
pet·ri·fy
  pet·ri·fied
  pet·ri·fy·ing
  pet·ri·fac·tion
pe·tro·chem·is·try

pe·trog·ra·phy
pet·rol
pe·tro·le·um
pe·trol·o·gy
pet·ti·coat
pet·ti·fog
  pet·ti·fogged
  pet·ti·fog·ging
pet·tish
  pet·tish·ness
pet·ty
  pet·ti·ly
  pet·ti·ness
pet·u·lant
  pet·u·lance
  pet·u·lan·cy
pe·tu·nia
pew·ter
pe·yo·te
pha·e·ton
pha·lanx
phal·lus
  phal·lic
phan·tasm
  phan·tas·mal
  phan·tas·ma·go·ria
  phan·tas·ma·gor·ic
phan·ta·sy
  phan·ta·sies
phan·tom
phar·aoh
phar·ma·ceu·ti·cal
  phar·ma·ceu·tic
  phar·ma·ceu·tics
phar·ma·cist
phar·ma·col·o·gy
  phar·ma·col·o·gist
phar·ma·co·poe·ia
  phar·ma·co·poe·ial
phar·ma·cy
phar·ynx
phase
  phased
  phas·ing
pheas·ant
phe·no·bar·bi·tal
phe·nom·e·non
  phe·nom·e·na

147

phe·nom·e·nal
phi·al
phi·lan·der
  phi·lan·der·er
phi·lan·thro·py
  phi·lan·thro·pies
  phil·an·throp·ic
  phil·an·throp·i·cal
  phi·lan·thro·pist
phi·lat·e·ly
  phi·a·tel·ic
  phi·lat·e·list
phil·har·mon·ic
Phil·ip·pine
phil·o·den·dron
phi·lol·o·gy
  phi·lol·o·gist
  phil·o·lo·gi·an
  phil·o·log·i·cal
phi·los·o·phy
  phi·los·o·pher
  phil·o·soph·i·cal
  phil·o·soph·ic
  phi·los·o·phize
phil·ter
phle·bi·tis
phle·bot·o·my
phlegm
phleg·mat·ic
  phleg·mat·i·cal
phlox
pho·bia
  pho·bic
phoe·be
phoe·nix
phone
  phoned
  phon·ing
pho·neme
  pho·ne·mic
pho·net·ics
  pho·net·ic
  pho·net·i·cal·ly
phon·ic
  phon·ics
pho·no·graph
pho·nol·o·gy
  pho·no·log·ic

pho·ny
  pho·ni·ness
phos·phate
phos·pho·resce
  phos·pho·res·cence
  phos·pho·resced
  phos·pho·resc·ing
  phos·pho·res·cent
phos·pho·rus
pho·to·copy
  pho·to·cop·ies
  pho·to·cop·ied
  pho·to·cop·y·ing
pho·to·en·grave
  pho·to·en·grav·ing
pho·to·gen·ic
pho·to·graph
  pho·tog·ra·pher
  pho·tog·ra·phy
  pho·to·graph·ic
pho·to·gra·vure
pho·to·stat
pho·to·syn·the·sis
phrase
  phrased
  phras·ing
phra·se·ol·o·gy
phre·net·ic
phre·nol·o·gy
  phre·nol·o·gist
phy·lac·tery
phy·log·e·ny
phy·lum
phys·ic
  phys·ick·ing
phys·i·cal
  phys·i·cal·ly
phy·si·cian
phys·ics
  phys·i·cist
phys·i·og·no·my
  phys·i·og·nom·i·cal
  phys·i·og·no·mist
phys·i·og·ra·phy
  phys·i·o·graph·ic
phys·i·ol·o·gy
  phys·i·o·log·i·cal
  phys·i·ol·o·gist

phys·i·o·ther·a·py
phy·sique
pi·a·nis·si·mo
pi·ano
pi·an·o·for·te
pi·az·za
pi·ca
pi·ca·dor
pic·a·resque
pic·a·yune
  pic·a·yun·ish
pic·ca·lil·li
pic·co·lo
picked
pick·er·el
pick·et
  pick·et·er
pick·ing
pick·le
  pick·led
  pick·ling
pick·pock·et
picky
  pick·i·est
pic·nic
  pic·nick·ing
  pic·nick·er
pic·to·ri·al
pic·ture
  pic·tured
  pic·tur·ing
pic·tur·esque
pid·dle
  pid·dled
  pid·dling
pidg·in
piece·meal
piece·work
pierce
  pierced
  pierc·ing
pi·e·ty
pi·geon·hole
pi·geon-toed
pig·gish
pig·gy·back
pig·head·ed
pig·ment

pig·men·ta·tion
pik·er
pi·las·ter
pile
  piled
  pil·ing
pil·fer
  pil·fer·age
  pil·fer·er
pil·grim
  pil·grim·age
pil·lage
  pil·laged
  pil·lag·ing
  pil·lag·er
pil·lar
pil·lion
pil·lo·ry
  pil·lo·ried
pil·low
pi·lot
  pi·lot·age
  pi·lot·less
pi·men·to
pim·ple
  pim·pled
  pim·ply
pin
  pinned
  pin·ning
pin·a·fore
pince-nez
pin·cers
pinch
pinch·er
pin·cush·ion
pine
  piney
  pined
  pin·ing
pine-ap·ple
pin·feath·er
ping·pong
pin·ion
pin·na·cle
pin·nate
pi·noch·le
pin·to

pin·wheel
pi·o·neer
pi·ous
  pi·ous·ness
pipe·line
pip·er
pi·pette
pip·ing
pip-squeak
pi·quant
  pi·quan·cy
  pi·quant·ness
pique
  piqued
  pi·quing
pi·ra·nha
pi·rate
  pi·rat·ed
  pi·rat·ing
  pi·rat·i·cal
  pi·ra·cy
pi·rogue
pir·ou·ette
  pir·ou·et·ted
  pir·ou·et·ting
pis·ca·to·ri·al
pis·ta·chio
pis·til
  pis·til·late
pis·tol
  pis·toled
  pis·tol·ing
pis·ton
pit
  pit·ted
  pit·ting
pitch·black
pitch·blende
pitch·er
pitch·fork
pitchy
pith
  pithy
  pith·i·ness
pit·man
pi·ton
pit·tance
pi·tu·i·tary

pity
  pit·ied
  pit·y·ing
  pit·e·ous
  pit·i·a·ble
  pit·i·ful
  pit·i·less
piv·ot
  piv·ot·al·ly
pixy
  pix·ie
  pix·ie·ish
piz·za
  piz·ze·ri·a
piz·zi·ca·to
plac·a·ble
  plac·a·bil·i·ty
  plac·a·bly
plac·ard
pla·cate
  pla·cat·ed
  pla·cat·ing
  pla·ca·tion
  pla·ca·tive
place
  plac·ed
  plac·ing
  pla·ce·bo
place·ment
pla·cen·ta
  pla·cen·tal
plac·er
plac·id
  pla·cid·i·ty
  plac·id·ness
  plac·id·ly
plack·et
pla·gia·rize
  pla·gia·rized
  pla·gia·riz·ing
  pla·gia·riz·er
  pla·gia·rism
  pla·gia·rist
  pla·gia·ris·tic
  pla·gia·ry
plague
  plagued
  pla·guing

plaid
plain
  plain·ness
plain·clothes man
plain·spo·ken
plain·tiff
plain·tive
  plain·tive·ly
plait
  plait·ing
plan
  planned
  plan·ning
  plan·less
plane
  planed
  plan·ing
plan·et
plan·e·tar·i·um
plan·e·tary
plan·e·toid
plan·ish
plank·ing
plank·ton
plant
plant·a·ble
  plant·er
plan·tain
plan·ta·tion
plaque
plas·ma
plas·ter
  plas·tered
  plas·ter·ing
  plas·ter·er
  plas·ter·work
plas·ter·board
plas·tic
  plas·ti·cal·ly
  plas·tic·i·ty
plat
  plat·ted
  plat·ting
plate
  plat·ed
  plat·ing
pla·teau
plate·ful

plate·let
plat·en
plat·form
plat·i·num
plat·i·tude
  plat·i·tu·di·nal
  plat·i·tu·di·nous
  plat·i·tu·di·nize
pla·ton·ic
  pla·ton·i·cal·ly
pla·toon
plat·ter
plat·y·pus
plau·dit
plau·si·ble
  plau·si·bil·i·ty
  plau·si·ble·ness
  plau·si·bly
play·act·ing
play·back
play·boy
play·ful
  play·ful·ly
play·ground
play·house
play·mate
play·wright
pla·za
plea
plead
  plead·ed
  plead·ing
  plead·a·ble
pleas·ant
  pleas·ant·ly
pleas·ant·ry
please
  pleased
  pleas·ing
  pleas·ing·ly
pleas·ure
  pleas·ur·a·ble
  pleas·ur·a·bly
pleat
  pleat·ed
plebe
ple·be·ian
pleb·i·scite

plec·trum
pledge
  pledged
  pledg·ing
  pledg·ee
Pleis·to·cene
ple·na·ry
ple·nip·o·tent
  plen·i·po·ten·ti·ary
plen·ty
  plen·i·tude
  plen·te·ous
  plen·ti·ful
  plen·ti·ful·ly
pleth·o·ra
pleu·ri·sy
plex·us
pli·a·ble
  pli·a·bil·i·ty
  pli·a·ble·ness
  pli·a·bly
pli·ant
  pli·an·cy
  pli·ant·ness
  pli·ant·ly
pli·ers
plight
plod
  plod·ded
  plod·ding
  plod·der
plop
  plopped
  plop·ping
plot
  plot·ted
  plot·ting
  plot·ter
plov·er
plow
  plow·a·ble
  plow·er
plow·share
pluck
plucky
  pluck·i·ly
  pluck·i·ness
plug

plugged
plug·ging
plum·age
plumb·er
plumb·ing
plume
plumed
plum·ing
plum·met
plump
plump·ish
plump·ly
plump·ness
plun·der
plun·der·er
plunge
plunged
plung·ing
plung·er
plu·ral
plu·ral·ly
plu·ral·ize
plu·ral·iza·tion
plu·ral·ism
plu·ral·ist
plu·ral·is·tic
plu·ral·i·ty
plu·ral·i·ties
plush
plush·i·ness
plushy
plush·i·est
plu·toc·ra·cy
plu·to·crat
plu·to·crat·ic
plu·to·ni·um
plu·vi·al
ply
plied
ply·ing
ply·wood
pneu·mat·ic
pneu·mat·i·cal·ly
pneu·mo·nia
poach
poach·er
pock·et·book
pock·et·ful

pock·et·knife
pock·mark
pod
pod·ded
pod·ding
pod·like
po·di·a·try
po·di·a·trist
po·di·um
po·em
po·et·ic
po·et·i·cal
po·et·i·cal·ly
po·e·sy
po·e·sies
po·et
po·et·ess
po·et·ize
po·et·lau·re·ate
po·et·ry
po·grom
poign·ant
poign·an·cy
poig·nant·ly
poin·ci·ana
poin·set·tia
point
point·ed
point·ed·ly
point·er
point·less
poin·til·lism
poise
poised
pois·ing
poi·son
poi·son·er
poi·son·ing
poi·son·ous
poke
poked
pok·ing
pok·er
poky
po·lar
Po·lar·is
po·lar·i·ty
po·lar·i·za·tion

po·lar·ize
po·lar·ized
po·lar·iz·ing
pole
poled
pol·ing
pole·less
po·lem·ic
po·lem·i·cal
po·lem·i·cist
po·lice
po·liced
po·lic·ing
pol·i·cy
pol·i·cies
pol·i·cy·hold·er
po·lio
pol·i·o·my·e·li·tis
pol·ish
po·lite
po·lite·ly
po·lite·ness
pol·i·tic
pol·i·tics
po·lit·i·cal
po·lit·i·cal·ly
pol·i·ti·cian
po·lit·i·cize
po·lit·i·cized
po·lit·i·ciz·ing
pol·i·ty
pol·ka
pol·kaed
pol·ka·ing
poll
poll·ee
poll·er
poll·ster
pol·len
pol·li·nate
pol·li·nat·ed
pol·li·nat·ing
pol·li·na·tion
pol·li·na·tor
pol·li·wog
pol·lute
pol·lut·ed

pol·lut·ing
pol·lu·tant
pol·lu·ter
pol·lu·tion
po·lo
po·lo·ist
pol·o·naise
pol·ter·geist
pol·y·an·dry
pol·y·an·drous
pol·y·chro·mat·ic
pol·y·chrome
pol·y·chro·mat·ic
pol·y·es·ter
pol·y·eth·yl·ene
po·lyg·a·my
po·lyg·a·mous
po·lyg·a·mist
pol·y·glot
pol·y·gon
po·lyg·o·nal
pol·y·graph
po·lyg·y·ny
po·lyg·y·nous
pol·y·he·dron
pol·y·mer
pol·y·mer·ize
po·lym·er·i·za·tion
pol·y·mor·phism
Poly·ne·sia
pol·y·no·mi·al
pol·yp
pol·y·phon·ic
po·lyph·o·ny
pol·y·sty·rene
pol·y·syl·lab·ic
pol·y·syl·la·ble
pol·y·tech·nic
pol·y·the·ism
pol·y·the·ist
pol·y·the·is·tic
pol·y·un·sat·u·rat·ed
po·made
pome·gran·ate
pom·mel
pom·meled
pom·mel·ing
pom·pa·dour

pom·pa·no
pom·pon
pomp·ous
pom·pos·i·ty
pon·cho
pon·der
pon·der·a·ble
pon·der·ous
pon·gee
pon·iard
pon·tiff
pon·tif·i·cal
pon·tif·i·cal·ly
pon·tif·i·cate
pon·tif·i·cat·ed
pon·tif·i·cat·ing
pon·toon
po·ny
po·nies
poo·dle
poor
poor·ish
poor·ly
pop·ery
pop·ish
pop·eyed
pop·in·jay
pop·lar
pop·lin
pop·per
pop·py
pop·pies
pop·py·cock
pop·u·lace
pop·u·lar
pop·u·lar·ly
pop·u·lar·i·ty
pop·u·lar·ize
pop·u·lar·ized
pop·u·lar·iz·ing
pop·u·lar·i·za·tion
pop·u·late
pop·u·lat·ed
pop·u·lat·ing
pop·u·la·tion
pop·u·lous
por·ce·lain
por·cine

por·cu·pine
pore
pored
por·ing
pork·er
por·nog·ra·phy
por·nog·ra·pher
por·no·graph·ic
por·no·graph·i·cal·ly
po·rous
po·ros·i·ty
po·rous·ness
por·poise
por·ridge
port·a·ble
port·a·bil·i·ty
port·a·bly
por·tage
por·taged
por·tag·ing
por·tal
por·tend
por·tent
por·ten·tous
por·ter
port·fo·lio
port·hole
por·ti·co
por·tion
port·ly
port·li·er
port·li·ness
por·trait
por·trait·ist
por·trai·ture
por·tray
por·tray·er
por·tray·al
Por·tu·gal
Por·tu·guese
pose
posed
pos·ing
pos·er
pos·seur
pos·it
po·si·tion
pos·i·tive

pos·i·tive·ly
pos·i·tive·ness
pos·i·tiv·ism
pos·i·tron
pos·se
pos·sess
  pos·ses·sor
pos·sessed
pos·ses·sion
pos·ses·sive
pos·si·bil·i·ty
pos·si·ble
pos·si·bly
pos·sum
post·age
post·date
  post·dat·ed
  post·dat·ing
post·er
pos·te·ri·or
  pos·te·ri·or·i·ty
pos·ter·i·ty
post·grad·u·ate
post·haste
post·hu·mous
pos·til·ion
post·lude
post·man
post·mark
post·mas·ter
  post·mis·tress
post me·rid·i·em
post mor·tem
post·na·sal
post·na·tal
post·paid
post·par·tum
post·pone
  post·poned
  post·pon·ing
  post·pon·a·ble
  post·pone·ment
post·script
pos·tu·lant
pos·tu·late
  pos·tu·lat·ed
  pos·tu·lat·ing
  pos·tu·la·tion

pos·tu·la·tor
pos·ture
  pos·tured
  pos·tur·ing
post·war
po·sy
  po·sies
pot
  pot·ted
  pot·ting
po·ta·ble
pot·ash
po·tas·si·um
po·ta·to
  po·ta·toes
pot·bel·ly
  pot·bel·lied
po·tent
po·ten·cy
po·tent·ly
po·ten·tate
po·ten·tial
  po·ten·ti·al·i·ty
  po·ten·tial·ly
pot·hole
po·tion
pot·luck
pot·pourri
pot·tage
pot·ter
pot·tery
pouch
  pouched
  pouchy
poul·tice
poul·try
pounce
  pounced
  pounc·ing
pound·age
pound-fool·ish
pour
  pour·a·ble
pout
pov·er·ty
pov·er·ty-strick·en
pow·der
  pow·dery

pow·er
pow·er·ful
  pow·er·ful·ly
  pow·er·ful·ness
pow·er·less
pow·wow
prac·ti·ca·ble
  prac·ti·ca·bil·i·ty
  prac·ti·ca·ble·ness
  prac·ti·ca·bly
prac·ti·cal
  prac·ti·cal·i·ty
  prac·ti·cal·ly
prac·tice
prac·ticed
prac·ti·tion·er
prae·di·al
prae·to·ri·an
prag·mat·ic
  prag·mat·i·cal
  prag·mat·i·cal·ly
prag·ma·tism
  prag·ma·tist
  prag·ma·tis·tic
prai·rie
praise
  praised
  prais·ing
praise·wor·thy
pra·line
prance
  pranced
  pranc·ing
prank
  prank·ish
  prank·ster
prate
  prat·ed
  prat·ing
prat·fall
prat·tle
  prat·tled
  prat·tling
prawn
  prawn·er
prayer
  prayer·ful
preach

preach·er
preach·ment
preachy
pre·ad·o·les·cence
  pre·ad·o·les·cent
pre·am·ble
pre·ar·range
  pre·ar·ranged
  pre·ar·rang·ing
  pre·ar·range·ment
pre·as·signed
pre·can·cel
pre·car·i·ous
  pre·car·i·ous·ness
pre·cau·tion
  pre·cau·tion·ary
pre·cede
  pre·ced·ed
  pre·ced·ing
  prec·e·dence
  prec·e·dent
pre·cept
  pre·cep·tive
  pre·cep·tor
  pre·cep·to·ri·al
pre·ces·sion
pre·cinct
pre·cious
  pre·ci·os·i·ty
  pre·cious·ness
prec·i·pice
  pre·cip·i·tous
pre·cip·i·tant
pre·cip·i·tate
  pre·cip·i·tat·ed
  pre·cip·i·tat·ing
  pre·cip·i·ta·tive
  pre·cip·i·ta·tor
pre·cip·i·ta·tion
pre·cip·i·tous
pre·cis
pre·cise
  pre·cise·ness
pre·ci·sion
  pre·ci·sion·ist
pre·clude
  pre·clud·ed

pre·clud·ing
pre·clu·sion
pre·clu·sive
pre·co·cious
  pre·co·cious·ness
  pre·coc·i·ty
pre·cog·ni·tion
  pre·cog·ni·tive
pre·con·ceive
  pre·con·ceiv·ing
  pre·con·cep·tion
pre·con·di·tion
pre·cook
pre·cur·sor
  pre·cur·so·ry
pre·date
pred·a·tor
  pred·a·to·ry
pre·de·cease
pred·e·ces·sor
pre·des·ti·nate
  pre·des·ti·nat·ed
  pre·des·ti·nat·ing
pre·des·ti·na·tion
pre·des·tine
  pre·des·tined
pre·de·ter·mine
  pre·de·ter·mined
  pre·de·ter·min·ing
  pre·de·ter·mi·na·tion
pred·i·ca·ble
  pred·i·ca·bil·i·ty
pre·dic·a·ment
pred·i·cate
  pred·i·ca·tion
  pred·i·ca·tive
pre·dict
  pre·dict·a·ble
  pre·dict·a·bly
  pre·dict·a·bil·i·ty
  pre·dic·tion
  pre·dic·tive
  pre·di·lec·tion
pre·dis·pose
  pre·dis·posed
  pre·dis·pos·ing
  pre·dis·po·si·tion
pre·dom·i·nant

pre·dom·i·nance
pre·dom·i·nan·cy
pre·dom·i·nate
  pre·dom·i·nat·ed
  pre·dom·i·nat·ing
  pre·dom·i·na·tion
pre·em·i·nent
  pre·em·i·nence
pre·empt
  pre·emp·tor
  pre·emp·tion
  pre·emp·tive
pre·ex·ist
  pre·ex·ist·ence
  pre·ex·ist·ent
pre·fab·ri·cate
  pre·fab·ri·cat·ed
  pre·fab·ri·cat·ing
  pre·fab·ri·ca·tion
pref·ace
  pref·aced
  pref·ac·ing
  pref·a·to·ry
pre·fer
  per·ferred
  pre·fer·ring
pref·er·a·ble
  pref·er·a·ble·ness
  pref·er·a·bil·i·ty
  pref·er·a·bly
pref·er·ence
pref·er·en·tial
pre·fer·ment
pre·fix
pre·flight
pre·form
preg·nant
  preg·nan·cy
  preg·na·bil·i·ty
pre·heat
pre·hen·sile
pre·his·tor·ic
pre·judge
  pre·judged
  pre·judg·ing
  pre·judg·ment
prej·u·dice
  prej·u·diced

prej·u·dic·ing
prej·u·di·cial
prel·ate
pre·lim·i·nary
  pre·lim·i·nar·ies
  pre·lim·i·nar·i·ly
prel·ude
  prel·ud·ing
pre·ma·ture
  pre·ma·ture·ness
  pre·ma·tu·ri·ty
pre·med·i·cal
pre·med·i·tate
  pre·med·i·tat·ed
  pre·med·i·tat·ing
  pre·med·i·ta·tive
  pre·med·i·ta·tion
pre·men·stru·al
pre·mier
pre·miere
prem·ise
  prem·ised
  prem·is·ing
pre·mi·um
pre·mo·ni·tion
  pre·mon·i·to·ry
  pre·mon·i·to·ri·ly
pre·na·tal
  pre·na·tal·ly
pre·oc·cu·py
  pre·oc·cu·pied
  pre·oc·cu·py·ing
  pre·oc·cu·pa·tion
pre·op·er·a·tive
pre·ordain
pre·pare
  pre·pared
  pre·par·ing
  prep·a·ra·tion
  pre·par·a·to·ry
  pre·par·a·to·ri·ly
pre·par·ed·ness
pre·pay
  pre·paid
  pre·pay·ing
  pre·pay·ment
pre·plan
  pre·planned

pre·plan·ning
pre·pon·der·ant
  pre·pon·der·ance
  pre·pon·der·an·cy
  pre·pon·der·ant·ly
pre·pon·der·ate
  pre·pon·der·at·ed
  pre·pon·der·at·ing
  pre·pon·der·at·ing·ly
  pre·pon·der·a·tion
prep·o·si·tion
pre·pos·sess
  pre·pos·sess·ing
  pre·pos·ses·sion
pre·pos·ter·ous
pre·puce
pre·re·cord
pre·req·ui·site
pre·rog·a·tive
pres·age
  pres·aged
  pres·ag·ing
Pres·by·te·ri·an
pres·by·tery
pre·school
pre·scind
pre·sci·ence
  pre·sci·ent
pre·scribe
  pre·scribed
  pre·scrib·ing
pre·script
pre·scrip·tion
  pre·scrip·tive
pre·sea·son
pres·ence
pre·sent
  pre·sent·er
pres·ent
pre·sent·a·ble
  pre·sent·a·bil·i·ty
  pre·sent·a·ble·ness
  pre·sent·a·bly
pres·en·ta·tion
pres·ent·ly
pre·serve
  pre·served

pre·serv·ing
pre·serv·a·ble
pres·er·va·tion
pre·serv·a·tive
pre·side
  pre·sid·ed
pre·sid·ing
pres·i·dent
  pres·i·den·tial
  pres·i·den·cy
pre·sid·i·um
pre·sig·ni·fy
press·ing
pres·sure
  pres·sured
  pres·sur·ing
  pres·su·rize
  pres·su·rized
  pres·su·riz·er
  pres·suri·za·tion
press·work
pres·ti·dig·i·ta·tion
  pres·it·dig·i·ta·tor
pres·tige
  pres·tig·ious
pres·tis·si·mo
pres·to
pre·sum·a·ble
  pre·sum·a·bly
pre·sume
  pre·sumed
  pre·sum·ing
  pre·sump·tion
  pre·sump·tive
  pre·sump·tu·ous
pre·sup·pose
  pre·sup·posed
  pre·sup·pos·ing
  pre·sup·po·si·tion
pre·tend
  pre·tend·ed
pre·tend·er
pre·tense
pre·ten·sion
  pre·ten·tious
pret·er·it
pret·er·i·tion
pre·ter·nat·u·ral

pre·test
pre·text
pret·ti·fy
   preti·ti·fi·ca·tion
pret·ty
   pret·ti·ly
   pret·ti·ness
pret·zel
pre·vail
   pre·vail·ing
prev·a·lent
   prev·a·lence
pre·vent
   pre·vent·a·ble
   pre·vent·a·bil·i·ty
pre·ven·ta·tive
   pre·ven·tion
pre·ven·tive
pre·view
pre·vi·ous
pre·vision
pre·war
prey
   prey·er
price·less
prick·le
   prick·ly
   prick·li·ness
pride
   prid·ed
   prid·ing
pride·ful·ly
prie-dieu
priest
   priest·ess
   priest·hood
priest·ly
   priest·li·ness
prig
   prig·gish
prim
   primmed
   prim·ming
   prim·ness
pri·ma·cy
pri·ma don·na
pri·ma fa·cie
pri·mal

pri·ma·ri·ly
pri·ma·ry
   pri·mar·ies
pri·mate
prime
   primed
   prim·ing
prime me·rid·i·an
prim·er
pri·me·val
prim·i·tive
pri·mo·gen·i·tor
pri·mo·gen·i·ture
pri·mor·di·al
prim·rose
prince·ly
   prince·li·ness
prin·cess
prin·ci·pal
   prin·ci·pal·ly
   prin·ci·pal·i·ty
   prin·ci·pal·i·ties
prin·ci·ple
   prin·ci·pled
print·a·ble
print·ing
print·out
pri·or
   pri·oress
pri·or·i·ty
   pri·or·i·ties
pri·ory
prism
   pris·mat·ic
pris·on
   pris·on·er
pris·sy
   pris·si·ness
pris·tine
pri·va·cy
pri·vate
   pri·vate·ly
pri·va·tion
priv·et
priv·i·lege
   priv·i·leged
   priv·i·leg·ing
privy

priv·ies
prize
   prized
   priz·ing
prize·fight·er
prob·a·ble
   prob·a·bly
   prob·a·bil·i·ty
   prob·a·bil·i·ties
pro·bate
   pro·bat·ed
   pro·bat·ing
pro·ba·tion
   pro·ba·tion·al
   pro·ba·tion·ary
   pro·ba·tion·al·ly
   pro·ba·tion·er
pro·ba·tive
   pro·ba·to·ry
probe
   probed
   prob·ing
prob·lem
   prob·lem·at·ic
   pro·lem·at·i·cal
pro·bos·cis
pro·ce·dure
   pro·ce·dur·al
   pro·ce·dur·al·ly
pro·ceed
   pro·ceed·ing
pro·ceeds
proc·ess
pro·ces·sion
   pro·ces·sion·al
pro·claim
   proc·la·ma·tion
pro·cliv·i·ty
   pro·cliv·i·ties
pro·con·sul
pro·cras·ti·nate
   pro·cras·ti·nat·ed
   pro·cras·ti·nat·ing
   pro·cras·ti·na·tion
   pro·cras·ti·na·tor
pro·cre·ate
   pro·cre·at·ed

pro·cre·at·ing
pro·cre·a·tion
pro·cre·a·tive
pro·cre·a·tor
pro·cre·ant
proc·tor
  proc·to·ri·al
pro·cure
  pro·cured
  pro·cur·ing
  pro·cur·a·ble
  pro·cur·ance
  pro·cure·ment
  pro·cur·er
prod
  prod·ded
  prod·ding
  prod·der
prod·i·gal
  prod·i·gal·i·ty
  prod·i·gal·ly
pro·di·gious
  pro·di·gious·ness
prod·i·gy
pro·duce
  pro·duced
  pro·duc·ing
  pro·duc·er
prod·uct
  pro·duc·tion
  pro·duc·tive
  pro·duc·tiv·i·ty
pro·fane
  pro·faned
  pro·fan·ing
  pro·fan·a·to·ry
  pro·fane·ness
  pro·fan·er
  pro·fan·i·ty
pro·fess
  pro·fessed
  pro·fess·ed·ly
pro·fes·sion
  pro·fes·sion·al
  pro·fes·sion·al·ism
  pro·fes·sion·al·ize
  pro·fes·sion·al·ized

pro·fes·sion·al·iz·ing
pro·fes·sor
  pro·fes·so·ri·al
  pro·fes·so·ri·al·ly
  pro·fes·sor·ship
prof·fer
pro·fi·cient
  pro·fi·cien·cy
pro·file
  pro·filed
  pro·fil·ing
prof·it
  prof·it·less
prof·it·a·ble
  prof·it·a·bil·i·ty
  prof·it·a·ble·ness
  prof·it·a·bly
prof·it·eer
prof·li·gate
  prof·li·ga·cy
pro·found
pro·fun·di·ty
pro·fuse
pro·fuse·ly
  pro·fu·sion
pro·gen·i·tor
prog·e·ny
prog·no·sis
  prog·nos·tic
prog·nos·ti·cate
  prog·nos·ti·cat·ed
  prog·nos·ti·cat·ing
  prog·nos·ti·ca·tion
  prog·nos·ti·ca·tive
  prog·nos·ti·ca·tor
pro·gram
  pro·grammed
  pro·gram·ming
  pro·gramed
  pro·gram·ing
  pro·gram·mer
  pro·gram·er
prog·ress
  pro·gres·sion
  pro·gres·sive
pro·hib·it
pro·hi·bi·tion
  pro·hi·bi·tion·ist

pro·hib·i·tive
pro·hib·i·to·ry
pro·ject
pro·jec·tile
pro·jec·tion
  pro·jec·tion·ist
pro·jec·tive
  pro·jec·tive·ly
  pro·jec·tiv·i·ty
pro·jec·tor
pro·le·tar·i·at
  pro·le·tar·i·an
pro·lif·er·ate
  pro·lif·er·at·ed
  pro·lif·er·at·ing
  pro·lif·er·a·tion
  pro·lif·er·a·tive
pro·lif·ic
  pro·lif·i·ca·cy
  pro·lif·ic·ness
  pro·lif·i·cal·ly
pro·lix
  pro·lix·i·ty
pro·loc·u·tor
pro·logue
pro·long
  pro·lon·ga·tion
prom·e·nade
  prom·e·nad·ed
  prom·e·nad·ing
  prom·e·nad·er
prom·i·nence
prom·i·nent
  prom·i·nent·ly
pro·mis·cu·ous
  pro·mis·cu·ous·ly
  pro·mis·cu·ous·ness
  pro·mis·cu·i·ty
prom·ise
  prom·ised
  prom·is·ing
  prom·ise·ful
prom·is·so·ry
prom·on·to·ry
pro·mote
  pro·mot·ed
  pro·mot·ing
  pro·mot·a·ble

pro·mot·er
pro·mo·tion
pro·mo·tive
prompt
prompt·er
prompt·ly
prompt·ness
promp·ti·tude
prom·ul·gate
prom·ul·gat·ed
prom·ul·gat·ing
prom·ul·ga·tion
prone
prone·ness
prong
pro·noun
pro·nounce
pro·nounced
pro·nounc·ing
pro·nounce·a·ble
pro·nun·ci·a·tion
pro·nounce·ment
pron·to
proof
proof·read·er
prop
propped
prop·ping
prop·a·gan·da
prop·a·gan·dist
prop·a·gan·dis·tic
prop·a·gan·dis·ti·cal·ly
prop·a·gan·dism
prop·a·gan·dize
prop·a·gan·dized
prop·a·gan·diz·ing
prop·a·gate
prop·a·gat·ed
prop·a·gat·ing
prop·a·ga·tive
prop·a·ga·tor
prop·a·ga·tion
prop·a·ga·tion·al
pro·pane
pro·pel
pro·pelled
pro·pel·ling
pro·pel·lant

pro·pel·ler
pro·pen·si·ty
pro·pen·si·ties
prop·er
prop·er·ly
prop·er·ty
prop·er·ties
prop·er·tied
proph·e·cy
proph·e·cies
proph·e·sy
proph·e·sied
proph·e·sy·ing
proph·et
pro·phet·ic
pro·phet·i·cal·ly
pro·phy·lac·tic
pro·phy·lax·is
pro·pin·qui·ty
pro·pi·ti·ate
pro·pi·ti·at·ed
pro·pi·ti·at·ing
pro·pi·ti·a·tion
pro·pi·ti·a·to·ry
pro·pi·tious
pro·pi·tious·ly
pro·po·nent
pro·por·tion
pro·por·tion·a·ble
pro·por·tion·a·bly
pro·por·tion·al
pro·por·tion·al·i·ty
pro·por·tion·ate
pro·pose
pro·posed
pro·pos·ing
pro·pos·al
pro·pos·er
prop·o·si·tion
pro·pound
pro·pri·e·tary
pro·pri·e·tor
pro·pri·e·tress
pro·pri·e·ty
pro·pri·e·ties
pro·pul·sion
pro·pul·sive
pro·rata

pro·rate
pro·rat·ed
pro·rat·ing
pro·ra·tion
pro·sa·ic
pro·sa·i·cal·ly
pro·sa·ic·ness
pro·scribe
pro·scribed
pro·scrib·ing
pro·scrib·er
pro·scrip·tion
pro·scrip·tive
pros·e·cute
pros·e·cut·a·ble
pros·e·cu·tion
pros·e·cu·tor
pros·e·lyte
pros·e·ly·tism
pros·e·ly·tize
pros·pect
pros·pec·tor
pro·spec·tive
pro·spec·tus
pros·per
pros·per·i·ty
pros·per·ous
pros·tate
pros·the·sis
pros·thet·ic
pros·tho·don·tics
pros·tho·don·tist
pros·ti·tute
pros·ti·tut·ed
pros·ti·tut·ing
pros·ti·tu·tion
pros·ti·tu·tor
pros·trate
pros·trat·ed
pros·trat·ing
pros·tra·tion
pro·tag·o·nist
pro·te·an
pro·tect
pro·tect·ing
pro·tec·tive
pro·tec·tive·ness
pro·tec·tor

pro·tec·tion
pro·tec·tion·ism
  pro·tec·tion·ist
pro·tec·tor·ate
pro·te·ge
pro·tein
Prot·er·o·zo·ic
pro·test
prot·es·ta·tion
Prot·es·tant
  Prot·es·tant·ism
pro·to·col
pro·ton
pro·to·plasm
pro·to·type
pro·to·zo·an
pro·tract
  pro·trac·tion
  pro·trac·tive
  pro·trac·tile
pro·trac·tor
pro·trude
  pro·trud·ed
  pro·trud·ing
  pro·trud·ent
  pro·tru·sion
  pro·tru·sive
pro·tu·ber·ance
  pro·tu·ber·ant
proud
  proud·ly
prove
  proved
  prov·en
  prov·ing
  prov·a·ble
  prov·a·bly
  prov·erb
  pro·ver·bi·al
pro·vide
  pro·vid·ed
  pro·vid·ing
  pro·vid·a·ble
  pro·vid·er
prov·i·dence
  prov·i·den·tial
  prov·i·dent
prov·ince

pro·vin·cial
  pro·vin·ci·al·i·ty
  pro·vin·cial·ly
  pro·vin·cial·ist
  pro·vin·cial·ize
  pro·vin·cial·ized
  pro·vin·cial·iz·ing
  pro·vin·cial·ism
pro·vi·sion
  pro·vi·sion·al
  pro·vi·sion·al·ly
  pro·vi·sion·ary
  pro·vi·so·ry
pro·vi·so
pro·voke
  pro·voked
  pro·vok·ing
  pro·vok·ing·ly
  prov·o·ca·tion
  pro·voc·a·tive
prov·ost
prow·ess
prowl
  prowl·er
prox·i·mal
prox·i·mate
prox·im·i·ty
proxy
  prox·ies
prude
  prud·ery
  prud·ish
pru·dence
  pru·dent
  pru·den·tial
prune
  pruned
  prun·ing
pru·ri·ent
  pru·ri·ence
  pru·ri·en·cy
pry
  pried
  pry·ing
psalm·book
psalm·ist
Psal·ter
pseu·do

pseu·do·nym
  pseu·don·y·mous
pseu·do·sci·ence
  pseu·do·sci·en·tif·ic
pshaw
pso·ri·a·sis
psy·che
psych·e·del·ic
psy·chi·a·try
  psy·chi·at·ric
  psy·chi·at·ri·cal·ly
  psy·chi·a·trist
psy·chic
  psy·chi·cal
  psy·chi·cal·ly
psy·cho·a·nal·y·sis
  psy·cho·an·a·lyt·ic
  psy·cho·an·a·lyt·i·cal
  psy·cho·an·a·lyze
  psy·cho·an·a·lyzed
  psy·cho·an·a·lyz·ing
  psy·cho·an·a·lyst
psy·cho·bi·ol·o·gy
psy·cho·dra·ma
psy·cho·dy·nam·ic
  psy·cho·dy·nam·i·cal·ly
psy·cho·gen·e·sis
  psy·cho·ge·net·ic
psy·cho·gen·ic
  psy·cho·gen·i·cal·ly
psy·cho·log·i·cal
  psy·cho·log·ic
  psy·cho·log·i·cal·ly
psy·chol·o·gy
psy·chol·o·gist
psy·cho·met·ric
  psy·cho·met·ri·cal·ly
psy·cho·mo·tor
psy·cho·neu·ro·sis
  psy·cho·neu·ro·ses
  psy·cho·neu·rot·ic
psy·cho·path
psy·cho·pa·thol·o·gy
  psy·cho·pa·thol·o·gist
  psy·cho·path·o·log·ic
  psy·cho·path·o·log·i·cal
psy·chop·a·thy
  psy·cho·path·ic

psy·cho·path·i·cal·ly
psy·cho·sis
  psy·cho·ses
  psy·chot·ic
  psy·chot·i·cal·ly
psy·cho·so·mat·ic
  psy·cho·so·mat·i·cal·ly
psy·cho·ther·a·py
  psy·cho·ther·a·peu·tics
  psy·cho·ther·a·peu·tic
  psy·cho·ther·a·peu·ti·cal·ly
  psy·cho·ther·a·pist
pto·maine
pu·ber·ty
  pu·bes·cence
  pu·bes·cen·cy
  pu·bes·cent
pu·bic
pub·lic
  pub·lic·ly
  pub·lic·ness
pub·li·cist
pub·lic·i·ty
pub·li·cize
  pub·li·cized
  pub·li·ciz·ing
pub·lish
  pub·lish·er
  pub·li·ca·tion
puck·er
pud·ding
pud·dle
  pud·dled
  pud·dling
pudgy
  pudg·i·ness
pueb·lo
pu·er·ile
  pu·er·il·i·ty
  pu·er·per·al
Puer·to· Ri·co
puff
  puff·i·ness
  puffy
pu·gil·ism
  pu·gil·ist
  pu·gil·is·tic
pug·na·cious

pug·na·cious·ness
pug·na·i·ty
puke
  puked
  puk·ing
pul·let
pul·ley
pul·mo·nary
pul·mo·tor
pulp
  pulp·i·ness
  pulpy
pul·pit
pul·sar
pul·sate
  pul·sat·ed
  pul·sat·ing
pul·sa·tion
pul·sa·tor
pulse
  pulsed
  puls·ing
pul·ver·ize
  pul·ver·ized
  pul·ver·iz·ing
  pul·ver·iz·a·ble
  pul·ver·i·za·tion
  pul·ver·iz·er
pu·ma
pum·ice
pum·mel
  pum·meled
  pum·melled
  pum·mel·ing
  pum·mel·ling
pump
  pump·a·ble
  pump·er
pum·per·nick·el
pump·kin
pun
  punned
  pun·ning
punch
punch-drunk
punc·til·io
  punc·til·i·ous
punc·tu·al

punc·tu·al·i·ty
punc·tu·al·ly
punc·tu·al·ness
punc·tu·ate
  punc·tu·at·ed
  punc·tu·at·ing
  punc·tu·a·tion
punc·ture
  punc·tured
  punc·tur·ing
  punc·tur·a·ble
pun·dit
pun·gent
  pun·gen·cy
  pun·gent·ly
pun·ish
  pun·ish·a·ble
  pun·ish·ment
pu·ni·tive
pun·ster
pu·ny
  pu·ni·er
  pu·ni·est
  pu·ni·ness
pu·pa
pu·pil
pup·pet
  pup·pet·eer
  pup·pet·ry
pup·py
  pup·pies
  pup·py·ish
pur·chase
  pur·chased
  pur·chas·ing
  pur·chas·a·ble
  pur·chas·er
pure
  pure·ly
  pure·ness
pu·ri·fy
pu·ri·ty
pu·ree
pur·ga·tive
  pur·ga·tion
pur·ga·to·ry
  pur·ga·to·ri·al

purge
  purged
  purg·ing
pu·ri·fy
  pu·ri·fied
  pu·ri·fy·ing
  pu·ri·fi·ca·tion
  pu·ri·fi·er
pur·ism
  pur·ist
  pu·ris·tic
pu·ri·tan
  pu·ri·tan·i·cal
  pu·ri·tan·i·cal·ly
pu·ri·ty
purl
pur·loin
  pur·loin·er
pur·ple
  pur·plish
pur·port
  pur·port·ed·ly
pur·pose
  pur·pose·ful·ly
  pur·pose·ly
  pur·pos·ive
purse
  pursed
  purs·ing
purs·er
pur·su·ant
  pur·su·ance
pur·sue
  pur·sued
  pur·su·ing
  pur·su·er
  pur·suit
pu·ru·lent
  pu·ru·lence
  pu·ru·len·cy
  pu·ru·lent·ly
pur·vey
  pur·vey·or
  pur·vey·ance
pur·view
pushy
  push·i·ly
  push·i·ness

push·cart
push·o·ver
pu·sil·lan·i·mous
  pu·sil·la·nim·i·ty
  pu·sil·lan·i·mous·ly
puss·y·foot
puss·y·wil·low
pus·tule
put
  put
  put·ting
pu·ta·tive
pu·tre·fy
  pu·tre·fied
  pu·tre·fy·ing
  pu·tre·fac·tion
pu·trid
  pu·trid·ness
putt
  putt·ed
  putt·ing
put·ter
put·ty
puz·zle
  puz·zled
  puz·zling
  puz·zler
  puz·zle·ment
pyg·my
py·lon
py·or·rhea
pyr·a·mid
  py·ram·i·dal
pyre
py·ro·ma·nia
  py·ro·ma·ni·ac
  py·ro·ma·ni·a·cal
py·rom·e·ter
py·ro·tech·nics
py·thon

Q

quack·ery
quad·ran·gle
  quad·ran·gu·lar
quad·rant
  quad·ran·tal

quad·rate
  quad·rat·ed
  quad·rat·ing
quad·rat·ic
  quad·rat·ics
quad·ra·ture
qua·dren·ni·al
quad·ri·lat·er·al
qua·drille
quad·ril·lion
  quad·ril·lionth
quad·roon
quad·ru·ped
quad·ru·ple
  quad·ru·pled
  quad·ru·pling
quad·ru·plet
quad·ru·pli·cate
quaff
quag·mire
quail
quaint·ly
quake
  quaked
  quak·ing
Quak·er
qual·i·fy
  qual·i·fied
  qual·i·fy·ing
  qual·i·fi·a·ble
  qual·i·fi·ca·tion
qual·i·ta·tive
qual·i·ty
  qual·i·ties
qualm
  qualm·ish
quan·da·ry
quan·ti·fy
  quan·ti·fied
  quan·ti·fy·ing
  quan·ti·fi·a·ble
  quan·ti·fi·ca·tion
quan·ti·ta·tive
quan·ti·ty
  quan·ti·ties
quan·tum
quar·an·tine
  quar·an·tin·a·ble

quar·rel
  quar·reled
  quar·rel·ing
quar·rel·some
quar·ry
  quar·ries
  quar·ried
  quar·ry·ing
quart
quar·ter
quar·ter·back
quar·ter·ing
quar·ter·ly
quar·ter·mas·ter
quar·tet
qua·sar
quash
qua·si
qua·si·ju·di·cial
qua·ter·nary
quat·rain
qua·ver
  quav·er·ing·ly
quay
quea·sy
  quea·si·ly
  quea·si·ness
queen
  queen·li·ness
  queen·ly
queer
  queer·ness
quell
quench
  quench·a·ble
quer·u·lous
que·ry
  que·ried
  que·ry·ing
quest
  quest·ing·ly
ques·tion
  ques·tion·er
ques·tion·a·ble
  ques·tion·a·ble·ness
  ques·tion·a·bil·i·ty
  ques·tion·a·bly
  ques·tion·naire

queue
  queued
  queu·ing
quib·ble
  quib·bled
  quib·bling
quick
  quick·en
  quick·ness
quick·freeze
quick·sand
quick·sil·ver
quick-tem·pered
quick-wit·ted
qui·es·cent
  qui·es·cence
qui·et
  qui·et·ly
  qui·et·ness
qui·e·tude
quill
quilt
  quilt·ing
quince
qui·nine
quin·quen·ni·al
quin·tes·sence
  quin·tes·sen·tial
quin·tet
quin·til·lion
  quin·til·lion·th
quin·tu·ple
  quin·tu·pled
  quin·tu·pling
quin·tu·plet
quip
  quipped
  quip·ping
  quip·ster
quirk
  quirk·i·ness
  quirky
quis·ling
quit
  quit·ted
  quit·ting
quit·claim
quit·tance

quite
quit·ter
quiv·er
quix·ot·ic
  quix·ot·i·cal·ly
quiz
  quiz·zes
  quizzed
  quiz·zing
quiz·zi·cal
quoit
quon·dam
Quon·set
quo·rum
quo·ta
  quo·ta·tion
quote
  quot·ed
  quot·ing
  quot·able
quo·tid·i·an
quo·tient

R

rab·bet
  rab·bet·ed
  rab·bet·ing
rab·bi
  rab·bis
rab·bin·i·cal
  rab·bin·i·cal·ly
rab·bit
rab·ble
rab·id
  rab·id·ly
ra·bies
race
  raced
  rac·ing
race·horse
rac·er
race·track
ra·cial
  ra·cial·ly
rac·ism
  ra·cial·ism
rac·ist

rack·et
rack·et·eer
rac·on·teur
racy
  rac·i·ly
  rac·i·ness
ra·dar
ra·di·al
  ra·di·al·ly
ra·di·ate
  ra·di·at·ed
  ra·di·at·ing
  ra·di·ance
  ra·di·an·cy
  ra·di·ant
  ra·di·a·tion
  ra·di·a·tor
rad·i·cal
  rad·i·cal·ly
  rad·i·cal·ism
ra·dio
  ra·di·oed
  ra·di·o·ing
  ra·di·o·ac·tive
  ra·di·o·ac·tiv·i·ty
  ra·di·o·fre·quen·cy
  ra·di·o·gram
  ra·di·o·graph
  ra·dio·iso·tope
  ra·di·ol·o·gy
    ra·di·ol·o·gist
  ra·di·os·co·py
rad·ish
ra·di·um
ra·di·us
ra·don
raf·fia
raf·fish
raft·er
rag
ragged
rag·a·muf·fin
rage
  raged
  rag·ing
rag·ged
  rag·ged·ness
rag·time

rag·weed
raid·er
rail·ing
rail·lery
rail·road
rail·way
rai·ment
rain·bow
rain·coat
rain·fall
rainy
  rain·i·er
  rain·i·ly
  rain·i·ness
  rainy
raise
  raised
  rais·ing
rai·sin
rake
  raked
  rak·ing
rak·ish
  rak·ish·ness
ral·ly
  ral·lied
  ral·ly·ing
ram
  rammed
  ram·ming
ram·ble
  ram·bled
  ram·bling
ram·bler
ram·bunc·tious
ram·i·fy
  ram·i·fied
  ram·i·fy·ing
  ram·i·fi·ca·tion
ram·page
  ram·paged
  ram·pag·ing
ramp·ant
  ram·pan·cy
  ram·pant·ly
ram·part
ram·rod
ram·shack·le

ran·cid
  ran·cid·i·ty
  ran·cid·ness
ran·cor
  ran·cor·ous
ran·dom
  ran·dom·ly
  ran·dom·ness
  ran·dom·ize
range
  ranged
  rang·ing
rangy
  rang·i·ness
ran·kle
  ran·kled
  ran·kling
ran·sack
ran·som
rant·er
rap
  rapped
  rap·ping
ra·pa·cious
  ra·pa·cious·ly
  ra·pac·i·ty
rape
  rap·ist
rap·id
  ra·pid·i·ty
  rap·id·ly
  rap·id·ness
rap·id-fire
ra·pi·er
rap·ine
rap·port
rap·proche·ment
rap·scal·lion
rapt
  rapt·ly
rap·ture
  rap·tur·ous
  rap·tur·ous·ly
rare
  rar·er
  rar·est
rare·bit
rar·e·fy

rar·e·fied
rar·e·fy·ing
rar·e·fac·tion
rar·e·fied
rare·ly
rar·i·ty
rar·i·ties
ras·cal
ras·cal·i·ty
ras·cal·ly
rash
rash·ly
rash·ness
rasp
rasp·ing·ly
raspy
rasp·ber·ry
rat
rat·ted
rat·ting
rat·a·ble
rate·a·ble
ratch·et
rate
rat·ed
rat·ing
rath·er
rat·i·fy
rat·i·fied
rat·i·fy·ing
rat·i·fi·ca·tion
rat·i·fi·er
ra·tio
ra·tios
ra·ti·oc·i·na·tion
ra·tion
ra·tion·al
ra·tion·al·i·ty
ra·tion·al·ly
ra·tion·ale
ra·tion·al·ism
ra·tion·al·ist
ra·tion·al·is·tic
ra·tion·al·is·ti·cal·ly
ra·tion·al·ize
ra·tion·al·ized
ra·tion·al·iz·ing
ra·tion·al·i·za·tion

ra·tion·al·iz·er
rat·tan
rat·tle
rat·tled
rat·tling
rat·tle·brain
rat·tler
rat·tle·snake
rat·ty
rat·ti·est
rau·cous
rau·cous·ly
raun·chy
raun·chi·er
rav·age
rav·aged
rav·ag·ing
rav·ag·er
rave
raved
rav·ing
rav·el
rav·eled
rav·el·ing
ra·ven
rav·en·ous
ra·vine
ra·vi·o·li
rav·ish
rav·ish·ment
rav·ish·ing
raw
raw·ness
ray·on
raze
razed
raz·ing
ra·zor
raz·zle-daz·zle
reach·able
re·act
re·ac·tive
re·ac·tion
re·ac·tion·ary
re·ac·ti·vate
re·ac·ti·vat·ed
re·ac·ti·vat·ing
re·ac·tor

read·a·ble
read·a·bil·i·ty
read·a·ble·ness
re·ad·just
re·ad·just·ment
ready
read·ied
read·y·ing
read·i·ly
read·i·ness
read·y·made
re·a·gent
re·al
re·al·ism
re·al·ist
re·al·is·tic
re·al·is·ti·cal·ly
re·al·i·ty
re·al·i·ties
re·al·ize
re·al·ized
re·al·iz·ing
re·al·iz·a·ble
re·al·i·za·tion
re·al·ly
realm
re·al·tor
re·al·ty
ream·er
re·an·i·mate
re·an·i·mat·ed
re·an·i·mat·ing
re·an·i·ma·tion
reap·er
re·ap·pear
re·ap·pear·ance
re·ap·por·tion
re·ap·por·tion·ment
rear ad·mi·ral
re·arm
re·ar·ma·ment
re·ar·range
re·ar·ranged
re·ar·rang·ing
re·ar·range·ment
rea·son
rea·son·er
rea·son·a·ble

rea·son·a·bil·i·ty
rea·son·a·ble·ness
rea·son·a·bly
rea·son·ing
re·as·sem·ble
re·as·sem·bled
re·as·sem·bling
re·as·sem·bly
re·as·sume
re·as·sump·tion
re·as·sure
re·as·sured
re·as·sur·ing
re·as·sur·ance
re·bate
re·bat·ed
re·bat·ing
reb·el
re·bel
re·belled
re·bel·ling
re·bel·lion
re·bel·lious
re·bel·lious·ness
re·birth
re·born
re·bound
re·buff
re·build
re·built
re·build·ing
re·buke
re·buked
re·buk·ing
re·but
re·but·ted
re·but·ting
re·but·ter
re·but·tal
re·cal·ci·trant
re·cal·ci·trance
re·cal·ci·tran·cy
re·call
re·cant
re·can·ta·tion
re·cap
re·capped

re·cap·ping
re·cap·able
re·ca·pit·u·late
re·ca·pit·u·lat·ed
re·ca·pit·u·lat·ing
re·ca·pit·u·la·tion
re·cap·ture
re·cap·tured
re·cap·tur·ing
re·cast
re·cede
re·ced·ed
re·ced·ing
re·ceipt
re·ceiv·a·ble
re·ceive
re·ceived
re·ceiv·ing
re·ceiv·er
re·ceiv·er·ship
re·cent
re·cent·ly
re·cen·cy
re·cent·ness
re·cep·ta·cle
re·cep·tion
re·cep·tion·ist
re·cep·tive
re·cep·tive·ly
re·cep·tive·ness
re·cep·tiv·i·ty
re·cess
re·ces·sion
re·ces·sion·ary
re·ces·sion·al
re·ces·sive
re·charge
re·charged
re·charg·ing
re·cid·i·vism
re·cid·i·vist
rec·i·pe
re·cip·i·ent
re·cip·i·ence
re·cip·i·en·cy
re·cip·ro·cal
re·cip·ro·cal·ly
re·cip·ro·cate

re·cip·ro·cat·ed
re·cip·ro·cat·ing
re·cip·ro·ca·tion
re·cip·ro·ca·tive
rec·i·proc·i·ty
re·ci·sion
re·cit·al
re·cite
re·cit·ed
re·cit·ing
rec·i·ta·tion
rec·i·ta·tive
reck·less
reck·less·ness
reck·on
reck·on·ing
re·claim
re·claim·able
rec·la·ma·tion
re·cline
re·clined
re·clin·ing
re·clin·er
rec·luse
re·clu·sion
re·clu·sive
rec·og·nize
rec·og·nized
rec·og·niz·ing
rec·og·niz·a·ble
rec·og·niz·a·bly
rec·og·ni·tion
re·cog·ni·zance
re·coil
re·coil·less
re·col·lect
rec·ol·lect
rec·ol·lec·tion
rec·om·mend
rec·om·mend·a·ble
rec·om·mend·er
rec·om·men·da·tion
re·com·mit
re·com·mit·tal
rec·om·pense
rec·om·pensed
rec·om·pens·ing
rec·on·cile

rec·on·ciled
rec·on·cil·ing
rec·on·cil·a·ble
rec·on·cil·a·bly
rec·on·cil·er
rec·on·cil·i·a·tion
rec·on·cile·ment
rec·on·dite
re·con·di·tion
re·con·firm
re·con·fir·ma·tion
re·con·noi·ter
re·con·noi·tered
re·con·noi·ter·ing
re·con·nais·sance
re·con·sid·er
re·con·sid·er·a·tion
re·con·sti·tute
re·con·struct
re·con·struc·tion
re·cord
rec·ord
re·cord·er
re·cord·ing
re·count
re·coup
re·course
re·cov·er
re·cov·ery
re·cov·er·able
rec·re·ant
re·cre·ate
re·cre·at·ed
re·cre·at·ing
re·cre·a·tion
rec·re·a·tion
rec·re·a·tion·al
rec·re·a·tive
re·crim·i·nate
re·crim·i·nat·ed
re·crim·i·nat·ing
re·crim·i·na·tion
re·crim·i·na·tive
re·crim·i·na·to·ry
re·cruit
re·cruit·er
re·cruit·ment
rec·tal

rec·tan·gle
rec·tan·gu·lar
rec·ti·fy
rec·ti·fied
rec·ti·fy·ing
rec·ti·fi·a·ble
rec·ti·fi·ca·tion
rec·ti·fi·er
rec·ti·lin·e·ar
rec·ti·tude
rec·tor
rec·to·ry
rec·tum
re·cum·bent
re·cum·ben·cy
re·cum·bent·ly
re·cu·per·ate
re·cu·per·at·ed
re·cu·per·at·ing
re·cu·per·a·tion
re·cu·per·a·tive
re·cur
re·curred
re·cur·ring
re·cur·rence
re·cur·rent
re·cy·cle
red
red·der
red·ness
red·den
red·dish
red-blood·ed
re·dec·o·rate
re·dec·o·rat·ed
re·dec·o·rat·ing
re·dec·o·ra·tion
re·ded·i·cate
re·ded·i·cat·ed
re·ded·i·cat·ing
re·ded·i·ca·tion
re·deem
re·deem·a·ble
re·deem·er
re·demp·tion
re·demp·tive
re·demp·to·ry
red-hand·ed

re·di·rect
re·di·rec·tion
re·dis·trib·ute
re·dis·tri·bu·tion
re·dis·trict
red-let·ter
re·do
re·did
re·done
re·do·ing
red·o·lent
red·o·lence
red·o·len·cy
re·dou·ble
re·dou·bled
re·dou·bling
re·doubt·a·ble
re·doubt·a·bly
re·dress
re·duce
re·duced
re·duc·ing
re·duc·er
re·duc·i·ble
re·duc·tion
re·dun·dant
re·dun·dance
re·dun·dan·cy
re·dun·dan·cies
re·dun·dant·ly
re·du·pli·cate
re·du·pli·cat·ed
re·du·pli·cat·ing
re·dup·li·ca·tion
re·echo
re·ech·o·ing
re·ech·oes
re·ed·u·cate
re·ed·u·ca·tion
reedy
reed·i·ness
re·e·lect
re·e·lec·tion
re·em·pha·size
re·em·pha·sized
re·em·pha·siz·ing
re·em·ploy
re·en·act

re·en·force
  re·en·forced
  re·en·forc·ing
  re·en·force·ment
re·en·list
  re·en·list·ment
re·en·ter
  re·en·trance
  re·en·try
re·es·tab·lish
  re·es·tab·lish·ment
re·ex·am·ine
  re·ex·am·ined
  re·ex·am·in·ing
  re·ex·am·i·na·tion
re·fer
  re·ferred
  re·fer·ring
  re·fer·a·ble
  re·fer·ral
ref·er·ee
  ref·er·eed
  ref·er·ee·ing
ref·er·ence
  ref·er·enced
  ref·er·enc·ing
ref·er·en·dum
ref·er·ent
  ref·er·en·tial
re·fer·ral
re·fill
  re·fill·a·ble
re·fi·nance
re·fine
  re·fined
  re·fin·ing
  re·fine·ment
re·fin·ery
re·fin·ish
re·fit
  re·fit·ted
  re·fit·ting
re·flect
  re·flec·tion
  re·flec·tive
  re·flec·tive·ly
re·flec·tor
re·flex

re·flex·ive
re·for·est
  re·for·est·a·tion
re·form
  re·formed
  re·form·er
  re·form·ist
ref·or·ma·tion
  re·form·a·to·ry
  re·form·a·tive
re·fract
  re·frac·tive
  re·frac·tion
re·frac·to·ry
  re·frac·to·ri·ness
re·frain
re·fran·gi·ble
re·fresh
  re·fresh·ing
  re·fresh·ment
re·frig·er·ate
  re·frig·er·at·ed
  re·frig·er·at·ing
  re·frig·er·ant
  re·frig·er·a·tion
  re·frig·er·a·tor
ref·uge
ref·u·gee
re·ful·gent
  re·ful·gence
re·fund
re·fur·bish
re·fuse
  re·fused
  re·fus·ing
  re·fus·al
ref·use
re·fute
  re·fut·ed
  re·fut·ing
  re·fut·a·ble
  ref·u·ta·tion
re·gain
re·gal
  re·gal·ly
re·gale
  re·galed
  re·gal·ing

re·ga·lia
re·gard
  re·gard·ful
  re·gard·ing
  re·gard·less
re·gat·ta
re·gen·cy
re·gen·er·ate
  re·gen·er·at·ed
  re·gen·er·at·ing
  re·gen·er·a·cy
  re·gen·er·a·tion
  re·gen·er·a·tive
re·gent
re·gime
reg·i·men
reg·i·ment
  reg·i·men·tal
  reg·i·men·ta·tion
re·gion
  re·gion·al
  re·gion·al·ly
reg·is·ter
  reg·is·tered
  reg·is·trant
  reg·is·trar
  reg·is·tra·tion
  reg·is·try
re·gress
  re·gres·sion
  re·gres·sive
re·gret
  re·gret·ted
  re·gret·ting
  re·gret·ta·ble
  re·gret·ta·bly
  re·gret·ful·ly
  re·gret·ful·ness
reg·u·lar
  reg·u·lar·i·ty
reg·u·late
  reg·u·lat·ed
  reg·u·lat·ing
  reg·u·la·tive
  reg·u·la·tor
  reg·u·la·to·ry
  reg·u·la·tion
re·gur·gi·tate

re·gur·gi·tat·ed
re·gur·gi·tat·ing
re·gur·gi·ta·tion
re·ha·bil·i·tate
  re·ha·bil·i·tat·ed
  re·ha·bil·i·tat·ing
  re·ha·bil·i·ta·tion
  re·ha·bil·i·ta·tive
re·hash
re·hears·al
re·hearse
  re·hearsed
  re·hears·ing
reign
re·im·burse
  re·im·bursed
  re·im·burs·ing
  re·im·burse·ment
rein
re·in·car·nate
  re·in·car·na·tion
rein·deer
re·in·fec·tion
re·in·force
  re·in·forced
  re·in·forc·ing
  re·in·force·ment
re·in·state
  re·in·stat·ed
  re·in·stat·ing
  re·in·state·ment
re·in·sur·ance
re·in·ter·pre·ta·tion
re·is·sue
re·it·er·ate
  re·it·er·at·ed
  re·it·er·at·ing
  re·it·er·a·tion
re·ject
  re·jec·tion
re·joice
  re·joiced
  re·joic·ing
re·join
  re·join·der
re·ju·ve·nate
  re·ju·ve·nat·ed
  re·ju·ve·nat·ing

re·ju·ve·na·tion
re·kin·dle
  re·kin·dled
  re·kin·dling
re·lapse
  re·lapsed
  re·laps·ing
re·late
  re·lat·ed
  re·lat·ing
re·la·tion
  re·la·tion·al
  re·la·tion·ship
rel·a·tive
  rel·a·tive·ly
rel·a·tiv·i·ty
re·lax
  re·lax·a·tion
re·lay
  re·laid
  re·lay·ing
re·lay
  re·layed
  re·lay·ing
re·lease
  re·leased
  re·leas·ing
rel·e·gate
  rel·e·gat·ed
  rel·e·gat·ing
  rel·e·ga·tion
re·lent
  re·lent·less
rel·e·vant
  rel·e·vance
  rel·e·van·cy
re·li·a·ble
  re·li·a·bil·i·ty
  re·li·a·ble·ness
  re·li·a·bly
re·li·ant
  re·li·ance
rel·ic
re·lief
re·lieve
  re·lieved
  re·liev·ing
  re·liev·a·ble

re·li·gion
  re·li·gi·os·i·ty
  re·li·gious
re·lin·quish
rel·ish
re·live
  re·lived
  re·liv·ing
re·lo·cate
  re·lo·cat·ed
  re·lo·cat·ing
  re·lo·ca·tion
re·luc·tant
  re·luc·tance
re·ly
  re·lied
  re·ly·ing
re·main
  re·main·der
re·mand
re·mark
re·mark·a·ble
  re·mark·a·ble·ness
  re·mark·a·bly
re·me·di·al
  re·me·di·a·ble
rem·e·dy
  rem·e·dies
  rem·e·died
  rem·e·dy·ing
re·mem·ber
  re·mem·brance
re·mind
  re·mind·er
rem·i·nisce
  rem·i·nisced
  rem·i·nisc·ing
  rem·i·nis·cence
  rem·i·nis·cent
re·miss
  re·mis·sion
re·mit
  re·mit·ted
  re·mit·ting
  re·mit·tance
rem·nant
re·mod·el
re·mon·strate

re·mon·strat·ed
re·mon·strat·ing
re·mon·strance
re·morse
re·morse·ful·ly
re·morse·less
re·mote
re·mote·ly
re·mote·ness
re·mount
re·move
re·moved
re·mov·ing
re·mov·a·ble
re·mov·al
re·mu·ner·ate
re·mu·ner·at·ed
re·mu·ner·at·ing
re·mu·ner·a·tion
re·mu·ner·a·tive
ren·ais·sance
re·nas·cence
re·nas·cent
rend
rend·ed
rend·ing
ren·der
ren·di·tion
ren·dez·vous
ren·dez·voused
ren·dez·vous·ing
ren·e·gade
re·nege
re·neged
re·neg·ing
re·new
re·new·al
re·nom·i·nate
re·nounce
re·nounced
re·nounc·ing
ren·o·vate
ren·o·vat·ed
ren·o·vat·ing
ren·o·va·tion
re·nown
re·nowned
rent·al

re·nun·ci·a·tion
re·or·gan·ize
re·or·gan·ized
re·or·gan·iz·ing
re·or·gan·i·za·tion
re·pair
rep·a·ra·ble
rep·a·ra·tion
rep·ar·tee
re·past
re·pa·tri·ate
re·pa·tri·at·ed
re·pa·tri·at·ing
re·pa·tri·a·tion
re·pay
re·paid
re·pay·ing
re·pay·ment
re·peal
re·peat
re·peat·a·ble
re·peat·ed
re·peat·er
re·pel
re·pelled
re·pel·ling
re·pel·lent
re·pent
re·pent·ance
re·pent·ant
re·per·cus·sion
rep·er·toire
rep·er·to·ry
rep·e·ti·tion
rep·e·ti·tious
re·pet·i·tive
re·place
re·placed
re·plac·ing
re·place·a·ble
re·place·ment
re·plen·ish
re·plete
re·ple·tion
rep·li·ca
re·ply
re·plied
re·ply·ing

re·plies
re·port
re·port·able
re·port·ed·ly
re·port·er
rep·or·to·ri·al
re·pose
re·posed
re·pos·ing
re·pos·i·tory
re·pos·sess
re·pos·ses·sion
rep·re·hend
rep·re·hen·si·ble
rep·re·hen·sion
rep·re·sent
rep·re·sen·ta·tion
rep·re·sent·a·tive
re·press
re·pres·sion
re·prieve
re·prieved
re·priev·ing
re·pri·mand
re·pris·al
re·proach
re·proach·ful·ly
rep·ro·bate
rep·ro·ba·tion
re·pro·duce
re·pro·duced
re·pro·duc·ing
re·pro·duc·tion
re·pro·duc·tive
re·proof
re·prove
re·proved
re·prov·ing
rep·tile
rep·til·i·an
re·pub·lic
re·pub·li·can
re·pu·di·ate
re·pu·di·at·ed
re·pu·di·at·ing
re·pu·di·a·tion
re·pug·nant
re·pug·nance

re·pug·nan·cy
re·pulse
  re·plused
  re·puls·ing
  re·pul·sion
  re·pul·sive
rep·u·ta·ble
  rep·u·ta·bly
  rep·u·ta·bil·i·ty
rep·u·ta·tion
re·pute
  re·put·ed
  re·put·ing
re·quest
req·ui·em
re·quire
  re·quired
  re·quir·ing
  re·quire·ment
req·ui·site
req·ui·si·tion
re·quit·al
re·quite
re·run
  re·run·ning
re·scind
re·scis·sion
res·cue
  res·cued
  res·cu·ing
re·search
  re·search·er
re·sem·ble
  re·sem·bled
  re·sem·bling
  re·sem·blance
re·sent
  re·sent·ful
  re·sent·ment
re·serve
  re·served
  re·serv·ing
  res·er·va·tion
re·serv·ist
res·er·voir
re·set
  re·set·ting
re·side

re·sid·ed
re·sid·ing
res·i·dence
res·i·den·cy
res·i·dent
res·i·den·tial
res·i·due
re·sid·u·al
re·sign
  res·ig·na·tion
  re·signed
re·sil·ient
  re·sil·ience
  re·sil·ien·cy
res·in
  res·in·ous
re·sist
  re·sist·er
  re·sist·i·ble
  re·sist·ance
  re·sist·ant
  re·sis·tor
res·o·lute
  res·o·lu·tion
re·solve
  re·solved
  re·solv·ing
res·o·nant
  res·o·nance
res·o·nate
  res·o·nat·ed
  res·o·nat·ing
  res·o·na·tor
re·sort
re·sound
re·source
re·spect
  re·spect·ful·ly
  re·spect·ful·ness
  re·spect·a·ble
  re·spect·a·bil·i·ty
  re·spect·ing
  re·spec·tive
res·pi·ra·tion
  res·pi·ra·to·ry
res·pi·ra·tor
re·spire
  re·spired

re·spir·ing
res·pite
re·splend·ent
  re·splend·ence
re·spond
re·spond·ent
re·sponse
  re·spon·sive
  re·spon·si·ble
  re·spon·si·bil·i·ty
  re·spon·si·bil·i·ties
res·tau·rant
res·tau·ra·teur
rest·ful·ly
res·ti·tu·tion
res·tive
re·store
  re·stored
  re·stor·ing
  res·to·ra·tion
  re·stor·a·tive
re·strained
re·straint
re·strict
  re·strict·ed
  re·stric·tion
  re·stric·tive
re·sult
  re·sult·ant
re·sume
  re·sumed
  re·sum·ing
  re·sump·tion
re·su·me
re·sur·gent
  re·sur·gence
res·ur·rect
  res·ur·rec·tion
re·sus·ci·tate
  re·sus·ci·tat·ed
  re·sus·ci·tat·ing
  re·sus·ci·ta·tion
  re·sus·ci·ta·tor
re·tail·er
re·tain·er
re·take
  re·took
  re·tak·en

re·tak·ing
re·tal·i·ate
  re·tal·i·at·ed
  re·tal·i·at·ing
  re·tal·i·a·tion
  re·tal·i·a·to·ry
re·tard
  re·tard·ant
  re·tar·da·tion
  re·tard·ed
retch
re·tell
  re·told
  re·tell·ing
re·ten·tion
re·ten·tive
  re·ten·tiv·i·ty
ret·i·cent
  ret·i·cence
re·tic·u·lar
ret·i·na
ret·i·nue
re·tire
  re·tired
  re·tir·ing
  re·tire·ment
re·tort
re·touch
re·trace
  re·traced
  re·trac·ing
re·tract
  re·trac·tion
  re·trac·tor
re·trac·tile
re·tread
re·treat
re·trench
  re·trench·ment
re·tri·al
ret·ri·bu·tion
re·trieve
  re·trieved
  re·triev·ing
  re·triev·er
ret·ro·ac·tive
ret·ro·fire
ret·ro·grade

ret·ro·gress
  ret·ro·gres·sion
  ret·ro·gres·sive
ret·ro·rock·et
ret·ro·spect
  ret·ro·spec·tion
  ret·ro·spec·tive
re·turn
  re·turn·a·ble
  re·turn·ee
re·un·ion
re·u·nite
  re·u·nit·ed
  re·u·nit·ing
rev
  revved
  rev·ving
re·value
  re·val·u·ate
  re·val·u·a·tion
re·vamp
re·veal
  rev·e·la·tion
rev·eil·le
rev·el
  rev·el·ry
re·venge
  re·venged
  re·veng·ing
  re·venge·ful
rev·e·nue
  rev·e·nu·er
re·ver·ber·ate
  re·ver·ber·at·ed
  re·ver·ber·at·ing
  re·ver·ber·a·tion
re·vere
  re·vered
  re·ver·ing
rev·er·ence
  rev·er·enced
  rev·er·enc·ing
rev·er·end
rev·er·ent
  rev·er·en·tial
rev·er·ie
re·ver·sal
re·verse

re·versed
re·vers·ing
re·vers·i·ble
re·ver·sion
re·vert
re·view
re·vile
  re·viled
  re·vil·ing
re·vise
  re·vised
  re·vis·ing
  re·vi·sion
  re·vi·sion·ist
re·vi·tal·ize
  re·vi·tal·iza·tion
re·viv·al
  re·viv·al·ist
re·vive
  re·vived
  re·viv·ing
  re·viv·i·fy
rev·o·ca·tion
re·voke
  re·voked
  re·vok·ing
rev·o·ca·ble
rev·o·ca·tion
re·volt
rev·o·lu·tion
  rev·o·lu·tion·ary
  rev·o·lu·tion·aries
  rev·o·lu·tion·ist
  rev·o·lu·tion·ize
re·volve
  re·volved
  re·volv·ing
re·volv·er
re·vue
re·vul·sion
re·wak·en
re·ward
re·wind
  re·wound
  re·wind·ing
re·write
  re·wrote
  re·writ·ten

re·writ·ing
rhap·sod·ic
  rhap·sod·i·cal·ly
rhap·so·dize
  rhap·so·dized
  rhap·so·diz·ing
rhap·so·dy
  rhap·so·dies
  rhap·so·dist
rhe·o·stat
rhe·sus
rhet·o·ric
  rhe·tor·i·cal·ly
rhet·o·ri·cian
rheu·mat·ic
  rheu·ma·tism
  rheu·ma·toid
rhine·stone
rhi·noc·er·os
rhi·zome
rho·do·den·dron
rhom·boid
rhom·bus
rhu·barb
rhyme
  rhymed
  rhym·ing
rhythm
  rhyth·mic
  rhyth·mi·cal
  rhyth·mi·cal·ly
rib
  ribbed
  rib·bing
rib·ald
  rib·ald·ry
rib·bon
ri·bo·fla·vin
rib·bo·nu·cle·ic
rich·es
rich·ness
rick·ets
rick·ety
  rick·et·i·ness
rick·shaw
ric·o·chet
  ric·o·cheted
  ric·o·chet·ing

rid
  rid·ded
  rid·ding
  rid·dance
rid·dle
  rid·dled
  rid·dling
ride
  rode
  rid·den
  rid·ing
  rid·er
ridge
  ridged
  ridg·ing
rid·i·cule
  rid·i·culed
  rid·i·cul·ing
ri·dic·u·lous
rif·fle
  rif·fled
  rif·fling
ri·fle
  ri·fled
  ri·fling
rig
  rigged
  rig·ging
rig·ger
right·eous
right·ful·ly
right·hand·ed
right-of-way
right·wing·er
rig·id
  ri·gid·i·ty
rig·ma·role
rig·or
  rig·or·ous
rig·or mortis
rile
  riled
  ril·ing
rim
  rimmed
  rim·ming
ring
  ringed

  ring·ing
ring
  rang
  rung
  ring·ing
ring·lead·er
ring·mas·ter
rinse
  rinsed
  rins·ing
Rio de Ja·nei·ro
ri·ot·er
ri·ot·ous
rip
  ripped
  rip·ping
ri·par·i·an
rip·en
  ripe·ness
rip·ple
  rip·pled
  rip·pling
rise
  rose
  ris·en
  ris·ing
ris·i·ble
ris·i·bil·i·ty
risky
  risk·i·er
  risk·i·ness
ris·que
rite
  rit·u·al
  rit·u·al·ism
  rit·u·al·ist
  rit·u·al·is·tic
ritzy
  ritz·i·er
ri·val
  ri·val·ry
  ri·val·ries
riv·er·side
riv·et·er
riv·i·er·a
riv·u·let
roach·es
road·bed

road·block
road·run·ner
roast·er
rob
  robbed
  rob·bing
  rob·ber
rob·bery
  rob·ber·ies
robe
  robed
  rob·ing
rob·in
ro·bot
  ro·bot·ics
ro·bust
rock·bound
rock·er
rock·et
  rock·et·ry
rock·ribbed
rocky
  rock·i·ness
ro·co·co
ro·dent
ro·deo
roent·gen
rogue
  ro·guish
  ro·guery
roist·er
roll·er bear·ing
roll·er coast·er
roll·er-skate
rol·lick
  rol·lick·ing
roll·ing mill
ro·ly-po·ly
ro·maine
ro·mance
  ro·manced
  ro·manc·ing
ro·man·tic
  ro·man·ti·cism
  ro·man·ti·cist
  ro·man·ti·cize
  ro·man·ti·cized
  ro·man·ti·ciz·ing

romp·er
roof·ing
rook·ery
rook·ie
room·mate
roomy
  room·i·er
  room·i·ness
roost·er
rope
  roped
  rop·ing
  ropy
ro·sa·ry
  ro·sa·ries
ro·se·ate
ro·sette
Rosh Ha·sha·nah
ros·in
ros·ter
ros·trum
rosy
  ros·i·ness
rot
  rot·ted
  rot·ting
  rot·ten
ro·tate
  ro·tat·ed
  ro·tat·ing
  ro·ta·ry
  ro·ta·tion
ro·tis·ser·ie
ro·tund
  ro·tun·di·ty
  ro·tun·da
rou·e
rouge
  rouged
  roug·ing
rough·age
rough-and-tum·ble
rough·en
  rough-hewed
rough·house
rough·neck
rough·rid·er
rough·shod

rou·lette
round·a·bout
round·ed
round·er
round-shoul·dered
rouse
  roused
  rous·ing
roust·a·bout
rout
route
  rout·ed
  rout·ing
rou·tine
  rou·tin·ize
  rou·tin·ized
  rou·tin·iz·ing
rove
  roved
  rov·ing
row·dy
  row·dies
  row·di·ly
  row·di·ness
roy·al
  roy·al·ly
  roy·al·ist
  roy·al·ty
  roy·al·ties
rub
  rubbed
  rub·bing
  rub·ber
  rub·bery
  rub·ber·ize
  rub·ber·ized
  rub·ber·iz·ing
rub·bish
rub·ble
ru·bel·la
ru·bi·cund
ru·bric
ru·by
  ru·bies
ruck·sack
ruck·us
rud·der
rud·dy

rud·di·ness
rude
  rude·ly
  rude·ness
ru·di·ment
  ru·di·men·tal
  ru·di·men·ta·ry
rue
  rued
  ru·ing
rue·ful·ly
  rue·ful·ness
ruf·fi·an
ruf·fle
  ruf·fled
  ruf·fling
rug·ged
  rug·ged·ness
ru·in
  ru·in·a·tion
  ru·in·ous
rule
  ruled
  rul·ing
rum·ba
rum·ble
  rum·bled
  rum·bling
ru·mi·nant
ru·mi·nate
  ru·mi·nat·ing
  ru·mi·na·tion
rum·mage
  rum·mag·ing
rum·my
ru·mor
ru·mor·mon·ger
rum·ple
  rum·pled
  rum·pling
rum·pus
run
  ran
  run
  run·ning
run·a·way
run·ner-up
run·ny

runt
  runty
  runt·i·est
run·way
rup·ture
  rup·tured
  rup·tur·ing
ru·ral
  ru·ral·ly
  ru·ral·ized
  ru·ral·i·za·tion
rus·set
Rus·sia
Rus·sian
rus·tic
rus·ti·cate
  rus·ti·cat·ed
  rus·ti·cat·ing
  rus·ti·ca·tion
  rus·tic·i·ty
rus·tle
  rus·tled
  rus·tling
rus·tler
rusty
  rust·i·ness
rut
  rut·ted
  rut·ting
ru·ta·ba·ga
ruth·less
  ruth·less·ness
rut·ty
  rut·ti·est

S

Sab·a·oth
Sab·bath
sab·bat·i·cal
sa·ber
sa·ble
sab·o·tage
  sab·o·taged
  sab·o·tag·ing
  sab·o·teur
sac·cha·rin
sac·cha·rine

sac·er·do·tal
sa·chet
sack·ful
sack·ing
sac·ra·ment
sa·cred
  sa·cred·ly
  sa·cred·ness
sac·ri·fice
  sac·ri·ficed
  sac·ri·fic·ing
  sac·ri·fi·cial
sac·ri·lege
  sac·ri·le·gious
sac·ris·ty
sac·ro·il·i·ac
sac·ro·sanct
  sac·ro·sanc·ti·ty
sad
  sad·der
  sad·ly
  sad·ness
  sad·den
sad·dle
  sad·dled
  sad·dling
sad·ism
  sad·ist
  sa·dis·tic
  sa·dis·ti·cal·ly
sa·fa·ri
safe
  saf·er
  saf·est
safe-con·duct
safe-de·pos·it
safe·keep·ing
safe·ty
saf·flow·er
saf·fron
sag
  sagged
  sag·ging
sa·ga
sa·ga·cious
  sa·gac·i·ty
sage
  sage·ness

Sag·it·ta·ri·us
sail·ing
sail·or
saint·hood
saint·ed
saint·ly
  saint·li·ness
sa·ke
sa·laam
sale·a·ble
  sal·a·bil·i·ty
sa·la·cious
sal·ad
sal·a·man·der
sa·la·mi
sal·a·ry
  sal·a·ries
sales·man
sales·per·son
sales·wom·an
sa·li·ent
  sa·li·ence
  sa·li·en·cy
  sa·li·ent·ly
  sa·li·ent·ness
sa·line
  sa·lin·i·ty
sa·li·va
  sal·i·vary
sal·i·vate
  sal·i·vat·ed
  sal·i·vat·ing
  sal·i·va·tion
sal·low
sal·ly
  sal·lied
salm·on
sal·mo·nel·la
sa·lon
sa·loon
salt·cel·lar
salt·ed
sal·tine
salt·shak·er
salt-wa·ter
salty
  salt·i·ness
sa·lu·bri·ous

sal·u·tary
sal·u·ta·tion
sa·lu·ta·to·ry
sa·lute
  sa·lut·ed
  sa·lut·ing
sal·vage
  sal·vaged
  sal·vag·ing
  sal·vage·a·ble
sal·va·tion
salve
  salved
  salv·ing
sal·vo
sam·ba
same·ness
sam·o·var
sam·ple
  sam·pled
  sam·pling
sam·pler
san·a·to·ri·um
sanc·ti·fy
  sanc·ti·fied
  sanc·ti·fy·ing
  sanc·ti·fi·ca·tion
sanc·ti·mo·ny
  sanc·ti·mo·ni·ous
sanc·tion
  sanc·tion·a·ble
sanc·ti·ty
sanc·tu·ary
sanc·tum
san·dal
sand·bag
  sand·bagged
  sand·bag·ging
sand-cast
  sand-cast·ed
  sand-cast·ing
sand·pa·per
sand·pi·per
sand·wich
sandy
  sand·i·ness
sane
  sane·ly

sane·ness
sang-froid
san·gria
san·gui·nary
san·guine
san·i·tar·i·um
san·i·tary
  san·i·tar·i·ly
  san·i·ta·tion
san·i·tize
  san·tized
  san·i·tiz·ing
san·i·ty
San·ta Claus
sap
  sapped
  sap·ping
sa·pi·ent
  sa·pi·ence
  sa·pi·en·cy
  sa·pi·en·tial
sap·ling
sap·phire
sap·py
sap·suck·er
sa·ran
sar·casm
  sar·cas·tic
  sar·cas·ti·cal·ly
sar·co·ma
sar·coph·a·gus
sar·dine
sar·don·ic
  sar·don·i·cal·ly
sa·ri
sa·rong
sar·sa·pa·ril·la
sar·to·ri·al
sa·shay
Sas·katch·e·wan
sas·sa·fras
sas·sy
  sas·si·ness
sa·tan·ic
  sa·tan·i·cal
satch·el
sate
  sat·ed

175

sat·ing
sa·teen
sat·el·lite
sa·ti·a·ble
  sa·ti·a·bly
  sa·ti·a·bil·i·ty
  sa·ti·a·ble·ness
sa·ti·ate
  sa·ti·at·ed
  sa·ti·at·ing
  sa·ti·a·tion
sa·ti·e·ty
sat·in
  sat·iny
sat·ire
  sa·tir·i·cal·ly
  sat·i·rist
sat·i·rize
  sat·i·rized
  sat·i·riz·ing
sat·is·fac·tion
sat·is·fac·to·ry
  sat·is·fac·to·ri·ly
sat·is·fy
  sat·is·fied
  sat·is·fy·ing
  sat·is·fi·a·ble
sat·u·rate
  sat·u·rat·ed
  sat·u·rat·ing
  sat·u·ra·ble
  sat·u·ra·tion
sat·ur·nine
sa·tyr
  sa·tyr·ic
sauce
sau·cer
sau·cy
  sau·ci·ness
Sau·di Ara·bia
sau·er·bra·tne
sau·er·kraut
sau·na
saun·ter
sau·sage
sau·te
  sau·teed
  sau·tee·ing

sau·terne
sav·age
  sav·age·ness
  sav·age·ry
sa·van·na
sa·vant
save
  saved
  sav·ing
sav·ior
sa·vior-faire
sa·vor
sa·vory
  sa·vor·i·ly
  sa·vor·i·ness
sav·vy
sax·o·phone
  sax·o·phon·ist
say
  said
  say·ing
scab
  scabbed
  scab·bing
scab·bard
scab·by
  scab·bi·ness
sca·bies
scaf·fold
scaf·fold·ing
scal·a·wag
scald
  scald·ing
scale
  scaled
  scal·ing
  scal·i·ness
scal·lion
scal·lop
scalp
  scalp·er
scal·pel
scaly
  scal·i·ness
scamp·er
scan
  scanned
  scan·ning

scan·ner
scan·dal
scan·dal·ize
  scan·dal·ized
  scan·dal·iz·ing
  scan·dal·i·za·tion
scan·dal·mon·ger
scan·dal·ous
Scan·di·na·via
scant
  scant·ness
scanty
  scant·i·ness
scape·goat
scap·u·la
scar
  scarred
  scar·ring
scar·ab
scarce
  scarce·ness
  scar·ci·ty
scare
  scared
  scar·ing
scarf
  scarfs
  scarves
scar·i·fy
  scar·i·fied
  scar·i·fy·ing
  scar·i·fi·ca·tion
scar·let
scarp
scary
  scar·i·er
  scar·i·est
scat
  scat·ted
  scat·ting
scathe
  scathed
  scath·ing
scat·ter
scat·ter·brained
scav·enge
  scav·enged
  scav·eng·ing

scav·en·ger
sce·nar·io
sce·nar·ist
scen·ery
sce·nic
  sce·ni·cal
scent
scep·ter
sched·ule
  sched·uled
  sched·ul·ing
sche·ma
  sche·mat·i·cal·ly
sche·ma·tize
  sche·ma·tized
  sche·ma·tiz·ing
scheme
  schem·er
  schem·ing
scher·zo
schism
  schis·mat·ic
  schis·mat·i·cal
schiz·oid
schiz·o·phre·nia
  schiz·o·phren·ic
schol·ar
  schol·ar·ly
  schol·ar·li·ness
schol·ar·ship
scho·las·tic
  scho·las·ti·cal
  scho·las·ti·cism
school board
school·ing
school·teach·er
schoon·er
sci·at·ic
  sci·at·i·ca
sci·ence
sci·en·tif·ic
  sci·en·tif·i·cal·ly
sci·en·tist
scim·i·tar
scin·til·la
scin·til·lant
scin·til·late
  scin·til·lat·ed

scin·til·lat·ing
scin·til·la·tion
sci·on
scis·sors
scle·ro·sis
scoff·er
scoff·ing·ly
scoff·law
scold·ing
scol·lop
sconce
scone
scoop·er
scoop·ful
scoot·er
scope
scorch
  scorched
  scorch·ing
score
  scored
  scor·ing
  score·less
  scor·er
score·keep·er
scorn
  scorn·er
  scorn·ful·ness
scor·pi·on
scot-free
scot·tie
scoun·drel
  scoun·drel·ly
scour
  scour·er
scourge
  scourged
  scourg·ing
scout·ing
scout·mas·ter
scowl
scrab·ble
  scrab·bled
  scrab·bling
scrag
  scragged
  scrag·ging
scrag·gly

scrag·gy
scram
  scrammed
  scram·ming
scram·ble
  scram·bled
  scram·bling
scrap
  scrapped
  scrap·ping
scrape
  scraped
  scrap·ing
scrap·per
scrap·py
  scrap·pi·ness
scratch
scratchy
  scratch·i·ness
scrawl
scrawny
  scrawn·i·ness
scream·er
scream·ing
screech
screen
  screen·er
  screen·ing
screw·driv·er
screwy
scrib·ble
  scrib·bled
  scrib·bling
  scrib·bler
scribe
  scribed
  scrib·ing
scrim·mage
  scrim·maged
  scrim·mag·ing
  scrim·mag·er
scrimpy
  scrimp·i·ness
scrim·shaw
script
scrip·ture
  scrip·tur·al
script·writ·er

scriv·en·er
scroll-work
scrooge
scro·tum
scrounge
  scroung·er
  scroung·ing
scrub
  scrubbed
  scrub·bing
scrub·by
  scruff·i·ness
scrump·tious
scru·ple
scru·pu·lous
  scru·pu·los·i·ty
  scru·pu·lous·ness
  scru·pu·lous·ly
scru·ta·ble
scru·ti·nize
  scru·ti·nized
  scru·ti·niz·er
  scru·ti·niz·ing·ly
scru·ti·ny
scu·ba
scuf·fle
  scuf·fled
  scuf·fling
scul·lery
sculp·tor
  sculp·tress
sculp·ture
  sculp·tured
  sculp·turing
  sculp·tur·al
scum
  scum·my
scup·per
scur·ri·lous
  scurril·i·ty
scurry
  scur·ried
  scurry·ing
scur·vy
  scur·vi·ness
scut·tle
  scut·tled

scut·tling
scut·tle-butt
scythe
  scythed
  scyth·ing
sea·far·ing
  sea·far·er
sea·go·ing
seal·ant
sea lam·prey
seal·skin
sea·man·ship
seam·stress
seamy
  seam·i·ness
se·ance
search
  search·er
  search·ing
search·light
sea·scape
sea·shell
sea·shore
sea·sick·ness
sea·side
sea·son
  sea·son·er
  sea·son·ing
  sea·son·a·ble
  sea·son·al
  sea·son·al·ly
seat·ing
sea·wor·thy
  sea·wor·thi·ness
se·ba·ceous
se·cant
se·cede
  se·ced·ed
  se·ced·ing
se·ces·sion
  se·ces·sion·ist
se·clude
  se·clud·ed
  se·clud·ing
  se·clud·ed·ness
se·clu·sion
  se·clu·sive
sec·ond

sec·ond·ary
  sec·ond·ar·i·ly
sec·ond-best
sec·ond-class
sec·ond-guess
sec·ond-hand
sec·ond-rate
se·cret
  se·cre·cy
sec·re·tari·at
sec·re·tary
  sec·re·taries
  sec·re·tari·al
se·crete
  se·cret·ed
  se·cret·ing
  se·cre·tion
  se·cre·tive
  se·cre·to·ry
sec·tari·an
  sec·tari·an·ism
sec·tion
  sec·tion·al
sec·tor
  sec·to·ri·al
sec·u·lar
  sec·u·lar·ism
sec·u·lar·ize
  sec·u·lar·ized
  sec·u·lar·iz·ing
  sec·u·lar·i·za·tion
se·cure
  se·cured
  se·cur·ing
  se·cur·a·ble
  se·cure·ness
se·cu·ri·ty
  se·cu·ri·ties
se·dan
se·date
  se·date·ness
se·da·tion
  se·dat·ed
  se·dat·ing
sed·a·tive
sed·en·tary
  sed·en·tari·ness
sed·i·ment

sed·i·men·ta·ry
sed·i·men·ta·tion
se·di·tion
se·di·tion·ary
se·di·tious
se·duce
se·duced
se·duc·ing
se·duc·er
se·duc·i·ble
se·duce·a·ble
se·duc·tion
se·duce·ment
se·duc·tive
sed·u·lous
se·du·li·ty
sed·u·lous·ness
see
saw
seen
see·ing
seed·ling
seedy
seed·i·er
seed·i·est
seed·i·ly
seed·i·ness
seek
sought
seek·ing
seem·ing
seem·ly
seem·li·est
seem·li·ness
seep
seepy
seep·age
se·er
seer·ess
seer·suck·er
see·saw
seethe
seethed
seeth·ing
seg·ment
seg·men·tal
seg·men·tary
seg·men·ta·tion

seg·re·gate
seg·re·gat·ed
seg·re·gat·ing
seg·re·ga·tion
seg·re·ga·tion·ist
seine
seined
sein·ing
seis·mic
seis·mo·graph
seis·mog·ra·phy
seis·mol·o·gy
seis·mol·o·gist
seize
seized
seiz·ing
sei·zure
sel·dom
se·lect
se·lect·ed
se·lec·tor
se·lec·tion
se·lec·tive
se·lec·tiv·i·ty
self
selves
self-a·base·ment
self-ab·ne·ga·tion
self-a·buse
self-ad·dressed
self-ad·just·ing
self-ag·gran·dize·ment
self-ag·gran·diz·ing
self-as·sur·ance
self-as·sured
self-cen·tered
self-col·lect·ed
self-com·posed
self-con·fessed
self-con·fi·dence
self-con·fi·dent
self-con·scious
self-con·scious·ness
self-con·tained
self-con·trol
self-con·trolled
self-cor·rect·ing
self-crit·i·cism

self-de·cep·tion
self-de·cep·tive
self-de·feat·ing
self-de·fense
self-de·ni·al
self-de·ter·mi·na·tion
self-dis·ci·pline
self-ed·u·cat·ed
self-ef·fac·ing
self-em·ployed
self-es·teem
self-ev·i·dent
self-ex·plan·a·to·ry
self-ex·pres·sion
self-ful·fill·ment
self-gov·ern·ment
self-gov·ern·ing
self-im·age
self-im·por·tance
self-im·posed
self-im·prove·ment
self-in·crim·i·na·tion
self-in·duced
self-in·dul·gence
self-in·flict·ed
self-in·ter·est
self·ish
self·ish·ness
self·less
self·less·ness
self-liq·ui·dat·ing
self-made
self-op·er·at·ing
self-per·pet·u·at·ing
self-pity
self-pol·li·na·tion
self-pos·sessed
self-pres·er·va·tion
self-pro·pelled
self-pro·tec·tion
self-re·al·i·za·tion
self-re·li·ance
self-re·spect
self-re·straint
self-right·eous
self-sac·ri·fice
self-sat·is·fied
self-sat·is·fac·tion

179

self-sat·is·fy·ing
self-serv·ice
self-serv·ing
self-suf·fi·cient
  self-suf·fi·cien·cy
self-sup·port
self-taught
sell
  sold
  sell·ing
sell·er
sell·out
sel·vage
selves
se·man·tics
  se·man·tic
  se·man·ti·cal
sem·a·phore
sem·blance
se·men
se·mes·ter
sem·i·an·nu·al
  sem·i·an·nu·al·ly
sem·i·ar·id
sem·i·au·to·mat·ic
sem·i·cir·cle
  sem·i·cir·cu·lar
sem·i·clas·si·cal
  sem·i·clas·sic
sem·i·co·lon
sem·i·con·duc·tor
  sem·i·con·duct·ing
sem·i·con·scious
sem·i·de·tached
sem·i·fi·nal
  sem·i·fi·nal·ist
sem·i·flu·id
sem·i·for·mal
sem·i·liq·uid
sem·i·month·ly
sem·i·nal
sem·i·nar
sem·i·nary
  sem·i·nar·i·an
sem·i·of·fi·cial
se·mi·ot·ic
sem·i·per·ma·nent
sem·i·per·me·a·ble

sem·i·pre·cious
sem·i·pri·vate
sem·i·pro·fes·sion·al
sem·i·pub·lic
sem·i·skilled
sem·i·sol·id
Sem·ite
Sem·it·ic
Sem·i·tism
sem·i·trail·er
sem·i·trop·ics
  sem·i·trop·i·cal
sem·i·week·ly
sem·i·year·ly
sen·a·ry
sen·ate
sen·a·tor
  sen·a·to·ri·al
send
  sent
  send·ing
se·nes·cent
  se·nes·cence
se·nile
  se·nil·i·ty
se·nior
  se·nior·i·ty
se·nor
  se·nors
se·no·ra
se·no·ri·ta
sen·sate
sen·sa·tion
sen·sa·tion·al
  sen·sa·tion·al·ly
  sen·sa·tion·al·ism
sense
  sensed
  sens·ing
sense·less
  sense·less·ness
sen·si·bil·i·ty
  sen·si·bil·i·ties
sen·si·ble
  sen·si·ble·ness
  sen·si·bly
sen·si·tive
  sen·si·tiv·i·ty

sen·si·tize
  sen·si·tized
  sen·si·tiz·ing
  sen·si·ti·za·tion
  sen·si·tiz·er
sen·sor
sen·so·ry
  sen·so·ri·al
sen·su·al
  sen·su·al·i·ty
  sen·su·al·ly
sen·su·al·ism
sen·su·al·ize
  sen·su·al·ized
  sen·su·al·iz·ing
  sen·su·al·i·za·tion
sen·su·ous
sen·tence
  sen·tenced
  sen·tenc·ing
sen·tient
sen·ti·ment
sen·ti·men·tal
  sen·ti·men·tal·ly
  sen·ti·men·tal·i·ty
  sen·ti·men·tal·i·ties
sen·ti·men·tal·ize
  sen·ti·men·tal·ized
  sen·ti·men·tal·iz·ing
  sen·ti·men·ta·li·za·tion
sen·ti·nel
sen·try
  sen·tries
sep·a·ra·ble
  sep·a·ra·bil·i·ty
  sep·a·ra·bly
sep·a·rate
  sep·a·rat·ed
  sep·a·rat·ing
  sep·a·rate·ness
  sep·a·ra·tion
sep·a·ra·tist
  sep·a·ra·tism
sep·a·ra·tive
sep·a·ra·tor
se·pi·a
sep·sis
sep·ten·ni·al

sep·tet
sep·tic
  sep·ti·cal·ly
  sep·tic·i·ty
sep·tu·a·ge·nar·i·an
sep·tu·ple
sep·ul·cher
  se·pul·chral
se·quel
se·quence
se·quen·tial
  se·quen·tial·ly
se·ques·ter
  se·ques·tered
  se·ques·tra·ble
  se·ques·tra·tion
se·quin
se·quoia
se·ra·pe
ser·aph
  ser·aphs
  ser·a·phim
  se·raph·ic
ser·e·nade
  ser·e·nad·ed
  ser·e·nad·ing
ser·en·dip·i·ty
se·rene
  se·ren·i·ty
serf·dom
serge
ser·geant
se·ri·al
  se·ri·al·ly
  se·ri·al·i·za·tion
  se·ri·al·ize
  se·ri·al·ized
  se·ri·al·iz·ing
se·ries
se·ri·ous
  se·ri·ous·ly
  se·ri·ous·ness
se·ri·ous-mind·ed
ser·mon
  ser·mon·ize
  ser·mon·ized
  ser·mon·iz·ing
  ser·mon·iz·er

se·rous
ser·pent
ser·pen·tine
ser·rate
  ser·rat·ed
  ser·rat·ing
  ser·ra·tion
se·rum
serv·ant
serve
  served
  serv·ing
serv·ice
  serv·iced
  serv·ic·ing
  serv·ice·a·ble
  serv·ice·a·bil·i·ty
  serv·ice·a·ble·ness
  serv·ice·a·bly
ser·vile
  ser·vil·i·ty
  ser·vile·ness
ser·vi·tude
ser·vo·mech·an·ism
ses·a·me
ses·qui·cen·ten·ni·al
ses·sion
set
  set
  set·ting
set·tee
set·ter
set·tle
  set·tled
  set·tling
  set·tle·ment
  set·tler
sev·en
  sev·enth
sev·en·teen
  sev·en·teenth
sev·en·ty
  sev·en·ti·eth
sev·er
  sev·er·a·bil·i·ty
  sev·er·a·ble
  sev·er·ance
sev·er·al

sev·er·al·ly
se·vere
  se·ver·est
  se·vere·ness
  se·ver·i·ty
sew·age
sew·er
sew·er·age
sew·ing ma·chine
sex·less
sex·tant
sex·tet
sex·ton
sex·tu·ple
sex·tu·plet
sex·u·al
  sex·u·al·ly
  sex·u·al·i·ty
sexy
  sex·i·er
  sex·i·est
  sex·i·ness
shab·by
  shab·bi·er
  shab·bi·ly
  shab·bi·ness
shack·le
  shack·led
  shack·ling
shade
  shad·ed
  shad·ing
shad·ow
  shad·owy
shady
  shad·i·er
  shad·i·ly
  shad·i·ness
shaft·ing
shag
  shagged
  shag·ging
  shag·ged
shag·gy
  shag·gi·er
  shag·gi·ly
  shag·gi·ness
shake

shook
shak·en
shak·ing
shak·er
Shake·speare·an
shaky
shak·i·ly
shak·i·ness
shal·lot
shal·low
shal·low·ness
sham
shammed
sham·ming
sha·man
sham·bles
shame
shamed
sham·ing
shame·faced
shame·ful
shame·ful·ly
shame·less
shame·less·ly
shame·less·ness
sham·mer
sham·poo
sham·pooed
sham·poo·ing
sham·rock
shang·hai
shang·haied
shang·hai·ing
shan·tung
shan·ty
shan·ties
shape
shaped
shap·ing
shap·a·ble
shap·er
shape·less
shape·ly
shape·li·est
shape·li·ness
share
shared
shar·ing

shar·er
share·crop
share·crop·per
share·cropped
share·crop·ping
share·hold·er
shark·skin
sharp·en
sharp·en·er
sharp·eyed
sharp·ie
sharp·shoot·er
sharp-tongued
sharp-wit·ted
shat·ter
shat·ter·proof
shave
shaved
shav·en
shav·ing
shawl
sheaf
sheaves
shear
sheared
shear·ing
sheath
sheathe
sheathed
sheath·ing
sheath·er
she·bang
shed
shed·ding
sheen
sheeny
sheep·herd·er
sheep·ish
sheep·skin
sheer
sheer·ness
sheet·ing
sheik
shelf
shelves
shell
shelled
shel·ly

shel·lac
shel·lacked
shel·lack·ing
shel·ter
shelve
shelved
shelv·ing
she·nan·i·gan
shep·herd
shep·herd·ess
sher·bet
sher·iff
sher·ry
shib·bo·leth
shield
shift
shift·ing·ness
shift·less
shifty
shift·i·er
shift·i·ly
shift·i·ness
shil·le·lagh
shil·ling
shi·ly-shal·ly
shim·mer
shim·mery
shim·my
shim·mied
shin
shinned
shin·ning
shin·dig
shine
shined
shone
shin·ing
shin·er
shin·gle
shin·gled
shin·gling
shin·gles
shin·ing
shiny
shin·i·ness
ship
shipped
ship·ping

ship·pa·ble
ship·build·ing
ship·mate
ship·ment
shirk
    shirk·er
shish ke·bab
shiv·er
    shiv·ery
shoal
shock·er
shock·ing
shod·dy
    shod·di·ly
    shod·di·ness
shoe·mak·er
shoe·string
shoot
    shot
    shoot·ing
shop
    shopped
    shop·ping
shop·lift·er
    shop·lift·ing
shop·per
shore·line
short
    short·ly
    short·ness
short·age
short-change
    short-changed
    short-chang·ing
short·cir·cuit
short·com·ing
short·cut
    short-cut·ting
short·en
short·en·ing
short·hand
short-hand·ed
short-lived
short-sight·ed
short-tem·pered
short-wind·ed
shot·gun
    shot·gunned

shot·gun·ning
should
shoul·der
shout·ing
shove
    shoved
    shov·ing
shov·el
    shov·eled
    shov·el·ing
show
    showed
    shown
    show·ing
show·case
    show·cased
    show·cas·ing
show·er
    show·ery
show·man·ship
showy
    show·i·ly
    show·i·ness
shrap·nel
shred
    shred·ded
    shred·ding
    shred·der
shrew
    shrew·ish
shrewd
    shrewd·ly
    shrewd·ness
shriek
shrill
    shril·ly
    shrill·ness
shrimp
shrine
shrink
    shrunk·en
    shrink·a·ble
    shrink·age
shrive
shriv·el
    shriv·eled
    shriv·el·ing
shroud

shrub·bery
shrug
    shrugged
    shrug·ging
shud·der
shuf·fle
    shuf·fled
    shuf·fling
shuf·fle·board
shun
    shunned
    shun·ning
    shun·ner
shunt
shut·ter
shut·tle
    shut·tled
    shut·tling
shy
    shied
    shy·ing
    shy·ly
    shy·ness
shy·ster
Si·a·mese
sib·i·lant
    sib·i·lance
sib·ling
sick·en
    sick·en·ing
sick·le
sick·ly
    sick·li·ness
sick·ness
sid·ed
side·line
    side·lined
    side·lin·ing
si·de·re·al
side·split·ting
side·step
    side·stepped
    side·step·ping
side·swipe
    side·swiped
    side·swip·ing
sid·ing
si·dle

si·dled
si·dling
siege
si·er·ra
si·es·ta
sieve
sift·er
sift·ings
sigh·ing
sight·ed
sight·less
sight·ly
sight-read·ing
sight·see·ing
  sight·see·er
sig·nal
  sig·naled
  sig·nal·ing
sig·na·to·ry
sig·na·ture
sig·net
sig·nif·i·cance
  sig·nif·i·cant
  sig·ni·fi·ca·tion
sig·ni·fy
  sig·ni·fied
  sig·ni·fy·ing
si·lage
si·lence
  si·lenced
  si·lenc·ing
si·lenc·er
si·lent
sil·hou·ette
  sil·hou·et·ted
  sil·hou·et·ting
sil·ica
sil·i·co·sis
sil·i·cone
silk·en
silky
  silk·i·est
  silk·i·ly
  silk·i·ness
sil·ly
  sil·li·er
  sil·li·est
  sil·li·ly

sil·li·ness
si·lo
  si·los
  si·loed
  si·lo·ing
silt
  sil·ta·tion
  silty
sil·ver
sil·ver·fish
sil·ver-tongued
sil·ver·ware
sil·very
  sil·ver·i·ness
sim·i·an
sim·i·lar
  sim·i·lar·i·ty
  sim·i·lar·i·ties
sim·i·le
si·mil·i·tude
sim·mer
si·mon·ize
  si·mon·ized
  si·mon·iz·ing
sim·per
  sim·per·ing·ly
sim·ple
  sim·pler
  sim·plest
  sim·ple·ness
sim·ple-mind·ed
sim·ple·ton
sim·plex
sim·plic·i·ty
sim·pli·fy
  sim·pli·fied
  sim·pli·fy·ing
  sim·pli·fi·ca·tion
sim·plis·tic
  sim·plis·ti·cal·ly
sim·ply
sim·u·late
  sim·u·lat·ed
  sim·u·lat·ing
  sim·u·la·tion
  sim·u·la·tive
  sim·u·la·tor
si·mul·cast

si·mul·ta·ne·ous
  si·mul·ta·ne·ous·ness
  si·mul·ta·ne·i·ty
sin
  sinned
  sin·ning
  sin·ner
Si·nai
sin·cere
  sin·cer·i·ty
si·ne·cure
sin·ew
  sin·ewy
sin·ful
  sin·ful·ly
  sin·ful·ness
sing
  sang
  sung
  sing·ing
singe
  singed
  singe·ing
sing·er
sin·gle
  sin·gled
  sin·gling
  sin·gle·ness
sin·gle-breast·ed
sin·gle-hand·ed
sin·gle-mind·ed
sin·gle-space
  sin·gle-spaced
  sin·gle-spac·ing
sin·gle·ton
sin·gle-track
sin·gly
sing·song
sin·gu·lar
  sin·gu·lar·i·ty
  sin·gu·lar·i·ties
sin·is·ter
sink
  sank
  sunk
  sink·ing
sink·a·ble
sink·er

sink·hole
sin·less
sin·ner
sin·u·ate
  sin·u·at·ed
  sin·u·at·ing
sin·u·ous
  sin·u·os·i·ty
  sin·u·ous·ness
si·nus
  si·nus·i·tis
sip
  sipped
  sip·ping
si·phon
sire
  sired
  sir·ing
si·ren
sir·loin
si·roc·co
sis·sy
sis·ter
  sis·ter·li·ness
  sis·ter·ly
sis·ter-in-law
sit
  sat
  sit·ting
sit·ter
sit·ting
sit·u·ate
  sit·u·at·ed
  sit·u·at·ing
sit·u·a·tion
six-shoot·er
six·teen
  six·teenth
sixth
six·ty
  six·ti·eth
siz·a·ble
  siz·a·ble·ness
  siz·a·bly
size
  sized
  siz·ing
siz·zle

siz·zled
siz·zling
skate
  skat·ed
  skat·ing
skein
skel·e·ton
  skel·e·tal
skep·tic
  skep·ti·cal
  skep·ti·cism
sketch
sketchy
  sketch·i·ly
  sketch·i·ness
skew·er
ski
  skied
  ski·ing
  ski·er
skid
  skid·ded
  skid·ding
skiff
skilled
skil·let
skill·ful·ly
skim
  skimmed
  skim·ming
skimp
  skimp·i·ly
  skimp·i·ness
  skimp·y
skin
  skinned
  skin·ning
skin-dive
  skin-dived
  skin-diving
skin·ny
  skin·ni·er
  skin·ni·est
skip
  skipped
  skip·ping
skip·per
skir·mish

skit·ter
skit·tish
skoal
skul·dug·ger·y
skulk·er
skunk
sky·div·ing
sky·jack·er
sky·rock·et
sky·scrap·er
sky·writ·ing
slab
  slabbed
  slab·bing
slack
  slack·ness
slack·en
slack·er
slake
  slaked
  slak·ing
sla·lom
slam
  slammed
  slam·ming
slan·der
  slan·der·er
  slan·der·ous
slang
  slang·i·ness
  slangy
slant
  slant·ways
  slant·wise
slap
  slapped
  slap·ping
slap·hap·py
slap·stick
slash·er
slash·ing
slat
  slat·ted
  slat·ting
slate
  slat·ed
  slat·ing
slat·tern

slat·tern·li·ness
slat·tern·ly
slaugh·ter
slave
  slaved
  slav·ing
  slav·ery
slav·ish
  sla·vish·ly
slay
  slew
  slain
  slay·ing
slea·zy
  slea·zi·ly
  slea·zi·ness
sled
  sled·ded
  sled·ding
sledge
sleek
  sleek·ness
sleep·less·ness
sleep·walk·ing
sleepy
  sleep·i·ly
  sleep·i·ness
sleet
  sleety
  sleet·i·ness
sleeve
  sleeved
  sleev·ing
  sleeve·less
sleigh
sleight
slen·der
slen·der·ize
sleuth
slice
  sliced
  slic·ing
slick·er
slick·ness
slide
  slid
  slid·ing
slight

slim
  slimmed
  slim·ming
  slim·mest
  slim·ness
slime
  slimy
  slim·i·ness
sling
  slung
  sling·ing
slink
  slunk
  slink·ing
  slinky
slip
  slipped
  slip·ping
slip·page
slip·per
slip·pery
  slip·peri·er
  slip·peri·est
  slip·peri·ness
slip·shod
slip·stream
slit
  slit·ting
slith·er
  slith·ery
sliv·er
slob·ber
sloe-eyed
slog
  slogged
  slog·ging
slo·gan
  slo·gan·eer
sloop
slop
  slopped
  slop·ping
slope
  sloped
  slop·ing
slop·py
  slop·pi·ly
  slop·pi·ness

sloshy
slot
  slot·ted
  slot·ting
sloth
  sloth·ful·ly
slouch
  slouch·i·ly
  slouchy
slough
  sloughy
slov·en
  slov·en·ly
  slov·en·li·ness
slow-down
slow-mo·tion
sludge
  sludgy
slug
  slugged
  slug·ging
slug·gard
  slug·gard·li·ness
slug·gish
sluice
  sluiced
  sluic·ing
slum
  slummed
  slum·ming
slum·ber
  slum·ber·er
  slum·ber·ous
slump
  slumped
slur
  slurred
  slur·ring
slush
  slush·i·ness
  slushy
slut
  slut·tish
sly
  sly·ly
  sly·ness
smack·ing
small·pox

smart
  smart·ness
smart al·eck
smash·ing
smat·ter·ing
smear
  smeary
  smear·i·ness
smell
  smelled
  smel·ling
  smelly
smelt
smelt·er
smid·gen
smile
  smil·ling·ly
smirch
smirk
  smirk·ing·ly
smite
  smote
  smit·ten
  smit·ting
smith·er·eens
Smith·so·ni·an
smock·ing
smog·gy
smoke
  smoked
  smok·ing
  smok·er
smoke·house
smoke·stack
smoky
  smok·i·ness
smol·der
smooth
  smooth·ness
  smooth·en
smor·gas·bord
smoth·er
smudge
  smudged
  smudg·ing
  smudg·i·ness
  smudgy
smug

smug·gest
smug·ly
smug·ness
smug·gle
  smug·gled
  smug·gling
  smug·gler
smut
  smut·ty
  smut·ti·ness
snaf·fle
sna·fu
  sna·fued
snag
  snagged
  snag·ging
  snag·gy
snail
snake
  snaked
  snak·ing
  snak·i·ly
  snaky
  snak·i·ness
snap
  snapped
  snap·ping
snap·drag·on
snap·py
  snap·pish
snare
  snared
  snar·ing
snarl
  snarly
snatch
  snatchy
snaz·zy
  snaz·zi·est
sneak·er
sneak·ing
sneaky
  sneak·i·ly
  sneak·i·ness
sneer
  sneer·ing·ly
sneeze
  sneezed

sneez·ing
sneezy
snick·er
snif·fle
  snif·fled
  snif·fling
snif·fy
  snif·fi·ly
snif·ter
snig·ger
snip
  snipped
  snip·ping
snipe
  sniped
  snip·ing
snip·py
  snip·pi·ness
snitch·er
sniv·el
  sniv·eled
  sniv·el·ing
snob
  snob·bery
  snob·bish·ness
snoop
  snoopy
  snoop·er
snooty
  snoot·i·ness
snooze
  snoozed
  snooz·ing
snore
  snored
  snor·ing
snor·kel
snort
  snort·ed
snot·ty
  snot·ti·ness
snout
snow·blow·er
snow·man
snow·mo·bile
snowy
  snow·i·er
  snow·i·ness

snub
  snubbed
  snub·bing
snuf·fle
  snuf·fled
  snuf·fling
snuffy
  snuff·i·ness
snug
  snugged
  snug·ging
  snug·ness
snug·gle
  snug·gled
  snug·gling
soak·ing
soap
  soapy
  soap·i·ness
soar
  soaring
sob
  sobbed
  sob·bing
so·ber
  so·ber·ness
so·bri·e·ty
so·bri·quet
soc·cer
so·cia·ble
  so·cia·bil·i·ty
  so·cia·ble·ness
  so·cia·bly
so·cial
  so·ci·al·i·ty
  so·cial·ly
so·cial·ism
  so·cial·ist
  so·cial·is·tic
so·cial·ite
so·cial·ize
  so·cial·ized
  so·cial·iz·ing
  so·cial·i·za·tion
so·ci·e·ty
  so·ci·e·ties
  so·ci·e·tal
so·ci·o·ec·o·nom·ic

so·ci·ol·o·gy
  so·ci·o·log·i·cal
  so·ci·ol·o·gist
so·ci·o·po·lit·i·cal
sock·et
sod
  sod·ded
  sod·ding
so·da
so·dal·i·ty
sod·den
  sod·den·ness
so·di·um
sod·omy
so·fa
soft
  soft·ness
  sof·ten
soft-heart·ed
soft-ped·al
  soft-ped·aled
  soft-ped·al·ing
soft-spo·ken
sog·gy
  sog·gi·ness
soi·ree
so·journ
sol·ace
  sol·aced
  sol·ac·ing
so·lar
so·lar·i·um
so·lar·ize
  so·lar·ized
  so·lar·iz·ing
  so·lar·i·za·tion
so·lar plex·us
sol·der
sol·dier
sol·e·cism
sole·ly
sol·emn
  sol·emn·ly
  sol·emn·ness
so·lem·ni·ty
sol·em·nize
  sol·em·nized
  sol·em·niz·ing

sol·em·ni·za·tion
sole·ness
so·le·noid
so·lic·it
  so·lic·i·ta·tion
  so·lic·i·tor
so·lic·i·tous
  so·lic·i·tude
sol·id
  so·lid·i·ty
  sol·id·ness
sol·i·dar·i·ty
so·lid·i·fy
  so·lid·i·fied
  so·lid·i·fy·ing
  so·lid·i·fi·ca·tion
sol·id·state
so·lil·o·quize
  so·lil·o·quized
  so·lil·o·quiz·ing
so·lil·o·quy
  so·lil·o·quies
sol·i·taire
sol·i·tary
  sol·i·tari·ness
sol·i·tude
so·lo
  so·loed
  so·lo·ing
  so·lo·ist
sol·stice
sol·u·ble
  sol·u·bil·i·ty
  sol·u·ble·ness
  sol·u·bly
sol·ute
so·lu·tion
solve
  solved
  solv·ing
  solv·a·ble
  solv·a·bil·i·ty
  solv·a·ble·ness
sol·vent
  sol·ven·cy
so·mat·ic
som·ber
  som·ber·ness

som·bre·ro
some·body
som·er·sault
some·thing
some·where
som·nam·bu·late
  som·nam·bu·lat·ed
  som·nam·bu·lat·ing
  som·nam·bu·lant
  som·nam·bu·la·tion
  som·nam·bu·lism
  som·nam·bu·list
som·no·lent
  som·no·lence
  som·no·len·cy
so·nant
so·nar
so·na·ta
song·ster
  song·stress
son·ic
son-in-law
son·net
son·ny
  son·nies
so·no·rous
  so·nor·i·ty
  so·no·rous·ness
soothe
  soothed
  sooth·ing
sooth·say·er
sooty
  soot·i·ness
sop
  sopped
  sop·ping
soph·ist
  soph·ism
  so·phis·tic
  so·phis·ti·cal
so·phis·ti·cate
  so·phis·ti·cat·ed
  so·phis·ti·cat·ing
  so·phis·ti·ca·tion
soph·ist·ry
soph·o·more
soph·o·mor·ic

sop·o·rif·ic
sop·py
so·prano
Sor·bonne
sor·cer·er
  sor·cer·ess
sor·cery
  sor·cer·ous
sor·did
  sor·did·ness
sore
  sor·est
  sore·ly
  sore·ness
sor·ghum
so·ror·i·ty
  so·ror·i·ties
sor·rel
sor·row
  sor·row·ful·ly
sorry
  sor·ri·ly
  sor·ri·ness
sort·a·ble
sor·tie
sot
  sot·ted
  sot·tish·ness
sot·to vo·ce
sou·bri·quet
souf·fle
  souf·fleed
sought
soul·ful
  soul·ful·ly
soul·search·ing
sound
  sound·a·ble
  sound·ly
  sound·ness
sound·ing
sound·less·ly
soupy
  soup·i·er
sour
  sour·ish
  sour·ness
source

souse
  soused
  sous·ing
south·east·er·ly
south·east·ern
south·er·ly
south·ern
south·ern·er
south·west·er·ly
south·west·ern
sou·ve·nir
sov·er·eign·
sov·er·eign·ty
so·vi·et
  so·vi·et·ism
sow
  sowed
  sown
  sow·ing
soy·bean
space
  spaced
  spac·ing
space·craft
space·ship
spa·cious
  spa·cious·ness
spack·le
  spack·led
  spack·ling
spade
  spad·ed
  spad·ing
  spade·ful
spa·ghet·ti
span
  spanned
  span·ning
span·gle
  span·gled
  span·gling
Spain
  Span·iard
  Span·ish
span·iel
spank·ing
spar
  sparred

spar·ring
spare
  spared
  spar·ing
  spare·ness
spar·ing·ness
spar·kle
  spar·kled
  spar·kling
spar·kler
spar·row
sparse
  sparse·ness
spasm
spas·mod·ic
  spas·mod·i·cal·ly
spas·tic
  spas·ti·cal·ly
spat
  spat·ted
  spat·ting
spa·tial
  spa·cial
  spa·ti·al·i·ty
  spa·tial·ly
spat·ter
spat·u·la
spav·in
spawn
speak
  spok·en
  speak·ing
speak-easy
speak·er
spear·head
spear·mint
spe·cial
  spe·cial·ly
spe·cial·ist
spe·cial·ize
  spe·cial·ized
  spe·cial·iz·ing
  spe·cial·i·za·tion
spe·cial·ty
  spe·cial·ties
spe·cie
spe·cif·ic
  spec·i·fi·able

spe·cif·i·cal·ly
spec·i·fic·i·ty
spec·i·fy
  spec·i·fied
  spec·i·fy·ing
  spec·i·fi·ca·tion
spec·i·men
spe·cious
  spe·ci·os·i·ty
  spe·cious·ness
speck·le
  speck·led
  speck·ling
spec·ta·cle
spec·tac·u·lar
spec·ta·tor
spec·ter
spec·tral
spec·tro·scope
  spec·tros·co·py
spec·trum
spec·u·late
  spec·u·lat·ed
  spec·u·lat·ing
  spec·u·la·tion
  spec·u·la·tor
  spec·u·la·tive
speech·i·fy
speech·less
speed
  speed·ed
  sped
  speed·ing
speed·om·e·ter
speedy
  speed·i·ly
  speed·i·ness
spe·le·ol·o·gy
  spe·le·ol·o·gist
spell
  spelled
  spell·ing
spell·bound
  spell·bind·ing
spe·lun·ker
spend
  spent
  spend·ing

spend·a·ble
spend·thrift
sper·ma·ce·ti
sper·mat·ic
sper·ma·to·zo·on
  sper·ma·to·zo·a
  sper·ma·to·zo·ic
spew·er
sphag·num
sphere
  sphered
  spher·ing
  spher·ic
  sphe·ric·i·ty
  spher·i·cal
sphe·roid
  sphe·roi·dal
sphinc·ter
sphinx
spice
  spiced
  spic·ing
spi·cule
spicy
  spic·i·er
  spic·i·est
  spic·i·ly
  spic·i·ness
spi·der
spi·dery
spiel
spiffy
  spiff·i·ness
spig·ot
spike
  spiked
  spiky
spill
  spilled
  spill·ing
spil·lage
spin
  spun
  spin·ning
spin·ach
spi·nal
spin·dle
  spin·dled

spin·dling
spin·dly
spine·less
spin·et
spin·na·ker
spin·ner
spin·ning
spin·ster
spiny
  spin·i·ness
spi·ra·cle
spi·ral
  spi·raled
  spi·ral·ing
  spi·ral·ly
spire
  spired
  spir·ing
spir·it
spir·it·ed
spir·it·less·ness
spir·i·tous
spir·it·u·al
  spir·it·u·al·ism
  spir·it·u·al·ist
  spir·it·u·al·i·ty
  spir·it·u·al·ize
  spir·it·u·al·ized
  spir·it·u·al·iz·ing
  spir·it·u·al·i·za·tion
spir·it·u·ous
  spir·it·u·os·i·ty
spi·ro·chete
spit
  spat
  spit·ting
spite
  spit·ing
  spite·ful
spit·tle
spit·toon
splash
  splashy
  splash·i·ness
splat·ter
splay·foot
spleen
  spleen·ful

sple·net·ic
splen·did
splen·dif·er·ous
splen·dor
splice
  spliced
  splic·ing
splin·ter
split
  split·ting
split-lev·el
split-sec·ond
splotch
  splotchy
splurge
  splurged
  splurg·ing
splut·ter
spoil
  spoiled
  spoil·ing
spoil·age
spoil·er
spoke
  spo·ken
spokes·man
  spokes·wom·an
spo·li·a·tion
sponge
  sponged
  spong·ing
spong·er
spon·gy
  spon·gi·ness
spon·sor
spon·ta·ne·i·ty
spon·ta·ne·ous
  spon·ta·ne·ous·ness
spook
  spooky
  spook·i·ness
spoon·er·ism
spoon-feed
  spoon-fed
spoon·fuls
spo·rad·ic
  spo·rad·i·cal·ly
spo·ran·gi·um

spore
sport
  sport·ful·ly
  sport·ing
  spor·tive
sports·cast·er
sports·man
sports·man·ship
sporty
  sport·i·ness
spot
  spot·ted
  spot·ting
spot·less·ness
spot·ty
  spot·ti·ly
  spot·ti·ness
spouse
sprained
sprawl
spray·er
spread
  spread·ing
spread-ea·gle
spread·er
sprig
spright·ly
  spright·li·ness
spring
  sprang
  sprung
  spring·ing
spring-clean·ing
spring·time
springy
  spring·i·ness
sprin·kle
  sprin·kled
  sprin·kling
  sprink·ler
sprint
  sprint·er
sprock·et
spruce
  spruced
  spruc·ing
  spruce·ly
spry

spry·ness
spume
  spumed
  spum·ing
  spum·ous
spunky
  spunk·i·ness
spur
  spurred
  spur·ring
spu·ri·ous
  spu·ri·ous·ness
spurner
spurt
  spur·tive
sput·nik
sput·ter
spu·tum
spy
  spies
  spied
  spy·ing
squab·ble
  squab·bled
  squab·bling
squad·ron
squal·id
  squal·id·ness
squall
  squally
squal·or
squan·der
square
  squared
  squar·ing
  square·ness
  squar·ish
square-danc·ing
squash
squashy
  squash·i·ness
squat
  squat·ted
  squat·ting
  squat·ness
squat·ter
squat·ty
squawk

squawky
squeak
  squeak·er
  squeak·ing·ly
  squeaky
squeal
  squeal·er
squeam·ish
  squeam·ish·ness
squee·gee
squeeze
  squeezed
  squeez·ing
  squeez·er
squelch
squib
squid
squig·gle
  squig·gled
  squig·gling
squint
  squint·er
  squint·ing·ly
  squinty
squire
squirm
  squirmy
squir·rel
squirt
squish
  squishy
stab
  stabbed
  stab·bing
  stab·ber
sta·bile
sta·bil·i·ty
  sta·bil·i·ties
sta·bi·lize
  sta·bi·lized
  sta·bi·liz·ing
  sta·bi·li·za·tion
  sta·bi·liz·er
sta·ble
  sta·bled
  sta·bling
stac·ca·to
sta·di·um

staff
stag
  stagged
  stag·ging
stage
  staged
  stag·ing
  stagy
stag·ger
  stag·ger·ing
stag·nant
  stag·nan·cy
stag·nate
  stag·nat·ed
  stag·nat·ing
  stag·na·tion
staid·ness
stain
  stained
stain·less
stake
  staked
  stak·ing
stake·hold·er
sta·lac·tite
sta·lag·mite
stale
  stale·ness
stale·mate
  stale·mat·ed
  stale·mat·ing
stalk
  stalked
  stalky
stalled
stal·lion
stal·wart
sta·men
stam·i·na
stam·mer
  stam·mer·ing·ly
stam·pede
  stam·ped·ed
  stam·ped·ing
stance
stand
  stand·ing
  stand·ard

stand·ard·ize
  stand·ard·ized
    stand·ard·iz·ing
    stand·ard·i·za·tion
stand·point
stan·za
staph·y·lo·coc·cus
sta·ple
  sta·pled
  sta·pling
  sta·pler
star
  starred
  star·ring
  starch·i·ness
star·dom
stare
  stared
  star·ing
star·gaze
  star·gazed
  star·gaz·ing
stark·ly
star·let
star·ling
star·ry
  star·ri·ness
star·ry-eyed
star-span·gled
start·er
star·tle
  star·tled
  star·tling
star·va·tion
starve
  starved
  starv·ing
starve·ling
sta·sis
state
  stat·ed
  stat·ing
  state·ment
state·craft
state·hood
state·less
state·ly

state·li·er
state·li·ness
states·man
  states·man·ship
stat·ic
  stat·i·cal·ly
sta·tion
  sta·tion·ary
  sta·tion·er
  sta·tion·ery
stat·ism
  stat·ist
sta·tis·tic
  sta·tis·ti·cal
  sta·tis·ti·cal·ly
  stat·is·ti·cian
  sta·tis·tics
sta·tor
stat·u·ary
stat·ue
stat·u·esque
stat·u·ette
stat·ure
sta·tus
  sta·tus quo
stat·ute
  stat·u·to·ry
staunch
stave
  staved
  stav·ing
stay
  stayed
  stay·ing
stead·fast
  stead·fast·ness
steady
  stead·ied
  stead·y·ing
  stead·i·ly
  stead·i·ness
steal
  stol·en
  steal·ing
stealth
  stealthy
  stealth·i·ly
  stealth·i·ness

steam·er
steam·fit·ter
steam·roll·er
steam·ship
steamy
  steam·i·ness
sted·fast
steel·work·er
steely
  steel·i·ness
steep
  steep·ly
  steep·ness
steep·en
stee·ple
stee·ple·chase
steer
  steer·a·ble
steer·age
stein
stel·lar
stem
  stemmed
  stem·ming
  stem·less
stem·wind·ing
stench
sten·cil
  sten·ciled
  sten·cil·ing
ste·nog·ra·pher
ste·nog·ra·phy
  sten·o·graph·ic
  sten·o·graph·i·cal·ly
sten·to·ri·an
step
  stepped
  step·ping
step·broth·er
step·child·ren
step·daugh·ter
step·fa·ther
step·lad·der
step·moth·er
steppe
step·ping·stone
stereo
ster·e·o·phon·ic

ster·e·o·phon·i·cal·ly
ster·e·o·scope
  ster·e·o·scop·ic
ster·e·o·type
  ster·e·o·typed
  ster·e·o·typ·ing
ster·ile
  ste·ril·i·ty
ster·i·lize
  ster·i·lized
  ster·i·liz·ing
  ster·i·li·za·tion
  ster·i·li·zer
ster·ling
stern
  stern·ly
  stern·ness
ster·num
ster·oid
steth·o·scope
ste·ve·dore
stew·ard
  stew·ard·ess
stick
  stuck
  stick·ing
stick·er
stick·ler
stick-to-it·ive·ness
stick·y
  stick·i·ness
stiff
  stiff·ness
  stiff·en
sti·fle
  sti·fled
  sti·fling
stig·ma
  stig·mat·ic
  stig·mat·i·cal·ly
stig·ma·tize
  stig·ma·tized
  stig·ma·tiz·ing
  stig·ma·ti·za·tion
stile
sti·let·to
still·born
still·ness

stilt·ed
stim·u·late
  stim·u·lat·ed
  stim·u·lat·ing
  stim·u·lant
  stim·u·la·tion
  stim·u·la·tive
stim·u·lus
  stim·u·li
sting
  stung
  sting·ing
stin·gy
  stin·gi·ness
stink
  stank
  stunk
  stink·ing
  stinky
stint·ing
sti·pend
stip·ple
  stip·pled
  stip·pling
stip·u·late
  stip·u·lat·ed
  stip·u·lat·ing
  stip·u·la·tion
  stip·u·la·to·ry
stir
  stirred
  stirring
stir·rup
stitch
stock·ade
stock·brok·er
stock·hold·er
stock·ing
stock·pile
  stock·piled
  stock·pil·ing
stock·y
  stock·i·ness
stodgy
  stodg·i·ness
sto·ic
  sto·i·cal
stoke

stoked
stok·ing
stol·id
  sto·lid·i·ty
  stol·id·ly
stom·ach
stom·ach·ache
stone
  stoned
  ston·ing
stone·ma·son
stony
  ston·i·er
  ston·i·ness
stop
  stopped
  stop·ping
stop·page
stop·per
stor·age
store
  stored
  stor·ing
sto·ried
stormy
  storm·i·ness
story
  sto·ries
sto·ry·tell·er
stout
  stout·ly
  stout·ness
stout-heart·ed
stove
  stoved
  stov·ing
stow·age
stow·a·way
strad·dle
  strad·dled
  strad·dling
strafe
  strafed
  straf·ing
strag·gle
  strag·gled
  strag·gling
  strag·gler

strag·gly
straight·a·way
straight-edge
straight·en
straight·for·ward
straight·way
strain·er
strait·en
strait·jack·et
strait-laced
strange
  strang·er
  strang·est
  strange·ly
  strange·ness
stran·ger
stran·gle
  stran·gled
  stran·gling
  stran·gler
stran·gu·la·tion
  stran·gu·late
  stran·gu·lat·ed
  stran·gu·lat·ing
strap
  strapped
  strap·ping
  strap·less
strat·a·gem
stra·te·gic
  stra·te·gi·cal·ly
strat·e·gy
  strat·e·gies
  strat·e·gist
strat·i·fy
  strat·i·fied
  strat·i·fy·ing
  strat·i·fi·ca·tion
stra·to·cu·mu·lus
strat·o·sphere
  strat·o·spher·ic
stra·tum
stra·tus
straw·ber·ry
  straw·ber·ries
stray·ing
streak
  streaky

stream·er
stream·line
  stream·lined
  stream·lin·ing
street·walk·er
strength·en
stren·u·ous
  stren·u·os·i·ty
  stren·u·ous·ly
strep·to·coc·cus
strep·to·my·cin
stress
  stress·ful·ly
stretch
  stretch·a·bil·i·ty
  stretch·a·ble
stretch·er
strew
  strewed
  strew·ing
stri·ate
  stri·at·ed
  stri·at·ing
  stri·a·tion
strick·en
strict
  strict·ly
  strict·ness
stric·ture
stride
  strode
  strid·den
  strid·ing
stri·dent
  stri·den·cy
strid·u·late
  strid·u·la·tion
  strid·u·lous
strife
  strife-less
strike‫
  struck
  strick·en
  strik·ing
strike·break·er
string
  strung
  string·ing

strin·gent
  strin·gen·cy
  strin·gent·ly
stringy
  string·i·ness
strip
  stripped
  strip·ping
strip-crop·ping
stripe
  striped
  strip·ing
strip·ling
strip·per
strip·tease
strive
  strove
  striv·en
  striv·ing
stro·bo·scope
  stro·bo·scop·ic
stroke
  stroked
  strok·ing
stroll·er
strong
  strong·ly
  strong·ness
strong-mind·ed
strop
  stropped
  strop·ping
struc·tural
  struc·tur·al·ly
struc·ture
  struc·tured
  struc·tur·ing
strug·gle
  strug·gled
  strug·gling
  strug·gler
strum
  strummed
  strum·ming
strum·pet
strut
  strut·ted
  strut·ting

strych·nine
stub
  stubbed
  stub·bing
  stub·by
stub·ble
  stub·bled
  stub·bly
stub·born
  stub·born·ly
  stub·born·ness
stuc·co
  stuc·coed
  stuc·co·ing
stud
  stud·ded
  stud·ding
stu·dent
stud·ied
  stud·ied·ness
stu·dio
stu·di·ous
  stu·di·ous·ly
  stu·di·ous·ness
study
  stud·ies
  stud·ied
  stud·y·ing
stuff·er
stuff·ing
stuffy
  stuff·i·ness
stul·ti·fy
  stul·ti·fied
    stul·ti·fy·ing
    stul·ti·fi·ca·tion
stum·ble
  stum·bled
  stum·bling
stump
  stumpy
stun
  stunned
  stun·ning
stunt
  stunt·ed
  stunt·ed·ness
stu·pe·fy

stu·pe·fied
stu·pe·fy·ing
stu·pe·fac·tion
stu·pen·dous
  stu·pen·dous·ly
  stu·pen·dous·ness
stu·pid
  stu·pid·i·ty
  stu·pid·ly
  stu·pid·ness
stu·por
  stu·por·ous
stur·dy
  stur·di·est
stur·geon
stut·ter
  stut·ter·ing·ly
style
  styled
  styl·ing
styl·ish
  styl·ish·ness
styl·ist
  sty·lis·tic
  sty·lis·ti·cal
  sty·lis·ti·cal·ly
styl·ize
  styl·ized
  styl·iz·ing
  styl·i·za·tion
sty·lus
sty·mie
  sty·mied
  sty·mie·ing
styp·tic
sty·rene
suave
  suave·ly
  suave·ness
  suav·i·ty
sub
  subbed
  sub·bing
sub·al·tern
sub·arc·tic
sub·as·sem·bly
  sub·as·sem·bler
sub·atom·ic

sub·base·ment
sub·chas·er
sub·com·mit·tee
sub·con·scious
  sub·con·scious·ness
sub·con·ti·nent
sub·con·trac·tor
sub·cul·ture
sub·cu·ta·ne·ous
sub·di·vide
  sub·di·vid·ed
  sub·di·vid·ing
sub·di·vi·sion
sub·due
  sub·dued
  sub·du·ing
sub·en·try
  sub·en·tries
sub·freez·ing
sub·group
sub·hu·man
sub·ject
  sub·jec·tion
sub·jec·tive
  sub·jec·tive·ly
  sub·jec·tive·ness
  sub·jec·tiv·i·ty
sub·join
sub·ju·gate
  sub·ju·gat·ed
  sub·ju·gat·ing
  sub·ju·ga·tion
sub·junc·tive
sub·lease
  sub·leased
  sub·leas·ing
sub·let
  sub·let·ting
sub·li·mate
  sub·li·mat·ed
  sub·li·mat·ing
  sub·li·ma·tion
sub·lime
  sub·lim·est
  sub·lime·ly
  sub·lime·ness
  sub·lim·i·ty
sub·lim·i·nal

sub·lim·i·nal·ly
sub·ma·chine
sub·mar·gin·al
sub·ma·rine
sub·merge
  sub·merged
  sub·merg·ing
  sub·mer·gence
  sub·mer·gi·ble
sub·merse
  sub·mersed
  sub·mers·ing
  sub·mers·i·ble
  sub·mer·sion
sub·mi·cro·scop·ic
sub·mis·sion
sub·mis·sive
  sub·miss·ive·ly
  sub·miss·ive·ness
sub·mit
  sub·mit·ted
  sub·mit·ting
sub·nor·mal
  sub·nor·mal·i·ty
sub·orbit·al
sub·or·di·nate
  sub·or·di·nat·ed
  sub·or·di·nat·ing
  sub·or·di·nate·ly
  sub·or·di·nate·ness
  sub·or·di·na·tion
  sub·or·di·na·tive
sub·orn
  sub·or·na·tion
sub·poe·na
  sub·poe·naed
  sub·poe·na·ing
sub·re·gion
sub·rosa
sub·scribe
  sub·scribed
  sub·scrib·ing
  sub·scrib·er
  sub·scrip·tion
sub·se·quent
  sub·se·quence
  sub·se·quent·ly
  sub·se·quent·ness

sub·ser·vi·ent
  sub·ser·vi·ence
  sub·ser·vi·en·cy
  sub·ser·vi·ent·ly
sub·side
  sub·sid·ed
  sub·sid·ing
  sub·sid·ence
sub·sid·i·ary
  sub·sid·i·ar·ies
sub·si·dize
  sub·si·dized
  sub·si·diz·ing
  sub·si·di·za·tion
sub·si·dy
  sub·si·dies
sub·sist
  sub·sist·ence
sub·soil
sub·son·ic
sub·spe·cies
sub·stance
sub·stand·ard
sub·stan·tial
  sub·stan·ti·al·i·ty
  sub·stan·tial·ly
  sub·stan·tial·ness
sub·stan·ti·ate
  sub·stan·ti·at·ed
  sub·stan·ti·at·ing
  sub·stan·ti·a·tion
  sub·stan·ti·a·tive
sub·stan·tive
  sub·stan·ti·val
  sub·stan·ti·val·ly
  sub·stan·tive·ly
  sub·stan·tive·ness
sub·sta·tion
sub·sti·tute
  sub·sti·tut·ed
  sub·sti·tut·ing
  sub·sti·tut·able
  sub·sti·tu·tion
  sub·sti·tu·tion·al
sub·stra·tum
  sub·stra·ta
sub·struc·ture
sub·sume

sub·sumed
sub·sum·ing
sub·sum·a·ble
sub·sump·tive
sub·sump·tion
sub·teen
sub·tend
sub·ter·fuge
sub·ter·ra·ne·an
  sub·ter·ra·ne·ous
sub·ti·tle
sub·tle
  sub·tle·ness
  sub·tle·ty
  sub·tle·ties
  sub·tly
  sub·tly
sub·tract
  sub·tract·er
  sub·trac·ion
  sub·trac·tive
sub·tra·hend
sub·trop·i·cal
  sub·trop·ic
sub·urb
  sub·ur·ban
  sub·ur·ban·ite
sub·ur·bia
sub·vene
  sub·ven·tion
sub·ver·sion
  sub·ver·sion·ary
sub·ver·sive
  sub·ver·sive·ly
  sub·ver·sive·ness
sub·vert
  sub·vert·er
sub·way
suc·ceed
  suc·ceed·ing
suc·cess
  suc·cess·ful·ly
  suc·cess·ful·ness
suc·ces·sion
  suc·ces·sion·al
suc·ces·sive
  suc·ces·sive·ly
  suc·ces·sive·ness

suc·ces·sor
suc·cinct
  suc·cinct·ly
  suc·cinct·ness
suc·cor
  suc·cor·er
suç·co·tash
suc·cu·lent
  suc·cu·lence
  suc·cu·len·cy
  suc·cu·lent·ly
suc·cumb
suck·er
suck·le
  suck·led
  suck·ling
su·crose
suc·tion
sud·den
  sud·den·ly
  sud·den·ness
sudsy
  suds·i·er
sue
  sued
  su·ing
  su·er
suede
su·et
suf·fer
  suf·fer·a·ble
  suf·fer·a·bly
  suf·fer·er
  suf·fer·ing
suf·fer·ance
suf·fice
  suf·ficed
  suf·fic·ing
suf·fi·cien·cy
  suf·fi·cien·cies
suf·fi·cient
  suf·fi·cient·ly
suf·fix
suf·fo·cate
  suf·fo·cat·ed
  suf·fo·cat·ing
  suf·fo·ca·tion
  suf·fo·ca·tive

suf·ra·gan
suf·frage
suf·fra·gette
suf·frag·ist
suf·fuse
  suf·fused
  suf·fus·ing
  suf·fu·sion
  suf·fu·sive
sug·ar
  sug·ary
sug·ar·coat
sug·gest
  sug·gest·i·ble
  sug·gest·i·bil·i·ty
sug·ges·tion
sug·ges·tive
  sug·ges·tive·ly
  sug·ges·tive·ness
su·i·cide
  su·i·cid·al
suit·a·ble
  suit·a·bil·i·ty
  suit·a·ble·ness
  suit·a·bly
suite
suit·ing
suit·or
sul·fa·nil·a·mide
sul·fate
sul·fide
sul·fur
sul·fu·ric
sul·fur·ous
sulky
  sulk·i·ly
  sulk·i·ness
sul·len
  sul·len·ly
  sul·len·ness
sul·ly
  sul·lied
  sul·ly·ing
sul·tan
  sul·tana
  sul·tan·ate
sul·try
  sul·tri·ly

sul·tri·ness
sum
  summed
  sum·ming
su·mac
sum·ma·rize
  sum·ma·rized
  sum·ma·riz·ing
  sum·ma·ri·za·tion
sum·ma·ry
  sum·ma·ries
  sum·mar·i·ly
  sum·mar·i·ness
sum·ma·tion
  sum·ma·tion·al
sum·mer
sum·mit
sum·mon
sum·mons
sump·tu·ary
sump·tu·ous
  sump·tu·ous·ly
  sump·tu·ous·ness
sun
  sunned
  sun·ning
sun·bathe
  sun·bathed
  sun·bath·ing
  sun·bath·er
sun·burn
  sun·burned
  sun·burnt
  sun·burn·ing
sun·dae
sun·der
  sun·der·ance
sun·di·al
sun·dry
  sun·dries
sun·flow·er
sun·glass·es
sunk·en
sun·ny
  sun·ni·er
  sun·ni·ness
sun·shine
sun·spot

sun·stroke
sup
  supped
  sup·ping
su·per·a·bun·dant
  su·per·a·bun·dance
  su·per·a·bun·dant·ly
su·per·an·nu·ate
  su·per·an·nu·at·ed
  su·per·an·nu·at·ing
  su·per·an·nu·a·tion
su·perb
  su·perb·ly
  su·perb·ness
su·per·car·go
su·per·charge
  su·per·charged
  su·per·charg·ing
su·per·charg·er
su·per·cil·i·ous
  su·per·cil·i·ous·ly
  su·per·cil·i·ous·ness
su·per·e·go
su·per·e·rog·a·to·ry
su·per·fi·cial
  su·per·fi·ci·al·i·ty
  su·per·fi·ci·al·i·ties
  su·per·fi·cial·ly
  su·per·fi·cial·ness
su·per·fine
su·per·flu·ous
  su·per·flu·i·ty
  su·per·flu·ous·ly
  su·per·flu·ous·ness
su·per·high·way
su·per·hu·man
su·per·im·pose
  su·per·im·posed
  su·per·im·pos·ing
  su·per·im·po·si·tion
super·in·duce
su·per·in·tend
  su·per·in·tend·ence
  su·per·in·tend·en·cy
  su·per·in·tend·ent
su·pe·ri·or
  su·pe·ri·or·i·ty
  su·pe·ri·or·ly

su·per·la·tive
  su·per·la·tive·ly
  su·per·la·tive·ness
su·per·man
su·per·market
su·per·nal
su·per·nat·u·ral
  su·per·nat·u·ral·ism
  su·per·nat·u·ral·ly
  su·per·nat·u·ral·ness
su·per·nu·mer·ary
su·per·pow·er
su·per·scribe
  su·per·scrip·tion
su·per·script
su·per·sede
  su·per·sed·ed
  su·per·sed·ing
su·per·son·ic
  su·per·son·i·cal·ly
su·per·sti·tion
su·per·sti·tious
  su·per·sti·tious·ly
  su·per·sti·tious·ness
su·per·struc·ture
su·per·tank·er
su·per·vene
  su·per·vened
  su·per·ven·ing
  super·ven·tion
su·per·vise
  su·per·vised
  su·per·vis·ing
  su·per·vi·sion
  su·per·vi·sor
  su·per·vi·so·ry
su·pine
  su·pine·ness
sup·per
sup·plant
  sup·plan·ta·tion
sup·ple
  sup·plest
  sup·ple·ness
sup·ple·ment
  sup·ple·men·tal
  sup·ple·men·ta·ry
  sup·ple·men·ta·tion

sup·pli·ant
sup·pli·cate
  sup·pli·cat·ed
  sup·pli·cat·ing
  sup·pli·cant
  sup·pli·ca·tion
  sup·pli·ca·to·ry
sup·ply
  sup·plied
  sup·ply·ing
  sup·plies
  sup·pli·er
sup·port
  sup·port·a·ble
  sup·port·a·bly
  sup·port·er
  sup·port·ive
sup·pose
  sup·posed
  sup·pos·ing
  sup·pos·a·ble
  sup·pos·a·bly
  sup·pos·ed·ly
sup·po·si·tion
  sup·po·si·tion·al·ly
sup·pos·i·to·ry
sup·press
  sup·press·i·ble
  sup·pres·sion
  sup·pres·sor
sup·pu·rate
  sup·pu·rat·ed
  sup·pu·rat·ing
  sup·pu·ra·tion
su·prem·a·cy
  su·prem·a·cist
su·preme
  su·preme·ly
  su·preme·ness
sur·cease
sur·charge
  sur·charged
  sur·charg·ing
sur·cin·gle
sure
  sur·er
  sur·est
  sure·ly

sure·ness
sure-foot·ed
sure·ty
surf
  surf·board
  surf·ing
sur·face
  sur·faced
  sur·fac·ing
sur·feit
surge
  surged
  surg·ing
sur·geon
sur·gery
  sur·gi·cal
  sur·gi·cal·ly
sur·ly
  sur·li·ly
  sur·li·ness
sur·mise
  sur·mised
  sur·mis·ing
sur·mount
  sur·mount·a·ble
sur·name
sur·pass
  sur·pass·a·ble
  sur·pass·ing
sur·plice
sur·plus
  sur·plus·age
sur·prise
  sur·prised
  sur·pris·ing
  sur·pris·al
sur·re·al·ism
  sur·re·al·ist
  sur·re·al·is·tic
  sur·re·al·is·ti·cal·ly
sur·ren·der
sur·rep·ti·tious
  sur·rep·ti·tious·ly
  sur·rep·ti·tious·ness
sur·rey
sur·ro·gate
  sur·ro·gat·ed
  sur·ro·gat·ing

sur·round
sur·round·ings
sur·tax
sur·veil·lance
  sur·veil·lant
sur·vey
  sur·vey·ing
  sur·vey·or
sur·vive
  sur·vived
  sur·viv·ing
  sur·viv·al
  sur·vi·vor
sus·cep·ti·ble
  sus·cep·ti·bil·i·ty
  sus·cep·ti·ble·ness
  sus·cep·ti·bly
sus·pect
sus·pend
  sus·pend·er
sus·pense
sus·pen·sion
sus·pi·cion
sus·pi·cious
  sus·pi·cious·ly
  sus·pi·cious·ness
sus·tain
  sus·tain·a·ble
  sus·tain·er
  sus·tain·ment
sus·te·nance
su·ture
  su·tured
  su·tur·ing
su·ze·rain
svelte
  svelte·ly
  svelte·ness
swab
  swabbed
  swab·bing
swad·dle
  swad·dled
  swad·dling
swag·ger
  swag·ger·ing
swal·low
swa·mi

swamp
  swampy
  swamp·i·ness
swank
  swank·i·ly
  swank·i·ness
  swanky
swan dive
swap
  swapped
  swap·ping
sward
swarthy
  swarth·i·er
  swarth·i·ness
swash·buck·ling
swas·ti·ka
swat
  swat·ted
  swat·ting
  swat·ter
swathe
  swathed
  swath·ing
sway
  sway·a·ble
  sway·backed
swear
  swore
  sworn
  swear·ing
  swear-er
sweat
  sweat·ing
  sweat·i·ly
  sweat·i·ness
  sweaty
  sweat·er
Swe·den
  Swed·ish
sweep
  swept
  sweep·ing
  sweep·ing·ness
sweep·stakes
sweet
  sweet·ish
  sweet·ly

sweet·ness
sweet·en
swell
swelled
swoll·en
swell·ing
swel·ter
swel·ter·ing
swerve
swerved
swerv·ing
swift
swift·ly
swift·ness
swig
swigged
swig·ging
swill
swim
swam
swum
swim·ming
swim·mer
swin·dle
swin·dled
swin·dling
swin·dler
swine
swin·ish
swing
swung
swing·ing
swing·a·ble
swing·er
swipe
swip·ed
swip·ing
swirl
swirl·ing·ly
swirly
swish
swishy
switch
switch·blade
switch·board
switch-hit·ter
Switz·er·land
swiv·el

swiv·eled
swiv·el·ing
swiz·zle
swoon
swoon·ed
swoon·ing·ly
swoop
swop
swopped
swop·ping
sword
swords·man
syc·a·more
syc·o·phant
syc·o·phan·cy
syc·o·phan·tic
syc·o·phan·ti·cal
syl·lab·ic
syl·lab·i·cate
syl·lab·i·ca·tion
syl·lab·i·fy
syl·lab·i·fi·ca·tion
syl·la·ble
syl·la·bus
syl·lo·gism
syl·lo·gis·tic
sylph-like
syl·van
sym·bi·o·sis
sym·bol
sym·bol·ic
sym·bol·i·cal
sym·bol·ism
sym·bol·ize
sym·bol·ized
sym·bol·iz·ing
sym·bol·i·za·tion
sym·me·try
sym·met·ric
sym·met·ri·cal
sym·pa·thet·ic
sym·pa·thet·i·cal·ly
sym·pa·thize
sym·pa·thized
sym·pa·thiz·ing
sym·pa·thiz·er
sym·pa·thiz·ing·ly
sym·pa·thy

sym·pa·thies
sym·pho·ny
sym·pho·nies
sym·phon·ic
sym·po·si·um
sym·po·sia
symp·tom
symp·to·mat·ic
symp·to·mat·i·cal
symp·to·mat·i·cal·ly
syn·a·gogue
syn·a·gog·al
syn·a·gog·i·cal
syn·chro·nism
syn·chro·nis·tic
syn·chro·nis·ti·cal
syn·chro·nis·ti·cal·ly
syn·chro·nize
syn·chro·nized
syn·chro·niz·ing
syn·chro·ni·za·tion
syn·chro·niz·er
syn·chro·nous
syn·chro·nous·ly
syn·chro·nous·ness
syn·chro·tron
syn·co·pate
syn·co·pat·ed
syn·co·pat·ing
syn·co·pa·tion
syn·co·pa·tor
syn·cre·tism
syn·cre·tic
syn·di·cate
syn·di·cat·ed
syn·di·cat·ing
syn·di·ca·tion
syn·di·ca·tor
syn·drome
syn·ec·do·che
syn·ecol·o·gy
syn·er·gism
syn·od
syn·od·al
syn·o·nym
syn·on·y·mous
syn·on·y·my
syn·op·sis

syn·op·tic
syn·tax
  syn·tac·tic
  syn·tac·ti·cal
syn·the·sis
  syn·the·sist
syn·the·size
  syn·the·sized
  syn·the·siz·ing
syn·thet·ic
  syn·thet·i·cal
  syn·thet·i·cal·ly
syph·i·lis
  syph·i·lit·ic
sy·ringe
syr·up
  syr·upy
system
sys·tem·at·ic
  sys·tem·at·i·cal
  sys·tem·at·i·cal·ly
  sys·tem·at·ic·ness
sys·tem·a·tize
  sys·tem·a·tized
  sys·tem·a·tiz·ing
  sys·tem·a·ti·za·tion
  sys·tem·a·tiz·er
sys·tem·ic
  sys·tem·i·cal·ly
sys·to·le
  sys·tol·ic

T

tab
  tabbed
  tab·bing
Ta·bas·co
tab·by
tab·er·na·cle
  tab·er·nac·u·lar
ta·ble
  ta·bled
  ta·bling
tab·leau
tab·le d'hote
ta·ble·spoon·fuls
tab·let

tab·loid
ta·boo
  ta·booed
  ta·boo·ing
ta·bor
tab·o·ret
tab·u·lar
  tab·u·lar·ly
tab·u·late
  tab·u·lat·ed
  tab·u·lat·ing
  tab·u·la·tion
  tab·u·la·tor
ta·chom·e·ter
tac·it
  tac·it·ly
  tac·it·ness
tac·i·turn
  tac·i·tur·ni·ty
tack
  tacked
  tack·ing
tack·le
  tack·led
  tack·ling
  tack·ler
tacky
  tack·i·ness
ta·cos
tact
  tact·ful·ly
  tact·ful·ness
  tact·less
tac·tics
  tac·ti·cal
  tac·ti·cian
tac·tile
  tac·til·i·ty
tad·pole
taf·fe·ta
taf·fy
tag
  tagged
  tag·ging
tail
  tailed
  tail·less
tail·gate

tail·gat·ed
tail·gat·ing
tai·lor
  tai·lored
  tai·lor·ing
taint
  taint·ed
take
  took
  tak·en
  tak·ing
take·off
tal·cum
tale·bear·ing
tal·ent
  tal·ent·ed
tal·is·man
talk·a·tive
  talk·a·tive·ly
  talk·a·tive·ness
talky
  talk·i·er
  talk·i·est
tal·low
  tal·lowy
tal·ly
  tal·lies
  tal·lied
  tal·ly·ing
tal·ly·ho
Tal·mud
  Tal·mud·ic
  Tal·mud·i·cal
tal·on
  tal·oned
ta·ma·le
tam·a·rack
tam·a·rind
tam·bour
tam·bou·rine
tame
  tamed
  tam·ing
  tam·a·ble
  tame·ly
  tame·ness
tam-o'-shan·ter
tam·per

tam·pon
tan
  tanned
  tan·ning
  tan·nish
tan·a·ger
tan·bark
tan·dem
tang
  tangy
  tang·i·er
tan·ge·lo
tan·gent
  tan·gen·cy
tan·gen·tial
tan·ge·rine
tan·gi·ble
  tan·gi·bil·i·ty
  tan·gi·ble·ness
  tan·gi·bly
tan·gle
  tan·gled
  tan·gling
  tan·gle·ment
tan·go
  tan·goed
  tan·go·ing
tank·age
tank·ard
tank·er
tan·nery
tan·nin
tan·ta·lize
  tan·ta·lized
  tan·ta·liz·ing
tan·ta·mount
tan·trum
tap
  tapped
  tap·ping
tape
  taped
  tap·ing
ta·per
  ta·per·ing·ly
tap·es·try
  tap·es·tries
  tap·es·tried

tap·es·try·ing
tap·i·o·ca
ta·pir
tar
  tarred
  tar·ring
  tar·ry
tar·an·tel·la
ta·ran·tu·la
  ta·ran·tu·las
  ta·ran·tu·lae
tar·dy
  tar·di·ly
  tar·di·ness
tar·get
tar·iff
tar·nish
  tar·nish·a·ble
ta·ro
tar·pau·lin
tar·pon
tar·ra·gon
tar·ry
  tar·ried
  tar·ry·ing
tart
  tart·ness
tar·tan
tar·tar
  tar·tar·ic
  tar·tar·ous
tas·sel
  tas·seled
  tas·sel·ing
taste
  tast·ed
  tast·ing
taste·ful
  taste·ful·ly
  taste·ful·ness
taste·less
  taste·less·ness
tasty
  tast·i·ness
tat
  tat·ted
  tat·ting
tat·ter·de·ma·lion

tat·tered
tat·tle
  tat·tled
  tat·tling
tat·tle·tale
tat·too
  tat·tooed
  tat·too·ing
taught
taunt
  taunt·ing·ly
taut
  taut·ly
  taut·ness
tau·tol·o·gy
  tau·to·log·i·cal
  tau·to·log·i·cal·ly
tav·ern
taw·dry
  taw·dri·ly
  taw·dri·ness
taw·ny
  taw·ni·ness
tax
  tax·a·bil·i·ty
  tax·a·ble
tax·a·tion
tax·ex·empt
taxi
tax·i·cab
tax·i·der·my
  tax·i·der·mic
  tax·i·der·mist
tax·on·o·my
  tax·o·nom·i·cal
  tax·o·nom·i·cal·ly
  tax·on·o·mist
tax·pay·er
teach
  taught
  teach·ing
teach·a·ble
  teach·a·ble·ness
  teach·a·bil·i·ty
teach·er
teak·wood
tea·ket·tle
team·mate

team·ster
tear
  tore
  torn
  tear·ing
tear·ful
  tear·ful·ly
  tear·ful·ness
  teary
tease
  teased
  teas·ing
tea·sel
  tea·seled
  tea·sel·ing
tea·spoon·fuls
teat
tech·ni·cal
  tech·ni·cal·ly
  tech·ni·cal·ness
  tech·ni·cal·i·ty
  tech·ni·cian
tech·nique
tech·noc·ra·cy
  tech·no·crat
  tech·no·crat·ic
tech·nol·o·gy
  tech·no·log·i·cal
  tech·no·log·ic
  tech·nol·o·gist
tec·ton·ic
te·di·ous
  te·di·ous·ly
  te·di·ous·ness
te·di·um
tee
  teed
  tee·ing
teem
  teem·ing
teen·ag·er
tee·pee
tee·ter
teethe
  teethed
  teeth·ing
tee·to·tal
  tee·to·tal·er

tee·to·tal·ist
tee·to·tal·ism
tee·to·tal·ly
teg·u·ment
tel·e·cast
  tel·e·cast·ing
  tel·e·cast·er
tel·e·com·mu·ni·ca·tion
tel·e·gram
tel·e·graph
  tel·e·graph·ic
  te·leg·ra·phy
tele·ki·ne·sis
tele·me·ter
te·le·ol·o·gy
te·lep·a·thy
  tel·e·path·ic
  tel·e·path·i·cal·ly
  tel·lep·a·thist
tel·e·phone
  tel·e·phoned
  tel·e·phon·ing
  tle·e·phon·ic
tel·e·pho·to
tel·e·pho·tog·ra·phy
  tel·e·pho·to·graph·ic
Tel·e·promp·ter
tel·e·ran
tel·e·scope
  tel·e·scoped
  tel·e·scop·ing
tel·e·scop·ic
  tel·e·scop·i·cal
tel·e·thon
Tel·e·type
tel·e·vise
  tel·e·vised
  tel·e·vis·ing
  tel·e·vi·sion
tell
  told
  tell·ing
tell·er
tem·blor
te·mer·i·ty
tem·per
  tem·per·a·bil·i·ty
  tem·per·a·ble

tem·pered
tem·per·er
tem·pera
tem·per·a·ment
tem·per·a·men·tal
tem·per·ance
tem·per·ate
  tem·per·ate·ly
  tem·per·ate·ness
tem·per·a·ture
tem·pest
tem·pes·tu·ous
  tem·pes·tu·ous·ly
  tem·pes·tu·ous·ness
tem·plate
tem·ple
tem·po
tem·po·ral
  tem·po·ral·i·ty
  tem·por·al·ly
  tem·por·ral·ness
tem·po·rary
  tem·po·rar·i·ty
  tem·po·rar·i·ness
tem·po·rize
  tem·po·ri·za·tion
  tem·po·riz·er
  tem·po·riz·ing·ly
tempt
tempt·a·ble
temp·ta·tion
tempt·ing
ten·a·ble
  ten·a·bil·i·ty
  ten·a·ble·ness
  ten·a·bly
te·na·cious
  te·na·cious·ly
  te·na·cious·ness
  te·nac·i·ty
ten·ant
  ten·an·cy
  ten·an·cies
  ten·ant·a·ble
ten·den·cy
  ten·den·cies
ten·den·tious
  ten·den·tious·ly

ten·den·tious·ness
ten·der
  ten·der·ly
  ten·der·ness
ten·der·foot
ten·der·ize
  ten·der·ized
  ten·der·iz·ing
  ten·der·iz·er
ten·der·loin
ten·don
ten·dril
te·neb·ri·ous
ten·e·ment
ten·et
ten·nis
ten·on
ten·or
tense
  tensed
  tens·ing
  tense·ly
  tense·ness
  ten·si·ty
ten·sile
  ten·sil·i·ty
ten·sion
  ten·sion·al
  ten·sion·less
  ten·sive
ten·ta·cle
  ten·ta·cled
  ten·tac·u·lar
ten·ta·tive
  ten·ta·tive·ly
  ten·ta·tive·ness
tenth
te·nu·i·ty
ten·u·ous
  ten·u·ous·ly
  ten·u·ous·ness
ten·ure
  ten·ured
  ten·u·ri·al
  ten·u·ri·al·ly
te·pee
tep·id
  te·pid·i·ty

tep·id·ness
te·qui·la
ter·cen·te·nary
  ter·cen·ten·ni·al
ter·gi·ver·sate
ter·i·ya·ki
ter·ma·gant
ter·mi·nal
  ter·mi·nal·ly
ter·mi·nate
  ter·mi·nat·ed
  ter·mi·nat·ing
  ter·mi·na·ble
  ter·mi·na·tion
  ter·mi·na·tive
  ter·mi·na·tor
ter·mi·nol·o·gy
  ter·mi·nol·o·gies
  ter·mi·no·log·i·cal
  ter·mi·no·log·i·cal·ly
ter·mi·nus
ter·mite
ter·na·ry
terp·sich·o·re·an
ter·race
  ter·raced
  ter·rac·ing
ter·ra-cot·ta
ter·ra fir·ma
ter·rain
Ter·ra·my·cin
ter·ra·pin
ter·rar·i·um
ter·raz·zo
ter·res·tri·al
  ter·res·tri·al·ly
ter·ri·ble
  ter·ri·ble·ness
  ter·ri·bly
ter·ri·er
ter·rif·ic
  ter·rif·i·cal·ly
ter·ri·fy
  ter·ri·fied
  ter·ri·fy·ing
ter·ri·to·ry
  ter·ri·to·ri·al
  ter·ri·to·ri·al·i·ty

ter·ror
  ter·ror·less
ter·ror·ism
ter·ror·ist
  ter·ror·is·tic
  ter·ror·less
ter·ror·ize
  ter·ror·ized
  ter·ror·iz·ing
  ter·ror·i·za·tion
  ter·ror·iz·er
ter·ry
terse
  ters·er
  terse·ly
  terse·ness
ter·ti·ary
tes·sel·late
  tes·sel·lat·ed
  tes·sel·lat·ing
  tes·sel·la·tion
tes·ta·ment
  tes·ta·men·ta·ry
tes·tate
tes·ta·tor
  tes·ta·trix
tes·ti·cle
  tes·tic·u·lar
tes·ti·fy
  tes·ti·fied
  tes·ti·fy·ing
tes·ti·mo·ni·al
tes·ti·mo·ny
  tes·ti·mo·nies
tes·tis
  tes·tes
tes·tos·ter·one
tes·ty
  tes·ti·ly
  tes·ti·ness
tet·a·nus
tete-a-tete
teth·er
tet·ra·eth·yl
tet·ra·he·dron
tex·tile
tex·tu·al
tex·ture

tex·tural
tex·tur·al·ly
tex·tured
thank
thank·ful·ly
thank·ful·ness
thank·less
thank·less·ly
thank·less·ness
thanks·giv·ing
thatch
thatch·ing
thaw
the·a·ter
the·a·tre
the·at·ri·cal
the·at·ri·cal·ism
the·at·ri·cal·i·ty
the·at·ri·cal·ly
the·ism
the·ist
the·is·tic
theme
the·mat·ic
the·mat·i·cal·ly
them·selves
thence·forth
the·oc·ra·cy
the·oc·ra·cies
the·o·crat
the·o·crat·ic
the·o·crat·i·cal
the·o·crat·i·cal·ly
the·ol·o·gy
the·ol·o·gies
the·o·lo·gian
the·o·log·ic
the·o·log·i·cal
the·o·log·i·cal·ly
the·o·rem
the·o·re·mat·ic
the·o·ret·i·cal
the·o·ret·ic
the·o·ret·i·cal·ly
the·o·rize
the·o·rized
the·o·riz·ing
the·o·re·ti·cian

the·o·rist
the·o·ri·za·tion
the·o·riz·er
the·o·ry
the·o·ries
the·os·o·phy
the·o·soph·ic
the·o·soph·i·cal
the·o·soph·i·cal·ly
the·os·o·phist
ther·a·peu·tic
ther·a·peu·ti·cal
ther·a·peu·ti·cal·ly
ther·a·peu·tics
ther·a·peu·tist
ther·a·py
ther·a·pist
there·fore
ther·mal
ther·mal·ly
ther·mo·dy·nam·ics
ther·mo·dy·nam·ic
ther·mo·dy·nam·i·cal
ther·mo·e·lec·tric
ther·mom·e·ter
ther·mo·met·ric
ther·mo·nu·cle·ar
ther·mo·plas·tic
ther·mos
ther·mo·stat
ther·mo·stat·ic
the·sau·rus
the·sis
the·ses
thes·pi·an
thi·a·mine
thick
thick·ish
thick·ly
thick·ness
thick·en
thick·et
thick·et·ed
thick-head·ed
thief
thieves
thieve
thieved

thiev·ing
thiev·ish
thiev·ish·ness
thiev·ery
thiev·er·ies
thim·ble
thin
thin·ner
thin·nest
thinned
thin·ning
thin·ly
thin·ness
thine
thing
think
thought
think·ing
third·ly
thirsty
thirst·i·er
thirst·i·est
thirst·i·ly
thirst·i·ness
thir·teen
thir·teenth
thir·ti·eth
thir·ty
thir·ties
this·tle
thith·er
thong
tho·rax
tho·ri·um
thorn
thorny
thorn·i·ness
thor·ough
thor·ough·ly
thor·ough·ness
thor·ough·bred
thor·ough·fare
thor·ough·go·ing
though
thought·ful
thought·ful·ly
thought·ful·ness
thought·less

thou·sand
  thou·santh
thrall
  thrall·dom
thrash·er
thrash·ing
thread
thread·bare
thready
  thread·i·ness
threat·en
  threat·en·ing·ly
three-deck·er
three-di·men·sion·al
three·fold
three-quar·ter
three·score
three·some
thren·o·dy
thresh·er
thresh·old
thrice
thrift·less
thrifty
  thrift·i·ly
  thrift·i·ness
thrill
  thrill·ing
thrive
  throve
  thrived
  thriven
  thriv·ing
throat
throaty
  throat·i·ly
  throat·i·ness
throb
  throbbed
  throb·bing
throe
throm·bo·sis
throne
throng
throt·tle
  throt·tled
  throt·tling
through

through·out
through·way
  thru·way
throw
  threw
  thrown
  throw·ing
  throw·a·way
  throw·back
thrum
  thrummed
  thrum·ming
thrust
  thrust·ing
thud
  thud·ded
  thud·ding
thug
  thug·gery
  thug·gish
thumb
thumb·nail
thumb·screw
thumb·tack
thump·ing
thun·der
  thun·der·ous
thun·der·bolt
thun·der·cloud
thun·der·head
thun·der·show·er
thun·der·storm
thun·der·struck
thwack
thwart
thyme
thy·mus
thy·roid
ti·ara
tib·ia
tic
tick
tick·er
tick·et
tick·ing
tick·le
  tick·led
  tick·ling

tick·lish
  tick·lish·ness
tick-tack-toe
ti·dal
tid·bit
tid·dly·winks
tide
tide·land
tide·water
ti·dings
ti·dy
  ti·di·ly
  ti·di·ness
tie
  tied
  ty·ing
tier
ti·ger
  ti·gress
  ti·ger·ish
tight
  tight·ly
  tight·ness
tight·en
tight-fist·ed
tight-lipped
tight·rope
tight·wad
til·de
tile
  tiled
  til·ing
till
  till·a·ble
till·age
tilt
  tilt·ed
tim·bal
tim·ber
  tim·bered
tim·ber·line
tim·bre
tim·brel
time
  timed
  tim·ing
time-con·sum·ing
time-hon·ored

time·keep·er
time·less·ness
time·out
time-shar·ing
time·ta·ble
tim·id
  tim·id·ly
  tim·id·i·ty
  tim·id·ness
tim·or·ous
  tim·or·ous·ly
  tim·or·ous·ness
tim·o·thy
tim·pa·ni
  tim·pa·nist
tin
  tinned
  tin·ning
tinc·ture
  tinc·tur·ing
tin·der
tinge
  tinged
  tinge·ing
tin·gle
  tin·gled
  tin·gling
  tin·gly
tink·er
tin·kle
  tin·kled
  tin·kling
tin·ny
  tin·ni·ly
  tin·ni·ness
tin·sel
  tin·seled
  tin·sel·ing
tint
  tint·er
  tint·ing
tin·tin·nab·u·la·tion
ti·ny
  ti·ni·er
  ti·ni·ness
tip
  tipped
  tip·ping

tip·ple
  tip·pled
  tip·pling
  tip·pler
tip·sy
  tip·si·ly
  tip·si·ness
tip·toe
  tip·toed
  tip·to·ing
tip·top
ti·rade
tire
  tired
  tir·ing
  tire·less
tire·some
  tire·some·ness
tis·sue
ti·tan
  ti·tan·ic
tithe
  tithed
  tith·ing
ti·tian
tit·il·late
  tit·il·lat·ed
  tit·il·lat·ing
  tit·il·la·tion
ti·tle
  ti·tled
tit·mouse
tit·ter
  tit·ter·ing
tit·u·lar
tiz·zy
toady
  toad·y·ing
  toad·y·ism
toast·er
toast·mas·ter
  toast·mis·tress
to·bac·co
to·bog·gan
toc·sin
to·day
tod·dle
  tod·dled

tod·dling
tod·dler
tod·dy
toe
  toed
  toe·ing
toe·nail
tof·fee
tog
  togged
  tog·ging
to·ga
to·geth·er
  to·geth·er·ness
tog·gle
  tog·gled
  tog·gling
toil·er
toi·let
  toi·let·ry
toil·some
to·ken·ism
To·kyo
tol·er·a·ble
  tol·er·a·ble·ness
  tol·er·a·bil·i·ty
  tol·er·a·bly
tol·er·ant
  tol·er·ance
tol·er·ate
  tol·er·at·ed
  tol·er·at·ing
  tol·er·a·tion
  tol·er·a·tive
toll·booth
tom·a·hawk
to·ma·to
tom·boy
  tom·boy·ish
tomb·stone
tom·cat
tom·fool·ery
to·mor·row
tom·tit
tom-tom
tone
  ton·al
  to·nal·i·ty

ton·al·ly
tone·less
tongue
tongue-lash
tongue-tied
ton·ic
to·night
ton·nage
ton·neau
ton·sil
ton·sil·lec·to·my
ton·sil·li·tis
ton·so·ri·al
ton·sure
  ton·sured
  ton·sur·ing
ton·tine
tool·mak·er
tooth
  teeth
tooth·ache
tooth·brush
tooth·less
tooth·paste
tooth·pick
tooth·some
toothy
  tooth·i·ness
top
  topped
  top·ping
to·paz
tope
  toped
  top·ing
  top·er
to·pi·ary
top·ic
top·i·cal
top·i·cal·i·ty
to·pog·ra·phy
  to·pog·ra·pher
  top·o·graph·i·cal
  top·o·graph·i·cal·ly
to·pol·o·gy
  top·o·log·i·cal
top·ping
top·pie

top·pled
top·pling
top·se·cret
top·sy-tur·vy
toque
To·rah
torch·bear·er
torch·light
tor·e·a·dor
to·re·ro
tor·ment
  tor·ment·ing
  tor·men·tor
tor·na·do
  tor·na·dos
  tor·nad·ic
tor·pe·do
  tor·pe·doed
  tor·pe·do·ing
tor·pid
  tor·pid·i·ty
  tor·pid·ly
tor·por
torque
tor·rent
  tor·ren·tial
tor·rid
  tor·rid·i·ty
  tor·rid·ness
  tor·rid·ly
tor·sion
  tor·sion·al
tor·so
tort
torte
tor·til·la
tor·toise
tor·to·ni
tor·tu·ous
  tor·tu·ous·ly
  tor·tu·ous·ness
tor·ture
  tor·tured
  tor·tur·ing
  tor·tur·er
  tor·ture·some
tossing
to·tal

to·taled
to·tal·ing
to·tal·i·tar·i·an
to·tal·i·tar·i·an·ism
to·tal·i·ty
to·tal·i·za·tor
to·tal·ly
tote
  tot·ed
  tot·ing
to·tem
  to·tem·ic
  to·tem·ism
  to·tem·ist
  to·tem·is·tic
tot·ter
  tot·ter·ing
tou·can
touch
  touched
  touch·ing
  touch·a·ble
  touchy
  touch·i·ness
touch·down
tou·ché
tough
  tough·ness
  tough·en
tou·pee
tour de force
tour·ism
tour·ist
tour·ma·line
tour·na·ment
tour·ney
tour·ni·quet
tou·sle
  tou·sled
tout·er
tow·age
to·ward
tow·boat
tow·el
  tow·eled
  tow·el·ing
tow·er
  tow·ered

tow·er·ing
tow-head·ed
town·ship
tox·e·mia
tox·ic
tox·ic·i·ty
tox·i·col·o·gy
  tox·i·co·log·i·cal
  tox·i·co·log·i·cal·ly
  tox·i·col·o·gist
tox·in
tox·oid
trace
  traced
  trac·ing
  trace·a·ble
  trace·a·bly
trac·ery
tra·chea
tra·che·ot·o·my
tra·cho·ma
track·age
track·er
tract
trac·ta·ble
  trac·ta·bil·i·ty
  trac·ta·ble·ness
  trac·ta·bly
trac·tion
  trac·tion·al
  trac·tive
trac·tor
trade
  trad·ed
  trad·ing
trade·mark
trades·man
tra·di·tion
tra·di·tion·al
  tra·di·tion·al·ism
  tra·di·tion·al·ist
  tra·di·tion·al·ly
tra·duce
  tra·duced
  tra·duc·ing
  tra·duce·ment
traf·fic
  traf·ficked

traf·fick·ing
traf·fick·er
tra·ge·di·an
tra·ge·di·enne
trag·e·dy
trag·e·dies
trag·ic
trag·i·cal
trag·i·cal·ly
trag·i·cal·ness
tragi·com·e·dy
trail·blaz·er
  trail·blaz·ing
trail·er
train
  train·a·ble
  train·er
  train·ing
traipse
  traipsed
  traips·ing
trait
trai·tor
  trai·tor·ous
  trai·tor·ous·ly
tra·jec·to·ry
  tra·jec·to·ries
tram·mel
  tram·meled
  tram·mel·ing
tramp·ing
tram·ple
  tram·pled
  tram·pling
tram·po·line
  tram·po·lin·ist
trance
tran·quil
  tran·quil·li·ty
  tran·quil·ly
  tran·quil·ness
tran·quil·ize
  tran·quil·ized
  tran·quil·iz·ing
  tran·quil·iz·er
trans·act
  trans·ac·tor
  trans·ac·tion

trans·ac·tion·al
trans·at·lan·tic
trans·ceiv·er
tran·scend
  tran·scend·ent
  tran·scen·den·tal
  tran·scen·den·tal·ly
  tran·scen·den·tal·ism
trans·con·ti·nen·tal
tran·scribe
  tran·scribed
  tran·scrib·ing
  tran·scrib·er
tran·script
  tran·scrip·tion
  tran·scrip·tion·al
  tran·scrip·tive
tran·sect
  trans·sec·tion
tran·sept
  tran·sep·tal
  tran·sep·tal·ly
trans·fer
  trans·ferred
  trans·fer·ring
  trans·fer·al
  trans·fer·a·ble
  trans·fer·ence
trans·fig·ure
  trans·fig·ured
  trans·fig·ur·ing
  trans·fig·ure·ment
  trans·fig·u·ra·tion
trans·fix
  trans·fixed
  trans·fix·ing
  trans·fix·ion
trans·form
  trans·form·a·ble
  trans·for·ma·tion
  trans·form·a·tive
trans·form·er
trans·fuse
  trans·fused
  trans·fus·ing
  trans·fus·a·ble
  trans·fu·sion
trans·gress

trans·gres·sive
trans·gres·sor
trans·gres·sion
tran·sient
tran·sience
tran·sis·tor
tran·sis·tor·ize
tran·sis·tor·ized
tran·sis·tor·iz·ing
trans·it
tran·si·tion
tran·si·tion·al
tran·si·tion·al·ly
tran·si·tive
tran·si·tive·ly
tran·si·tive·ness
tran·si·tiv·i·ty
tran·si·to·ry
tran·si·to·ri·ly
tran·si·to·ri·ness
trans·late
trans·lat·ed
trans·lat·ing
trans·lat·a·bil·i·ty
trans·lat·a·ble
trans·lat·or
trans·la·tion
trans·la·tion·al
trans·la·tive
trans·lit·er·ate
trans·lit·er·at·ed
trans·lit·er·at·ing
trans·lit·er·a·tion
trans·lu·cent
trans·lu·cence
trans·lu·cen·cy
trans·lu·cent·ly
trans·me·rid·i·o·nal
trans·mi·grate
trans·mi·grat·ed
trans·mi·grāt·ing
trans·mi·gra·tion
trans·mi·gra·tor
trans·mi·gra·to·ry
trans·mis·sion
trans·mis·si·bil·i·ty
trans·mis·siv·i·ty
trans·mis·si·ble

trans·mis·sive
trans·mit
trans·mit·ted
trans·mit·ting
trans·mit·ta·ble
trans·mit·tal
trans·mit·ter
trans·mute
trans·mut·ed
trans·mut·ing
trans·mut·er
trans·mut·a·ble·ness
trans·mut·a·bil·i·ty
trans·mut·a·bly
trans·mu·ta·tion
trans·mut·a·ble
trans·o·ce·an·ic
tran·som
tran·son·ic
trans·pa·cif·ic
trans·par·ent
trans·par·en·cy
trans·par·en·cies
trans·par·ent·ly
trans·par·ent·ness
tran·spire
tran·spired
tran·spir·ing
tran·spi·ra·tion
trans·plant
trans·plant·a·ble
trans·plan·ta·tion
trans·port
trans·port·a·bil·i·ty
trans·port·a·ble
trans·port·er
trans·por·ta·tion
trans·pose
trans·posed
trans·pos·ing
trans·pos·a·ble
trans·po·si·tion
trans·ship
trans·shipped
trans·ship·ping
trans·ship·ment
trans·verse
trans·verse·ly

trans·ves·tism
trans·ves·tite
trap
trapped
trap·ping
tra·peze
tra·pe·zi·um
trap·e·zoid
trap·per
trap·pings
trap·shoot·ing
trash
trash·i·est
trash·i·ness
trashy
trau·ma
trau·mat·ic
trau·mat·i·cal·ly
trau·ma·tize
tra·vail
trav·el
tra·vel·ed
tra·vel·ing
trav·e·logue
trav·e·log
tra·verse
trav·ersed
trav·ers·ing
tra·vers·a·ble
tra·vers·al
trav·es·ty
trawl·er
treach·er·ous
treach·er·ous·ly
treach·er·ous·ness
treach·ery
treach·er·ies
tread
trod
trod·den
tread·ing
trea·dle
trea·son
trea·son·a·ble
trea·son·ous
trea·son·a·bly
treas·ure
treas·ured

treas·ur·ing
treas·ur·a·ble
treas·ur·er
treas·ur·y
treas·ur·ies
treat
treat·a·ble
treat·ment
trea·tise
trea·ty
trea·ties
tre·ble
tre·bled
tre·bling
tre·bly
tre·foil
trek
trekked
trek·king
trel·lis
trem·ble
trem·bled
trem·bling
trem·bly
tre·men·dous
tre·men·dous·ly
tre·men·dous·ness
trem·o·lo
trem·or
trem·or·ous
trem·u·lous
trem·u·lous·ly
trem·u·lous·ness
trench·ant
trench·an·cy
trench·ant·ly
trench·er
trend
trendy
tre·pan
tre·panned
tre·pan·ning
trep·an·a·tion
tre·phine
trep·i·da·tion
tres·pass
tres·pass·er
tres·tle

tri·ad
tri·ad·ic
tri·al
tri·an·gle
tri·an·gu·lar
tri·an·gu·lar·i·ty
tri·an·gu·lar·ly
tri·an·gu·late
tri·an·gu·lat·ed
tri·an·gu·lat·ing
tri·an·gu·la·tion
tribe
trib·al
tribes·men
trib·u·la·tion
trib·u·nal
trib·une
trib·u·tary
trib·u·tar·ies
trib·u·tar·i·ly
trib·ute
trice
tri·ceps
trich·i·no·sis
tri·chot·o·my
trick·ery
trick·le
trick·led
trick·ling
trick·ster
tricky
trick·i·er
trick·i·ly
trick·i·ness
tri·col·or
tri·cus·pid
tri·cy·cle
tri·dent
tri·den·tate
tri·di·men·sion·al
tri·en·ni·al
tri·en·ni·um
tri·fle
tri·fled
tri·fling
trif·ler
tri·fling·ness
tri·fo·cals

trig·ger
trig·o·nom·e·try
trig·o·no·met·ric
trig·o·no·met·ri·cal
trig·o·no·met·ri·cal·ly
tri·lin·gual
tril·lion
tril·lionth
tril·o·gy
trim
trimmed
trim·ming
trim·mer
trim·mest
trim·ly
trim·ness
tri·mes·ter
tri·mes·tral
tri·mes·tri·al
tri·month·ly
Trin·i·tar·i·an
Trin·i·ty
trin·ket
trio
trip
tripped
trip·ping
tri·par·tite
trip·ham·mer
tri·ple
tri·pled
tri·pling
tri·ply
trip·let
trip·li·cate
trip·li·cat·ed
trip·li·cat·ing
trip·li·ca·tion
tri·pod
trip·tych
tri·sect
tri·sec·tion
tri·sec·tor
trite
trite·ly
trite·ness
trit·u·rate
tri·umph

tri·um·phal
tri·um·phal·ly
tri·um·phant
tri·um·phant·ly
tri·um·vi·rate
triv·et
triv·ia
triv·i·al
  triv·i·al·i·ty
  triv·i·al·i·ties
  triv·i·al·i·za·tion
  triv·i·al·ly
tri·week·ly
tro·che
trog·lo·dyte
troi·ka
troll
trol·ley
trol·lop
trom·bone
  trom·bon·ist
troop·er
tro·phy
  tro·phies
trop·ic
  trop·i·cal
trop·o·sphere
trot
  trot·ted
  trot·ting
trot·ter
trou·ba·dour
trou·ble
  trou·bled
  trou·bling
trou·ble·mak·er
trou·ble·shoot·er
trou·ble·some
trough
trounce
  trounced
  trounc·ing
troupe
  trouped
  troup·ing
troup·er
trou·sers
trous·seau

trow·el
tru·ant
tru·an·cy
tru·an·cies
tru·ant·ry
truck·age
truck·er
truck·ing
truc·u·lent
  truc·u·lence
  truc·u·lent·ly
trudge
  trudged
  trudg·ing
true
  tru·er
  tru·est
  true·ness
truf·fle
tru·ism
  tru·is·tic
tru·ly
trump
  trump·er·y
trum·pet
  trum·pet·er
trun·cate
  trun·cat·ed
  trun·cat·ing
  trun·ca·tion
trun·cheon
trun·dle
  trun·dled
  trun·dling
truss
  truss·ing
trust
trus·tee
  trus·teed
  trus·tee·ing
  trus·tee·ship
trust·ful
  trust·ful·ly
trust·wor·thy
  trust·wor·thi·ly
  trust·wor·thi·ness
trusty
  trust·i·est

trust·i·ness
truth·ful
  truth·ful·ly
  truth·ful·ness
try
  tried
  try·ing
tryst
tsu·na·mi
tu·ba
tu·bal
tub·by
  tub·bi·ness
tube
  tubed
  tub·ing
tu·ber
tu·ber·cle
tu·ber·cu·lo·sis
  tu·ber·cu·lar
tu·ber·ous
tu·bu·lar
tu·bule
tuck-point
tuft·ed
tu·i·tion
tu·la·re·mia
tu·lip
tulle
tum·ble
  tum·bled
  tum·bling
tum·ble-down
tum·bler
tum·ble·weed
tu·mes·cent
tu·mid
  tu·mid·i·ty
tu·mor
tu·mor·ous
tu·mult
tu·mul·tu·ous
tu·mul·tu·ous·ly
tu·mul·tu·ous·ness
tu·na
tun·dra
tune
  tuned

tun·ing
tun·a·ble
tune·ful
tung·sten
tu·nic
tun·nel
tun·neled
tun·nel·ing
tuque
tur·ban
tur·bid
tur·bid·i·ty
tur·bid·ness
tur·bine
tur·bo
tur·bo·fan
tur·bo·jet
tur·bo·prop
tur·bot
tur·bu·lent
tur·bu·lence
tru·bu·len·cy
tu·reen
turf
tur·gid
tur·gid·i·ty
tur·gid·ness
tur·key
tur·mer·ic
tur·moil
turn·coat
turn·ing
tur·nip
turn·key
turn·pike
turn·ta·ble
tur·pen·tine
tur·pi·tude
tur·quoise
tur·ret
tur·tle
tur·tle·dove
tur·tle·neck
tusk
tusked
tus·sle
tus·sled
tus·sling

tu·te·lage
tu·tor
tu·tor·age
tu·to·ri·al
tu·ti-fru·ti
tu·tu
tux·e·do
twad·dle
twain
twang
twangy
tweak
tweed
tweedy
tweed·i·ness
tweet·er
tweez·ers
tweeze
tweezed
tweez·ing
twelve
twelfth
twen·ty
twen·ties
twen·ti·eth
twid·dle
twid·dled
twid·dling
twig
twig·gy
twi·light
twilled
twin
twinned
twin·ning
twine
twined
twin·ing
twinge
twinged
twing·ing
twin·kle
twin·kled
twin·kling
twirl
twirl·er
twirly
twist·er

twit
twit·ted
twit·ting
twitch
twit·ter
twit·tery
two-di·men·sion·al
two-faced
two-fist·ed
two-sid·ed
two·some
two-time
ty·coon
tym·pan·ic
type
typed
typ·ing
typ·ist
type·face
type·set·ter
type·set
type·write
type·writ·ten
type·writ·ing
type·writ·er
ty·phoid
ty·phoon
ty·phus
typ·i·cal
typ·i·cal·ly
typ·i·cal·ness
typ·i·cal·i·ty
typ·i·fy
typ·i·fied
typ·i·fy·ing
typ·i·fi·ca·tion
ty·pog·ra·phy
ty·pog·ra·pher
ty·po·graph·ic
ty·po·graph·i·cal
ty·po·graph·i·cal·ly
ty·pol·o·gy
ty·ran·ni·cal
ty·ran·nic
ty·ran·ni·cal·ly
tyr·an·nous
tyr·an·nize
tyr·an·nized

tyr·an·niz·ing
tyr·an·niz·er
tyr·an·ny
ty·rant
ty·ro

U

ubiq·ui·ty
  ubiq·ui·tous
  ubiq·ui·tary
  ubiq·ui·tous·ly
  ubiq·ui·tous·ness
ud·der
ug·ly
  ug·li·er
  ug·li·est
  ug·li·ly
  ug·li·ness
uku·le·le
ul·cer
  ul·cer·ous
ul·cer·ate
  ul·cer·at·ed
  ul·cer·at·ing
  ul·cer·a·tion
ul·ster
ul·te·ri·or
  ul·te·ri·or·ly
ul·ti·mate
  ul·ti·mate·ly
  ul·ti·mate·ness
ul·ti·ma·tum
ul·tra
ul·tra·con·serv·a·tive
ul·tra·fash·ion·a·ble
ul·tra·lib·er·al
ul·tra·ma·rine
ul·tra·mod·ern
ul·tra·re·li·gious
ul·tra·son·ic
ul·tra·vi·o·let
ul·u·late
  ul·u·la·tion
um·bel
um·ber
um·bil·i·cal
um·bra

um·brage
  um·bra·geous
  um·bra·geous·ly
  um·bra·geous·ness
um·brel·la
u·mi·ak
um·laut
um·pire
  um·pired
  um·pir·ing
un·a·bashed
un·a·ble
un·a·bridged
un·ac·cep·ta·ble
un·ac·com·pa·nied
un·ac·count·ed
un·ac·count·a·ble
  un·ac·count·a·bly
un·ac·cus·tomed
un·ac·quaint·ed
un·a·dorned
un·a·dul·ter·at·ed
un·ad·vised
  un·ad·vis·ed·ly
  un·ad·vis·ed·ness
un·af·fect·ed
  un·af·fect·ed·ly
  un·af·fect·ed·ness
un·a·fraid
un·aligned
un-A·mer·i·can
unan·i·mous
  una·nim·i·ty
  unan·i·mous·ly
  unan·i·mous·ness
un·an·swer·a·ble
  un·an·swered
un·ap·peal·a·ble
  un·ap·peal·ing
un·ap·pe·tiz·ing
un·ap·pre·ci·at·ed
  un·ap·pre·ci·a·tive
un·ap·pro·pri·at·ed
un·ap·proach·a·ble
  un·ap·proach·a·ble·ness
un·armed
un·a·shamed
un·asked

un·a·spir·ing
un·as·sail·a·ble
  un·as·sailed
un·as·sum·ing
un·at·tached
un·at·tain·a·ble
  un·at·tained
un·at·tended
un·au·thor·ized
un·a·vail·a·ble
  un·a·vail·a·bil·i·ty
  un·a·vail·a·bly
un·a·void·a·ble
  un·a·void·a·bil·i·ty
  un·a·void·a·bly
un·a·ware
  un·a·ware·ness
un·a·wares
un·backed
un·bal·anced
un·bar
  un·barred
  un·barring
un·bear·a·ble
  un·bear·a·ble·ness
  un·bear·a·bly
un·beat·en
  un·beat·a·ble
un·be·com·ing
  un·be·com·ing·ness
un·be·known
un·be·lief
un·be·liev·a·ble
  un·be·liev·a·bly
un·be·liev·er
  un·be·liev·ing
un·bend
  un·bend·ed
  un·bend·ing
  un·bend·ing·ness
un·be·seem·ing
un·bi·ased
un·bid·den
un·bind
un·blem·ished
un·blush·ing
un·blot
un·born

un·bos·om
un·bound
  un·bound·ed
  un·bound·ed·ness
un·bowed
un·bred
un·break·a·ble
un·bri·dled
un·bro·ken
un·buck·le
un·bur·den
un·but·ton
un·called-for
un·can·ny
  un·can·ni·ly
  un·can·ni·ness
un·cap
  un·capped
  un·cap·ping
un·ceas·ing
  un·ceas·ing·ly
  un·ceas·ing·ness
un·cere·mo·ni·ous
  un·cere·mo·ni·ous·ly
  un·cere·mo·ni·ous·ness
un·cer·tain
  un·cer·tain·ly
  un·cer·tain·ness
  un·cer·tain·ty
un·chal·lenged
un·change·a·ble
  un·changed
  un·chang·ing
un·char·i·ta·ble
  un·char·i·ta·ble·ness
  un·char·i·ta·bly
un·chart·ed
un·chris·tian
un·cir·cum·cised
un·civ·il
  un·civ·il·ly
  un·civ·i·lized
un·clad
un·class·i·fi·a·ble
  un·clas·si·fied
un·cle
un·clear
  un·clean·ly

un·clean·li·ness
un·clothe
  un·clothed
un·clut·tered
un·com·fort·a·ble
  un·com·fort·a·ble·ness
  un·com·fort·a·bly
un·com·mit·ted
un·com·mon
  un·com·mon·ly
  un·com·mon·ness
un·com·mu·ni·ca·tive
  un·com·mu·ni·ca·tive·ness
un·com·pre·hend·ing
un·com·pro·mis·ing
  un·com·pro·mised
  un·com·pro·mis·ing·ly
  un·com·pro·mis·ing·ness
un·con·cerned
  un·con·cern·ed·ly
  un·con·cern·ed·ness
un·con·di·tion·al
  un·con·di·tion·al·ly
un·con·firmed
un·con·for·mi·ty
un·con·nect·ed
  un·con·nect·ed·ness
un·con·quer·a·ble
  un·con·quered
un·con·scion·a·ble
  un·con·scion·a·ble·ness
  un·con·scion·a·bly
un·con·scious
  un·con·scious·ly
  un·con·scious·ness
un·con·sti·tu·tion·al
  un·con·sti·tu·tion·al·i·ty
  un·con·sti·tu·tion·al·ly
un·con·strained
un·con·test·ed
un·con·trol·la·ble
  un·con·trolled
un·con·ven·tion·al
  un·con·ven·tion·al·i·ty
  un·con·ven·tion·al·ly
un·count·ed
un·cou·ple
un·cour·te·ous

un·couth
  un·couth·ly
  un·couth·ness
un·cov·er
  un·cov·ered
un·crit·i·cal
unc·tion
unc·tu·ous
un·daunt·ed
  un·daunt·ed·ly
  un·daunt·ed·ness
un·de·ceived
un·de·ceiv·ing
un·de·cid·ed
  un·de·cid·ed·ness
un·de·fined
un·de·fin·a·ble
un·de·mon·stra·tive
  un·de·mon·stra·tive·ly
  un·de·mon·stra·tive·ne
un·de·nied
  un·de·ni·a·ble
  un·de·ni·a·ble·ness
  un·de·ni·a·bly
un·de·pend·a·ble
  un·de·pend·a·bil·i·ty
  un·de·pend·a·ble·ness
un·der·a·chiev·er
  un·der·a·chiev·ment
un·der·act
un·der·age
un·der·arm·ed
un·der·bid
un·der·brush
un·der·car·riage
un·der·charge
un·der·class·man
un·der·clothes
un·der·coat·ing
un·der·cov·er
un·der·cur·rent
un·der·cut
  un·der·cut·ting
un·der·de·vel·oped
  un·der·de·vel·op·ing
un·der·dog
un·der·es·ti·mate
  un·der·es·ti·mat·ed

un·der·es·ti·ma·tion
un·der·ex·pose
un·der·go
  un·der·went
  un·der·gone
  un·der·go·ing
un·der·grad·u·ate
un·der·ground
un·der·growth
un·der·hand·
un·der·hand·ed
  un·der·hand·ed·ness
un·der·lie
  un·der·lay
  un·der·lain
  un·der·ly·ing
un·der·line
  un·der·lined
  un·der·lin·ing
un·der·ling
un·der·mine
  un·der·mined
  un·der·min·ing
un·der·most
un·der·neath
un·der·nourished
un·der·paid
un·der·pass
un·der·pin·ning
un·der·play
un·der·priv·i·leged
un·der·rate
  un·der·rat·ed
un·der·score
  un·der·scored
  un·der·scor·ing
un·der·sea
un·der·sec·re·tary
  un·der·sec·re·taries
un·der·sell
  un·der·sold
un·der·shirt
un·der·shoot
un·der·side
un·der·signed
un·der·sized
un·der·slung
un·der·stand

un·der·stood
un·der·stand·ing
un·der·stand·a·bil·i·ty
un·der·stand·a·ble
un·der·stand·a·bly
un·der·state
  un·der·stat·ed
  un·der·stat·ing
  un·der·state·ment
un·der·study
  un·der·stud·ied
  un·der·stud·y·ing
un·der·take
  un·der·took
  un·der·tak·en
  un·der·tak·ing
un·der·tak·er
un·der-the-coun·ter
un·der·tone
un·der·tow
un·der·val·ue
un·der·wa·ter
un·der·wear
un·der·weight
un·der·world
un·der·write
  un·der·wrote
  un·der·writ·ten
  un·der·writ·ing
  un·der·writ·er
un·de·sign·ing
un·de·sir·a·ble
  un·de·sir·a·bil·i·ty
  un·de·sir·a·ble·ness
  un·de·sir·a·bly
un·de·ter·minded
un·de·vel·oped
un·di·gest·i·ble
un·dip·lo·mat·ic
  un·dip·lo·mat·i·cal·ly
un·di·rect·ed
un·dis·ci·plined
un·dis·closed
un·dis·posed
un·dis·tin·guished
un·di·vid·ed
un·do
  un·did

un·done
un·do·ing
un·doubt·ed
  un·doubt·ed·ly
  un·doubt·ing
un·dress
  un·dressed
  un·dress·ing
un·due
un·du·lant
un·du·late
  un·du·lat·ed
  un·du·lat·ing
  un·du·la·tion
  un·du·la·tory
un·du·ly
un·dy·ing
un·earned
un·earth
un·earth·ly
  un·earth·li·ness
un·easy
  un·ease
  un·eas·i·ly
  un·eas·i·ness
un·ed·u·cat·ed
un·em·ployed
  un·em·ploy·ment
  un·em·ploy·a·ble
un·end·ing
un·e·qual
  un·e·qual·ly
  un·e·qualed
un·e·quiv·o·cal
  un·e·quiv·o·cal·ly
un·err·ing
  un·err·ing·ly
un·es·sen·tial
un·eth·i·cal
  un·eth·i·cal·ly
un·e·ven
  un·e·ven·ly
  un·e·ven·ness
un·event·ful
un·ex·am·pled
un·ex·cep·tion·al
  un·ex·cep·tion·a·ble
un·ex·pect·ed

un·ex·pect·ed·ly
un·ex·pect·ed·ness
un·ex·pres·sive
un·fail·ing
un·fail·ing·ly
un·fair·ness
un·faith·ful
un·faith·ful·ly
un·faith·ful·ness
un·fa·mil·iar
un·fa·mil·i·ar·i·ty
un·fas·ten
un·fath·om·a·ble
un·fa·vor·a·ble
un·fa·vor·a·ble·ness
un·fa·vor·a·bly
un·feel·ing
un·feel·ing·ly
un·feel·ing·ness
un·feigned
un·fet·ter
un·fet·tered
un·fin·ished
un·fit
un·fit·ness
un·fit·ting
un·flat·ter·ing
un·flinch·ing
un·fold
un·for·get·ta·ble
un·for·get·ta·bly
un·for·giv·a·ble
un·formed
un·for·tu·nate
un·for·tu·nate·ly
un·for·tu·nate·ness
un·found·ed
un·fre·quent·ed
un·friend·ly
un·friend·li·ness
un·fruit·ful
un·gain·ly
un·gain·li·ness
un·gen·er·ous
un·god·ly
un·god·li·ness
un·gov·ern·a·ble
un·grace·ful

un·gra·cious
un·gra·cious·ly
un·gra·cious·ness
un·gram·mat·i·cal
un·grate·ful
un·grate·ful·ly
un·grate·ful·ness
un·grudg·ing
un·guard·ed
un·guent
un·ham·pered
un·handy
un·hap·py
un·hap·pi·ly
un·hap·pi·ness
un·harmed
un·healthy
un·health·i·ness
un·heard
un·heed·ed
un·heed·ful
un·heed·ing
un·hinge
un·ho·ly
un·ho·li·ly
un·ho·li·ness
un·hook
un·hur·ried
uni·cel·lu·lar
uni·corn
uni·cy·cle
uni·form
uni·formed
uni·form·i·ty
uni·form·ly
uni·form·ness
uni·fy
uni·fied
uni·fy·ing
uni·fi·ca·tion
uni·lat·er·al
uni·lat·er·al·ly
un·im·ag·i·na·ble
un·im·paired
un·im·peach·a·ble
un·im·peach·a·bly
un·im·por·tance
un·im·por·tant

un·im·proved
un·in·hib·it·ed
un·in·tel·li·gent
un·in·tel·li·gi·ble
un·in·ten·tion·al
un·in·ter·est·ed
un·in·ter·est·ing
un·in·ter·rupt·ed
un·ion
un·ion·ism
un·ion·ist
un·ion·ize
un·ion·ized
un·ion·iz·ing
un·ion·i·za·tion
unique
unique·ly
unique·ness
uni·sex
uni·son
unit
Uni·tar·i·an
unite
unit·ed
unit·ing
United Arab Emirates
Unit·ed King·dom
Unit·ed Na·tions
Unit·ed States
uni·ty
uni·valve
uni·ver·sal
uni·ver·sal·i·ty
uni·ver·sal·ly
uni·ver·sal·ness
uni·verse
uni·ver·si·ty
uni·ver·si·ties
un·just
un·just·ly
un·just·ness
un·kempt
un·kind
un·kind·ly
un·kind·ness
un·kind·li·ness
un·know·ing
un·known

218

un·law·ful
  un·law·ful·ly
  un·law·ful·ness
un·learn
  un·learned
un·learn·ed
un·leash
un·less
un·let·tered
un·like
  un·like·ness
un·like·ly
  un·like·li·hood
  un·like·li·ness
un·lim·ber
un·lim·it·ed
un·list·ed
un·load
un·lock
un·looked-for
un·loose
  un·loos·en
un·lucky
  un·luck·i·est
  un·luck·i·ly
  un·luck·i·ness
un·make
  un·made
  un·mak·ing
  un·mak·er
un·man·ly
un·manned
un·man·ner·ly
un·mask
un·mean·ing
  un·mean·ing·ly
un·men·tion·a·ble
un·mer·ci·ful
  un·mer·ci·ful·ly
un·mind·ful
un·mis·tak·a·ble
  un·mis·tak·a·bly
un·mit·i·gat·ed
un·nat·u·ral
  un·nat·u·ral·ly
  un·nat·u·ral·ness
un·nec·es·sary
  un·nec·es·sar·i·ly

un·nerve
  un·nerved
  un·nerv·ing
un·num·bered
un·ob·jec·tion·a·ble
un·ob·tru·sive
un·oc·cu·pied
un·or·gan·ized
un·or·tho·dox
un·pack
un·par·al·leled
un·par·don·a·ble
un·pleas·ant
  un·pleas·ant·ly
  un·pleas·ant·ness
un·plumbed
un·pop·u·lar
  un·pop·u·lar·i·ty
un·prec·e·dent·ed
un·pre·dict·a·ble
un·prej·u·diced
un·pre·ten·tious
un·prin·ci·pled
un·print·a·ble
un·pro·fes·sion·al
un·prof·it·a·ble
un·prom·is·ing
un·qual·i·fied
  un·qual·i·fied·ly
un·ques·tion·a·ble
  un·ques·tion·a·bly
un·ques·tioned
un·rav·el
  un·rav·eled
  un·rav·el·ing
un·ready
  un·read·i·ness
un·re·al
un·re·al·is·tic
un·re·al·i·ty
un·rea·son·a·ble
  un·rea·son·a·ble·ness
  un·rea·son·a·bly
un·rea·son·ing
un·re·con·struct·ed
un·re·fined
un·re·gen·er·ate
un·re·lat·ed

un·re·lent·ing
un·re·mit·ting
un·re·serve
  un·re·serv·ed·ly
un·rest
un·re·strained
un·ri·valed
un·ruf·fled
un·ru·ly
  un·ru·li·ness
un·sad·dle
un·said
un·sat·u·rat·ed
un·sa·vory
un·scathed
un·schooled
un·sci·en·tif·ic
un·scram·ble
un·screw
un·scru·pu·lous
  un·scru·pu·lous·ness
un·seal
un·sea·son·a·ble
  un·sea·son·a·bly
un·seat
un·seem·ly
  un·seem·li·ness
un·seg·re·gat·ed
un·self·ish
un·set·tle
  un·set·tled
  un·set·tling
un·sheathe
un·shod
un·sight·ly
  un·sight·li·ness
un·skilled
un·skill·ful
un·snap
  un·snapped
  un·snap·ping
un·snarl
un·so·phis·ti·cat·ed
  un·so·phis·ti·ca·tion
un·sought
un·sound
  un·sound·ness
un·spar·ing

un·speak·a·ble
un·spot·ted
un·sta·ble
  un·sta·ble·ness
un·steady
  un·stead·i·ly
un·stop
  un·stopped
  un·stop·ping
un·stressed
un·strung
un·stud·ied
un·suc·cess·ful
un·suit·a·ble
un·sung
un·tan·gle
un·taught
un·think·a·ble
un·think·ing
un·ti·dy
  un·ti·di·ness
un·tie
  un·tied
  un·ty·ing
un·til
un·time·ly
  un·time·li·ness
un·to
un·told
un·touch·a·ble
un·to·ward
un·truth·ful
un·tu·tored
un·used
un·u·su·al
  un·u·su·al·ness
un·ut·ter·a·ble
un·var·nished
un·veil
un·war·rant·ed
un·wary
  un·war·i·ness
un·well
un·whole·some
un·wieldy
  un·wield·i·ness
un·will·ing
  un·will·ing·ness

un·wind
  un·wound
  un·wind·ing
un·wise
un·wit·ting
  un·wit·ting·ly
un·wont·ed
un·world·li·ness
un·wor·thy
  un·wor·thi·ly
  un·wor·thi·ness
un·wrap
  un·wrapped
  un·wrap·ping
un·writ·ten
un·yield·ing
up-and-com·ing
up-and-down
up·beat
up·braid
up·bring·ing
up·com·ing
up·coun·try
up·date
  up·dat·ed
  up·dat·ing
up·grade
  up·grad·ed
  up·grad·ing
up·heav·al
up·heave
up·hold
  up·held
  up·hold·ing
up·hol·ster
up·hol·stery
up·keep
up·land
up·most
up·on
up·per·class
up·per·cut
up·per·most
up·pish·ness
up·pi·ty
up·raise
  up·raised
  up·rais·ing

up·rear
up·right
  up·right·ness
up·ris·ing
up·roar
up·roar·i·ous
up·root
up·set·ting
up·shot
up·stage
  up·staged
  up·stag·ing
up·stairs
up·stand·ing
up·start
up·state
up·stream
up·swing
up·take
up-to-date
up·town
up·trend
up·turn
up·ward
ura·ni·um
Ura·nus
ur·ban
ur·bane
  ur·bane·ness
  ur·ban·i·ty
ur·ban·ize
  ur·ban·ized
  ur·ban·iz·ing
  ur·ban·i·za·tion
ur·chin
ure·mia
ure·ter
ure·thra
urge
  urged
  urg·ing
ur·gent
  ur·gen·cy
  ur·gent·ly
uri·nal
uri·nal·y·sis
uri·nary
uri·nate

uri·na·tion
urine
urol·o·gy
uro·log·ic
Uru·guay
us·a·ble
　us·a·ble·ness
　us·a·bil·i·ty
us·age
use
　used
　us·ing
use·ful
　use·ful·ly
　use·ful·ness
use·less·ness
ush·er
usu·al
　usu·al·ly
usurp
　usur·pa·tion
　usurp·er
usu·ry
　usu·ri·ous
uten·sil
uter·us
util·i·tar·ian
util·i·ty
　util·i·ties
uti·lize
　uti·lized
　uti·liz·ing
　uti·li·za·tion
ut·most
Uto·pia
　Uto·pi·an
ut·ter
　ut·ter·a·ble
ut·ter·ance
ut·ter·most
uvu·la
ux·o·ri·ous

V

va·can·cy
　va·can·cies
va·cant

va·cate
　va·cat·ed
　va·cat·ing
va·ca·tion
vac·ci·nate
　vac·ci·nat·ed
　vac·ci·nat·ing
　vac·ci·na·tion
vac·cine
vac·il·late
　vac·il·lat·ed
　vac·il·lat·ing
　vac·il·la·tion
　vac·il·la·tor
va·cu·i·ty
vac·u·ous
　vac·u·ous·ness
vac·u·um
vag·a·bond
　vag·a·bond·age
va·gary
　va·gar·i·ous
va·gi·na
　vag·i·nal
va·grant
　va·gran·cy
vague
　vague·ness
vain
　vain·ly
　vain·ness
vain·glo·ry
　vain·glo·ri·ous
　vain·glo·ri·ous·ness
val·ance
　val·anced
val·e·dic·tion
　val·e·dic·to·ri·an
　val·e·dic·to·ry
va·lence
　va·len·cy
val·en·tine
val·et
val·iant
　val·iant·ly
　val·iant·ness
val·id
　val·id·ly

val·id·ness
val·i·date
　val·i·dat·ed
　val·i·dat·ing
　val·i·da·tion
va·lid·i·ty
va·lise
val·ley
　val·leys
val·or
　val·or·ous
　val·or·ous·ly
　val·or·ous·ness
val·or·ize
　val·or·i·za·tion
val·u·a·ble
　val·u·a·ble·ness
　val·u·a·bly
val·u·a·tion
　val·u·a·tion·al
val·ue
　val·ued
　val·u·ing
　val·ue·less
valve
　valve·less
val·vu·lar
va·moose
vam·pire
　vam·pir·ic
van·dal
van·dal·ism
　van·dal·ize
　van·dal·ized
　van·dal·iz·ing
vane
　vaned
　vane·less
van·guard
va·nil·la
van·ish
van·i·ty
　van·i·ties
van·quish
　van·quish·a·ble
　van·quish·er
van·tage
vap·id

va·pid·i·ty
vap·id·ness
vap·id·ly
va·por
va·por·er
va·por·ish
va·por·ish·ness
va·por·es·cence
va·por·ize
va·por·ized
va·por·iz·ing
va·por·i·za·tion
va·por·iz·er
va·por·ous
va·por·ous·ly
va·que·ro
var·i·a·ble
var·i·a·bil·i·ty
var·i·a·ble·ness
var·i·a·bly
var·i·ance
var·i·ant
var·i·a·tion
var·i·a·tion·al
var·i·a·tion·al·ly
var·i·col·ored
var·i·cose
var·i·cos·i·ty
var·ied
var·ied·ness
var·i·e·gate
var·i·e·gat·ed
var·i·e·gat·ing
var·i·e·ga·tion
va·ri·e·tal
va·ri·e·tal·ly
va·ri·e·ty
va·ri·e·ties
var·i·o·rum
var·i·ous
var·i·ous·ly
var·i·ous·ness
var·mint
var·nish
var·si·ty
var·si·ties
vary
var·ied

var·y·ing
var·y·ing·ly
vas·cu·lar
vas·cu·lar·i·ty
vas·ec·to·my
Vas·e·line
vas·o·mo·tor
vas·sal
vas·sal·age
vast·ness
vas·ti·tude
vat
vat·ted
vat·ting
Vat·i·can
vaude·ville
vaude·vil·lian
vault
vault·ed
vault·er
vault·ing
vaunt
vaunt·er
vaunt·ing·ly
vec·tor
vec·to·ri·al
veering
veg·e·ta·ble
veg·e·tal
veg·e·tar·i·an
veg·e·tari·an·ism
veg·e·tate
veg·e·tat·ed
veg·e·tat·ing
veg·e·ta·tion
veg·e·ta·tion·al
veg·e·ta·tion·less
veg·e·ta·tive
ve·he·ment
ve·he·mence
ve·he·men·cy
ve·hi·cle
ve·hic·u·lar
veil
veiled
veil·ing
vein
veiny

vein·ing
vel·lum
ve·loc·i·ty
ve·loc·i·ties
vel·our
ve·lum
vel·vet
vel·vet·ed
vel·vety
vel·vet·een
ve·nal
ve·nal·i·ty
ve·nal·ly
ve·na·tion
ve·na·tion·al
vend·er
vend·or
ven·det·ta
vend·i·ble
vend·i·bil·i·ty
ve·neer
ve·neer·ing
ven·er·a·ble
ven·er·a·bil·i·ty
ven·er·a·ble·ness
ven·er·a·bly
ven·er·ate
ven·er·a·tion
ven·er·a·tor
ve·ne·re·al
venge·ance
venge·ful
venge·ful·ness
ve·ni·al
ve·ni·al·i·ty
ve·ni·al·ness
ve·ni·al·ly
ven·i·son
ven·om
ven·om·ous
ven·om·ous·ness
ve·nous
ve·nous·ly
ve·nous·ness
vent
vent·ed
vent·ing
ven·ti·late

222

ven·ti·lat·ed
ven·ti·lat·ing
ven·ti·la·tion
ven·ti·la·tor
ven·tral
ven·tri·cle
ven·tril·o·quism
  ven·tril·o·qui·al
ven·tril·o·quist
ven·tril·o·quize
  ven·tril·o·quized
  ven·tril·o·quiz·ing
ven·ture
ven·ture·some
ven·tur·ous
  ven·tur·ous·ness
ven·ue
ve·ra·cious
  ve·ra·cious·ness
ve·rac·i·ty
  ve·rac·i·ties
ve·ran·da
ver·bal
  ver·bal·ly
ver·bal·ize
  ver·bal·ized
  ver·bal·iz·ing
  ver·bal·i·za·tion
ver·ba·tim
ver·be·na
ver·bi·age
ver·bose
  ver·bose·ness
  ver·bos·i·ty
ver·bo·ten
ver·dant
  ver·dan·cy
ver·dict
ver·di·gris
ver·dure
  ver·dured
  ver·dur·ous
verge
  verged
  verg·ing
ver·i·fy
  ver·i·fied
  ver·i·fy·ing

ver·i·fi·a·bil·i·ty
ver·i·fi·a·ble·ness
ver·i·fi·a·ble
ver·i·fi·ca·tion
ver·i·fi·er
ver·i·si·mil·i·tude
ver·i·ta·ble
  ver·i·ta·ble·ness
  ver·i·ta·bly
ver·i·ty
  ver·i·ties
ver·meil
ver·mi·cel·li
ver·mic·u·lar
ver·mic·u·late
ver·mi·fuge
ver·mil·ion
ver·min
  ver·min·ous
ver·mouth
ver·nac·u·lar
  ver·nac·u·lar·ism
ver·nal
  ver·nal·ly
ver·ni·er
Ver·sailles
ver·sa·tile
  ver·sa·tile·ness
  ver·sa·til·i·ty
versed
ver·si·fy
  ver·si·fi·ca·tion
ver·sion
  ver·sion·al
ver·sus
ver·te·bra
  ver·te·brae
ver·te·bral
ver·te·brate
ver·tex
  ver·tex·es
ver·ti·cal
  ver·ti·cal·i·ty
  ver·ti·cal·ness
  ver·ti·cal·ly
ver·ti·go
  ver·tig·i·nous
verve

ves·i·cant
vas·pers
ves·sel
ves·tal
vest·ed
ves·ti·bule
ves·tige
  ves·tig·i·al
  ves·tig·i·al·ly
vest·ment
vest-pock·et
ves·try
  ves·tries
vet·er·an
vet·er·i·nar·i·an
vet·er·i·nary
ve·to
  ve·toed
  ve·to·ing
  ve·to·er
vex
  vexed
  vex·ing
vex·a·tion
vex·a·tious
vi·a·ble
  vi·a·bil·i·ty
  vi·a·bly
vi·a·duct
vi·al
vi·and
vi·brant
  vi·bran·cy
vi·brate
  vi·brat·ed
  vi·brat·ing
  vi·bra·tion
vi·bra·to
vi·bra·tor
vi·bra·to·ry
vi·bur·num
vic·ar
  vic·ar·age
vi·car·i·ous
  vi·car·i·ous·ly
  vi·car·i·ous·ness
vice-ad·mi·ral
vice-chan·cel·lor

vice-con·sul
  vice-con·su·lar
  vice-con·su·late
  vice-con·sul·ship
vice-pres·i·dent
  vice-pres·i·den·cy
  vice-pres·i·den·cies
  vice-pres·i·den·tial
vice·roy
vice ver·sa
vi·chys·soise
vi·cin·i·ty
  vi·cin·i·ties
vi·cious
  vi·cious·ly
  vi·cious·ness
vi·cis·si·tude
vic·tim
vic·tim·ize
  vic·tim·ized
  vic·tim·iz·ing
  vic·tim·i·za·tion
vic·tor
Vic·to·ri·an
vic·to·ri·ous
  vic·to·ri·ous·ly
  vic·to·ri·ous·ness
vic·to·ry
  vic·to·ries
vict·ual
vi·cu·na
vid·eo
vid·e·o·tape
  vid·e·o·taped
  vid·e·o·tap·ing
vie
  vied
  vy·ing
  vi·er
Vi·et·nam·ese
view·er
view·point
vig·il
vig·i·lance
vig·i·lant
vig·i·lan·te
  vig·i·lan·tism
vi·gnette

vig·or
vig·or·ous
  vig·or·ous·ly
Vi·king
vile
  vil·er
  vil·est
  vile·ly
vil·i·fy
  vil·i·fied
  vil·i·fy·ing
  vil·i·fi·ca·tion
vil·la
vil·lage
vil·lain
vil·lain·ous
  vil·lain·ous·ly
  vil·lain·ous·ness
vil·lainy
  vil·lain·ies
vil·lein
vil·lous
vin·ai·grette
vin·ci·ble
  vin·ci·bil·i·ty
vin·di·cate
  vin·di·cat·ed
  vin·di·cat·ing
  vin·di·ca·tion
  vin·di·ca·tor
vin·dic·tive
  vin·dic·tive·ly
  vin·dic·tive·ness
vin·e·gar
  vin·e·gary
vine·yard
vi·ni·cul·ture
vi·nous
vin·tage
vint·ner
vi·nyl
vi·ol
vi·o·la
  vi·o·list
vi·o·la·ble
  vi·o·la·bil·i·ty
vi·o·late
  vi·o·lat·ed

vi·o·lat·ing
vi·o·la·tor
vi·o·la·tion
vi·o·lence
vi·o·lent
vi·o·let
vi·o·lin
  vi·o·lin·ist
vi·o·list
vi·o·lon·cel·lo
  vi·o·lon·cel·list
vi·per
vi·ra·go
vi·ral
vireo
vir·gin
  vir·gin·al
  vir·gin·al·ly
  vir·gin·i·ty
vir·gule
vir·ile
  vi·ril·i·ty
vi·rol·o·gy
  vi·rol·o·gist
vir·tu·al
  vir·tu·al·ly
vir·tue
vir·tu·os·i·ty
vir·tu·o·so
vir·tu·ous
  vir·tu·ous·ly
  vir·tu·ous·ness
vir·u·lent
  vir·u·lence
  vir·u·len·cy
vi·rus
  vi·rus·es
vi·sa
vis·age
vis-a-vis
vis·cera
  vis·ceral
vis·cid
  vis·cid·i·ty
  vis·cid·ly
  vis·cid·ness
vis·cos·i·ty
  vis·cos·i·ties

vis·count
  vis·count·ess
vis·cous
vis·i·bil·i·ty
vis·i·ble
vi·sion
vi·sion·ary
vis·it
  vis·i·tant
  vis·it·a·tion
  vis·it·ing
  vis·i·tor
vi·sor
vis·ta
vis·u·al
  vis·u·al·ly
vis·u·al·ize
  vis·u·al·ized
  vis·u·al·iz·ing
  vis·u·al·i·za·tion
vi·tal
  vi·tal·ly
  vi·tal·i·ty
vi·tal·ize
  vi·tal·ized
  vi·tal·iz·ing
  vi·tal·i·za·tion
vi·tals
vi·ta·min
vi·ti·ate
  vi·ti·at·ed
  vi·ti·at·ing
  vi·ti·a·tion
vit·re·ous
  vit·re·os·i·ty
vit·ri·fy
  vit·ri·fied
  vit·ri·fy·ing
  vit·ri·fi·a·ble
  vit·ri·fi·ca·tion
vit·ri·ol
  vit·ri·ol·ic
vit·tles
vi·tu·per·ate
  vi·tu·per·at·ed
  vi·tu·per·at·ing
  vi·tu·per·a·tion
vi·va

vi·va·cious
vi·vac·i·ty
vi·var·i·um
vi·va vo·ce
viv·id
viv·i·fy
  viv·i·fied
  viv·i·fy·ing
  viv·i·fi·ca·tion
vi·vip·a·rous
vivi·sect
  vivi·sec·tion
vix·en
vi·zier
vi·zor
vo·cab·u·lary
  vo·cab·u·lar·ies
vo·cal
  vo·cal·ic
  vo·cal·ist
  vo·cal·ize
  vo·cal·ized
  vo·cal·iz·ing
  vo·cal·i·za·tion
vo·ca·tion
  vo·ca·tion·al
vo·cif·er·ate
  vo·cif·er·ous
vod·ka
vogue
  vogu·ish
voice
  voiced
  voic·ing
  voice·print
void·a·ble
voile
vol·a·tile
  vol·a·til·i·ty
vol·can·ic
  vol·can·i·cal·ly
vol·ca·no
  vol·ca·noes
  vol·ca·nos
vo·li·tion
vol·ley
  vol·leys
  vol·leyed

  vol·ley·ing
vol·ley·ball
volt·age
vol·ta·ic
vol·u·ble
  vol·u·bly
  vol·u·bil·i·ty
vol·ume
vo·lu·mi·nous
  vo·lu·mi·nous·ly
  vo·lu·mi·nous·ness
vol·un·tary
  vol·un·tar·i·ly
vol·un·teer
vo·lup·tu·ary
vo·lup·tu·ous
vo·lute
vom·it
voo·doo
  voo·doo·ism
  voo·doo·ist
  voo·doo·is·tic
vo·ra·cious
  vo·rac·i·ty
vor·tex
  vor·tex·es
  vor·ti·ces
vo·ta·ry
  vo·ta·ries
vote
  vot·ed
  vot·ing
  vot·er
vo·tive
vouch·er
vouch·safe
  vouch·safed
  vouch·saf·ing
vow·el
vox po·pu·li
voy·age
  voy·aged
  voy·ag·ing
  voy·ag·er
vo·yeur
  vo·yeur·ism
  voy·eur·is·tic
vul·can·ize

vul·can·ized
vul·can·iz·ing
vul·can·i·za·tion
vul·gar
vul·gar·ism
vul·gar·i·ty
vul·gar·ize
vul·gar·ized
vul·gar·iz·ing
vul·gar·i·za·tion
Vul·gate
vul·ner·a·ble
vul·ner·a·bil·i·ty
vul·ner·a·bly
vul·ture
vul·tur·ous
vul·va

W

wab·ble
wab·bled
wab·bling
wacky
wack·i·er
wack·i·est
wack·i·ly
wack·i·ness
wad
wad·ded
wad·ding
wad·dle
wad·dled
wad·dling
wad·dler
wad·dly
wade
wad·ed
wad·ing
wa·fer
waf·fle
waft
wag
wagged
wag·ging
wage
waged
wag·ing

wa·ger
wag·gery
wag·gish
wag·gle
wag·gled
wag·gling
wag·on
wa·hi·ne
Wai·ki·ki
wain·scot
wain·scot·ing
wain·wright
waist·band
waist·coat
waist·line
wait·er
wait·ress
wait·ing
waive
waived
waiv·ing
waiv·er
wake
waked
wok·en
wak·ing
wake·ful
wake·ful·ly
wake·ful·ness
wak·en
wale
waled
wal·ing
walk·a·way
walk·er
walk·ie-talk·ie
walk·out
walk·o·ver
walk·up
walk·way
wal·la·by
wal·la·bies
wall·board
wal·let
wall·flow·er
wal·lop
wall·pa·per
wall-to-wall

wal·nut
wal·rus
waltz
wam·pum
wan
wan·ner
wan·ness
wan·der
wan·der·lust
wane
waned
wan·ing
wan·gle
wan·gled
wan·gling
want·ing
wan·ton
war
warred
war·ring
war·ble
war·bled
war·bling
war·bler
war·den
ward·er
ward·robe
ware·house
war·fare
war·head
warm
warm·er
warm·est
warm-blood·ed
warm-heart·ed
war·mon·ger
warmth
warn·ing
war·path
war·rant
war·ran·ty
war·ren
war·ri·or
war·ship
war·time
wary
war·i·er
war·i·est

war·i·ly
war·i·ness
wash·a·ble
wash·ba·sin
wash·bowl
wash·cloth
wash·er
wash·ing
Wash·ing·ton
wash·out
wash·room
wash·tub
wasp·ish
  wasp·ish·ness
was·sail
wast·age
waste
  wast·ed
  wast·ing
  waste·ful
waste·bas·ket
waste·land
waste·pa·per
wast·rel
watch·dog
watch·ful
watch·man
watch·tow·er
watch·word
wa·ter·borne
wa·ter·col·or
wa·ter·course
wa·ter·cress
wa·ter·fall
wa·ter·fowl
wa·ter·front
wa·ter·less
wa·ter lev·el
wa·ter lily
wa·ter line
wa·ter·logged
wa·ter main
wa·ter·mark
wa·ter·mel·on
wa·ter moc·ca·sin
wa·ter·pow·er
wa·ter·proof
wa·ter-re·pel·lent

wa·ter·side
wa·ter·ski
  wa·ter-skied
  wa·ter-ski·ing
wa·ter·spout
wa·ter·tight
wa·ter·works
wa·tery
  wa·ter·i·ness
watt·age
watt-hour
wat·tle
  wat·tled
  wat·tling
wave
  waved
  wav·ing
wave·length
wave·let
wa·ver
wav·y
  wav·i·ly
  wav·i·ness
wax
  waxed
  wax·ing
wax·en
wax·wing
wax·work
waxy
  wax·i·er
  wax·i·ness
way·far·er
way·far·ing
way·lay
  way·laid
  way·lay·ing
way·side
way·ward
weak·en
weak-kneed
weak·ling
weak·ly
  weak·li·er
  weak·li·ness
weak-mind·ed
weak·ness
wealthy

wealth·i·er
wealth·i·est
wealth·i·ness
wean
weap·on
weap·on·ry
wear
  wore
  worn
  wear·ing
wea·ri·some
wea·ry
  wea·ried
  wea·ry·ing
  wea·ri·ly
  wea·ri·ness
wea·sel
weath·er
weath·er·a·bil·i·ty
weath·er-beat·en
weath·er·cock
weath·er·glass
weath·er·ing
weath·er·man
weath·er·proof
weath·er·vane
weave
  wove
  weaved
  wov·en
  weav·ing
web
  webbed
  web·bing
web-foot·ed
wed·ding
wedge
  wedged
  wedg·ing
wed·lock
weedy
  weed·i·er
  weed·i·ness
week·day
week·end
week·ly
weep
  wept

weep·ing
wee·vil
weigh
weight
weighty
  weight·i·er
  weight·i·est
  weight·i·ness
weird
  weird·er
  weird·est
wel·come
  wel·comed
  wel·com·ing
wel·fare
well-ad·vised
well-be·ing
well-born
well-bred
well-dis·posed
well-done
well-found·ed
well-groomed
well-ground·ed
well-known
well-mean·ing
well-off
well-read
well-spo·ken
well·spring
well-timed
well-to-do
well-wish·er
well-worn
wel·ter
wel·ter·weight
were·wolf
west·er·ly
west·ern
West·ern·er
west·ern·ize
  west·ern·ized
  west·ern·iz·ing
  west·ern·i·za·tion
west·ern·most
west·ward
wet
  wet·ter

wet·test
wet·ting
wet·back
whale
  whaled
  whal·ing
whale·boat
whale·bone
whal·er
wharf
  wharves
wharf·age
what·ev·er
what·not
what·so·ev·er
wheal
wheat
whee·dle
  whee·dled
  whee·dling
wheel·bar·row
wheel·chair
wheeled
wheel·house
wheeze
  wheezed
  wheez·ing
wheezy
  wheez·i·ness
whelm
whelp
whence·so·ev·er
when·ev·er
where·a·bouts
where·as
where·by
where·fore
where·in
where·on
where·so·ev·er
where·to
where·up·on
wher·ev·er
where·with
where·with·al
wher·ry
whet
  whet·ted

whet·ting
wheth·er
whet·stone
which·ev·er
while
whim·per
whim·sy
  whim·si·cal
whine
  whin·ed
  whin·ing
whin·ny
  whin·nied
  whin·ny·ing
whip
  whipped
  whip·ping
whip·lash
whip·per·snap·per
whip·pet
whip·poor·will
whir
  whirred
  whir·ring
whirl·i·gig
whirl·pool
whirl·wind
whisk·er
whis·key
  whis·ky
whis·per
whist
whis·tle
  whis·tled
  whis·tling
whis·tler
white
  whit·er
  whit·ish
white-col·lar
white-faced
whit·en
white·wash
whith·er
whit·tle
  whit·tled
  whit·tling
whiz

whizzed
whiz·zing
whiz·zes
whoa
who·ev·er
whole·heart·ed
whole·sale
  whole·sal·ing
  whole·sal·er
whole·some
whol·ly
whom·ev·er
whom·so·ev·er
whoop·ing
whop·per
whop·ping
whore
whorled
whose·so·ev·er
who·so·ev·er
wick·ed
wick·er·work
wick·et
wide
  wid·er
  wid·est
wide-a·wake
wide-eyed
wid·en
wide·spread
widg·eon
wid·ow
wid·ow·er
width
wield·er
wieldy
wie·ner
wife·ly
  wife·li·ness
wig·gle
  wig·gled
  wig·gling
  wig·gly
  wig·gli·est
wig·wag
  wig·wagged
  wig·wag·ging
wig·wam

wild·cat
  wild·cat·ted
  wild·cat·ting
wil·der·ness
wild-eyed
wild·fire
wild·fowl
wild·life
wild·wood
wile
wil·i·ly
wil·i·ness
wily
willed
will·ful·ly
will·ing
will-o'-the-wisp
wil·low
wil·lowy
wil·ly-nil·ly
win
  won
  win·ning
wince
  winc·ing
wind
  wound
  wind·ing
wind·break
wind·ed
wind·fall
wind·jam·mer
wind·lass
wind·mill
win·dow
win·dow·pane
win·dow-shop
  win·dow·shop·ping
wind·pipe
wind·shield
wind·storm
wind·up
wind·ward
windy
  wind·i·er
  wind·i·ness
wine
  wined

win·ing
win·ery
winged
wing·span
wing·spread
win·na·ble
win·ner
win·ning
win·now
win·some
win·ter
win·ter·green
win·ter·ize
  win·ter·ized
  win·ter·iz·ing
  win·ter·i·za·tion
win·try
  win·ter·y
  win·tri·ness
wipe
  wiped
  wip·ing
wire-haired
wire·less
wire·tap
  wire·tapped
  wire·tap·ping
  wire·tap·per
wir·ing
wiry
  wir·i·er
  wir·i·ness
wis·dom
wise
  wis·er
  wis·est
wise·ly
wise·crack
wish·bone
wish·ful·ly
wish·y-washy
wisp
  wispy
  wisp·i·er
wis·te·ria
wist·ful·ly
witch·craft
witch·ery

witch·ing
with·al
with·draw
  with·drew
  with·drawn
  with·draw·ing
with·draw·al
with·er
with·hold
  with·held
  with·hold·ing
with·in
with·out
with·stand
  with·stood
  with·stand·ing
wit·less
wit·ness
wit·ti·cism
wit·ting
  wit·ting·ly
wit·ty
  wit·ti·est
  wit·ti·ly
  wit·ti·ness
wiz·ard
  wiz·ard·ry
wiz·en
  wiz·ened
wob·ble
  wob·bled
  wob·bling
  wob·bly
woe·be·gone
woe·ful·ly
wolf·hound
wolf·ram
wol·ver·ine
wom·an
  wom·en
wom·an·ly
  wom·an·li·ness
wom·an·hood
wom·an·ish
wom·an·kind
womb
won·der·ful
won·der·land

won·der·ment
won·drous
wont·ed
wood·bine
wood·chuck
wood·cock
wood·craft
wood·ed
wood·en
wood·land
wood·peck·er
wood·pile
woods·man
woodsy
wood·wind
wood·work
woody
woo·er
woof·er
wool·en
wool·gath·er·ing
wool·ly
  wool·li·ness
  wool·ly-head·ed
woozy
  wooz·i·ly
  wooz·i·ness
word·ing
word·less
wordy
  word·i·est
  word·i·ly
  word·i·ness
work·a·ble
  work·a·bil·i·ty
work·a·day
work·bench
worked-up
work·er
work·horse
work·ing
work·ing·man
work·man
work·man·like
work·man·ship
work·out
work·room
work·shop

work·ta·ble
world·ly
  world·li·er
  world·li·est
  world·li·ness
world·ly-wise
world-wea·ry
world-wide
worm-eat·en
wormy
worn-out
worri·some
worry
  wor·ried
  worry·ing
  worries
  worri·er
worry-wart
wors·en
worship
  wor·ship·ful
wor·sted
worth·less
worth·while
worthy
  wor·thi·er
  wor·thi·est
  wor·thi·ly
  wor·thi·ness
would-be
wound·ed
wrack
wraith
wran·gle
  wran·gled
  wran·gling
wran·gler
wrap
  wrapped
  wrap·ping
wrap·per
wrath·ful
wreak
wreath
wreathe
  wreathed
  wreath·ing
wreck·age

wrench
wres·tle
  wres·tled
  wres·tling
wretch
wretch·ed
wrig·gle
  wrig·gled
  wrig·gling
  wrig·gly
  wrig·gler
wring
  wrung
  wring·ing
wring·er
wrin·kle
  wrin·kled
  wrin·kling
  wrin·kly
write
  wrote
  writ·ten
  writ·ing
  writ·er
writhe
  writhed
  writh·ing
wrong·do·er
  wrong·do·ing
wronged
wrong·ful·ly
wrong-head·ed
wrought
wry
  wri·er
  wri·est
  wry·ly

X

xan·thous
xe·bec
xe·non
xen·o·phobe
  xen·o·pho·bia
X-ray
  x·ray
xy·lem

xy·lo·graph
  xy·log·ra·phy
xy·loid
xy·lo·phone
  xy·lo·phon·ist

Y

yacht
  yacht·ing
  yachts·man
ya·hoo
yak
yam
yam·mer
yank
Yan·kee
yap
  yapped
  yap·ping
yard·age
yard·arm
yard·mas·ter
yard·stick
yarn
yar·row
yawl
yawn
year·book
year·ling
year·long
year·ly
yearn
  yearn·ing
year-round
yeast
  yeasty
yel·low
  yel·low·ish
  yel·low·bird
  yel·low fe·ver
  yel·low·ham·mer
  yel·low jack·et
yelp
yen
  yenned
  yen·ning
yeo·man

yeo·men
ye·shi·va
yes·ter·day
yes·ter·year
yew
Yid·dish
yield
  yield·ing
yip
  yipped
  yip·ping
yo·del
  yo·deled
  yo·del·ing
  yo·del·er
yo·ga
yo·gi
yo·gurt
yoke
  yoked
  yok·ing
yo·kel
yolk
Yom Kip·pur
yon·der
yore
young
  young·er
  young·ish
young·ling
young·ster
your·self
  your·selves
youth·ful
  youth·ful·ly
yowl
yuc·ca
yule·tide

Z

za·ny
  za·nies
  za·ni·er
  za·ni·est
  za·ni·ly
  za·ni·ness
zeal

zeal·ot
zeal·ous
ze·bra
ze·bu
ze·nith
zeph·yr
zep·pe·lin
ze·ro
  ze·ros
  ze·roes
zest
  zesty
  zest·i·er
  zest·ful
  zest·ful·ly
zig·zag
  zig·zagged
  zig·zag·ging

zinc
  zinced
  zinc·ing
zing
zin·nia
Zi·on
Zi·on·ism
  Zi·on·ist
zip
  zipped
  zip·ping
zip·per
zip·py
  zip·pi·er
  zip·pi·est
zir·con
zir·co·ni·um
zith·er

zo·di·ac
  zo·di·a·cal
zom·bie
zon·al
  zon·al·ly
zone
  zoned
  zon·ing
zoo
  zoos
zoo·ge·og·ra·phy
zo·ol·o·gy
  zo·o·log·ical
  zo·o·log·i·cal·ly
  zo·ol·o·gist
zuc·chet·to
zuc·chi·ni
zwie·back
zy·gote

NOTES

NOTES

NOTES

NOTES

NOTES

NOTES

NOTES

<u>NOTES</u>

NOTES

NOTES

NOTES

NOTES

NOTES

NOTES

NOTES

NOTES